Presbyterian Records
of
Baltimore City Maryland
1765-1840

Henry C. Peden, Jr., M.A.

HERITAGE BOOKS
2008

HERITAGE BOOKS
AN IMPRINT OF HERITAGE BOOKS, INC.

Books, CDs, and more—Worldwide

For our listing of thousands of titles see our website
at
www.HeritageBooks.com

Published 2008 by
HERITAGE BOOKS, INC.
Publishing Division
100 Railroad Ave. #104
Westminster, Maryland 21157

Copyright © 1995 Henry C. Peden, Jr., M.A.

All rights reserved. No part of this book may be reproduced or transmitted in any form or by any means, electronic or mechanical, including photocopying, recording or by any information storage and retrieval system without written permission from the author, except for the inclusion of brief quotations in a review.

International Standard Book Numbers
Paperbound: 978-1-58549-400-2
Clothbound: 978-0-7884-7162-9

TABLE OF CONTENTS

Introduction v

First Presbyterian Church
    Births and Baptisms, 1765-1801 1
    Marriages, 1767-1801 71
    Marriages, 1802-1819, by Rev. Inglis 83
    Marriages, 1820-1835, by Rev. Nevins 90
    Marriages, 1836-1840, by Rev. Backus 96
    Baptisms, 1802-1820, by Rev. Inglis 97
    Baptisms, 1820-1835, by Rev. Nevins 127
    Baptisms, 1836-1840, by Rev. Backus 146
    Births prior to 1840, baptized after 1840 149
    Burials, 1820-1835, by Rev. Nevins 150
    Burials, 1836-1838, by Rev. Backus 161
    Communicants, 1802-1840 162
    Office holders, 1763-1840 186

Second Presbyterian Church
    Membership (and others), 1803-1830 190
    Membership rolls, 1826-1840 194

Fifth Presbyterian Church
    Members and communicants, 1838-1840 211

Names on Westminster Graveyard Tablet 221

Westminster Presbyterian Church Cemetery Records 224

Glendy Graveyard Tombstone Inscriptions 229

First United Presbyterian Church (Montebello)
    Communicants, 1826-1840 233
    Baptisms, 1826-1840 237

Index 243

INTRODUCTION

The early history of the Presbyterian Church in Baltimore City is involved in some obscurity. As early as 1715 a few Presbyterians were gathered into a congregation which was ministered by Rev. Hugh Conn. In all likelihood this first congregation worshipped in their private homes. In the early 1700's there was also a small number of Presbyterians scattered over the Baltimore region who had migrated from Pennsylvania during the border troubles between that colony and Maryland. In 1740, Mr. Whitefield had preached to Presbyterians in Baltimore County, and related that he found "a close opposition from the Presbyterians in Baltimore Town." In 1751, Rev. Samuel Davis noted "a considerable revival or first plantation of religion in Baltimore County." There are no extant records for these early years of the Presbyterian congregations in the Baltimore area.

In 1760, the Presbytery appointed John Steele to preach one Sunday in Baltimore. Dr. William Lyon, and others who had formed the Presbyterian Church, had resided in Baltimore for a number of years, but it was not until 1761 that a regular congregation was formed. In that year "a few Presbyterian families that had removed from Pennsylvania with two or three of the same persuasion that had emigrated directly from Europe, formed themselves into a regular society, and had occasional supplies, assembling into private houses, though liable to persecution on this account, as the province groaned under a religious establishment." Among those to come from Pennsylvania were John Smith and William Buchanan, who removed to Baltimore from Carlisle in 1760. They were followed in 1761 by William Smith and James Sterrett from Lancaster County, and soon after by Mark Alexander, John Brown, Benjamin Griffith, and Robert Purviance, all from Pennsylvania; Dr. John Stevenson and Dr. Henry Stevenson, from Ireland; and, Jonathan Plowman, from England. These men, and the noted Dr. William Lyon, were the founders of the Presbyterian Church in Baltimore City.

In 1761, Rev. Hector Allison preached to the congregation on several Sundays, and application was made by the Presbyterians of Baltimore Town to the Presbytery of New Castle in his behalf; yet, in November, 1761, it was judged best to refuse the application [no reason stated]. In May, 1763, and again in August, the congregation requested the Presbytery of Philadelphia to send the Rev. Patrick Allison to preach to them, and although invited at the same time to become the pastor of what was then a much larger church in New Castle, Delaware, he accepted the call to Baltimore, where he remained until his death in 1802.

Shortly after the arrival of Rev. Allison, the congregation leased two lots on December 5, 1763, located on East Street (now Fayette) in the rear of the edifice formerly occupied by the Christ P. E. Church, on the southwest corner of Gay and Fayette Streets. There they erected a small log church, which they sold about two years later to Charles Ridgely. In March, 1765, they purchased ground from Alexander Lawson at the northwest corner of Fayette and North Streets, adding to it in 1772 another lot which they leased and then purchased from Andrew Buchanan. Here they erected a plain brick church, 45 feet long by 35 feet wide, containing 36 pews. The building was completed in November, 1766, and all but two pews were rented. In 1771 the church was enlarged so as to contain 50 pews. A parsonage was erected on what is now North Street in 1781.

On July 20, 1789, a lottery was advertised for the purpose of building a larger Presbyterian Church and 7,500 tickets were issued at $4 each. The managers were Robert Gilmor, David Stewart, Stephen Wilson, Samuel Smith, Samuel Sterrett, David Plunkett, Christopher Johnston, John Swan, William Taylor, John Brown, John Stricker, Thomas McElderry, Hercules Courtenay, Andrew Skinner Ennals, Henry Schroeder, William McCreery, William Wilson, William McLoughlin, Charles Ghequiere, Cyprian Wells, Patrick Bennett, Peter Hoffman, Martin Eichelberger, Baltzer Schaeffer, and George Lindenberger. The edifice was ready for occupancy in 1791.

On January 20, 1798, the church committee (elders and deacons) was incorporated by an Act of the Legislature under the title of "Committee of the Presbyterian Church in the City of Baltimore." From a review of the operations of the church in 1792, "the visible results of the work since 1764 may be thus summed up: three church edifices had been erected, one had been enlarged, a parsonage had been built, the lots for these buildings had been bought, a burial ground had been purchased, two enclosed, the annual salaries had been collected with unusual accuracy, and the inferior expenses defrayed without applying to the congregation or the public fund."

Following the death of the Rev. Dr. Patrick Allison on August 21, 1802, the Rev. James Inglis, of New York, became pastor of the First Presbyterian Church and served until his death on August 15, 1819. The pastorate remained vacant for about a year until the Rev. William Nevins, of Norwich, Connecticut, was called to the church in Baltimore in October, 1820. He also served until his death on September 14, 1835. The fourth pastor was the Rev. John C. Backus, of Philadelphia, who was elected on April 11, 1836, and installed the following September.

Upon the election of the Rev. James Inglis to the pastorate of the First Church in 1802, a large minority of the congregation withdrew and formed the Second Church. A plain but very ample and substantial church edifice was erected in 1804 on Baltimore and Loyd Streets, and Dr. John Glendy was called to the pastorate. On January 1, 1805, a lottery was then announced for the purpose of building the Second Presbyterian Church and 11,000 tickets were issued at $5 each. The managers were Thomas McElderry, James Biays, James Armstrong, James Sloan, Hugh McCurdy, John McKim, Jr., Thomas Dickson, and Kennedy Long.

In 1826 the Rev. Dr. John Glendy was compelled by infirmities of age (born in Ireland in 1755) to ask for an assistant. The Rev. John Breckenridge, of Kentucky, was chosen as his colleague. After a short time, Dr. Glendy gave up the charge entirely and moved to Philadelphia where he died October 4, 1832. Dr. John Breckenridge served until November 22, 1832, when he was succeeded by the Rev. Dr. Robert J. Breckenridge, his brother, who served until 1845. The graveyard of the Second Church, known as the Glendy Graveyard, was situated at the head of Broadway, fronting on Gay Street. It had about 3 acres, which were purchased in 1807. "Within the last few years [1880] this city of the dead has been forced to give way before the city of the living, and the remains of those interred there have been removed to other resting places."

The Third Presbyterian Church was organized around 1819 and a church building erected on Eutaw Street above Saratoga soon after. In 1851 a new edifice was erected, which was sold in 1861 to St. Mark's English Lutheran congregation.

The Franklin Square Presbyterian Church was originally the Fourth Church, which occupied for some years the Winans' Chapel on

West Baltimore Street, between Fremont and Poppleton Streets. It began as a Sunday School enterprise of the First Presbyterian Church in 1833. The first pastor was Rev. James Purviance who served until 1856. The church was incorporated as the Franklin Square Church in 1862.

The Fifth Presbyterian Church was organized in 1833. The building on Hanover Street, near Lombard Street, was erected in 1836. "It was sold to the Hebrews in 1858, and is now [1880] used as a synagogue." The Rev. Dr. John G. Hamner was its first pastor.

The First United Presbyterian Church was organized in 1826. The original church edifice was erected in 1828 and was situated on Courtland Street between Saratoga and Pleasant. The present edifice [in 1880], at the corner of Madison Avenue and Biddle Street, was dedicated in 1861. The first pastor in 1828 was the Rev. Archibald Whyte, and he was succeeded by the Rev. John G. Smart, who served until 1850. "Their form of worship is very similar to that of the Covenanters, or Caledonian Church."

The Reformed Presbyterian, or Church of the Covenanters, was organized in 1818 as the "Society of the Covenanters of Baltimore" and incorporated in 1821. Their church at the junction of Aisquith Street and Harford Avenue was purchased in 1833. "The members are almost exclusively Scotch, or north of Ireland people, or their descendants. They are connected with the Philadelphia Presbytery. Their mode of worship is simple to severity; the church is devoid of steeple, bell, or organ, no instrumental music is tolerated in the services, and only the psalms of David are sung."

The Associate Reformed Presbyterian Church was organized in 1797 and in 1803 had a large enough congregation to build a church at the corner of Pitt (now East Fayette) and Aisquith Streets. The Rev. R. Annan was their pastor, who served until March, 1812, when the Rev. John Mason Duncan was elected as his successor. In 1814 they erected a larger church on Tammany (now West Fayette) Street between Charles and Liberty Streets. The congregation continued its connection with the "Associated Reformed Church in North America" until May, 1822, when a union took place between this church and the "Presbyterian Church in the United States." However, troubles soon arose over the government of the church. The Synod met on October 27, 1825, in Baltimore, and Rev.

John M. Duncan and Rev. Charles G. McLean both formally withdrew from all connection with the "Presbyterian Church in the United States." The congregation supported their pastors' decision and have since [1880] maintained their independent organization.

The foregoing information about the early history of the Presbyterian Church in Baltimore from 1760 through 1840 was taken primarily from J. Thomas Scharf's *History of Baltimore City and County*, Volume II (1881). Naturally, there are other references to consult for more information, such as the following: Rev. Dr. John H. Gardner, Jr.'s *The First Presbyterian Church of Baltimore: A Two Century Chronicle* (1962); William Reynolds' *A Brief History of the First Presbyterian Church* (1913); *Manual for the First Presbyterian Church, Baltimore* (printed by the Session, 1877); T. H. Walker's *History of the Second Presbyterian Church, 1802-1902* (1902); J. E. P. Bouldin's *Presbyterians of Baltimore* (1875); *Maryland Historical Magazine*, Vol. 35 (1940); and, *Patriotic Marylander*, Vol. 2 (1916).

The information contained herein was gleaned from records that were available at the Library of the Maryland Historical Society in Baltimore, and the Maryland State Archives in Annapolis. There may be other records not known or available to this compiler, and my apologies for their omission. The vast majority of the records in this book pertain to the First Presbyterian Church prior to 1840, namely marriages, 1767-1840; births and baptisms, 1765-1840; births prior to 1840 with baptisms after 1840; burials, 1820-1840; office holders, 1763-1840; and, communicants, 1802-1840. The register of baptisms began in late 1765, but there are births recorded for some children born in the 1750's listed among the subsequent baptisms in the 1760's and 1770's. Also, included are membership rolls of the Second Presbyterian Church, 1803-1840; communicants (and others) of the Fifth Presbyterian Church, 1833-1840; and, communicants and baptisms of the First United Presbyterian Church (now Montebello Presbyterian Church), 1826-1840. Also, burial records were gleaned from Westminster Presbyterian Church cemetery records and Glendy Graveyard (Second Presbyterian Church Cemetery) inscriptions. These burial records, however, appear to be incomplete and may require one to do additional research to correct any inherent mistakes.

As with my other books on early Maryland church records, I trust this book on Baltimore's early Presbyterian church records will prove beneficial to genealogists and church historians.

                                                            Henry C. Peden, Jr.
                                                            Bel Air, Maryland
                                                            June 1, 1995

PRESBYTERIAN RECORDS OF BALTIMORE CITY, MARYLAND, 1765-1840

FIRST PRESBYTERIAN CHURCH, RECORD OF BIRTHS AND BAPTISMS, 1765-1801

[Although the record of baptisms began in 1765, there are births of many children in the 1750's and early 1760's listed in the record.]

John Anderson, son of Thomas and Ann Anderson, born 1 May 1769, baptized 27 October 1769

Syme Arrison, son of Thomas Cox and Mary Arrison, born 19 September 1772, baptized 1 November 1772

Mary Anderson, daughter of James and Mary Anderson, born 19 October 1783, baptized 27 February 1784

Samuel Allen, son of James and Catharine Allen, born 19 January 1784, baptized 27 February 1784

John William Allen, son of James and Catharine Allen, born 27 September 1785, baptized 12 February 1786

Anne Aitken, daughter of Andrew and Elizabeth Aitken, born 4 August 1785, baptized 5 November 1787

Andrew Aitken, son of Andrew and Elizabeth Aitken, born 17 July, 1787, baptized 5 November 1787

Mary Allen, daughter of James and Catharine Allen, born 30 August 1787, baptized 9 December 1787

Elizabeth Aitken, daughter of Andrew and Elizabeth Aitken, born 1 June 1789, baptized 17 June 1789

James Williams Allen, son of James and Catharine Allen, born 25 June 1789, baptized 3 January 1790

Robert Aitken, son of Andrew and Elizabeth Aitken, born 31 August, 1790, baptized 28 September 1790

James Angell, son of James and Mary Angell, born 24 December 1789, baptized 13 September 1791

William Henry Angell, son of James and Mary Angell, born 24 July 1791, baptized 13 September 1791

Solomon Allen, son of Solomon and Catherine Allen, born 17 November 1788, baptized 1 January 1792

Eliza Allen, daughter of Solomon and Catherine Allen, born 19 November 1791, baptized 1 January 1792

Esther Allison, daughter of Patrick and Mary Allison, born 17 Feb 1792, baptized 15 April 1792 by Dr. Muir, Alexandria

George Aitken, son of Andrew and Elizabeth Aitken, born 11 June 1792, baptized 22 July 1792

John Allen, son of James and Catherine Allen, born 14 December 1791, baptized 7 November 1792

Joshua Barney Angell, son of James and Mary Angell, born 16 November 1792, baptized 20 April 1793

Thomas Andrews, son of William and Isabella Andrews, born 1 January 1794, baptized 2 February 1794

Maria Aitken, daughter of Andrew and Elizabeth Aitken, born 1 January 1794, baptized 11 May 1794

James Angell, son of James and Mary Angell, born 26 August 1794, baptized 8 January 1795

Eliza Aitken, daughter of Andrew and Elizabeth Aitken, born 18 February 1795, baptized 24 May 1795

John Andrews, son of William and Isabella Andrews, born 5 November 1795, baptized 27 March 1796

Betty Alexander, daughter of William and Jane Alexander, born 28 August 1796, baptized 25 September 1796

Cornelia Andrews, daughter of Nathaniel and Cornelia Andrews, born 27 July 1796, baptized 4 December 1796

Agness Anderson, daughter of William and Mary Anderson, born 14 February 1794, baptized 17 February 1797

Andrew Anderson, son of William and Mary Anderson, born 3 January 1796, baptized 17 February 1797

James Aitken, son of Andrew and Elizabeth Aitken, born 22 September 1796, baptized 30 April 1797

John Barney Sweeting Angell, son of James and Mary Angell, born 28 August 1797, baptized 22 October 1797

Elizabeth Armstrong, daughter of James and Jane Armstrong, born 18 October 1791, baptized 12 November 1797

Thomas Armstrong, son of James and Jane Armstrong, born 1 January 1794, baptized 12 November 1797

John Armstrong, son of James and Jane Armstrong, born 25 April 1796, baptized 12 November 1797

Hannah Buckler Andrews, daughter of Nathaniel and Cornelia Andrews, born 10 February 1798, baptized 16 April 1798

Francis Armstrong, son of James and Jane Armstrong, born 23 November 1798, baptized 12 February 1799

Rebecca Aitken, daughter of Andrew and Elizabeth Aitken, born 26[?] June 1799, baptized 14[?] April 1799

Fanny Hughes Andrews, daughter of Nathaniel and Cornelia Andrews, born 30 November 1799, baptized 3 April 1800

John Anderson, son of William and Mary Anderson, born 29 January 1799, baptized 14 November 1800

Jane Armstrong, daughter of James and Jane Armstrong, born 14 October 1800, baptized 5 January 1801

Eliza Polly Anderson, daughter of Henry and Eliza Anderson, born 24 October 1800, baptized 20 January 1801

Joseph Biays Allender, son of Joseph and Mary Allender, born 13 December 1800, baptized 12 July 1801

John Smith Buchanan, son of William and Esther Buchanan, born 12 August 1766, baptized 20 August 1766

Elizabeth Buchanan, daughter of John and Jane Buchanan, born 28 August 1765, baptized 26 August 1766

James Buchanan, son of William and Esther Buchanan, born 17 October 1768, baptized 20 October 1768

Honor Bosler, daughter of Jacob and Rachel Bosler, born 23 December 1759, baptized 15 October 1769

Mary Bosler, daughter of Jacob and Rachel Bosler, born 28 November 1763, baptized 15 October 1769

Mary Beatty, daughter of Arthur and Eleanor Beatty, born 25 January 1770, baptized 13 March 1770

Robert Barnhell, son of David and Jane Barnhell, born 31 December 1769, baptized 29 April 1770

James Syme Brown, son of Samuel and Jane Brown, born 12 June 1770, baptized 16 June 1770

Catharine Bain, daughter of Daniel and Margaret Bain, born 16 January 1770, baptized 19 September 1770

Rebecca Bosler, daughter of Jacob and Rachel Bosler, born 28 November 1770, baptized 9 June 1771

John Bennet, son of James and Jane Bennet, born 22 September 1771, baptized 12 November 1771

Boyd Buchanan, son of William and Esther Buchanan, born 10 February [1772?], baptized 23 February 1772

Sarah Brown, wife of John Brown, baptized 20 November 1772

James Brown, son of John and Sarah Brown, born 29 October 1772, baptized 20 November 1772

Elizabeth Bailey, daughter of James and Hannah Bailey, born 7 February 1773, baptized 19 July 1773

Robert Bailey, son of William and Margaret Bailey, born ---- [blank], baptized 17 September 1773

Thomas Bailey, son of William and Margaret Bailey, born ---- [blank], baptized 17 September 1773

Elizabeth Esther Buchanan, daughter of William and Esther Buchanan, born 16 February 1774, baptized 6 March 1774

James Burke, son of John and Janit Burke, born 22 March 1774, baptized 7 May 1774

James Bennet, son of James and Jane Bennet, born 25 May 1774, baptized 10 June 1774

William Brown, son of John and Sarah Brown, born 22 October 1774, baptized 15 November 1774

William Bennet, son of James and Jane Bennet, born 7 November 1775, baptized 13 February 1776

Hannah Brown, daughter of John and Sarah Brown, born 19 February 1777, baptized 1 June 1777

Samuel Bennet, son of James and Jane Bennet, born 16 August 1777, baptized 15 September 1777

Margaret Brown, daughter of Alexander and Margaret Brown, born 10 December 1778, baptized 16 December 1778 (twin)

John Brown, son of Alexander and Margaret Brown, born 10 December 1778, baptized 16 December 1778 (twin)

John Brown, son of John and Sarah Brown, born 1 April 1780, baptized 20 May 1780

James Bryson, son of John and Elizabeth Bryson, born 26 July 1780, baptized 27 August 1780

Susanna Bull, daughter of John and Rachel Bull, born 2 August 1780, baptized 27 August 1780

William Barnard, son of John and Priscilla Barnard, born 29 August 1781, baptized 14 January 1782

Elizabeth Biays, daughter of Joseph and Mary Biays, born 27 January 1780, baptized 29 January 1782

Mary Biays, daughter of Joseph and Mary Biays, born -- [December?], 1781, baptized 29 January 1782

John Bryson, son of John and Elizabeth Bryson, born 17 February 1782, baptized 14 April 1782

Susanna Brown, daughter of Justus and Grace Brown, born 5 May 1782, baptized 15 July 1782

FIRST PRESBYTERIAN CHURCH

Elizabeth Bull, daughter of John and Rachel Bull, born 19 August 1782, baptized 29 September 1782

Alexander Boyd, son of Andrew and Mary Boyd, born 2 November 1782, baptized 8 December 1782

Sarah Brown, daughter of John and Sarah Brown, born 4 December 1782, baptized 17 January 1783

William Bryson, son of John and Elizabeth Bryson, born 15 February 1784, baptized 16 February 1784

Callendar Randal Burke, son of Thomas and Margaret Burke, born 16 February 1784, baptized 25 February 1784

Jane Brown, daughter of George and Rose Brown, born 12 March 1784, baptized 24 July 1784

Margaret Biays, daughter of Joseph and Mary Biays, born 15 September 1783, baptized 4 August 1784

James Burnside, son of James and Elizabeth Burnside, born 10 October 1784, baptized 11 October 1784

Elizabeth Brown, daughter of Justus and Grace Brown, born 4 August 1784, baptized -- [blank] October, 1784

James Bryden [?], son of James and Mary [Bryden?, illegible], born ---- [illegible], 1784, baptized 17 January 1785

Judien [?] Bull, daughter of John and Rachel Bull, born 16 November 1784, baptized 17 February 1785

Abraham Biays, son of James and Sarah Biays, born 4 June 1785, baptized 20 July 1785

Matthew Biays, son of Joseph and Mary Biays, born 24 September 1785, baptized 5 November 1785

John Biays, son of John and Agness Biays, born 18 May 1786, baptized 15 June 1786

Thomas Jameson Brown, son of John and Sarah Brown, born 18 December 1785, baptized 21 September 1786

Mary Burton, daughter of Richard and Margaret Burton, born 13 September [1782?], baptized 1 February 1787

Matthew Biays, son of James and Sarah Biays, born 4 April 1787, baptized 1 June 1787

Susanna Biays, daughter of Joseph and Mary Biays, born 11 March 1787, baptized 1 June 1787

Teresa Blaney, daughter of Nathanael and Elizabeth Blaney, born -- [blank] January 1787, baptized 17 July 1787

John Bryden, son of James and Mary Bryden, born 23 July 1787, baptized 10 September 1787

George John Brown, son of George and Rose Brown, born 4 October 1787, baptized 16 November 1787

Rachel Bull, daughter of John and Rachel Bull, born 3 September 1787, baptized 26 December 1787

Jesse Brown, son of John and Sarah Brown, born 14 May 1788, baptized 1 June 1788

Joseph Biays, son of James and Sarah Biays, born 23 March 1788, baptized 12 June 1788

James Burney, son of John and Mary Burney, born 6 May 1788, baptized 7 July 1788

Eleanor Boyer, daughter of John and Agness Boyer, born 19 September 1788, baptized 13 October 1788

Joseph Biays, son of Joseph and Mary Biays, born ---- [illegible] ----, baptized ---- 1789

William Burn, son of James and Hannah Burn, born 2 November 1789, baptized 25 December 1789

Mary Burney, daughter of John and Mary Burney, born 2 January 1790, baptized 14 January 1790

Elizabeth Bryden, daughter of James and Mary Bryden, born 21 February 1790, baptized 7[?] March 1790

Anne Biays, daughter of James and Sarah Biays, born 18 May 1790, baptized 5 June 1790

William Barney, son of Joshua and Anne Barney, born 7 December ----

Louis Barney, son of Joshua and Anne Barney, born 12 January 1783

John Barney, son of Joshua and Anne Barney, born 18 January 1785
  The above three were "Baptized in Philadelphia" [no date given].

Caroline Barney, daughter of Joshua and Anne Barney, born 21 January 1787, baptized 9 August 1790

Henry Barney, son of Joshua and Anne Barney, born 28 April 1790, baptized 9 August 1790

Thomas Brown, son of Justus and Grace Brown, born 17 October 1786, baptized 13 August 1790

William Brown, son of Justus and Grace Brown, born 13 August 1789, baptized 13 August 1790

John Burke, son of David and Elizabeth Burke, born 13 February 1791, baptized 15 March 1791

Margaret Burney, daughter of John and Mary Burney, born 23 March 1791, baptized 5 May 1791

James Biays, son of Joseph and Mary Biays, born 25 May 1791, baptized 3 June 1791

FIRST PRESBYTERIAN CHURCH

John Brown, son of George and Rose Brown, born 6 March 1791, baptized 9 June 1791

Janit Bryden, daughter of James and Mary Bryden, born 5 June 1791, baptized 17 July 1791

Susanna Beers, daughter of William and Mary Beers, born 9 July 1791, baptized 1 August 1791

Alexander Brown, son of George and Rose Brown, born 10 April 1792, baptized 3 June 1792

Margaret Brown, daughter of John and Sarah Brown, born 17 November 1791, baptized 11 August 1792

Arrabella Burke, daughter of David and Elizabeth Burke, born 26 October 1792, baptized 16 December 1792

Martha Burney, daughter of John and Mary Burney, born 25 August 1792, baptized 22 January 1793

Joseph Biays, son of Joseph and Mary Biays, born 6 April 1792, baptized 5 May 1793

Agness Bryden, daughter of James and Mary Bryden, born 7 May 1793, baptized 7 July 1793

Elizabeth Buckler, daughter of William and Anne Buckler, born 21 August 1793, baptized 2 October 1793

Anne Maria Buchanan, daughter of James A. and Elizabeth Buchanan, born 28 September 1793, baptized 24 November 1793

John Biays, son of Joseph and Mary Biays, born 7 July 1794, baptized 10 August 1794

Joseph Mather Brown, son of John and Sarah Brown, born 6 July 1794, baptized 10 September 1794

Esther Smith Buchanan, daughter of James A. and Elizabeth Buchanan, born 4 September 1794, baptized 26 September 1794

Anne Biays, daughter of James and Sarah Biays, born 16 December 1794, baptized 29 December 1794

Harriot Burke, daughter of David and Elizabeth Burke, born 20 September 1795, baptized 10 February 1795

Robert Bryson, son of William and Winifred Bryson, born 28 January 1790, baptized 4 March 1795

Agness Bryson, daughter of William and Winifred Bryson, born -- [blank] September 1792, baptized 4 March 1795

Maria Barry, daughter of Standish and Agness Barry, born 9 May 1790, baptized [12 June 1795?] by Mr. Slemons

George Barry, son of Standish and Agness Barry, born 31 August 1792, baptized 12 June 1795

John L. Barry, son of Standish and Agness Barry, born 9 January 1795, baptized 12 June 1795

Grace Brown, daughter of George and Rose Brown, born 6 September 1794, baptized 5 September 1795

James Bryson, son of William and Winifred Bryson, born 1 May 1794, baptized 5 September 1795

William Boyd Buchanan, son of James A. and Elizabeth Buchanan, born 9 September 1795, baptized 7 November 1795

John Buckler, son of William and Anne Buckler, born 30 August 1795, baptized 7 November 1795

Anne Biays, daughter of Joseph and Mary Biays, born 17 October 1795, baptized 6 December 1795

Nancy Brown, adult, baptized 29 December 1795

David Brown, son of David and Nancy Brown, born 11 December 1795, baptized 29 December 1795

Mary Bryden, daughter of James and Mary Bryden, born 29 June 1796, baptized 12 July 1796

William Biays, son of James and Sarah Biays, born 6 March 1796, baptized 28 July 1796

John Stevenson Bryson, son of John and Elizabeth Bryson, born 11 February 1796, baptized 17 September 1796

Eleanor Burn, daughter of James and Hannah Burn, born 6 October 1791, baptized 16 December 1796

Jane Burn, daughter of James and Hannah Burn, born 14 March 1796, baptized 16 December 1796

Mary Ann Brown, daughter of George and Rose Brown, born 18 March 1796, baptized 6 January 1797

David Burke, son of David and Elizabeth Burke, born 11 September 1796, baptized 1 April 1797

Bateman Beatty, son of John and Mary Beatty, born 5 October 1796, baptized 8 May 1797

Ann Vetch Bayden [Bryden?], daughter of William and Ann, born 1 August 1797, baptized 21 September 1797

Airy Ann Bayson [Bryson?], daughter of John and Elizabeth, born 12 November 1797, baptized 1 December 1797

Martha Biggar, daughter of Samuel and Margaret Biggar, born 22 October 1797, baptized 5 March 1798

Philip Biays, son of James and Sarah Biays, born 18 August 1797, baptized 9 April 1798

Margaretta Brown, daughter of Stewart and Sarah Brown, born 19 March 1798, baptized 14 April 1798

Rachel Biays, daughter of Joseph and Elizabeth Biays, born 7 August 1797, baptized 27 July 1798

Rebecca Ensor Briggs, daughter of James and Temperance Briggs, born 16 September 1798, baptized 20 October 1798

James Calhoun Buchanan, son of James A. and Elizabeth Buchanan, born 29 July 1798, baptized 23 October 1798

Ann Hepburn Buckler, daughter of William and Ann Buckler, born 22 July 1798, baptized 6 November 1798

George Washington Burke, son of David and Elizabeth Burke, born 21 September 1798, baptized 20 May 1799

Eliza Biays, daughter of James and Sarah Biays, born 21 [31?] December 1799, baptized 1 January 1800

Mary Beatty, daughter of John and Mary Beatty, born 23 November 1799, baptized 15 January 1800

William Harman Brown, son of Stewart and Sarah Brown, born 8 February 1800, baptized 26 March 1800

Elizabeth Sidney Buchanan, daughter of James A. and Elizabeth, born 22 December 1799, baptized 7 April 1800

Henry Karclaw Behn, son of John H. and Violet Behn, born 28 August 1799, baptized 17 April 1800

Robert Patterson Brown, son of George and Rose Brown, born 13 October 1800, baptized 22 April 1800

Agness Bryson, daughter of John and Elizabeth Bryson, born 8 June 1800, baptized 16 November 1800

Mary Cook Bedford, daughter of Peter and Mary Bedford, born 11 December 1789, baptized 22 February 1801

Jefferson Burke, son of David and Elizabeth Burke, born 23 September 1800, baptized 26 February 1801

Samuel Smith Biays, son of James and Mary Biays, born 8 January 1801, baptized 26 February 1801

Anne Lydia Buchanan, daughter of James A. and Elizabeth Buchanan, born 31 December 1800, baptized 10 May 1801

Jane Johnson Buckler, daughter of William and Anne Buckler, born 19 February 1801, baptized 4 July 1801

Elizabeth Bunker, daughter of George and Mary Bunker, born 30 April 1798, baptized 9 July 1801

Edward Bryson, son of John and Elizabeth Bryson, born 12 September 1801, baptized 13 September 1801

Elizabeth Caldwell, daughter of James and Elizabeth Caldwell, born 15 August 1765, baptized 15 September 1765

Mark Alexander Coxe, son of James and Mary Coxe, born 25 May 1766, baptized 6 August 1766

Jane Caldwell, daughter of James and Elizabeth Caldwell, born 13 September 1767, baptized 22 October 1767

Rebecca Coxe, daughter of James and Mary Coxe, born 31 May 1768, baptized 30 June 1768

James Clement, son of John and Jane Clement, born 6[?] October, 1768, baptized 22 October 1768

John Carmichael, son of Duncan and Agness Carmichael, born 21 March 1769, baptized 3 April 1769

Samuel Caldwell, son of James and Elizabeth Caldwell, born 10 March 1769, baptized 8 June 1769

John Cross, son of Samuel and Susanna Cross, born 8 November 1769, baptized 17 November 1769

James Coxe, son of James and Mary Coxe, born 27 June 1770, baptized 10 August 1770

Comfort Cromwell, daughter of Nathan and Phebe Cromwell, born 1 December 1769, baptized 19 August 1770

James Caldwell, son of James and Elizabeth Caldwell, born 30 November 1770, baptized 10 January 1771

Archibald Carmichael, son of Duncan and Agness Carmichael, born 3[?] February 1771, baptized 28 February 1771

John Clement, son of John and Jane Clement, born 25 November 1770, baptized 7 May 1771

Margaret Crawford, daughter of Alexander and Jane Crawford, born 16 January 1772, baptized 7 June 1772

William Coxe, son of James and Mary Coxe, born 30 December 1772, baptized 16 February 1773

Nicholas Clement, son of John and Jane Clement, born 16 January 1773, baptized 16 February 1773

Susanna Caldwell, daughter of James and Elizabeth Caldwell, born 30 December 1772, baptized 7 March 1773

Robert Clark, son of John and Rebecca Clark, born 29 January 1773, baptized 20 March 1773

Nathan Cromwell, son of Nathan and Phebe Cromwell, born 21 September 1772, baptized 5 September 1773

Edward Nicol Clopper, son of Cornelius and Rachel Clopper, born 8 November 1773, baptized 9 December 1773

FIRST PRESBYTERIAN CHURCH 11

Mary Carmichael, daughter of Daniel and Anne Carmichael, born 9 November 1773, baptized 12 December 1773

Elizabeth Calhoun, daughter of James and Agness Calhoun, born 26 April 1774, baptized 26 June 1774

Mary Coxe, daughter of James and Mary Coxe, born 31 December 1775, baptized 23 January 1775

Hugh Cameron, son of James and Elizabeth Cameron, born 17 September 1775, baptized 8 October 1775

Sarah Clark, daughter of John and Rebecca Clark, born 18 November 1776, baptized 3 January 1776

Abraham Duryee Clopper, son of Cornelius and Rachel Clopper, born 17 February 1776, baptized 17 march 1776

Sidney and Sarah Clement, twins of John and Jane Clement, born 23 March 1776, baptized 17 June 1776

Rachel Clark, daughter of John and Rebecca Clark, born 21 February 1778, baptized 23 April 1778

Jehu Cannon, son of Isaac and Mary Cannon, born 25 January 1778, baptized 10 August 1778

Priscilla Calhoun, daughter of John and Margaret Calhoun, born 9 April 1779, baptized 29 April 1779

Elizabeth Crawford, daughter of Robert and Anne Crawford, born 23 February 1777, baptized 27 August 1779

James Crawford, son of Robert and Anne Crawford, born 10 June 1779, baptized 27 August 1779

John Cunningham, son of John and Frances Cunningham, born 29 March 1778, baptized 23 October 1780

Robert Crawford, son of Robert and Anne Crawford, born 11 December 1781, baptized 23 October 1782

Jane Grable, daughter of Jacob and Martha Grable, born 10 February 1783, baptized 29 June 1783

Isaac Causten, son of Isaac and Jane Causten, born 14 July 1783, baptized 7 September 1783

Samuel Chambers, son of Arthur and Sarah Chambers, born 7 May 1784, baptized 4 July 1784

James Carmichael, son of Alexander and Margaret Carmichael, born 21 December 1785, baptized 9 January 1786

Joseph Causten, son of Isaac and Jane Causten, born 13 October 1785, baptized 1 March 1786

Arabella Cunningham, daughter of John and Margaret Cunningham, born 28 November 1787, baptized 20 December 1787

Leah Clopper, daughter of John and Elizabeth Clopper, born 14 August 1787, baptized 26 December 1787

Hugh Edward Brown, son of Edward and Alice Brown, born 15 February 1786, baptized 31 January 1788

Andrew Cooper, son of John and Agness Cooper, born 22 March 1788, baptized 27 April 1788

James Causten, son of Isaac and Jane Causten, born 26 September 1787, baptized 7 May 1788

Mary Anne Conn, daughter of Edward and Alice Conn, born 3 April 1788, baptized 12 August 1788

Hannah Coulter, daughter of John and Mary Coulter, born 23 October 1788, baptized 11 January 1789

William Cooper Chambers, son of Arthur and Sarah Chambers, born 30 September 1788, baptized 26 July 1789

Louisa Coulter, daughter of John and Mary Coulter, born 12 October 1789, baptized 25 December 1789

Elizabeth Calquhaun, daughter of Lamont and Janit Calquhaun, born 22 April 1790, baptized 7 May 1790

Joseph Cooper, son of John and Agness Cooper, born 20 June 1790, baptized 28 June 1790

William Carson, son of Andrew and Jane Carson, born 5 June 1790, baptized 26 October 1790

Peter Clark, son of Matthew and Janit Clark, born 18 November 1790, baptized 9 December 1790

John Mather Cunningham, son of John and Margaret Cunningham, born 23 April 1791, baptized 5 May 1791

Matilda, John, and Elizabeth Chambers, children [triplets] of Arthur and Sarah Chambers, born 26 March, baptized 29 May 1791

Joseph Causten, son of Isaac and Jane Causten, born 16 March 1792, baptized 15 April 1792

John Alexander Coulter, son of John and Mary Coulter, born 3 January 1792, baptized 13 May 1792

Samuel Carlile, son of James and Agness Carlile, born 16 January 1792, baptized 20 May 1792

Rachel Clinton, daughter of Isaac and Elizabeth Clinton, born 3[?] July 1792, baptized 14 July 1792

Thomas Clark, son of Thomas and Ann Clark, born 3 November 1792, baptized 14 November 1792

John Carson, son of Andrew and Jane Carson, born 22 January 1792, baptized 13 January 1793

FIRST PRESBYTERIAN CHURCH 13

Margaret Clarke, daughter of Matthew and Janit Clarke, born 29 January 1793, baptized 29 March 1793

Henry Campbell, son of Robert and Catherine Campbell, born 28 January 1793, baptized 5 May 1793

John Parks Coulter, son of Alexander and Hetty Coulter, born 11 March 1793, baptized 5 May 1793

Elizabeth and Mary Coulter, twins of John and Mary Coulter, born 17 April 1793, baptized 9 May 1793 [1792?]

Joseph Mather Cunningham, son of John and Margaret Cunningham, born 5 July 1793, baptized 19 July 1793

John Chesnut, son of James and Lydia Chesnut, born 26 October 1794, baptized 2 November 1794

John Clarke, son of Matthew and Janit Clarke, born 30 November 1794, baptized 21 December 1794

John Brown Cunningham, son of John and Margaret Cunningham, born 5 March 1795, baptized 19 March 1795

John Campbell, son of Robert and Catherine Campbell, born 14 August 1795, baptized 5 April 1795

Josiah and George Crosby, twins of Josiah and Hannah Crosby, born 21 November 1782, baptized 19 April 1795

Hannah Crosby, daughter of Josiah and Hannah Crosby, born 19 July 1784, baptized 19 April 1795

Henry Payson Crosby, son of Josiah and Hannah Crosby, born 18 April 1786, baptized 19 April 1795

Caroline Crosby, daughter of Josiah and Hannah Crosby, born 5 September 1794, baptized 19 April 1795

Hannah Coulter, daughter of John and Mary Coulter, born 16 April 1795, baptized 17 May 1795

Alexander Coulter, son of Alexander and Ester Coulter, born 27 January 1795, baptized 24 May 1795

Sarah Carson, daughter of Andrew and Jane Carson, born 9 April 1794, baptized 25 July 1795

James Carlile, son of James and Agness Carlile, born 24 September 1795, baptized 5 October 1795

Jane Williams Clopper, daughter of Peter and Mary Clopper, born 7 July 1795, baptized 7 February 1796

Alexander John Calhoun, son of Alexander and Sarah Calhoun, born ---- [blank], baptized 6 June 1796

James Chesnut, son of James and Lydia Chesnut, born 25 August 1796, baptized 2 September 1796

Andrew Coulter, son of Alexander and Esther Coulter, born 7 July 1796, baptized 4 September 1796

Esther and Louisa Coulter, twins of John and Mary Coulter, born 11 July 1796, baptized 16 December 1796

Edward Nicols Clopper, son of Peter and Mary Clopper, born 19 October 1796, baptized 2 April 1797

William Caldwell, son of John and Mary Caldwell, born 21 May 1797, baptized 15 June 1797

Margaret Cross, daughter of Robert and Catharine Cross, born 7 March 1797, baptized 16 July 1797

Macdonald Cox, son of James and Catharine Cox, born 11 October 1797, baptized 6 December 1797

Jane Augusta Wilson Cunningham, daughter of John and Margaret, born 23 December 1797, baptized 13 January 1798

Mary Coulter, daughter of John and Margaret Coulter, born 14 January 1798, baptized 15 January 1798

Catharine Gough Cantwell, daughter of Thomas and Sarah Cantwell, born 12 January 1798, baptized 27 March 1798

Ann Cole, daughter of John and Mary Cole, born 11 February 1798, baptized 1 April 1798

Ann Carson, daughter of Andrew and Jane Carson, born 5 December 1797, baptized 9 April 1798

Susan Coulter, daughter of John and Mary Coulter, born 12 March 1798, baptized 7 December 1798

Mifflin Coulter, son of Alexander and Esther Coulter, born 27 November 1798, baptized 12 April 1799

Mary Cross, daughter of Robert and Catharine Cross, born 18 April 1800, baptized 3 May 1800

John Coulter, son of John and Mary Coulter, born 9 November 1800, baptized 19 March 1801

Hannah Daugherty, daughter of Hugh and Hannah Daugherty, born 5 February 1765, baptized 8 October 1765

Margaret Downey, daughter of Thomas and Mary Downey, born 13 July 1766, baptized 30 November 1766

John Duffy, son of John and Mary Duffy, born 2 November 1767, baptized 2 December 1767

Margaret Doran, daughter of James and Margaret Doran, born 12 April 1768, baptized 14 May 1768

William Doran, son of James and Margaret Doran, born 16 May 1768, baptized 2 August 1769

FIRST PRESBYTERIAN CHURCH

William Drummond, son of John and Mary Drummond, born 7 June 1772, baptized 23 August 1772

John and Anne Deaver, adults, baptized 14 November 1771

John Deaver, son of John and Anne Deaver, born 15[?] April 1759, baptized 14 November 1771

Martha Deaver, daughter of John and Anne Deaver, born 3 February 1762, baptized 14 November 1771

Mary Deaver, daughter of John and Anne Deaver, born 31 October 1765, baptized 14 November 1771

Nathan Deaver, son of John and Anne Deaver, born 25 July 1771, baptized 14 November 1771

Mary Duncan, daughter of William and Rebecca Duncan, born 7 April 1772, baptized 17 May 1772

Esther Duncan, daughter of William and Rebecca Duncan, born 26 September 1773, baptized 25 October 1773

John Dewitt, son of Thomas and Elizabeth Dewitt, born 31 December 1773, baptized 13 March 1774

Abigail Duncan, daughter of William and Rebecca Duncan, born 15 May 1775, baptized 5 June 1775

Agness Duncan, daughter of William and Rebecca Duncan, born 22 January 1776, baptized 13 February 1776

James Dunlap, son of James and Sarah Dunlap, born 26 December 1777, baptized 2 January 1778

Elizabeth Duncan, daughter of William and Rebecca Duncan, born 7 April 1778, baptized 6 May 1778

Joseph Donaldson, son of Joseph and Frances Donaldson, born 17 July 1780, baptized 7 September 1780

Joseph Dorrity, son of Joseph and Margaret Dorrity, born 13 July 1781, baptized 1 September 1781

Cornelius Dysard, son of John and Ruth Dysard, born 12 June 1783, baptized 26 June 1783

Janit Duncan, daughter of William and Rebecca Duncan, born 15 February 1784, baptized 3 July 1784

John Paul Dumerte, son of John and Elizabeth Dumerte, born 9 December 1783, baptized 15 August 1784

Elizabeth Duham, adult, baptized 14 April 1784

Jacob Duham, son of Samuel and Elizabeth Duham, born 3 March 1778, baptized 14 April 1785

Samuel Johnston Donaldson, son of Joseph and Frances Donaldson, born 18 April 1785, baptized 14 May 1785

John Duncan, son of William and Rebecca Duncan, born 7 December 1785, baptized 7 January 1786

Anna Elizabeth Dumerte, daughter of John and Elizabeth Dumerte, born 1 February 1786, baptized 12 May 1786

Sarah Duncan, daughter of William and Rebecca Duncan, born 26 September 1787, baptized 5 October 1787

Cumberland Dugan, son of Cumberland and Margaret Dugan, born 14 September 1787, baptized 6 October 1787

Sophia Dumerte, daughter of John and Elizabeth Dumerte, born 13 September 1787, baptized 18 December 1787

Francis Donaldson, son of Joseph and Frances Donaldson, born 30 September 1786, baptized ---- [blank], by Dr. West

John Johnston Donaldson, son of Joseph and Frances Donaldson, born 27 August 1788, baptized 20 November 1788

Rebecca Dugan, daughter of Cumberland and Margaret Dugan, born 22 October 1788, baptized 15 December 1788

Hugh Duncan, son of William and Rebecca Duncan, born 17 February 1789, baptized 11 March 1789

David Duncan, son of William and Rebecca Duncan, born 29 October 1790, baptized 18 November 1790

Hugh Duncan, son of William and Mary Duncan, born 2 August 1791, baptized 6 August 1791

William Davison, son of Samuel and Jane Davison, born 19 December 1787 [1789?], baptized 12 September 1791

Jane Dick, daughter of David and Elizabeth Dick, born 27 March 1792, baptized 3 June 1792

Samuel Duncan, son of William and Mary Duncan, born 6 July 1792, baptized 19 July 1792

Samuel Duncan, son of William and Mary Duncan, born 24 February 1794, baptized 6 March 1794

Mary Magdalane Dagan, daughter of George and Fanny Dagan, born 23 March 1794, baptized 27 April 1794

Mary Dick, daughter of David and Elizabeth Dick, born 28 April 1794, baptized 27 July 1794

Samuel Henry Dunsmore, son of Thomas and Charlotte Dunsmore, born 28 August 1794, baptized 28 October 1794

William Scott Duncan, son of William and Mary Duncan, born 19 February 1795, baptized 22 February 1795

Elizabeth Glen Davies, daughter of John and Sarah Davies, born 20 December 1794, baptized 5 March 1795

FIRST PRESBYTERIAN CHURCH 17

Debby Duncan, daughter of William and Mary Duncan, born 15 March 1795, baptized 2 April 1795
Harriet Daniels, daughter of Anthony and Anna Maria Daniels, born 17 May 1795, baptized 12 August 1795
John Dick, son of David and Elizabeth Dick, born 17 October 1795, baptized 24 January 1796
Jacob Davies, son of John and Sarah Davies, born 29 May 1796, baptized 4 September 1796
Charlotte Dunsmoore, daughter of Thomas and Charlotte Dunsmoore, born 13 September 1796, baptized 20 September 1795
Agness Davidson, daughter of Andrew and Mary Davidson, born 12 May 1796, baptized 28 October 1796
Rebecca Dobson Duncan, daughter of William and Rebecca Duncan, born 12 November 1796, baptized 5 December 1796
Mary Dick, daughter of David and Elizabeth Dick, born 13 April 1797, baptized 21 April 1797
James Somervell Dykes, son of William and Margaret Dykes, born 26 October 1796, baptized 9 September 1797
William Glen Davies, son of John and Sarah Davies, born 30 August 1797, baptized 26 October 1797
John Daniels, son of Anthony and Ann Daniels, born 23 November 1797, baptized 20 December 1797
Margaret Davidson, daughter of Andrew and Mary Davidson, born 14 September 1797, baptized 14 June 1798
Elizabeth Dashiels, daughter of Richard and Rachel Dashiels, born 27 October 1796, baptized 27 September 1798
Maria Dashiels, daughter of Richard and Rachel Dashiels, born 1 March 1798, baptized 27 September 1798
Sarah Davidson, daughter of Andrew and Mary Davidson, born 19 December 1798, baptized 1 June 1799
Joseph Doaks, son of James and Mary Doaks, born 2 July 1797, baptized 30 June 1799
Jane Doaks, daughter of James and Mary Doaks, born 14 October 1798, baptized 2 June 1799
Edward Duncan, son of William and Mary Duncan, born 7 February 1799, baptized 11 November 1799
Elizabeth Genevieve Dumerte, daughter of John and Elizabeth Dumerte born 31 March 1793, baptized abroad
Catharine Virginia Dumerte, daughter of John and Elizabeth Dumerte, born 28 December 1795, baptized 1 March 1801

George Keeports Dumerte, son of John and Elizabeth Dumerte, born 16 January [1796?], baptized 1 March 1801
Jacob Adrain Dumerte, son of John and Elizabeth Dumerte, born 8 April 1798, baptized 1 March 1801
Henrietta Maria Dumerte, daughter of John and Elizabeth Dumerte, born 12 June 1799, baptized 1 March 1801
Ann Maria Duncan, daughter of William and Mary Duncan, born 17 June 1801, baptized 14 July 1801
Margaret English, daughter of Robert and Janit English, born 26 June 1767, baptized 26 July 1767
William English, son of Robert and Janit English, born 8 July 1769, baptized 13 August 1769
Thomas English, son of George and Elizabeth English, born 1 September 1771, baptized 18 October 1771
Mary Emmit, daughter of David and Jane Emmit, born 22 June 1779, baptized 19 July 1779
Margaret Emmit, daughter of David and Jane Emmit, born 9 November 1780, baptized 8 January 1781
John Emmit, son of David and Jane Emmit, born 14 June 1784, baptized 17 July 1784
William Adams Edwards, son of Thomas and Mary Edwards, born 15 August 1788, baptized 12 January 1789
Eliza Edwards, daughter of Thomas and Mary Edwards, born 24 November 1790, baptized 12 April 1791
Elizabeth Elvins, adult, baptized 1 January 1800
William Reed Rogers, son of William and Elizabeth Rogers, born 26 July 1794, baptized 1 January 1800
Hugh Fraser, son of Robert and Christiana Fraser, born 16 December 1771, baptized 14 March 1772 by Mr. Ewing Ph.D.
Alexander Fraser, son of Hugh and Ruth Fraser, born 3 December 1769, baptized 2 September 1772
Mary Anne Fraser, daughter of Hugh and Ruth Fraser, born 29 February 1772, baptized 2 September 1772
Sarah Fleming, daughter of William and Anne Fleming, born 7 August 1773, baptized 5 November 1773
William Fraser, son of James and Elizabeth Fraser, born 5 July 1773, baptized 8 July 1774
James Fraser, son of James and Elizabeth Fraser, born 5 March 1775, baptized 14 May 1775

FIRST PRESBYTERIAN CHURCH

William Fraser, son of William and Mary Fraser, born 17 April 1775, baptized 14 May 1775

Mary Fraser, daughter of William and Mary Fraser, born 23 April 1777, baptized 8 June 1777

Mary French, daughter of Robert and Mary French, born 3 October 1778, baptized 4 February 1779

Margaret Finlater, daughter of Alexander and Mary Finlater, born 12 June 1782, baptized 3 July 1782

Mary Folger, daughter of Frederic and Isabella Folger, born 6 March 1783, baptized 18 August 1783

Franklin Folger, son of Frederic and Isabella Folger, born 17 November 1784, baptized 21[?] April 1785

James Finlater, son of Alexander and Mary Finlater, born 30 January 1786, baptized 11 February 1786

Frederic Folger, son of Frederic and Isabella Folger, born 21 March 1786, baptized 6 April 1786

Elizabeth Finlater, daughter of Alexander and Mary Finlater, born 17 October 1787, baptized 14 November 1787

Sophia Maria Folger, daughter of Frederic and Isabella Folger, born 21 [31?] March 1788, baptized 16 December 1788

Thomas Cale Folger, son of Frederic and Isabella Folger, born 28 June 1790, baptized 9 August 1790

Mary Finlater, daughter of Alexander and Mary Finlater, born 28 August 1791, baptized 9 August 1790

Sarah Emory Forman, daughter of William Lee and Jane Forman, born 17 May 1792, baptized 31 January 1793

Isabella Folger, daughter of Frederic and Isabella Folger, born 12 September 1792, baptized 17 March 1793

Jane Finlater, daughter of Alexander and Mary Finlater, born ---- [blank], baptized 30 June 1793

Margaret Forman, daughter of William Lee and Jane Forman, born 9 June 1793, baptized 26 January 1794

William Spear Forman, son of William Lee and Jane Forman, born 28 August 1794, baptized 21 September 1794

Anne Finlater, daughter of Alexander and Mary Finlater, born 19 December 1795, baptized 7 January 1796

Polly Finley, daughter of Ebenezer and Jenny Finley, born 20 February 1797, baptized 30 April 1797

Sophia Forman, daughter of William Lee and Jane Forman, born 26 March 1796, baptized -- [blank] April 1796

Eliza Forman, daughter of William Lee and Jane Forman, born 11 April 1797, baptized 6 May 1797

Stephen Wilson Falls, son of Moor and Rebecca Falls, born 26 July 1797, baptized 8 September 1797

Jane Finlater, daughter of Alexander and Mary Finlater, born 3 August 1797, baptized 24 September 1797

Daniel Fackner, son of James and Jane Fackner, born 30 June 1797, baptized 8 April 1798

John Spear Forman, son of William Lee and Jane Forman, born 4 January 1799, baptized 13 March 1799

Rebecca Falls, daughter of Moor and Rebecca Falls, born 1 September 1798, baptized 21 April 1799

Thomas Cousins Fry, son of Thomas and Isabella Fry, born 26 July 1796, baptized 5 April 1800

Elizabeth Jane Fry, daughter of Thomas and Isabella Fry, born 15 July 1798, baptized 5 April 1800

William Irvin Fry, son of Thomas and Isabella Fry, born 15 March 1800, baptized 5 April 1800

Jane Falls, daughter of Moor and Rebecca Falls, born 4 September 1799, baptized 8 January 1801

Jane Hollins Forman, daughter of William Lee and Jane Forman, born 18 July 1800, baptized 16 January 1801

Sarah Falls, daughter of Moor and Rebecca Falls, born 27 April 1801, baptized 25 June 1801

Joseph Washington Finley, son of Ebenezer and Jenny Finley, born 28 April 1801, baptized 12 July 1801

Mary Gibson, daughter of Robert and Elizabeth Gibson, born 13 June 1770, baptized 17 June 1770

James Galloway, son of James and Mary Galloway, born 9 June 1770, baptized 8 July 1770

Susanna Galloway, daughter of James and Mary Galloway, born 26 August 1772, baptized 4 September 1772

John Garretson, son of Cornelius and Mary Garretson, born 3 February 1773, baptized 26 June 1774

Anne Galloway, daughter of James and Mary Galloway, born 16 July 1774, baptized 26 July 1774

James Greier, son of Alexander and Alice Greier, born 21 December 1774, baptized 4 January 1775

Mary and Anne Gordon, twins of John and Catharine Gordon, born 9 December 1774, baptized 15 January 1775

William Martin Garretson, son of Cornelius and Mary Garretson, born 14 October 1775, baptized 5 November 1775
Sarah Gordon, daughter of John and Catharine Gordon, born 19 August 1776, baptized 6[?] September 1776
Moses Galloway, son of James and Mary Galloway, born 23 October 1776, baptized 30 October 1776
Janit Galloway, daughter of James and Mary Galloway, born 4 February 1778, baptized 1 March 1778
John Gordon, son of John and Catharine Gordon, born 3 April 1778, baptized 31 May 1778
Independent Gist, son of Mordecai and Mary Gist, born 8 January 1779, baptized 31 January 1779
Mary Garretson, daughter of Cornelius and Mary Garretson, born 14 December 1778, baptized 14 February 1779
Elizabeth Gilmor, daughter of Robert and Louisa Gilmor, born 11 May 1779, baptized 17 June 1779
Charles Gordon, son of John and Catharine Gordon, born 8 October 1779, baptized 11 June 1780
Jane Gilmor, daughter of Robert and Louisa Gilmor, born 27 December 1780, baptized 25 February 1781
Sabrey [?] Gordon, daughter of John and Catharine Gordon, born 5 August 1781, baptized 17 August 1781
Thomas Gilmor, son of Robert and Louisa Gilmor, born 15 January 1782, baptized 21 April 1782
George Gordon, son of John and Catharine Gordon, born ---- [blank], baptized 27 October 1782
Benjamin Garrison, son of John and Hannah Garrison, born 13 January 1784, baptized 27 October 1784
Harriet Gordon, daughter of John and Catharine Gordon, born 6 August 1784, baptized 19 January 1785
William Gordon, son of John and Catharine Gordon, born 21 September 1785, baptized 10 October 1785
Louisa Gittings, daughter of Richard and Mary Gittings, born 29 December 1789, baptized 12 May 1790
Elizabeth Gallagher, daughter of Alexander and Elizabeth Gallagher, born 8 June 1791, baptized 4 December 1791
Peter Gallagher, son of Alexander and Elizabeth Gallagher, born 26 December 1788, baptized 4 December 1791
James Gallagher, son of Alexander and Elizabeth Gallagher, born 6 September 1790, baptized 4 December 1791

Maria Golden, daughter of John and Susanna Golden, born 29 November 1791, baptized 6 May 1792

Thomas Gill, son of John and Esther Gill, born 14 January 1792, baptized 26 February 1793

Martha Gallagher, daughter of Alexander and Elizabeth Gallagher, born 28 May 1793, baptized 7 July 1793

Thomas Gallagher, son of Alexander and Elizabeth Gallagher, born 25 July 1795, baptized 10 October 1795

Sarah Girkey, daughter of Frederic and Margaret Girkey, born 1 October 1795, baptized 1 November 1795

Alexander Gibson, son of James and Elizabeth Gibson, born 1 December 1796, baptized 12 March 1797

Hugh Gallagher, son of Alexander and Elizabeth Gallagher, born 15 October 1797, baptized 12 December 1797

Mary Bunker Gardner, daughter of Timothy and Margaret Gardner, born 16 November 1787, baptized 13 January 1798

William Henry Gardner, son of Obed and Elizabeth Gardner, born 23 November 1796, baptized 13 January 1798

John Graham, son of Robert and Mary Graham, born 24 January 1798, baptized 25 February 1798

Elizabeth Grant, daughter of Angus and Janit Grant, born 7 February 1798, baptized 26 March 1798

Hamilton Graham, son of Hamilton and Mary Graham, born 10 November 1797, baptized 23 July 1798

Elizabeth Gibson, daughter of James and Elizabeth Gibson, born 24 August 1798, baptized 20 April 1799

Frances Jane Grant, daughter of Daniel and Isabella Grant, born 19 March 1797, baptized 30 June 1799

Jenny Graham, daughter of Robert and Mary Graham, born 16 May 1799, baptized 8 December 1799

Louisa Guishard, daughter of Mark and Catharine Guishard, born 20 June 1798, baptized 1 January 1800

Pamela Guishard, daughter of Mary and Catharine Guishard, born 7 July 1799, baptized 1 January 1800

George Washington Gallagher, son of Alexander & Elizabeth Gallagher born -- [?] December, 1799, baptized 13[?] February, 1800

Robert Hamilton, son of James and Mary Hamilton, born 9 December 1765, baptized 31 August 1766

Eleanor Hamilton, daughter of James and Mary Hamilton, born 16 March 1768, baptized 12 June 1768

FIRST PRESBYTERIAN CHURCH

Alexander Hooks, son of Andrew and Margaret Hooks, born 31 July 1766, baptized 30 November 1768

Margaret Harris, daughter of Matthew and Sooty Harris, born 31 July 1766, baptized 30 November 1768

Mary Helm, daughter of George and Frances Helm, born 17 August 1769, baptized 31 December 1769

David Harris, son of William and Sarah Harris, born 23 July 1770, baptized 12 August 1770

William Holliday, son of James and Mary Holliday, born 27 July 1770, baptized 26 August 1770

Henry Helm, son of George and Frances Helm, born 24 February 1771, baptized 21 April 1771

Charles Holliday, son of James and Mary Holliday, born 23 November 1771, baptized 1 December 1771

Jonathan Haslet, son of William and Elizabeth Haslet, born 12 October 1771, baptized 7 June 1772

Henry Helm, son of George and Frances Helm, born 26 November 1772, baptized 7 December 1772

John Hall, son of Philip and Sarah Hall, born 10 August 1772, baptized 17 January 1773

Sarah Harris, daughter of William and Sarah Harris, born 27 April 1773, baptized 12 May 1773

Janit Holliday, daughter of James and Mary Holliday, born 10 July 1773, baptized 15 August 1773

John Hawkins, son of John and Agness Hawkins, born 27 November 1773, baptized 10 December 1773

Isabella Hannah, daughter of William and Grissel Hannah, born 1 September 1774, baptized 5 October 1774

Alexander Fraser Hall, son of Philip and Sarah Hall, born 6 June 1774, baptized 18 October 1774

George Helm, son of George and Frances Helm, born 16 October 1774, baptized 20 January 1775

Mary Haslet, daughter of Samuel and Kissinah Haslet, born 31 January 1775, baptized 19 March 1775

Matthew Hawkins, son of John and Agness Hawkins, born 1 August 1775, baptized 7 August 1775

George Harris, son of Charles and Rebecca Harris, born 8 November 1775, baptized 17 December 1775

Philip Hall, son of Philip and Sarah Hall, born 10 April 1776, baptized 4 August 1776

Elizabeth Hannah, daughter of William and Grissel Hannah, born 15 June 1777, baptized 25 August 1777

Anne Helm, daughter of George and Frances Helm, born 9 June 1777, baptized 29 August 1777

Benjamin Harris, son of Charles and Rebecca Harris, born 31 January 1778, baptized 22 February 1778

Mary Hawkins, daughter of John and Agness Hawkins, born 31 December 1778, baptized 7 January 1779

Sarah Haslet, daughter of Moses and Sarah Haslet, born 10 March 1779, baptized 19 April 1779

William Hannah, son of William and Grissel Hannah, born 18 February 1779, baptized 17 May 1779

Robert Henderson, son of Robert and Elizabeth Henderson, born 6 July 1779, baptized 13 July 1779

Anne Haslet, daughter of Samuel and Kessina Haslet, born 4 July 1777, baptized 4 June 1780

Joseph Haslet, son of Samuel and Kessina Haslet, born 5 June 1779, baptized 4 June 1780

John Haslet, son of Moses and Sarah Haslet, born 21 May 1780, baptized 18 June 1780

Frances Hawkins, daughter of William and Frances Hawkins, born 16 September 1780, baptized 23 October 1780

Mary Bond Hay, daughter of John and Martha Hay, born 14 March 1781, baptized 8 April 1781

Elizabeth Henderson, daughter of Robert and Elizabeth Henderson, born 30 April 1781, baptized 9 May 1781

Eliza Harris, daughter of David and Sarah Harris, born 20 March 1781, baptized 3 July 1781

Thomas Hannah, son of William and Grissel Hannah, born 21 January 1781, baptized 16 July 1781

Margaret Helm, daughter of George and Frances Helm, born 16 July 1781, baptized 23 July 1781

Daniel Hughes, son of Daniel and Susanna Hughes, born 2 September 1781, baptized 9 April 1782

Molly Harris, daughter of David and Sarah Harris, born 7 February 1782, baptized 28 April 1782

Solomon Haslet, son of Moses and Sarah Haslet, born 8 April 1782, baptized 12 May 1782

George Hall, son of Philip and Sarah Hall, born 2 September 1778, baptized 22 July 1782

Eleanor Hall, daughter of Philip and Sarah Hall, born 25 March 1782, baptized 22 July 1782

John Hay, son of John and Martha Hay, born 28 January 1783, baptized 3 March 1783

John Henderson, son of Robert and Elizabeth Henderson, born 13 May 1783, baptized 16 May 1783

Elizabeth Smith Hall, daughter of Josias Carvil and Janit Hall, born 19 June 1783, baptized 8 July 1783

John Harris, son of David and Sarah Harris, born 1 July 1783, baptized 7 September 1783

Hannah Haslet, daughter of Moses and Sarah Haslet, born 26 January 1784, baptized 19 December 1784

Samuel Haslet, son of Samuel and Kissinah Haslet, born 5 July 1782, baptized 22 January 1785

Sarah Haslet, daughter of Samuel and Kissinah Haslet, born 2 January 1785, baptized 22 January 1785

Andrew Haslet, son of Moses and Sarah Haslet, born 11 September 1785, baptized 1 October 1785

Matthew Hamilton, son of John and Bridget Hamilton, born 11 July 1785, baptized 20 November 1785

Hannah Elizabeth Hall, daughter of Josias Carvil and Janit Hall, born 28 November 1785, baptized 10 May 1786

Andrew Hay, son of John and Martha Hay, born 18 July 1786, baptized 15 April 1787

William Haslet, son of Moses and Sarah Haslet, born 26 February 1787, baptized 13 May 1787

John Smith Collins, son of John and Janit Collins, born 9 October 1787, baptized 4 November 1787

John Agnew Hamilton, son of John Agnew and Margaret Hamilton, born 9 November 1787, baptized 9 February 1788

Bell Hutton, daughter of William and Margaret Hutton, born 27 October 1788, baptized 15 November 1788

William Hollins, son of John and Janit Hollins, born 24 February 1789, baptized 10 March 1789

Julia Honora, daughter of John Anthony and Mary Honora, born 15 May 1789, baptized 13 August 1789

Martha Hill, daughter of Jonas and Jane Hill, born 7 July 1788, baptized 18 December 1789

Jeremiah Hill, daughter of Jonas and Jane Hill, born 26 October 1784, baptized 18 December 1789

William Hill, son of Jonas and Jane Hill, born 24 October 1786, baptized 18 December 1789

Joseph Hill, son of Jonas and Jane Hill, born 21 March 1790, baptized 8 April 1790

George Salmon Haslet, son of Moses and Sarah Haslet, born 26 February 1790, baptized 24 April 1790

Benedict William Hall, son of Josiah Carvil and Janit Hall, born 6 May 1790, baptized 15 May 1790

Molly Buchanan Hollins, daughter of John and Janit Hollins, born 5 August 1790, baptized 29 August 1790

Lydia Harvey, daughter of James and Anne Harvey, born 10 October 1790, baptized 12 November 1790

Mary Henry, daughter of John and Christian Henry, born 28 July 1790, baptized 22 July 1791

Richard von den Heavell, son of Romelis Wilhelmus and Remptje von den Heavell, born 1 August 1791, baptized 4 September 1791

Margaret Harvey, daughter of James and Anne Harvey, born 6 April 1792, baptized 17 June 1792

Anne Holmes, daughter of John and Anne Holmes, born 21 August 1791, baptized 2 November 1792

Molly Buchanan Hollins, daughter of John and Janit Hollins, born 13 December 1792, baptized 17 March 1793

Mary Hill, daughter of Jonas and Jane Hill, born 23 February 1791, baptized 28 May 1793

Mary Hannah, daughter of Caleb and Mary Hannah, born 29 April 1792, baptized 15 September 1793

William Haslet, son of Alexander and Rachel Haslet, born 12 September 1793, baptized 17 November 1793

Catharine Harnaugh, daughter of John and Christian Harnaugh, born ----- [blank], baptized 27 April 1794

Thomas Henry Hunter, son of William and Hannah Hunter, born ---- [illegible], baptized -- May 1795

George Henderson, son of William and Isabella Henderson, born 4 August 1795, baptized 7 November 1795

Elizabeth Haslet, daughter of Alexander and Rachel Haslet, born 7 October 1795, baptized 3 January 1796

Jane Hammet, daughter of Thomas and Maria Rosanna Hammet, born 25 March 1796, baptized 8 June 1796

Robert Hollins, son of John and Janit Hollins, born 29 June 1797, baptized 9 July 1797

FIRST PRESBYTERIAN CHURCH

John Lewis Houston, son of John and Elizabeth Houston, born 14 March 1798, baptized 18 March 1798

Jane Catharine Hannah, daughter of Edward and Rebecca Hannah, born 1 March 1798, baptized 17 June 1798

Margaretta Hollins, daughter of John and Janit Hollins, born 16 August 1798, baptized 31 August 1798

Thomas Hammett, son of Thomas and Rosanna Hammett, born 16 February 1798, baptized 3 September 1798

Susanna Haslet, daughter of Alexander and Elizabeth Haslet, born 10 January 1799, baptized 14 April 1799

Margaret Hunter, daughter of John and Agness Hunter, born 31 May 1798, baptized 26 October 1799

George Nicholas Hollins, son of John and Janit Hollins, born 20 September 1799, baptized 24 November 1799

William Duncan Haslet, son of Alexander and Elizabeth Haslet, born 25 September 1800, baptized 5 January 1801

Margaret Hammett, daughter of Jesse and Jane Hammett, born 20 April 1800, baptized 20 January 1801

Mary Jane Hollins, daughter of John and Janit Hollins, born 20 March 1801, baptized 15 May 1801

Margaret Hunter, daughter of John and Agness Hunter, born 30 May 1801, baptized 7 June 1801

Mary Hall, daughter of Alexander F. and Mary Hall, born 21 November 1800, baptized 12 July 1801

John Irvin, son of John and Sarah Irvin, born 25 September 1777, baptized 28 September 1777

John Johnston, son of Edward and Margaret Johnston, born 21 January 1766, baptized 15 January 1769

William Johnston, son of Hannah Johnston [father not named], born 11 August 1770, baptized 14 April 1771

Mary Stith Johnston, daughter of Christopher and Susanna Johnston, born 6 March 1781, baptized 8 April 1781

John Johnston, son of Christopher and Susanna Johnston, born 11 February 1783, baptized 23 March 1783

Janit Johnston, daughter of Christopher and Susanna Johnston, born 4 September 1784, baptized 10 October 1784

John Griffin Johnston, son of Christopher and Susanna Johnston, born 7 October 1786, baptized 17 December 1786

Elizabeth Jenney, daughter of Nathanael and Sarah Jenney, born 26 May 1788, baptized 21 September 1788

Robert Nelson Johnston, son of Christopher and Susanna Johnston, born 29 October 1788, baptized 19 November 1788

Susanna Johnston, daughter of Christopher and Susanna Johnston, born 6 January 1791, baptized 23 January 1791

Elizabeth Johnston, daughter of Christopher and Susanna Johnston, born 16 April 1793, baptized 12 May 1793

Elizabeth Johnston, daughter of Christopher and Susanna Johnston, born 31 July 1795, baptized 24 August 1795

Anna Maria Jenney, daughter of Nathanael and Sarah Jenney, born 31 December 1791, baptized 13 September 1795

John Jenney, son of Nathanael and Sarah Jenney, born 1 January 1794, baptized 13 September 1795

Margaret James, daughter of William and Janit James, born 30 September 1795, baptized 29 December 1795

Margaret Jaffries, daughter of John and Sarah Jaffries, born 5 June 1791, baptized 25 February 1797

James Jaffries, son of John and Sarah Jaffries, born 11 March 1794, baptized 5 February 1797

John Jackson, son of Collin and Jane Jackson, born --- [illegible], baptized ---- [illegible], 1797

Ann Elizabeth Johnston, daughter of John and Ann Johnston, born -- [blank] April, 1798, baptized 3 July 1798

James Jackson, son of Collin and Jane Jackson, born 19 October 1798, baptized 24 March 1799

David Hezekiah Johnson, son of Caleb and Jane Johnson, born 9 July 1798, baptized 21 October 1798

John James, son of William and Elizabeth James, born 9 May 1799, baptized 13 May 1799

Caleb ---- [illegible] Johnson, son of Caleb and Jane Johnson, born 14 January 1800, baptized 27 April 1800

Christopher Johnston, son of Christopher and Susanna Johnston, born 4 May 1800, baptized 20 July 1800, by Dr. Muir. ("On the information of the parents of the child last above named and at their instance and request I certify that there is an error in the record of his birth which happened on the 18th and not the 4th of May. This entry is made May 19, 1807. James Inglis, Pastor.")

Sarah Kelso, daughter of James and Rebecca Kelso, born 7 October 1767, baptized 14 October 1767

John Kelso, son of James and Rebecca Kelso, born 31 October 1770, baptized 14 December 1770

Hugh Kidd, son of John and Anne Kidd, born 18 January 1771, baptized 24 March 1771

William Knox, son of William and Elizabeth Knox, born 1 February 1782, baptized 13 March 1782

Thomas Kingan, son of Thomas and Elizabeth Kingan, born 17 April 1783, baptized 13 August 1783

Charity Kennedy, adult, baptized 14 April 1785

Jane Key, daughter of Andrew and Margaret Key, born 19 December 1785, baptized 30 December 1785

Margaret Key, daughter of Andrew and Margaret Key, born 19 February 1788, baptized 5 April 1788

James King, son of William and Elizabeth Anne King, born 22 July 1788, baptized 9 November 1788

George Peter Kingston, son of Nathaniel and Abigail Kingston, born 20 October 1788, baptized 13 August 1789

Joseph Kerr, son of William and Agness Kerr, born 5 April 1786, baptized 15 November 1789

Harriet Kerr, daughter of William and Agness Kerr, born 22 January 1789, baptized 15 November 1789

Marand [?] Key, son of Andrew and Margaret Key, born 26 October 1790, baptized 27 October 1790

Harriet Kingston, daughter of William and Margaret Kingston, born 16 January 1795, baptized 20 May 1795

John Pendleton Kennedy, son of John and Nancy Kennedy, born 25 October 1796, baptized 3 January 1796

Rebecca Knap, daughter of Samuel and Rebecca Knap, born 24 February 1797, baptized 11 June 1797

Thomas Key, son of Thomas and Jane Key, born 23 March 1797, baptized 9 July 1797

Andrew Kennedy, son of John and Nancy Kennedy, born 28 July 1797, baptized 12 December 1797

James and William Kennedy, twins of John and Agness Kennedy, born 8 October 1797, baptized 26 June 1798

Eliza Kearney, daughter of Richard and Ann Kearney, born 14 November 1798, baptized 2 April 1799

Elizabeth Kirkpatrick, daughter of Jeremiah and Elizabeth Kirkpatrick, born 30 July 1798, baptized 14 July 1799

Joseph Kerr, son of Thomas and Jane Kerr, born 17 December 1799, baptized 13 April 1780

John Kennedy, son of John and Agness Kennedy, born 13 February 1800, baptized 12 July 1801

Robert McNight Lawry, son of Thomas and Mary Lawry [Lowry?], born 12 February 1766, baptized 10 March 1766

Elizabeth Long, daughter of Thomas and Jane Long, born 27 February 1766, baptized 26 August 1766

Andrew Linn, son of [David?] and Rachel Linn, born 29 September 1766, baptized 12 December 1766

Thomas Lockard, son of Francis and Jane Lockard, born 25 November 1766, baptized 25 March 1767

John Long, son of Thomas and Jane Long, born 26 April 1768, baptized 26 June 1768

Jane Lockard, daughter of Francis and Jane Lockard, born 25 November 1768, baptized 8 January 1769

John Edwards Long, son of Robert and Elizabeth Long, born 11 March 1769, baptized 3 April 1769

Robert Lawry, son of Robert and Margaret Lawry [Lowry?], born 18 June 1769, baptized 16 July 1769

Robert Lawry, son of John and Anne Lawry [Lowry?], born 5 July 1769, baptized 20 July 1769

William Lockard, son of Francis and Jane Lockard, born 26 March 1771, baptized 14 April 1771

Mary Long, daughter of Thomas and Jane Long, born 31 October 1770, baptized 21 April 1771

Margaret Long, daughter of Thomas and Jane Long, born 30 June 1773, baptized 10 July 1773

Martha Lockard, daughter of Francis and Jane Lockard, born 1 August 1773, baptized 5 September 1773

Mary Lawrence, daughter of Daniel and Rachel Lawrence, born 25 September 1773, baptized 9 December 1773

Mary Anne Lindsay, daughter of Adam and Mary Lindsay, born 2 August 1775, baptized 14 September 1775

Elizabeth Laughlin, daughter of Robert and Jane Laughlin, born 2 October 1780, baptized 7 December 1780

Harriet Little, daughter of Alexander and Martha Little, born 29 December 1782, baptized 27 April 1783

William Lyon, son of Robert and Susanna Lyon, born 30 September 1784, baptized 17 December 1784

John Lemmond, son of William and Martha Lemmond, born 23 November 1785, baptized 12 February 1786

FIRST PRESBYTERIAN CHURCH 31

Elihu Hall Lyon, son of Robert and Susanna Lyon, born 2 January 1786, baptized 23 February 1786

Charles Grahame Lyon, son of Robert and Susanna Lyon, born 3 November 1787, baptized 17 December 1787

John Myer Lawrence, son of Richard and Elizabeth Lawrence, born 26 September 1787, baptized 24 December 1787

Thomas Leggat Lawrence, son of Richard and Elizabeth Lawrence, born 10 March 1789, baptized 18 April 1789

Alexander Liggat, son of Samuel and Jane Liggat, born 27 September 1788, baptized 1 June 1789

Catharine Lyon, daughter of Robert and Susanna Lyon, born 21 June 1789, baptized 25 September 1789

David Howland Lawrence, son of Richard and Elizabeth Lawrence, born 12 June 1791, baptized 28 July 1791

Elizabeth Longhead, daughter of Adam and Sarah Longhead [Langhead?] born 18 August 1791, baptized 7 November 1791

Jane Landes, daughter of Alexander and Mary Landes, born 3 January 1791, baptized 26 January 1792

Robert Lyon, son of Robert and Susanna Lyon, born 16 September 1791, baptized 15 November 1792

Jane Lowry, daughter of William and Olivia Lowry, born 1 December 1792, baptized 17 March 1793

Anne Landes, daughter of Alexander and Mary Landes, born 13 September 1793, baptized 21 September 1793

Olivia Lowry, daughter of William and Olivia Lowry, born 21 November 1793, baptized 1 December 1793

Thomas Langhead, son of Adam and Sarah Langhead [Longhead?], born 31 October 1793, baptized 26 January 1794

Francis Lason, son of Francis and Marieanna Lambert Lason, born 7 January 1794, baptized 30 March 1794

Mary Landes, daughter of Alexander and Mary Landes, born 10 August 1794, baptized 21 September 1794

Joseph Lyon, son of Robert and Susanna Lyon, born 3 June 1795, baptized 21 July 1795

Mary Crawford Law, daughter of James and Elizabeth Law, born 17 May 1796, baptized 4 September 1796

Jacob Davies Law, son of James and Elizabeth Law, born 18 June 1797, baptized 13 July 1797

William Barron Lewis, son of Charles and Margaret Lewis, born 1 January 1798, baptized 18 April 1798

Mary Lyon, daughter of Robert and Susanna Lyon, born 6 September 1797, baptized 3 May 1798

Rachel Davies Law, daughter of James and Elizabeth Law, born 13 November 1798, baptized 14 November 1798

George Hunter Longborn, son of Kennedy and Elizabeth Longborn, born 8 August 1799, baptized 13 September 1799

Frances Landes, daughter of Alexander and Mary Landes, born 31 Mar 1797, "Not returned in time and the date of baptism forgotten."

John Landes, son of Alexander and Mary Landes, born 14 July 1798, "Not returned in time and the date of baptism forgotten."

Mary Ann Landes, daughter of Alexander and Mary Landes, born 2 October 1800, baptized 16 November 1800

Charles George Lewis, son of Charles and Margaret Lewis, born 16 December 1799, baptized 23 February 1801

Edward Dorsey Lyon, son of Robert and Susanna Lyon, born 10 May 1800, baptized 14 June 1801

William Lyon, son of Samuel and Hester Lyon, born 14 February 1801 ("Baptized by Rev. Nathl. Snowden of Harrisburg then at Baltimore as appears by information of said Samuel Lyon, and I make this entry on the 20th day of July, 1804. James Inglis, Minister.")

Balcher Myers, son of Balcher and Barbara Myers, born 18 February 1766, baptized 17 April 1766

Mary McMechen, daughter of Alexander and Elizabeth McMechen, born 10 March 1766, baptized 24 April 1766

John Morrison, son of John and Eleanor Morrison, born 15 November 1766, baptized 25 March 1767

Elizabeth McLellan, daughter of John McLellan, born 7 February 1767, baptized 20 April 1767

Frederic Myers, son of Frederic and Catharine Myers, born 1 July 1767, baptized 14 July 1767

Mary McRea, daughter of Samuel and Jane McRea, born 2 January 1768, baptized 24 January 1768

Catherine Myers, daughter of Balcher and Barbara Myers, born 12 March 1768, baptized 17 March 1768

Elizabeth McMechen, daughter of Alexander and Elizabeth McMechen, born 5 April 1768, baptized 15 May 1768

Mary McLellan, daughter of David and Janit McLellan, born 6 February 1769, baptized 5 April 1769

John McLellan, son of John and Mary McLellan, born 6 June 1769, baptized 31 July 1769

John McNight, son of William and Martha McNight, born 2 July 1769, baptized 11 September 1769

Mary McRea, daughter Samuel and Jane McRea, born 22 February 1770, baptized 11 March 1770

Elizabeth McLellan, daughter of David and Janit McLellan, born 30 March 1770, baptized 6 April 1770

Rebecca McMechen, daughter of Alexander and Elizabeth McMechen, born 17 April 1770, baptized 6 May 1770

Hugh McIlvaine, son of Gilbert and Rosanna McIlvaine, born 20 August 1770, baptized 9 September 1770

Joseph McGrew, son of Robert and Dolly McGrew, born 7 June 1770, baptized 9 September 1770

Mary Morrison, daughter of John and Eleanor Morrison, born 22 October 1769, baptized 14 October 1770

Agness McKim, daughter of Robert and Mary McKim, born 7 November 1770, baptized 7 January 1771

Andrew McBeath, son of James and Jane McBeath, born 5 February 1771, baptized 24 February 1771

Duncan McPherson, son of Malcolm and Mary McPherson, born 22 February 1771, baptized 28 February 1771

William McNight, son of William and Martha McNight, born 23 July 1771, baptized 10 September 1771

William McLellan, son of David and Janit McLellan, born 18 October 1771, baptized 19 November 1771

Thomas Major, son of Robert and Rebecca Major, born 30 December 1771, baptized 10 May 1772

James Morgan McMechen, son of Alexander and Elizabeth McMechen, born 20 January 1772, bapt. 20 February 1772 by Mr. Ewing, Phila.

John Mack, son of James and Hannah Mack, born 8 February 1772, baptized 2 August 1772

Agness McGrew, daughter of Robert and Dorothy McGrew, born 16 September 1772, baptized 18 October 1772

Mary Marshall, daughter of James and Anne Marshall, born 14 October 1772, baptized 22 November 1772

Thomas McCabe, son of John and Phebe McCabe, born 12 April 1773, baptized 27 April 1773

David McLellan, son of David and Janit McLellan, born 20 April 1773, baptized 14 May 1773

George McCandless, son of George and Sarah McCandless, born 10 April 1773, baptized 24 June 1773

Mary Mossman, daughter of Archibald and Elizabeth Mossman, born 26 September 1773, baptized 11 October 1773

Elizabeth Marshall, daughter of James and Anne Marshall, born 16 January 1774, baptized 27 February 1774

Sarah McMechen, daughter of Alexander and Elizabeth McMechen, born 30 June 1774, baptized 10 July 1774

Ellen Mack, daughter of James and Hannah Mack, born 7 May 1774, baptized 24 August 1774

Robina Kennedy McHossey, daughter of James and Janit McHossey, born 24 April 1775, baptized 2 May 1775

Walter McLellan, son of David and Janit McLellan, born 4 June 1775, baptized 8 June 1775

Margaret McLure, daughter of David and Elizabeth McLure, born 24 July 1775, baptized 30 July 1775

Anne Marshall, daughter of James and Anne Marshall, born 2 October 1775, baptized 19 November 1775

Alexander McIlroy, son of Fergus and Alice McIlroy, born 7 January 1776, baptized 1 March 1776

Janit McDonough, daughter of John and Elizabeth McDonough, born 26 May 1775, baptized 31 July 1776

James McCandless, son of George and Sarah McCandless, born 5 August 1776, baptized 24 November 1776

Sarah Marshall, daughter of James and Anne Marshall, born 5 January 1777, baptized 23 March 1777

Archibald McBride, son of Archibald and Florence McBride, born 29 March 1777, baptized 20 April 1777

James May, son of James and Mary May, born 29 May 1777, baptized 12 June 1777

John McNeill, son of James and Mary McNeill, born 24 June 1775, baptized 16 July 1777

Mary McDonough, daughter of John and Elizabeth McDonough, born 5 July 1777, baptized 31 August 1777

Elizabeth Moore, daughter of Robert and Susanna Moore, born 27 August 1777, baptized 12 October 1777

John McCabe, son of John and Phebe McCabe, born 11 September 1777, baptized 20 October 1777

James McNeill, son of James and Mary McNeill, born 4 January 1778, baptized 7 March 1778

Anne McNight, daughter of James and Mary McNight, born 25 March 1778, baptized 22 May 1778

FIRST PRESBYTERIAN CHURCH

David Moorehead, son of Michael and Jane Moorehead, born 15 May 1779, baptized 9 June 1779
James and Fanny Marshall, twins of James and Anne Marshall, born 21 May 1779, baptized 27 June 1779
Jane May, daughter of James and Mary May, born 10 March 1779, baptized 17 August 1779
Robert Mather, son of John and Dorothy Mather, born 5 July 1779, baptized 10 September 1779
Margaret Mack, daughter of James and Hannah Mack, born 24 December 1778, baptized 3 October 1779
John McDonough, son of John and Elizabeth McDonough, born 29 December 1779, baptized 13 February 1780
William Blair Martin, son of John and Elizabeth Martin, born 22 December 1779, baptized 1 May 1780
Michael Moorehead, son of Michael and Jane Moorehead, born ---- [blank], baptized 19 March 1781
Richard Tellies Morrison, son of Samuel and Susanna Morrison, born 2 April 1781, baptized 17 June 1781
Susanna Moore, daughter of Robert and Susanna Moore, born 23 May 1781, baptized 24 June 1781
Dorothy Mather, daughter of John and Dorothy Mather, born 1 August 1781, baptized 3 October 1781
Rebecca Marshall, daughter of James and Anne Marshall, born 5 January 1782, baptized 5 May 1782
Rebecca Martin, daughter of John and Elizabeth Martin, born 21 April 1782, baptized -- August 1782, by Mr. Linn
Joseph Morrison, son of Hans and Elizabeth Morrison, born -- [blank] March 1782, baptized 21 October 1782
James Morrison, son of Hugh and Margaret Morrison, born 22 December 1781, baptized 23 October 1782
Hans Hohnes Morrison, son of Samuel and Susanna Morrison, born 17 February 1783, baptized 30 March 1783
Joseph McDonough, son of John and Elizabeth McDonough, born 7 February 1783, baptized 27 April 1783
William Moore, son of Stephen and Ruth Moore, born 30 June 1776, baptized 16 May 1783
Robert Moore, son of Robert and Susanna Moore, born ---- [blank], baptized 22 October 1783, by Mr. Keith
Hugh Holmes Morrison, son of Hugh and Margaret Morrison, born 12 September 1783, baptized 2 January 1784

Mary McGuire, daughter of Anthony and Mary McGuire, born 24 July 1784, baptized 9 August 1784

Robert Mather, son of John and Dorothy Mather, born 23 February 1784, baptized 9 August 1784

Mary Mosher, daughter of Philip and Elizabeth Mosher, born 19 July 1784, baptized 27 September 1784

John Martin, son of John and Elizabeth Martin, born 20 July 1784, baptized 24 October 1784, by Mr. Linn

Benjamin May, son of Benjamin and Elizabeth May, born 11 October 1784, baptized 7 November 1784

Grace McHenry, daughter of James and Margaret McHenry, born 2 November 1784, baptized 4 December 1784

James McChord, son of John and Isabella McChord, born 29 March 1785, baptized 13 April 1785

Isabella Moore, daughter of Robert and Susanna Moore, born 20 March 1785, baptized 17 April 1785

William Mack, son of James and Hannah Mack, born ---- [blank], baptized 19 August 1785

Daniel McDonnel, son of Andrew and Catherine McDonnel, born 18 September 1785, baptized 20 October 1785

James Mosher, son of Philip and Elizabeth Mosher, born 9 October 1785, baptized 8 January 1786

Phebe McAlister, daughter of John and Agness McAlister, born 26 November 1786, baptized 22 February 1786

Isabella McMillan, daughter of John and Janit McMillan, born 4 March 1786, baptized 26 March 1786

Daniel William McHenry, son of James and Margaret McHenry, born 12 November 1786, baptized 26 November 1786

Abraham May, son of Benjamin and Elizabeth May, born 15 November 1787, baptized 28 January 1787

Hannah Martin, daughter of James and Mary Martin, born 5 October 1785, baptized 25 February 1787

Anney McChord, daughter of John and Isabella McChord [McChard?], born 22 February 1787, baptized 12 March 1787

Francis Mosher, son of Philip and Elizabeth Mosher, born 18 October 1787, baptized 18 November 1787

James Jennings McFaddon, son of James and Rebecca McFaddon, born 4 June 1787, baptized 2 February 1788

Catharine Jarold Myers, daughter of Charles and Elizabeth Myers, born 31 October 1787, baptized 13 April 1788

FIRST PRESBYTERIAN CHURCH

Elisabetth McCandley, daughter of John and Jane McCandley, born 4 March 1788, baptized 22 April 1788
Abraham Duryee May, son of Benjamin and Elizabeth May, born 22 March 1788, baptized 18 May 1788
John McElderry, son of Thomas and Elizabeth McElderry, born 12 May 1788, baptized 29 May 1788
Elizabeth McFanin, daughter of John and Jane McFanin, born 13 October 1787, baptized 8 June 1788
Samuel Mosher, son of James and Anne Mosher, born 25 September 1788, baptized 16 November 1788
Anne Mather, daughter of John and Dorothy Mather, born 13 October 1787, baptized 18 December 1788
Agness McHenry, daughter of James and Margaret McHenry, born 20 November 1788, baptized 4 January 1789
Matilda Myers, daughter of Charles and Elizabeth Myers, born 15 January 1789, baptized 2 May 1789
Sarah McCulloch, daughter of James and Margaret McCulloch, born 21 March 1789, baptized 5 July 1789
Elizabeth Mosher, daughter of Philip and Elizabeth Mosher, born 6 November 1789, baptized 17 January 1790
James McDonough, son of John and Elizabeth McDonough, born 15 August 1789, baptized 24 July 1790
Alexander McIntosh, son of Duncan and Elizabeth McIntosh, born 19 July 1790, baptized 20 August 1790
Margaret McElderry, daughter of Thomas and Elizabeth McElderry, born 26 October 1790, baptized 5 November 1790
Mary McCohn, daughter of Dennis and Anne McCohn, born 15 October 1790, baptized 19 November 1790
John McFaddon, son of James and Rebecca McFaddon, born 9 March 1790, baptized 30 December 1790
Nelson Murphy, son of John and Eleanor Murphy, born 6 January 1791, baptized 15 March 1791
Anney Mosher, daughter of James and Anne Mosher, born 1 March 1791, baptized 10 April 1791
John McHenry, son of James and Margaret McHenry, born 27 March 1791, baptized 7 May 1791
Janit Mactier, daughter of Alexander and Frances Mactier, born 20 April 1791, baptized 15 May 1791
Frances Mosher, daughter of Philip and Elizabeth Mosher, born 12 August 1791, baptized 23 August 1791

Abbey May, daughter of Benjamin and Elizabeth Mosher, born 24 August 1791, baptized 9 September 1791

Letitia McCarty, daughter of William and Margaret McCarty, born 27 August 1791, baptized 21 September 1791

Jane McElderry, daughter of Thomas and Elizabeth McElderry, born 23 November 1791, baptized 25 December 1791

Elizabeth McAlister, daughter of John and Agness McAlister, born 11 July 1791, baptized 8 February 1792

Elizabeth Mahollin, daughter of Charles and Elizabeth Mahollin, born 13 January 1792, baptized 29 February 1792

James Hugh McCulloch, son of James and Margaret McCulloch, born 4 December 1791, baptized 15 April 1792, by Dr. Muir

Mary McConky, daughter of William and Rebecca McConky, born 19 November 1791, baptized 20 May 1792

Bethea Moore, daughter of William and Sarah Moore, born 27 September 1792, baptized 16 December 1792

Robert McIlvain, son of Alexander and Sarah McIlvain, born 24 September 1792, baptized 27 January 1793

John Murphy, adult, baptized 27 March 1793

Anne Murphy, daughter of John and Eleanor Murphy, born 16 March 1793, baptized 27 March 1793

Dorothy Mactier, daughter of Alexander and Frances Mactier, born 14 April 1793, baptized 9 May 1793

Rachel Anne May, daughter of Benjamin and Elizabeth May, born 13 March 1793, baptized 10 May 1793

John McFerran, son of John and Jane McFerran, born 18 October 1792, baptized 7 July 1793

Jane Mosher, daughter of James and Anne Mosher, born 18 August 1793, baptized 6 October 1793

Hugh McElderry, son of Thomas and Elizabeth McElderry, born 8 August 1793, baptized 13 October 1793

James Martin, son of James and Mary Martin, born 14 April 1793, baptized 6 October 1793

Margaret McDonough, daughter of John and Elizabeth McDonough, born 6 December 1792, baptized 17 November 1793

John William Boyles Murray, son of William and Olivia Murray, born 18 May 1793, baptized 1 December 1793

Margaretta McHenry, daughter of James and Margaret McHenry, born 9 March 1794, baptized 27 March 1794

John McFadon, son of William and Ann McFadon, born 19 February 1794, baptized 22 July 1794
Hugh McCulloch, son of James and Margaret McCulloch, born 8 September 1793, baptized 23 July 1794
David Telfair McKim, son of John and Margaret McKim, born 22 May 1794, baptized 14 September 1794
Isabella Mosher, daughter of Philip and Johanna Mosher, born 22 June 1794, baptized 14 September 1794
Juliann May, daughter of Benjamin and Elizabeth May, born 10 January 1794, baptized 5 April 1795
Hellen Ranney Moore, daughter of William and Sarah Moore, born 5 April 1795, baptized 7 June 1795
James Mosher, son of James and Anne Mosher, born 9 August 1795, baptized 11 October 1795
John Myers, son of Robert and Mary Myers, born 14 September 1795, baptized 18 October 1795
James Rodgers McFerran, son of John and Jane McFerran, born 13 May 1795, baptized 8 November 1795
Elizabeth McElderry, daughter of Thomas and Elizabeth McElderry, born 1 September 1795, baptized 8 November 1795
Jane McKim, daughter of John and Margaret McKim, born 7 August 1795, baptized 13 December 1795
Anne Martin, daughter of George and Anne Martin, born 9 February 1796, baptized 22 February 1796
Jane Malloy, daughter of Peter and Grissell Malloy, born 19 January 1796, baptized 25 February 1796
Elizabeth McKeen, daughter of John and Ann McKeen, born 15 January 1796, baptized 27 March 1796
Jeremiah McNeilly, son of John and Agness McNeilly, born 3 December 1795, baptized 29 April 1796
Anne McCammon, daughter of Joseph and Sarah McCammon, born 21 July 1795, baptized 16 May 1796
Nancy Martin, daughter of Alexander and Francis Martin, born 25 February 1796, baptized 5 June 1796
William McDonough, son of John and Elizabeth McDonough, born 26 February 1796, baptized 8 June 1796
Eliza Murphy, daughter of John and Eleanor Murphy, born 19 March 1795, baptized 25 June 1796
Andrew McIlvain, son of Alexander and Sarah McIlvain, born 5 February 1795, baptized 29 June 1796

Hugh Morrow, son of Kennedy and Mary Morrow, born 7 June 1796, baptized 28 June 1796

Anne Marshall, daughter of John and Martha Marshall, born 6 April 1796, baptized 13 July 1796

William McConkey, son of James and Agness McConkey, born 26 June 1796, baptized 25 September 1796

Philip Mosher, son of Philip and Johanna Mosher, born 4 January 1797, baptized 2 February 1797

Mary McElderry, daughter of Thomas and Elizabeth McElderry, born 9 February 1797, baptized 23 April 1797

George McIlvain, son of Alexander and Sarah McIlvain, born 27 February 1797, baptized 30 April 1797

Elizabeth McKim, daughter of John and Margaret McKim, born 17 March 1797, baptized 9 July 1797

James Mahool, son of Thomas and Elizabeth Mahool, born 21 August 1797, baptized 18 September 1797

Elizabeth Mayer, daughter of Robert and Mary Mayer, born 10 September 1797, baptized 29 October 1797

Letitia Grace McCurdy, daughter of Hugh and Grace McCurdy, born 25 September 1797, baptized 13 November 1797

William McConkey, son of William and Rebecca McConkey, born 6 February 1794, baptized 28 November 1797

John McConkey, son of William and Rebecca McConkey, born 17 September 1797, baptized 28 November 1797

Ann Maria McKeen, daughter of John and Ann McKeen, born 7 November 1797, baptized 12 December 1797

Mary McDowell, daughter of George and Susanna McDowell, born 25 June 1797, baptized 17 December 1797

George Martin, son of George and Ann Martin, born 19 September 1797, baptized 20 December 1797

Ignatius Perry McCandless, son of Robert and Rachel McCandless, born 22 July 1797, baptized 21 December 1797

Susanna Miller, daughter of Alexander and Susanna Miller, born 28 May 1797, baptized 10 April 1798

Samuel McFerran, son of John and Jane McFerran, born 29 September 1797, baptized 22 April 1798

John McNeilly, son of John and Agness McNeilly, born 20 February 1798, baptized 14 June 1798

Agness Moore, daughter of William and Sarah Moore, born 18 March 1798, baptized 10 June 1798

FIRST PRESBYTERIAN CHURCH 41

William Mosher, son of James and Anne Mosher, born 13 March 1798, baptized 22 July 1798

James McConkey, son of James and Agness McConkey, born 6 July 1798, baptized 29 July 1798

Alexander Mactier, son of Alexander and Frances Mactier, born 13 December 1797, baptized 16 August 1798

Elizabeth McCay, daughter of John and Agness McCay, born 10 August 1797, baptized 19 August 1798

Isabella McKim, daughter of John and Margaret McKim, born 29 July 1798, baptized 28 October 1798

Ann Mosher, daughter of Philip and Johanna Mosher, born 28 November 1798, baptized 14 April 1799

William McElderry, son of Thomas and Elizabeth McElderry, born 19 January 1799, baptized 5 May 1799

William Marron, son of William and Catharine Marron, born 2 May 1798, baptized 13 May 1799

Adeline Murphy, daughter of John and Ellen Murphy, born 15 December 1797, baptized 12 June 1799

James Moody, son of James and Elizabeth Moody, born 27 October 1798, baptized 12 July 1799

William McDowell, son of George and Susanna McDowell, born 23 August 1799, baptized 24 November 1799

Thomas McConkey, son of James and Agness McConkey, born 14 August 1799, baptized 1 December 1799

Margaretta McFaden, daughter of John and Priscilla McFaden, born 17 October 1799, baptized 12 January 1800

William Swan McKeen, son of John and Ann McKeen, born 15 November 1799, baptized 12 January 1800

Isabella Maholl, daughter of Thomas and Elizabeth Maholl, born 14 February 1800, baptized 8 April 1800

John McKim, son of John and Margaret McKim, born 11 February 1800, baptized 10 April 1800

Mary Ann Miller, daughter of Alexander and Susanna Miller, born ---- [blank], baptized 5 May 1800

Washington McLenahan, son of Elijah and Mary McLenahan, born 1 August 1800, baptized 2 November 1800

Louis Mosher, son of James and Ann Mosher, born 9 June 1800, baptized 27 June 1800

George Clarke Munson, son of Joel and Ann Munson, born 1 September 1800, baptized 16 November 1800

Mary Martin, daughter of George and Ann Martin, born 27 January 1800, baptized 19 November 1800

Robert McElderry, son of Thomas and Elizabeth McElderry, born 4 April 1800, baptized -- August 1800, by Mr. Sinclair

John Pinkerton McKenzie, son of Colin and Sarah McKenzie, born 8 April 1800, baptized 10 December 1800

Mary McCandless, daughter of Robert and Rachel McCandless, born 11 September 1800, baptized 23 December 1800

Eliza Mactier, daughter of Alexander and Frances Mactier, born 23 October 1799, baptized 26 December 1800

Eliza Maitland Mitchell, daughter of Alexander and Elizabeth Mitchell, born 6 February 1801, baptized 19 April 1801

Elizabeth McDowell, daughter of George and Elizabeth McDowell, born 6 March 1801, baptized 10 May 1801

William Lynch Murphy, son of John and Eleanor Murphy, born 20 November 1800, baptized 12 May 1801

John McLellan, son of Robert and Ann McLellan, born 23 July 1797, baptized 9 July 1801

Effe McLellan, daughter of Robert and Ann McLellan, born 8 December 1800, baptized 9 July 1801

John Mosher, son of James and Ann Mosher, born 15 June 1801, baptized 12 July 1801

George Mosher, son of Philip and Johanna Mosher, born 27 November 1800, baptized 14 July 1801

Agness Night, daughter of Edward and Sarah Night, born 16 January 1773, baptized 25 August 1773

Elizabeth Neill, daughter of William and Isabella Neill, born 20 September 1774, baptized 23 October 1774

Christian Nucoll, son of William and Grizel Nucoll, born 20 December 1765, baptized 11 February 1776

Mary Neill, daughter of William and Isabella Neill, born 17 July 1776, baptized 26 October 1776

William Nucoll, son of William and Grizel Nucoll, born 18 March 1778, baptized 28 April 1778

Alexander Neill, son of William and Isabell Neill, born 22 December 1778, baptized 19 January 1779

Mary Nicholas, daughter of George and Mary Nicholas, born 23 October 1780, baptized 26 November 1780

Robert Callender Neill, son of William and Isabell Neill, born 6 April 1781, baptized 13 May 1781

Thomas Nucoll, son of William and Grizel Nucoll, born 13 May 1782, baptized 23 June 1782

Isabella Neill, daughter of William and Isabella Neill, born 8 March 1783, baptized 18 May 1783

Phebe Neill, daughter of John and Margaret Neill, born 16 June 1785, baptized 23 February 1786

Mary Buchanan Nicholas, daughter of Wilson Cary and Margaret Nicholas, born 12 November 1785, baptized 14 May 1786

Margaretta Nicholas, daughter of George and Mary Nicholas, born 8 June 1789, baptized 2 July 1789

Thomas Young Nucoll, son of William and Grizel Nucoll, born 17 March 1789, baptized 22 November 1789

Agness Neill, daughter of Hugh and Rachel Neill, born 17 March 1786, baptized 4 November 1792

Cinthia Neill, daughter of Hugh and Rachel Neill, born 4 August 1787, baptized 4 November 1792

George Neill, son of Hugh and Rachel Neill, born 2 April 1789, baptized 4 November 1792

Frances Neill, daughter of Hugh and Rachel Neill, born 9 February 1792, baptized 4 November 1792

James Nesbit, son of John and Margaret Nesbit, born 22 February 1793, baptized 14 July 1793

Cary Ann Nicholas, daughter of Wilson Cary and Margaret Nicholas, born 19 April 1790, baptized 2 June 1794

Wilson Cary Nicholas, son of Wilson Cary and Margaret Nicholas, born 10 March 1794, baptized 2 June 1794

Mary Nugent, daughter of David and Mary Nugent, born 1 May 1792, baptized 29 August 1794

John Nicholas Turner, son of William and ---- [blank] Turner, born ---- [blank], baptized 8 July 1794

Cinthia Neill, daughter of Hugh and Rachel Neill, born 11 June 1794, baptized 28 December 1794

Gilbert Neilson, son of James and Jane Neilson, born 8 September 1796, baptized 10 October 1796

John Smith Neill, son of Hugh and Rachel Neill, born 17 February 1797, baptized 28 April 1797

Ann Nugent, daughter of John and Sarah Nugent, born 24 February 1797, baptized 19 June 1797

Elisa Martin Needles, daughter of Stephen and Nancy Needles, born 29 March 1797, baptized 22 April 1798

Margaret Nicholas, daughter of Wilson Cary and Margaret Nicholas, born 16 March 1796, baptized 30 November 1798

Jane Nicholas, daughter of Wilson Cary and Margaret Nicholas, born 16 January 1798, baptized 30 November 1798

Catharine Nicoll, daughter of David and Dorcas Nicoll, born 21 January 1799, baptized 17 February 1799

William Neill, son of Hugh and Rachel Neill, born 15 October 1799, baptized 13 February 1800

David Nicoll, son of David and Dorcas Nicoll, born 2 March 1800, baptized 20 April 1800

Robert Carter Nicholas, son of Philip N. and Mary Nicholas, born 16 November 1799, baptized 16 January 1801

William Orrick, son of Nicholas and Mary Orrick, born 25 February 1770, baptized 30 April 1770

Sydnee Orrick, daughter of Nicholas and Mary Orrick, born 13 July 1771, baptized 8 September 1771

George Oliver, son of Robert and Eliza Oliver, born 29 August 1787, baptized 30 September 1787

Hugh Thompson Oliver, son of Robert and Eliza Oliver, born 28 March 1789, baptized 16 April 1789

Mary O'Donnell, daughter of John and Sarah O'Donnell, born 1 May 1790, baptized 14 May 1790

Peggy Oliver, daughter of Robert and Eliza Oliver, born 12 October 1790, baptized 4 November 1790

Henry O'Donnell, son of John and Sarah O'Donnell, born 13 August 1791, baptized 19 August 1791

Charles Oliver, son of Robert and Eliza Oliver, born 8 February 1792, bapt. 15 April 1792 by Dr. Muir, Alexandria

Sarah Osborne, daughter of James and Eleanor Osborne, born 24 August 1789, baptized 26 August 1792

James Haly Osborne, son of James and Eleanor Osborne, born 24 June 1792, baptized 26 August 1792

Columbus O'Donnell, son of John and Sarah O'Donnell, born 1 October 1792, baptized 8 October 1792

John Stevenson Ogier, son of John and Mary Ogier, born 11 June 1793, baptized 24 June 1793

Eliza and Robert Oliver, twins of Robert and Eliza Oliver, born 24 September 1793, baptized 25 September 1793

Deborah O'Donnell, daughter of John and Sarah O'Donnell, born 6 August 1794, baptized 4 September 1794

FIRST PRESBYTERIAN CHURCH

John Oliver, son of Robert and Eliza Oliver, born 10 February 1795, baptized 13 February 1795

Francis Canoze Ogier, son of John and Mary Ogier, born 2 October 1795, baptized 3 January 1796

Henry Oliver, son of Robert and Eliza Oliver, born 3 April 1796, baptized 6 April 1796

John O'Donnell, son of John and Sarah O'Donnell, born 30 August 1796, baptized 29 September 1796

Elliot O'Donnell, son of John and Sarah O'Donnell, born 21 March 1798, baptized 2 May 1798

Jane Oliver, daughter of Robert and Eliza Oliver, born 9 December 1798, baptized 21 December 1798

George Oliver, son of Robert and Eliza Oliver, born 9 February 1800, baptized 17 February 1800

Elisa White O'Donnell, daughter of John and Sarah O'Donnell, born 13 March 1800, baptized 3 April 1800

Mary Plowman, daughter of Jonathan and Rebecca Plowman, born 13 August 1765, baptized 2 October 1766

Jonathan Plowman, son of Jonathan and Rebecca Plowman, born 28 August 1766, baptized 2 October 1766

Margaret Paisley, daughter of David and Margaret Paisley, born 10 April 1765, baptized 20 April 1767

Sarah Patton, daughter of Abraham and Martha Patton, born 8 May 1770, baptized 26 June 1770

Sarah Plowman, daughter of Jonathan and Rebecca Plowman, born 19 October 1770, baptized 10 November 1770

James Purviance, son of Robert and Frances Purviance, born 19 February 1772, baptized 22 February 1772 by Mr. Ewing

Susanna Purviance, son of Samuel and Susanna Purviance, born 4 September 1772, baptized 17 October 1772

Jane Patton, daughter of Abraham and Martha Patton, born 21 June 1773, baptized 4 July 1773

John Purviance, son of Robert and Frances Purviance, born 5 July 1774, baptized 17 July 1774

Anne Plowman, daughter of Jonathan and Rebecca Plowman, born 3 October 1773, baptized 8 August 1774

Robert Pierson, son of John and Mary Pierson, born 30 August 1773, baptized 18 December 1774

Elizabeth Pierson, adult, baptized 25 December 1774

Rebecca Pierson, daughter of Thomas and Elizabeth Pierson, born 5 December 1773, baptized 25 December 1774

Margaret Patton, daughter of Abraham and Martha Patton, born 25 March 1775, baptized 18 April 1775

Samuel Purviance, son of Robert and Frances Purviance, born 9 October 1775, baptized 22 October 1775

Matthew Patton, son of Matthew and Rebecca Patton, born 18 May 1776, baptized 19 August 1776

John Hancock Poe, son of David and Elizabeth Poe, born 25 August 1776, baptized 13 September 1776

Anne Pierson, daughter of John and Mary Pierson, born 10 September 1776, baptized 31 October 1776

Jane Purviance, daughter of Robert and Frances Purviance, born 3 December 1776, baptized 22 December 1776

Hugh Purviance, son of Robert and Frances Purviance, born 17 November 1777, baptized 7 December 1777

William Young Purviance, son of Robert and Francs Purviance, born 1 December 1778, baptized 16 December 1778

Mary Patton, daughter of Matthew and Rebecca Patton, born 26 November 1779, baptized 1 January 1779

Isabella Purviance, daughter of Samuel and Catharine Purviance, born 4 June 1779, baptized 4 July 1779

William Poe, son of David and Elizabeth Poe, born 2 March 1780, baptized 14 April 1780

Robert Purviance, son of Robert and Frances Purviance, born 28 April 1780, baptized 21 May 1780

William Patterson, son of William and Dorcas Patterson, born 22 March 1780, baptized 22 June 1780

John Dyer Patton, son of Matthew and Rebecca Patton, born 28 January 1781, baptized 10 June 1781

Frances Purviance, daughter of Robert and Frances Purviance, born 26 November 1781, baptized 11 December 1781

Margaret Pannell, daughter of John and Elizabeth Pannell, born 1 December 1781, baptized 4 January 1782

William Patton, son of Matthew and Rebecca Patton, born 23 January 1782, baptized 15 March 1782

Robert Patterson, son of William and Dorcas Patterson, born 16 July 1781, baptized 5 May 1782

George Washington Poe, son of David and Elizabeth Poe, born 21 August 1782, baptized 6 October 1782

FIRST PRESBYTERIAN CHURCH

John Patterson, son of William and Dorcas Patterson, born 24 March 1783, baptized 11 May 1783

Hugh Pannell, son of John and Elizabeth Pannell, born 24 September 1783, baptized 17 February 1784

Esther Patton, daughter of Matthew and Rebecca Patton, born 17 April 1784, baptized 6 July 1784

David Poe, son of David and Elizabeth Poe, born 18 July 1784, baptized 21 September 1784

Elizabeth Patterson, daughter of William and Dorcas Patterson, born 6 February 1785, baptized 3 April 1785

James Pannell, son of Edward and Sarah Pannell, born 21 May 1784, baptized 23 April 1785

Benjamin Pannell, son of John and Elizabeth Pannell, born 31 August 1785, baptized 17 November 1785

Hugh Pannell, son of Edward and Sarah Pannell, born 11 April 1786, baptized 29 January 1786

Rebecca Patton, daughter of Matthew and Rebecca Patton, born 22 September 1786, baptized 18 October 1786

Joseph Wilson Patterson, son of William and Dorcas Patterson, born 6 December 1786, baptized 11 February 1787

Samuel Poe, son of David and Elizabeth Poe, born 21 December 1787, baptized 17 February 1788

William Pannell, son of Edward and Sarah Pannell, born 18 June 1788, baptized 1 January 1789

John Pannell, son of John and Elizabeth Pannell, born 21 March 1788, baptized 18 April 1789

Benjamin Patton, son of Matthew and Rebecca Patton, born 14 December 1788, baptized 17 March 1789

William Pollock, son of George and Susanna Pollock, born 27 December 1788, baptized 13 October 1789

Agness Pollock, daughter of George and Susanna Pollock, born 12 August 1789, baptized 13 October 1789

Edward Patterson, son of William and Dorcas Patterson, born 14 July 1789, baptized 25 October 1789

Edward Pannell, son of John and Elizabeth Pannell, born 28 October 1789, baptized 9 December 1789

Mary Poe, daughter of David and Elizabeth Poe, born 17 March 1790, baptized 6 June 1790

James Patton, son of Matthew and Rebecca Patton, born 17 March 1791, baptized 29 May 1791

John Pogue, son of James and Elizabeth Pogue, born 27 May 1791, baptized 3 July 1791

Elizabeth Pannell, daughter of Edward and Sarah Pannell, born 13 August 1791, baptized 29 December 1791

Augusta Sophia Patterson, daughter of William and Dorcas Patterson, born 27 November 1791, baptized 18 March 1792

John Pollock, son of George and Susanna Pollock, born 8 October 1791, bapt. 15 April 1792, by Dr. Muir, Alexandria

Eliza Pannell, daughter of John and Elizabeth Pannell, born 11 March 1792, baptized 6 June 1792

Elizabeth Poe, daughter of David and Elizabeth Poe, born 26 September 1792, baptized 16 December 1792

James Pogue, son of James and Elizabeth Pogue, born 16 October 1792, baptized 16 December 1792

Margaretta Patterson, daughter of William and Dorcas Patterson, born 20 March 1793, baptized 9 May 1793

Rebecca Patterson, daughter of John and Esther Patterson, born 7 November 1787, baptized 11 July 1793

George Patterson, son of John and Esther Patterson, born 25 January ---- [blank], baptized 11 July 1793

John Patterson, son of John and Esther Patterson, born 15 January 1793, baptized 11 July 1793

Benjamin Prat, son of James and Sarah Prat, born 26 February 1794, baptized 2 March 1794

Edward Pannell, son of Edward and Sarah Pannell, born 10 January 1794, baptized 31 March 1794

Susanna Pollock, daughter of George and Susanna Pollock, born 15 November 1793, baptized 20 April 1794

Esther Patterson, daughter of John and Esther Patterson, born 2 December 1793, baptized 11 May 1794

William Pogue, son of James and Elizabeth Pogue, born 29 October 1794, baptized 15 March 1795

Sarah Prat, daughter of James and Sarah Prat, born 16 March 1795, baptized 29 April 1795

Mary Pierson, daughter of Henry and Mary Pierson, born 17 March 1796 and baptized 17 March 1796

George Washington Pannell, son of Edward and Sarah Pannell, born 18 March 1796, baptized 14 May 1796

Polly Porter, daughter of David and Rebecca Porter, born 5 May 1789, baptized 5 July 1796

FIRST PRESBYTERIAN CHURCH 49

Peggy Porter, daughter of David and Rebecca Porter, born 16 August 1791, baptized 5 July 1796

John Porter, son of David and Rebecca Porter, born 5 October 1793, baptized 5 July 1796

Tarissa and Luisa Porter, twin daughters of David and Rebecca Porter, baptized 5 July 1796. Tarissa was born 31 May 1793, and Luisa was born 1 June 1793.

Robert Pogue, son of James and Elizabeth Pogue, born 7 April 1796, baptized 10 September 1796

George Patterson, son of William and Dorcas Patterson, born 19 August 1796, baptized 29 October 1796

Eliza Prat, daughter of James and Sarah Prat, born 5 February 1797, baptized 12 March 1797

William Pierce, son of Israel and Letitia Pierce, born 1 September 1797, baptized 7 September 1797

Betsy Williamson Pierce, daughter of Israel and Letitia Pierce, born 15 ---- [blank], baptized 7 September 1797

George Pogue, son of James and Elizabeth Pogue, born 28 December 1797, baptized 18 March 1798

Caroline Patterson, daughter of William and Dorcas Patterson, born 30 June 1798, baptized 28 July 1798

George Washington Parks, son of Andrew and Harriet Parks, born 26 November 1798, baptized 6 February 1799

George Washington Pannell, son of Edward and Sarah Pannell, born 13 May 1798, baptized 16 May 1799

Hugh Young Purviance, son of James and Eliza Purviance, born 22 March 1799, baptized 30 June 1799

Elizabeth Pogue, daughter of James and Elizabeth Pogue, born 17 August 1799, baptized 13 February 1800

William Patterson, son of Walter and Ann Patterson, born 12 September 1800, baptized 18 January 1801

Joseph Pogue, son of James and Elizabeth Pogue, born 25[?] October 1800, baptized 30[?] January 1801

Henry Patterson, son of William and Dorcas Patterson, born 6 November 1800, baptized 30 January 1801

Ann Pierce Pannell, daughter of Edward and Sarah Pannell, born 18 January 1800, baptized 23 February 1801

Wilson Cary Purviance, son of James and Eliza Purviance, born 28 September 1800, baptized 11 July 1801

William Rusk, son of David and Mary Rusk, born 8 September 1765, baptized 14 October 1766

Samuel Rusk, son of David and Mary Rusk, born 30 June 1767, baptized 3 July 1767

Anne Plat Rodgers, daughter of John and Elizabeth Rodgers, born 7 March 1769, baptized 31 March 1769

Helen Rusk, daughter of David and Mary Rusk, born 2 July 1768, baptized 13 May 1769

David Rusk, son of David and Mary Rusk, born 20 August 1770, baptized 12 September 1770

Margaret Ross, daughter of John and Sarah Ross, born 11 July 1771, baptized 20 July 1771

John Rodgers, son of John and Elizabeth Rodgers, born 11 July 1771, baptized 9 August 1771

Sarah Rusk, daughter of David and Mary Rusk, born 2 August 1771, baptized 16 August 1771

Mary Rusk, daughter of David and Mary Rusk, born 19 April 1773, baptized 17 August 1773

Janit Richardson, daughter of Samuel and Mary Richardson, born 27 December 1773, baptized 25 January 1774

Anne Ross, daughter of John and Sarah Ross, born 20 February 1774, baptized 15 April 1774

Alexander Rodgers, son of John and Elizabeth Rodgers [Rogers?], born 3 October 1773, baptized 4 October 1774

Elam Rusk, son of David and Mary Rusk, born 27 February 1775, baptized 17 April 1775

Elizabeth Rogers, daughter of John and Elizabeth Rogers [Rodgers?], born 27 April 1776, baptized 8 June 1776

Elizabeth Rusk, daughter of David and Mary Rusk, born 28 March 1777, baptized 20 March 1781

David Lewis Rusk, son of David and Mary Rusk, born 23 August 1779, baptized 20 march 1781

Rachel Rogers, daughter of John and Elizabeth Rogers [Rodgers?], born ---- [blank], baptized 1 June 1781

Harriet Robinson, daughter of Andrew and Agness Robinson, born 11 June 1781, baptized 16 September 1781

Mary Richardson, daughter of William and Elizabeth Richardson, born 9 July 1781, baptized 19 July 1782

James Ramsay, son of Thomas and Elizabeth Ramsay, born 23 February 1784, baptized 2 May 1784

FIRST PRESBYTERIAN CHURCH 51

Samuel Rusk, son of David and Mary Rusk, born 26 August 1781, baptized 15 May 1784

John Rice, son of John and Mary Rice, born 24 June 17783, baptized 21 November 1784

Alexander Reney, son of Alexander and Sarah Reney, born 21 September 1785, baptized 10 October 1785

Mary Rice, daughter of John and Mary Rice, born 1 September 1785, baptized 16 October 1785

Nancy Robinson, daughter of Andrew and Agness Robinson, born ---- [blank], baptized 27 January 1786

Maria Riddell, daughter of Robert and Mary Riddell, born 24 January 1787, baptized 11 March 1787

Elizabeth Ramsay, daughter of Thomas and Elizabeth Ramsay, born 26 September 1785, baptized 28 March 1787

Agness Robison, daughter of Ephraim and Eve Robison, born 14 April 1787, baptized 15 July 1787

Catherine Rice, daughter of John and Mary Rice, born 24 November 1787, baptized 9 June 1788

Nancy Riddell, daughter of Robert and Mary Riddell, born 21 May 1788, baptized 7 July 1788

Mary Reney, daughter of Alexander and Sarah Reney, born 4 July 1787, baptized 23 August 1788

Elizabeth Robison, daughter of Ephraim and Eve Robison, born 12 February 1789, baptized 18[?] March 1789

Harriet Robinson, daughter of Alexander and Priscilla Robinson, born 19 March 1789, baptized 10 May 1789

James Ross, son of John and Hannah Ross, born 31 August 1789, baptized 3 January 1790

Thomas Ratien, son of Dederick and Wilhemina Dorothea Ratien, born 25 March 1790, baptized 25 April 1790

Matilda Frances Sherbourne Ridley, daughter of Matthew and Catherine Ridley, born 19 November 1789, baptized 21 June 1790

Louisa Riddell, daughter of Robert and Mary Riddell, born 10 September 1790, baptized 26 September 1790

Mary Richart, daughter of William and Sarah Richert, born 12 August 1790, baptized 11 October 1790

Jesse Robison, son of Ephraim and Eve Robison, born 9 March 1791, baptized 5 June 1791

James Russell, son of Robert and Jane Russell, born 4 June 1791, baptized 5 October 1791

Betsey Richart, daughter of William and Sarah Richart, born 5 November 1791, baptized 20 November 1791

Alexander Hawkesworth Riddell, son of Robert and Mary Riddell, born 16 July 1792, baptized 2 December 1792

John Rany, son of Robert and Jane Rany, born 20 November 1792, baptized 8 March 1793

Elizabeth Robinson, daughter of John and Catherena Robinson, born 16 November 1792, baptized 7 April 1793

Jane Ross, daughter of Thomas and Mary Ross, born 19 October 1792, baptized 10 April 1793

Anne Robison, daughter of Ephraim and Eve Robison, born 20 April 1794, baptized 1 July 1794

Amelia Riddell, daughter of Robert and Mary Riddell, born 11 September 1794, baptized 22 October 1794

Catharine Robb, daughter of William and Elizabeth Robb, born 1 October 1794, baptized 25 December 1794

David Elphinston Robb, son of Patrick and Rebecca Robb, born 21 July 1795, baptized 25 July 1795

Alexander Robinson, son of Alexander and Angelica Robinson, born 17 July 1795, baptized 31 July 1795

Mary Ann Robb, daughter of William and Elizabeth Robb, born 20 September 1795, baptized 8 November 1795

Robert Russell, son of Robert and Jane Russell, born 17 March 1793, baptized 22 November 1795

Thomas Russell, son of Robert and Jane Russsell, born 8 October 1795, baptized 22 November 1795

Mary Fraser Riddell, daughter of Robert and Mary Riddell, born 15 October 1795, baptized 13 December 1795

Catharine Robinson, daughter of John and Catharine Robinson, born 10 June 1795, baptized 3 January 1796

Charlotte Christena Robison, daughter of Ephraim and Eve Robison, born 15 April 1796, baptized 8 June 1796

Charles Gartry Robb, son of William and Elizabeth Robb, born 31 October 1796, baptized 4 December 1796

Margaret Robeson, daughter of John and Johanna Robeson, born 14 July 1791, baptized 2 February 1797

William James Reside, son of Edward and Jane Reside, born 3 January 1797, baptized 24 March 1797

Robert Lyles Robinson, son of Alexander and Priscilla Robinson, born 9 June 1796, baptized 9 June 1797

FIRST PRESBYTERIAN CHURCH 53

Priscilla Robeson, daughter of Alexander and Angelica Robeson, born 8 January 1797, baptized 9 June 1797
Charles Robinson, son of John and Catharine Robinson, born 23 June 1797, baptized 27 August 1797
Esther Robison, daughter of Ephraim and Eve Robison, born 2 May 1798, baptized 10 June 1798
Ephraim Allen Rothrock Robison, son of John and Catharine Robison, born 2 May 1798, baptized 10 June 1798
Anabella [Arrabella?] Ramsay, daughter of Thomas and Elizabeth Ramsay, born 11 November 1788, baptized 17 June 1798
William Richards, son of William and Sarah Richards, born 8 April 1796, baptized 25 December 1798
Archibald Robinson, son of Alexander and Priscilla Robinson, born 10 November 1798, baptized 30[?] January 1799
Jane Russell, daughter of Robert and Jane Russell, born 31 October 1797, baptized 9 October 1799
Oliver Bond Ross, son of James and Rose Ross, born 10 November 1799, baptized 20 November 1799
George Robb, son of William and Elizabeth Robb, born 24 September 1799, baptized 24 November 1799
Moses Elvins Rogers, son of William and Elizabeth Rogers, born 26 June 1800, baptized 1 January 1800
Agness Eve Robison, daughter of Ephraim and Eve Robison, born 2 February 1800, baptized 13 March 1800
Angelica Robinson, daughter of Alexander and Angelica Robinson, born 24 October 1790, baptized 6 July 1801
William Buchanan Smith, son of William and Elizabeth Smith, born 19 June 1766, baptized 26 September 1766
Robert Spear, son of William and Elizabeth Spear, born 15 September 1766, baptized 7 October 1766
George Pitt Stevenson, son of Henry and Frances Stevenson, born 20 May 1766, baptized 1 January 1767
Esther Smith, daughter of John and Mary Smith, born 5 March 1767, baptized 8 March 1767
Rebecca Smith, daughter of John and Mary Smith, born 22 October 1767, baptized 31 January 1768
Campbell Smith, son of William and Elizabeth Smith, born 8 April 1768, baptized 15 May 1768
John Conrad Smith, son of Conrad and Margaret Smith, born 9 June 1768, baptized 19 June 1768

James Stevenson, son of William and Rachel Stevenson, born 16 August 1767, baptized 12 August 1768

Mary Spear, daughter of William and Elizabeth Spear, born 6 September 1768, baptized 17 September 1768

George Sterett, son of James and Mary Sterett, born 3 July 1768, baptized 2 October 1768

Lina Smith, daughter of John and Rebecca Smith, born 31 October 1768, baptized 23 February 1769

William Henry Stevenson, son of Henry and Frances Stevenson, born 12 January 1769, baptized 28 August 1769

Margaret Stuart, daughter of Robert and Margaret Stuart, born 25 April 1767, baptized 4 September 1769

Barbara Spear, daughter of William and Elizabeth Spear, born 5 March 1770, baptized 9 March 1770

Mary Smith, daughter of William and Jane Smith, born 8 March 1761, baptized 14 October 1770

Jane Smith, daughter of William and Jane Smith, born 24 April 1767, baptized 14 October 1770

Samuel Smith, son of William and Elizabeth Smith, born 6 November 1770, baptized 10 November 1770

Nancy Stiles, daughter of Joseph and Phebe Stiles, born 3 October 1770, baptized 8 April 1771

John Smith, son of Hannah Smith, "patre ignoto," born 9 December 1770, baptized 5 May 1771

Joseph Sterett, son of James and Mary Sterett, born 15 July 1771, baptized 4 August 1771

Rachel Stevenson, daughter of William and Rebecca Stevenson, born 6 August 1771, baptized 6 September 1771

Rachel Sinclair, daughter of William and Margaret Sinclair, born 16 November 1791, baptized 7 December 1771

Mary Sterett, daughter of John and Deborah Sterett, born 1 September 1772, baptized 23 October 1772

Rachel Stevenson, daughter of William and Rachel Stevenson, born 9 March 1773, baptized 4 June 1773

David Smith, son of John and Elizabeth Smith, born 11 June 1774, baptized 8 July 1774

Frances Stevenson Smith, daughter of Nathaniel and Sarah Smith, born 21 August 1774, baptized 4 September 1774

McLure Sterett, son of John and Deborah Sterett, born 24 October 1774, baptized 13 November 1774

Robert Saunderson, son of Francis and Margaret Saunderson, born 29 January 1775, baptized 9 April 1775
Susanna Sinclair, daughter of William and Margaret Sinclair, born 7 August 1775, baptized 1 October 1775
Harriet Sterett, daughter of John and Deborah Sterett, born 26 November 1775, baptized 13 December 1775
Betsey Stiles, daughter of Joseph and Phebe Stiles, born 30 October 1775, baptized 4 April 1776
Samuel Steigar, son of Andrew and Mary Anne Steigar, born 6 July 1776, baptized 19 January 1777
John Stewart, son of David and Elizabeth Stewart, born 28 February 1777, baptized 16 March 1777
Jesse Lukens Saunderson, son of Frances and Margaret Saunderson, born 10 March 1777, baptized 13 July 1777
Andrew Mease Sinclair, son of William and Margaret Sinclair, born 27 August 1777, baptized 27 September 1777
Andrew Sterett, son of John and Deborah Sterett, born 27 January 1778, baptized 16 March 1778
Anne Henry Stevenson, daughter of Henry and Anne Stevenson, born 5 August 1775, baptized 17 January 1779
Eliza Sterett, daughter of John and Deborah Sterett, born 3 July 1779, baptized 15 August 1779
Lewis Buchanan Smith, son of Samuel and Margaret Smith, born 5 November 1779, baptized 12 December 1779
Mary Stewart, daughter of David and Elizabeth Stewart, born 17 November 1779, baptized 19 December 1779
Mary Spear, daughter of John and Elizabeth Spear, born 10 July 1780, baptized 27 August 1780
Juliet Sterett, daughter of John and Deborah Sterett, born 20 August 1780, baptized 10 September 1780
St. John Smith, son of Samuel and Margaret Smith, born 8 March 1781, baptized 29 April 1781
William Plunket Stewart, son of David and Elizabeth Stewart, born 8 May 1781, baptized 15 July 1781
David Brown Shields, son of Caleb and Jane Shields, born 15 August 1780, baptized 20 July 1781
James Shepherd, son of John and Anne Shepherd, born 18 February 1782, baptized 23 February 1782
John Porter Smith, son of Nathaniel and Sarah Smith, born 21 November 1781, baptized 17 March 1782

Charles Ridgely Sterett, son of John and Deborah Sterett, born 7 March 1782, baptized 25 March 1782

Elizabeth Spear, daughter of John and Elizabeth Spear, born 25 May 1782, baptized 2 June 1782

Alexander Wilson Stewart, son of Hugh and Susanna Stewart, born 20 June 1782, baptized 14 August 1782

Elizabeth Smith, daughter of Samuel and Margaret Smith, born 7 March 1783, baptized 6 April 1783

James Sterett, son of John and Deborah Sterett, born 23 August 1783, baptized 8 November 1783

Catharine Isabella Stewart, daughter of David and Elizabeth Stewart, born 11 September ---- [1783?], baptized 18 July 1784

Agness Shipley, daughter of Henry and Eleanor Shipley, born 17 February 1783, baptized 18 July 1784

James Sloan, son of James and Elizabeth Sloan, born 28 January 1784, baptized 29 September 1784

John Sterett, son of John and Deborah Sterett, born 3 December 1784, baptized 9 January 1785

William Spear Smith, son of Samuel and Margaret Smith, born 6 March 1786, baptized 24 April 1786

James Smith, son of John and Elizabeth Smith, born 5 February 1783, baptized 9 May 1783

Matthew Swan, son of Matthew and Anne Swan, born 28 June 1785, baptized 21 August 1785

Anne Philpot Stewart, daughter of David and Elizabeth Stewart, born 6 June 1785, baptized 2 October 1785

William Stewart, son of William and Peggy Stewart, born 3 May 1785, baptized 27 November 1785

William Scott, son of William and Mary Scott, born 31 October 1785, baptized 15 January 1786

James Sloon, son of James and Elizabeth Sloon, born 5 February 1786, baptized 16 April 1786

Mary Smith, daughter of Joseph and Sarah Smith, born 5 December 1785, baptized 10 May 1786

Sophia Sterett, daughter of John and Deborah Sterett, born 29 October 1786, baptized 4 November 1786

John Smith, son of Samuel and Margaret Smith, born 2 November 1786, baptized 8 January 1797

Catherine Stricker, daughter of John and Martha Stricker, born 27 September 1786, baptized 10 January 1787

Gertrude Stevenson, daughter of Henry and Anne Stevenson, born 26 March 1787, baptized 1 April 1787

William Swann, son of Matthew and Anne Swann, born 11 May 1787, baptized 10 June 1787

William Smith, son of William and Henrietta Smith, born 22 March 1784, baptized 1 August 1787

Catherine Smith, daughter of William and Henrietta Smith, born 7 August 1786, baptized 1 August 1787

Andrew Scott, son of William and Mary Scott, born 1 June 1787, baptized 19 August 1787

Anne Brent Smith, daughter of Johnston and Mary Smith, born 27 February 1786, baptized 19 August 1787

James Smith, son of James and Sarah Smith, born 15 August 1787, baptized 11 March 1788

William Sloon, son of James and Elizabeth Sloon, born 15 February 1788, baptized 23 March 1788

Jane Steel, daughter of Archibald and Jane Steel, born 2 March 1777, baptized 24 April 1788

James Caldwell Stewart, son of David and Elizabeth Stewart, born 4 March 1788, baptized 22 June 1788

Robert Swan, son of John and Elizabeth Swan, born 29 June 1788, baptized 10 July 1788

Anne Stewart, daughter of Robert and Susanna Stewart, born 17 December 1788, baptized 11 January 1789

Mary Buchanan Smith, daughter of Samuel and Margaret Smith, born 22 November 1788, baptized 1 February 1789

Anne Elizabeth Stricker, daughter of John and Martha Stricker, born 11 February 1789, baptized 12 March 1789

John Swan, son of Matthew and Anne Swan, born 15 March 1789, baptized 7 June 1789

Harriet Stiles, daughter of George and Anne Stiles, born 25 August 1787, baptized 13 September 1789

John Steel Stiles, son of George and Anne Stiles, born 21 November 1788, baptized 13 September 1789

John Stewart, son of James and Anne Stewart, born 24 September 1789, baptized 29 November 1789

John Stirling, son of James and Elizabeth Stirling, born 8 December 1789, baptized 9 May 1790

John Swan, son of John and Elizabeth Swan, born 4 May 1790, baptized 16 May 1790

Elizabeth Slappy, daughter of Jacob and Jane Slappy, born 28 September 1790, baptized 31 October 1790

Margaretta Galbraith Smith, daughter of Samuel and Margaret Smith, born 25 August 1790, baptized 31 October 1790

Susanna Stricker, daughter of John and Martha Stricker, born 13 March 1791, baptized 31 March 1791

George Clingon Simpson, son of James and Jane Simpson, born 5 March 1791, baptized 24 April 1791

John Maxwell Swan, son of Joseph and Agness Swan, born 4 July 1791, baptized 24 July 1791

James Stevens, son of James and Rebecca Stevens, born 16 July 1791, baptized 26 July 1791

Mary Stewart, daughter of Robert and Susanna Stewart, born 10 May 1791, baptized 7 September 1791

Thomas Swan, son of Matthew and Anne Swan, born 27 March 1791, baptized 6 November 1791

Thomas Stewart, son of Cowden and Mary Stewart, born 27 October 1790, baptized 18 December 1791

Elizabeth Louisa Smith, daughter of Robert and Margaret Smith, born 14 September 1791, baptized 25 December 1791

George Pitt Stevenson, son of George Pitt and Esther Stevenson, born 14 December 1791, baptized 17 February 1792

George Maxwell Swan, son of John and Elizabeth Swan, born 28 November 1791, baptized 4 March 1792

Elizabeth Sterling, daughter of James and Elizabeth Sterling, born 4 February 1792, bapt 15 April 1792, by Dr. Muir, Alexandria

Joseph Graybell Stiles, son of George and Anne Stiles, born 16 July 1791, baptized 13 May 1792

Joseph Elliott Smith, son of Joseph and Sarah Smith, born 2 June 1788, baptized 31 July 1792

James Stewart, son of James and Anne Stewart, born 20 August 1792, baptized 25 August 1792

Mary Scott, daughter of Robert and Elizabeth Scott, born 25 January 1793, baptized 27 January 1793

Eleanor Stewart, daughter of Archibald and Sarah Stewart, born 30 August 1792, baptized 16 February 1793

Laura Sophia Smith, daughter of Samuel and Margaret Smith, born 27 November 1792, baptized 18 February 1793

Mary Stevens, daughter of James and Rebecca Stevens, born 4 January 1793, baptized 10 March 1793

FIRST PRESBYTERIAN CHURCH

George Bedford Stricker, son of John and Martha Stricker, born 12 February 1793, baptized 7 April 1793
James Swan, son of John and Elizabeth Swan, born 10 November 1792, baptized 11 April 1793
Agness Slappy, daughter of Jacob and Jane Slappy, born 24 May 1793, baptized 7 July 1793
Elizabeth Sloan, daughter of James and Elizabeth Sloan, born 17 March 1793, baptized 9 August 1793
Louisa Stiles, daughter of George and Anne Stiles, born 26 March 1793, baptized 17 August 1793
Andrew Stewart, son of John Couden and Mary Stewart, born 1 May 1793, baptized 18 August 1793
William Glassell Swan, son of Joseph and Ann Swan, born 29 July 1793, baptized 13 October 1793
Elizabeth Swan, daughter of Matthew and Ann Swan, born 18 July 1793, baptized 6 October 1793 ("returned after ye preceeding entry.")
Mary Scroggs, daughter of John and Frances Scroggs, born 1 April 1788, baptized 9 November 1793
Margaret Scroggs, daughter of John and Frances Scroggs, born 3 January 1790, baptized 9 November 1793
Allen Scroggs, son of John and Frances Scroggs, born 30 December 1791, baptized 9 November 1793
George Maxwell Swan, son of John and Elizabeth Swan, born 28 November 1793, baptized 31 January 1794
David Boyd Simpson, son of James and Jane Simpson, born 7 January 1794, baptized 20 April 1794
Anna Maria Stiles, daughter of George and Anne Stiles, born 6 June 1794, baptized 2 July 1794
William Solomon, son of Elkins and Abigail Solomon, born 2 December 1793, baptized 27 July 1794
William John Stewart, son of James and Ann Stewart, born 18 August 1794, baptized 6 September 1794
John Buchanan Smith, son of Robert and Margaret Smith, born 25 June 1794, baptized 14 September 1794
Sidney Smith, daughter of Samuel and Margaret Smith, born 15 August 1794, baptized 21 September 1794
Mary Sterett, daughter of Samuel and Rebecca Sterett, born 1 September 1794, baptized 3 October 1794

Thomas Stirling, son of James and Elizabeth Stirling, born 4 June 1794, baptized 6 October 1794

George Smith, son of Richard and Mary Smith, born 7 February 1793, baptized 29 October 1794

John Stewart, son of John Couden and Mary Stewart, born 28 October 1794, baptized 2 November 1794

O'Neal Scott, son of Robert and Elizabeth Scott, born 4 December 1794, baptized 6 December 1794

Mary Stewart, daughter of Archibald and Sarah Stewart, born 21 August 1794, baptized 14 December 1794

Jacob Summers, son of James and Jane Summers, born 22 January 1795, baptized 1 February 1795

Jane Henrietta Stricker, daughter of John and Martha Stricker, born 15 October 1794, baptized 8 March 1795

Caroline Smith, daughter of Richard and Mary Smith, born 3 March 1795, baptized 14 June 1795

James Sleppy [Slappy?], son of Jacob and Jane Slappy, born 26 September 1795, baptized 7 November 1795

Mary Sloan, daughter of James and Elizabeth Sloan, born 1 October 1795, baptized 14 December 1795

William Stevens, son of James and Rebecca Stevens, born 20 December 1789, baptized 1 January 1790 ("omitted in its proper place.")

Alexander Stevens, son of James and Rebecca Stevens, born 29 December 1795, baptized 31 January 1796

David Carroll S----, son of ---- and ---- S---- [illegible], born 13 March 1796, baptized 3 April 1796

Augusta Temple Sterett, daughter of Samuel and Rebecca Sterett, born 29 December 1795, baptized 25 May 1796

William Smith, son of Robert and Margaret Smith, born 9 March 1796, baptized 19 June 1796

James Stewart, son of Robert and Susanna Stewart, born 3 July 1796, baptized 15 July 1796

John Scott, son of Robert and Elizabeth Scott, born 1 September 1796, baptized 9 September 1796

Ednery Solomon, daughter of Elkins and Abigail Solomon, born 27 March 1795, baptized 15 September 1796

Eliza Starr, daughter of Obadiah and Ruth Starr, born 24 June 1796, baptized 2 October 1796

Eliza Smiley, daughter of Isaac and Margaret Smiley, born 30 July 1796, baptized 28 October 1796

FIRST PRESBYTERIAN CHURCH 61

Couden Stewart, son of John Cowden [sic] and Mary Stewart, born 29 May 1796, baptized 6 November 1796

Jane Hollins Smith, daughter of Samuel and Margaret Smith, born 22 October 1796, baptized 28 December 1796

Julianna Stricker, daughter of John and Martha Stricker, born 21 December 1796, baptized 22 February 1797

William Shaw, son of Robert and Lucy Shaw, born 7 December 1796, baptized 19 March 1797

Frances Scroggs, adult, baptized 21 March 1797

John Scroggs, son of John and Frances Scroggs, born 9 June 1794, baptized 21 March 1797

David Reed Stewart, son of James and Ann Stewart, born 9 March 1797, baptized 8 May 1797

Anna Maria Smith, daughter of John and Elizabeth Smith, born 11 February 1797, baptized 6 June 1797

Eloisa Bentalou Sanger, daughter of Seth and Catharine Sanger, born 9 December 1796, baptized 9 July 1797

William Story, son of John and Mary Story, born 20 April 1797, baptized 3 September 1797

Jane Scroggs, daughter of Alexander and Ann Scroggs, born 27 August 1797, baptized 30 September 1797

Robert Smith, son of Robert and Margaret Smith, born 18 September 1797, baptized 13 November 1797

Mary Ann Smith, daughter of Richard and Mary Smith, born 11 November 1796, baptized 13 January 1798

Margaret Stewart, daughter of Robert and Susanna Stewart, born 20 February 1798, baptized 2 March 1798

William Sleppy [Slappy?], son of Jacob and Jane Slappy, born 8 January 1798, baptized 18 March 1798

Charles and Jane Sloan, twins of James and Elizabeth Sloan, born 18 March 1798, baptized 8 April 1798

Margaret Deaver Starr, daughter of Obadiah and Ruth Starr, born 14 June 1798, baptized 16 July 1798

Elizabeth Scott, daughter of Robert and Elizabeth Scott, born 5 August 1798, baptized 6 August 1798

Amelia Stabler, daughter of William and Margaret Stabler, born 13 August 1798, baptized 21 October 1798

Anne Smith, daughter of Samuel and Margaret Smith, born 26 September 1798, baptized 9 October 1798

Archibald Stirling, son of James and Elizabeth Stirling, born 13 July 1798, baptized 30 November 1798

Sarah Solomon, daughter of Elkins and Abigail Solomon, born 11 February 1799, baptized 13 February 1799

Charlotte Stricker, daughter of John and Martha Stricker, born 4 November 1798, baptized 10 March 1799

Juliana Snuggress, daughter of William and Catharine Snuggress, [Snodgrass?], born 21 September 1798, baptized 11 April 1799

Mary Ann Smiley, daughter of Isaac and Margaret Smiley, born 6 March 1799, baptized 5 May 1799

Lucy Margaret Sanger, daughter of Seth and Catharine Sanger, born 18 February 1799, baptized 26 May 1799

John Stephens Smith, son of John and Elizabeth Smith, born 11 August 1799, baptized 25 September 1799

William Carvil Smith, son of Robert and Margaret Smith, born 14 August 1799, baptized 25 September 1799

Elizabeth Smull, adult, baptized 3 December 1799

Richard Johns Smull, son of Jacob and Elizabeth Smull, born 13 December 1797, baptized 3 December 1799

David Burke Smull, son of Jacob and Elizabeth Smull, born 18 November 1799, baptized 3 December 1799

Edward Stewart, son of James and Ann Stewart, born 12 December 1799, baptized 15 January 1800

Louisa Starr, daughter of Obadiah and Ruth Starr, born 4 September 1799, baptized 25 January 1800

Robert Clement Shermerdine, son of Joseph and Sarah Shermerdine, born 24 November 1799, baptized 26 January 1800

Meron Sandison, daughter of Alexander and Jane Sandison, born 26 March 1800, baptized 27 April 1800

Elkin Solomon, son of Elkin [Elkins] and Abigail Solomon, born 29 April 1800, baptized 2 May 1800

Samuel Smith, son of Robert and Margaret Smith, born 12 August 1800, baptized 16 November 1800

Letitia Jane Stewart, daughter of David and Jane Stewart, born 3 April 1800, baptized 16 November 1800

Sally Sleppy [Slappy?], Jacob and Jane Sleppy, born 29 June 1800, baptized 16 November 1800

William Stewart, son of Couden and Mary Stewart, born 11 December 1800, baptized 22 December 1800

FIRST PRESBYTERIAN CHURCH 63

David Stewart, son of John and Helena Stewart, born 13 September 1800, baptized 24 December 1800

Robert Stirling, son of James and Elizabeth Stirling, born 20 April 1800, baptized 12 January 1801

Joseph Spear, son of Joseph and Barbara Spear, born 23 May 1800, baptized 16 January 1801

Eliza Scott, daughter of John and Jane Scott, born 2 May 1800, baptized 21 January 1801

William Scott Young, son of William and Catharine Young, born 29 January 1801, baptized 19 February 1801

John Stricker, son of John and Martha Stricker, born 26 July 1800, baptized 22 February 1801

Ann Barbara Sweeting, daughter of Thomas and Catharine Sweeting, born 26 October 1800, baptized 24 February 1801

Mary Ann Scroggs, daughter of Alexander and Ann Scroggs, born 29 February 1800, baptized 27 February 1801

Eleanor Reed Stewart, daughter of James and Ann Stewart, born 22 February 1801, baptized 19 March 1801

William Cooper Stabler, son of William and Margaret Stabler, born 9 March 1801, baptized 10 May 1801

Isabella Stewart, daughter of Archibald and Sarah Stewart, born 16 September 1801, baptized 14 May 1801

Robert Joseph Swan, son of Joseph and Agness Swan, born 27 June 1801, baptized 5 July 1801

Elizabeth Ann Stewart, daughter of David and Jane Stewart, born 28 May 1801, baptized 10 July 1801

Mary Taylor, daughter of Isaac and Martha Taylor, born 3 June 1766, baptized 19 October 1766

Anne Taylor, daughter of Isaac and Martha Taylor, born 9 January 1768, baptized 20 July 1768

Martha Taylor, daughter of Isaac and Martha Taylor, born 29 January 1771, baptized 22 August 1771

Frances Thompson, daughter of John and Jane Thompson, born 26 March 1772, baptized 21 June 1772

John Turner, son of Samuel and Jane Turner, born 24 February 1779, baptized 2 May 1779

James Torrance, son of Charles and Elizabeth Torrance, born 26 July 1780, baptized 9 August 1780

James Tumblesome, son of William and Janit Tumblesome, born 11 August 1780, baptized 23 August 1780

Mary Thompson, daughter of John and Jane Thompson, born 12 July 1781, baptized 4 October 1781

Anne Torrance, daughter of Charles and Elizabeth Torrance, born 23 February 1781, baptized 23 April 1781

William Tumblesome, son of William and Janit Tumblesome, born 25 November 1781, baptized 1 June 1782

Mary Tumblesome, daughter of James and Elizabeth Tumblesome, born 10 February 1782, baptized 1 June 1782

Mary Tumblesome, daughter of William and Janit Tumblesome, born 7 April 1783, baptized 9 December 1783

John Thompson, son of John and Jane Thompson, born 23 October 1783, baptized 31 January 1784

Dorcas Torrance, daughter of Charles and Elizabeth Torrance, born 24 November 1783, baptized 3 May 1784

Samuel Tumblesome, son of William and Janit Tumblesome, born 10 March 1785, baptized 20 July 1785

Mary Torrance, daughter of Charles and Elizabeth Torrance, born 16 October 1785, baptized 26 November 1785

Elizabeth Thompson, daughter of John and Jane Thompson, born 18 March 1786, baptized 11 May 1786

John Tumblesome, son of William and Janit Tumblesome, born 27 October 1786, baptized 19 November 1786

Agness Tate, daughter of Andrew and Jane Tate, born 29 January 1779, baptized 27 April 1787

Mary and Margaret Tate, twins of Andrew and Jane Tate, born 30 September 1783, baptized 27 April 1787

Elizabeth Tate, daughter of Andrew and Jane Tate, born 17 July 1785, baptized 27 April 1787

Robert Thompson, son of Alexander and Jane Thompson, born 28 October 1786, baptized 30 April 1787

Rebecca Travers, daughter of Matthew and Jane Travers, born 26 July 1787, baptized 12 June 1788

Charles Torrance, son of Charles and Elizabeth Torrance, born 20 April 1788, baptized 14 July 1788

Lydia Towson, daughter of Jacob and Jane Towson, born 25 February 1789, baptized 26 April 1789

George Torrance, son of Charles and Elizabeth Torrance, born 9 January 1790, baptized 15 May 1790

James Duncan Taylor, son of Joseph and Esther Taylor, born 28 June 1790, baptized 7 September 1790

FIRST PRESBYTERIAN CHURCH 65

Harriet Torrance, daughter of Charles and Elizabeth Torrance, born 24 May 1791, baptized 28 July 1791

Elizabeth Tagart, daughter of John and Mary Lyon Tagart, born 15 August 1791, baptized 25 December 1791

Elizabeth Travers, daughter of Matthew and Jane Travers, born 4 November 1791, baptized 13 May 1792

William Tuston, son of Septimus and Elizabeth Tuston, born 4 July 1792, baptized 11 July 1792

William Thornell, son of Robert and Jane Thornell, born 6 November 1790, baptized 16 July 1792

Mary Tagart, daughter of John and Mary Lyon Tagart, born 15 January 1794, baptized 6 April 1794

James Torrance, son of Charles and Elizabeth Torrance, born 11 May 1793, baptized 5 May 1794

Jane Etting Taylor, daughter of Robert and Frances Taylor, born 3 December 1793, baptized 11 July 1794

Albert Tuston, son of Septimus and Elizabeth Tuston, born 14 March 1794, baptized 27 July 1794

Sally Turnbull, daughter of Andrew and Hannah Turnbull, born 14 July 1794, baptized 3 August 1794

Ann Thompson, daughter of Robert and Sarah Thompson, born 16 February 1794, baptized 10 August 1794

John Torrance, son of Charles and Elizabeth Torrance, born 24 November 1794, baptized 1 December 1794

George Thornell, son of Robert and Jane Thornell, born 5 November 1792, baptized 25 April 1795

Sarah Thornell, daughter of Robert and Jane Thornell, born 24 February 1795, baptized 25 April 1795

Catharine Taylor, daughter of Robert and Frances Taylor, born 18 July 1795, baptized 29 December 1795

John Thompson, son of Robert and Sarah Thompson, born 11 April 1796, baptized 12 September 1796

Anne Thompson, daughter of George and Mary Thompson, born 1 January 1796, baptized 3 February 1797

Anne Calwell Tagart, daughter of John and Mary Lyon Tagart, born 18 October 1796, baptized 9 February 1797

James Thompson, son of Nathaniel and Eliza Thompson, born 28 March 1796, baptized 1 April 1797

Mary Travers, daughter of Matthew and Jane Travers, born 11 December 1796, baptized 11 July 1797

Elizabeth Turnbull, daughter of Andrew and Hannah Turnbull, born 25 May 1797, baptized 12 July 1797
Louisa Torrance, daughter of Charles and Elizabeth Torrance, born 15 May 1797, baptized 15 July 1797
William Thompson, son of William and Margaret Thompson, born 16 February 1797, baptized 13 October 1797
William Tagart, son of John and Mary Lyon Tagart, born 30 January 1798, baptized 14 April 1798
George Thompson, son of William and Maria Thompson, born 10 March 1798, baptized 28 September 1798
Mary Ann Thompson, daughter of Nathaniel and Elizabeth Thompson, born 18 July 1798, baptized 9 July 1799
Jane Travers, daughter of Matthew and Jane Travers, born 11 March 1799, baptized 1 January 1800
Ann Thompson, daughter of George and Mary Thompson, born 11 November 1799, baptized 1 January 1800
Jane Turnbull, daughter of Andrew and Hannah Turnbull, born 8 September 1799, baptized 15 January 1800
Julian Taylor, daughter of William and Maria Taylor, born 3 February 1800, baptized 13 April 1800
Louisa Watson Taylor, daughter of John and Louisa Taylor, born 21 March 1800, baptized 9 November 1800
John Thomson, son of William and Eleanor Thomson, born 20 August 1800, baptized 16 November 1800
James Vansant, son of Isaiah and Mary Vansant, born 27 July 1756, baptized 18 November 1771
Susanna Vansant, daughter of Isaiah and Mary Vansant, born 23 October 1758, baptized 18 November 1771
Rebecca Vansant, daughter of Isaiah and Mary Vansant, born 28 August 1760, baptized 18 November 1771
Elizabeth Vansant, daughter of Isaiah and Mary Vansant, born 16 August 1762, baptized 18 November 1771
Eleanor Vansant, daughter of Isaiah and Mary Vansant, born 19 September 1765, baptized 18 November 1771
Agness Vansant, daughter of Isaiah and Mary Vansant, born 1 September 1768, baptized 18 November 1771
Dorothy Vickery, daughter of Stephen and Elizabeth Vickery, born 15 October 1791, baptized 25 October 1791
Stephen Vickery, son of Stephen and Elizabeth Vickery, born 14 September 1793, baptized 27 July 1794

Eleanor Vickery, daughter of Stephen and Elizabeth Vickery, born 3 February 1796, baptized 15 September 1796

Abraham Van Bibber, son of Abraham and Mary Van Bibber, born 16 May 1797, baptized 9 July 1797

Nathaniel Westby, son of William and Rebecca Westby, born 11 February 1767, baptized 28 March 1767

Sarah Webster, daughter of John and Hannah Webster, born 4 October 1759, baptized 11 May 1767

Elizabeth Webster, daughter of John and Sarah Webster, born 21 February 1767, baptized 11 May 1767

Elizabeth Williams, daughter of George and Mary Williams, born 27 March 1758, baptized 25 April 1768

Mary Williams, daughter of George and Mary Williams, born 12 November 1760, baptized 25 April 1768

John Williams, son of George and Mary Williams, born 7 March 1762, baptized 25 April 1768

William Williams, son of George and Mary Williams, born 9 February 1764, baptized 25 April 1768

George Williams, son of George and Mary Williams, born 20 March 1768, baptized 25 April 1768

Elizabeth Walker, daughter of James and Jane Walker, born 8 May 1768, baptized 31 August 1768

Susanna Westby, daughter of William and Rebecca Westby, born 19 April 1769, baptized 3 May 1769

Joseph Walker, son of Robert and Isabella Walker, born 27 September 1769, baptized 20 October 1769

Jemima Weimer, daughter of Matthias and Agness Weimer, born 5 October 1767, baptized 2 December 1769

Eleanor Weer, daughter of William and Catherine Weer, born 1 March 1771, baptized 14 April 1771

Thomas Westby, son of William and Rebecca Westby, born 2 April 1771, baptized 20 April 1771

George Weimer, son of Matthias and Agness Weimer, born 4 February 1770, baptized 26 June 1771

Rebecca Westby, daughter of William and Rebecca Westby, born 16 July 1773, baptized 30 July 1773

Mary Welch, daughter of George and Margaret Welch, born 23 November 1774, baptized 23 January 1775

James Wilkins, son of Thomas and Mary Wilkins, born 14 November 1774, baptized 2 February 1775

Robert White, son of Robert and Mary White, born 22 August 1775, baptized 23 August 1775

James Wilson, son of William and Jane Wilson, born 3 December 1765, baptized 18 February 1776

John Welch, son of George and Margaret Welch, born 12 January 1776, baptized 17 February 1776

Robert White, son of Robert and Margaret White, born 11 April 1777, baptized 7 May 1777

Eleanor Westby, daughter of William and Rebecca Westby, born 26 November 1777, baptized 17 December 1777

Jane Wallace, son of John and Eleanor Wallace, born 5 May 1778, baptized 6 May 1778

George Welch, son of George and Margaret Welch, born 11 December 1778, baptized 27 September 1779

Elizabeth Wallace, daughter of John and Eleanor Wallace, born 22 February 1780, baptized 23 February 1780

Thomas Wilson, son of James and Jane Wilson, born 27 August 1777, baptized 5 June 1780

Hannah Wilson, daughter of James and Jane Wilson, born 8 July 1779, baptized 5 June 1780

Robert Westby, son of William and Rebecca Westby, born 29 April 1780, baptized 17 June 1780

David Smith Welch, son of George and Margaret Welch, born 11 July 1780, baptized 30 July 1780

Zipporah Wilson, daughter of Jesse and Eleanor Wilson, born ---- [blank], baptized 23 January 1781

James Wilson, son of Jesse and Eleanor Wilson, born 8 January 1781, baptized 23 January 1781

Elizabeth Wilson, daughter of David and Anne Wilson, born 22 October 1778, baptized 23 January 1781

Rebecca Wilson, daughter of James and Jane Wilson, born 22 April 1781, baptized 26 August 1781

James Cox Welch, son of George and Margaret Welch, born 19 December 1781, baptized 20 January 1782

Rebecca Welch, daughter of George and Margaret Welch, born 8 February 1783, baptized 20 April 1783

William Wilson, son of James and Jane Wilson, born 25 December 1782, baptized 28 April 1783

John Wall, son of John and Anne Wall, born 25 January 1781, baptized 21 September 1783

FIRST PRESBYTERIAN CHURCH

Anne Wall, daughter of John and Anne Wall, born 15 September 1783, baptized 21 September 1783

Robert White, son of Robert and Kissina White, born 10 December 1783, baptized 17 February 1784

Eleanor Wilson, daughter of David and Anne Wilson, born 22 June 1784, baptized 6 October 1784

John Wilson, son of David and Anne Wilson, born 30 September 1784, baptized 6 October 1784

Hugh Wilson, son of Hugh and Eleanor Wilson, born 30 July 1784, baptized 14 October 1784

Andrew White, son of Joseph and Susanna White, apprentice of John McChord, born 1770, baptized 13 April 1785

Robert Smith Williams, son of Otho Holland and Mary Williams, born 25 July 1786, baptized 10 September 1786

Betsey White, daughter of Edward and Letitia White, born 9 March 1785, baptized 25 February 1787

James White, son of Edward and Letitia White, born 5 October 1785, baptized 25 February 1787

Andrew Work, son of William and Nancy Work, born 29 September 1786, baptized 8 May 1787

Elizabeth Wilson, daughter of Stephen and Rebecca Wilson, born 27 December 1786, baptized 27 December 1787

William Elie Williams, son of Otho Holland and Mary Williams, born 10 December 1787, baptized 10 February 1788

Edward Greene Williams, son of Otho Holland and Mary Williams, born 23 March 1789, baptized 27 April 1789

Isabella Wilson, daughter of Stephen and Rebecca Wilson, born 3 June 1789, baptized 14 August 1789

Sarah Watson, daughter of Joseph and Frances Watson, born 1 January 1790, baptized 7 January 1790

Samuel White, son of John and Rebecca White, born 22 January 1790, baptized 23 March 1790

George Gillespie Wallace, son of Andrew and Ruth Wallace, born 19 February 1790, baptized 9 April 1790

William Williams, son of John and Margaret Williams, born 6 April 1791, baptized 12 June 1791

Robert Wilson, son of Stephen and Rebecca Wilson, born 29 June 1791, baptized 29 July 1791

Frances Anne Watson, daughter of Joseph and Frances Watson, born 8 March 1791, baptized 7 August 1791

Henry Lee Williams, son of Otho Holland and Mary Williams, born 23 December 1791, baptized 4 March 1792

Mary Watson, daughter of Francis and Agness Watson, born and baptized 19 May 1792

William Wallace, son of Andrew and Ruth Wallace, born 18 February 1793, baptized 5 May 1793

Armenella Wilson, daughter of Stephen and Rebecca Wilson, born 21 April 1793, baptized 7 April 1794

Otho Holland Williams, son of Otho Holland and Mary Williams, born 15 May 1794, baptized 2 June 1794

Isabella Watson, daughter of David and Mary Watson, born 20 June 1794, baptized 20 July 1794

Thomas Wooden, son of Richard and Letitia Wooden, born 21 March 1795, baptized 4 April 1795

Francis Watson, son of Francis and Agness Watson, born 2 February 1795, baptized 21 June 1795

Elizabeth Whitelock, daughter of Moses and Agness Whitelock, born 15 October 1795, baptized 10 April 1796

James A. Waddle, son of William and Sarah Waddle, born 23 November 1795, baptized 20 February 1797

Mary Ann Wooden, daughter of Richard and Letitia Wooden, born 6 June 1797, baptized 19 June 1797

Andrew Wallace, son of Andrew and Ruth Wallace, born 24 March 1797, baptized 14 July 1797

Robert Wilson, son of Robert and Anna Wilson, born 3 September 1797, baptized 30 November 1797

Anna Wilson, adult, baptized 30 November 1797

David Waddle, son of William and Sarah Waddle, born 27 October 1797, baptized 26 June 1798

Zechariah Crawford Wilson, son of Benoni and Elizabeth Wilson, born 25 November 1798, baptized 25 March 1799

Jesse Wheeler, son of Jesse and Agness Wheeler, born 25 March 1799, baptized 23 June 1799

Mary West, daughter of James and Maria L. West, born 15 February 1799, baptized 27 June 1799

James Wilson, son of Robert and Anna Wilson, born 12 October 1799, baptized 11 December 1799

William Waddle, son of William and Sarah Waddle, born 4 June 1799, baptized 12 January 1800

Harriet West, daughter of James and Maria L. West, born 20 October 1800, baptized 24 December 1800
Anne Eliza Wheeler, daughter of Jesse and Agness Wheeler, born 16 April 1801, baptized 17 May 1801
Martha Whitelock, daughter of Moses and Agness Whitelock, born 24 June 1799, baptized 21 June 1801
Decimus White, son of John Campbell and Elizabeth White, born 3 December 1800, baptized 21 June 1801
Maurice Williams, son of Jacob and Mary Williams, born 9 October 1800, baptized 12 July 1801
Eliza Young, daughter of Hugh and Mary Young, born 7 November 1779, baptized 26 December 1779
Carey Young, son of Hugh and Mary Young, born 22 November 1781, baptized 27 January 1782
James Young, son of Hugh and Mary Young, born 26 November 1783, baptized 2 July 1784
Elizabeth Young, daughter of Jesse and Jane Young, born 17 December 1796, baptized 4 February 1797
William Young, son of Hugh and Rebecca Young, born 20 February 1798, baptized 4 March 1798
Robert Young, son of Hugh and Rebecca Young, born 4 July 1799, baptized 10 July 1799
McClintock Young, son of Hugh and Rebecca Young, born 21 March 1801, baptized 7 April 1801

FIRST PRESBYTERIAN CHURCH, MARRIAGE RECORDS, 1767-1801

John Allison and Elizabeth Wilkins married 3 November 1768, PA
James Anderson and Mary Clark married 3 January 1775
Robert Allison and Anne Ramsey married 26 June 1777, VA
Patrick Allison and Mary Buchanan married 15 March 1787 by Rev. Isaac S. Keith, VA
James Angell and Mary Barney married 25 December 1788
John Armstrong and Patience Lorton married 18 November 1790
John Allridge and Margaret Limes married 1 May 1792
William Anderson and Mary McDonald married 1 February 1793
William Armstrong and Esther Dungen married 21 February 1796

PRESBYTERIAN RECORDS OF BALTIMORE, MD

Andrew Albright and Elizabeth Cobenheifer married 11 July 1796
Henry Anderson and Eliza Crawford married 23 October 1799
Joseph Allender and Mary Biays married 30 January 1800
Thomas Allen and Elizabeth Egnew married 18 December 1800
James Bennett and Jane Weer married 15 November 1769
John Boyd and Anne Little married 8 May 1777
John Brown and Elizabeth Davies married 7 May 1778
James Bearing and Patience Hipsley married 22 August 1779
Thomas Brown and Mary Ellicot married 17 October 1785
James Bumrides and Margaret Slater married 24 November 1785
James Buchanan and Susanna Young married 26 November 1787
John Beach and Catherine Wolf married 13 January 1789
Josiah Brown and Jehosheba Kirk married 16 August 1790
Gilbert Bigges and Rebecca Short married 14 August 1791
William Boyle and Mary Evans married 9 December 1792
James A. Buchanan and Elizabeth Calhoun married 1 January 1793
Joseph Belt and Ellin Randall married 8 October 1793
Nicholas Bisho and Nancy Turine married 12 December 1794
Alexander Brown and Anne Jones married 24 March 1795
Jesse Bonsell and Mary Stapleton married 2 June 1795
John Burtes and Ellin Price married 5 September 1795
Jacob Burgoine and Ann Gardner married 1 May 1796
James Biays and Sarah Trimble married 12 May 1796
Robert P. Bail and Mary Ann Davies married 10 October 1796
Henry Buldge and Elizabeth Price married 10 March 1797
Joseph Biays and Elizabeth May married 26 March 1797
Jennis Helming Baker and Susanna Johanna Gerardina Van Noemes married 29 May 1797
Sylvanus Bourne and Rebecca Mercer Haslett married 17 October 1797
James Briggs and Temperance Ensor married 5 December 1797
Moses Bunker and Margaret Franciscus married 8 May 1798
Joseph Bennett and Elizabeth Lindon married 11 June 1798
John H. Behn and Violet Bryden married 18 September 1798
Thomas Burk and Sarah Hines married 4 October 1798
Thomas Barklie and Jane McCormick married 1 November 1798
Ferdinand Broke and Hannah Cornwall married 2 April 1799
James Bond and Julia McCard married 11 July 1799
John Bowering and Margaret Martin married 7 October 1799
Nathan Gregg Bryson and Susanna Prentiss married 20 October 1799
Thomas Burk and Rebecca North married 26 June 1795

Hugh Carr and Eleanor Weer married 12 May 1767
Daniel Chamier and Ashsah Carman married 25 February 1768
Robert Crawford and Anne Wells married 7 May 1776
John Councilman and Mary Turnpaugh married 6 August 1778
Robert Caulfield and Phebe Hayes married 10 December 1778
John Coale and Elizabeth Stevens married 23 May 1779
James Coxe and Sophia Kennedy married 7 September 1780
Daniel Cartee and Susanna Griffee married 30 November 1783
Moses Cohoun and Eleanor Stewart married 28 April 1784
William Coleman and Anne Labesius married 31 July 1784
John Chiseley and Elizabeth Flanagan married 30 October 1784
Samuel Cox and Elizabeth Hopkins married 10 November 1785
James Conn and Agness Sparks married 2 January 1786
William Carron and Anne Aldridge married 13 February 1786
John Cunningham and Margaret Mather married 30 January 1787
John Coulter and Mary McCaskey married 3 February 1788
James Campbell and Frances Moody married 6 January 1790
John Carlyle and Elizabeth Lane married 18 February 1790
Barton Cross and Ruth Cross married 4 November 1790
Alexander Coulter and Hetty McCaskey married 29 March 1792
James Conway and Amelia Elizabeth Atkinson married 24 November 1792
Samuel Church and Hannah Pitcher married 27 July 1793
Alexander Calhoun and Sarah Clemments married 27 March 1794
Barnett Cantle and Catharine McLaughlin married 15 April 1794
Jeremiah Capoot and Mary Taylor married 6 August 1794
Peter Clopper and Mary Goulding married 11 September 1794
James Courtenay and Mary Mitcheson married 18 November 1794
Robert Cross and Catharine Hildebrand married 3 March 1795
Thomas Clifton and Lydia Hopkins married 18 July 1795
Thomas Cantwell and Sally Smith married 27 August 1795
Oliver Clark and Sophia North married 3 September 1795
John Calwell and Mary Purle married 11 February 1796
Josiah Caswell and Nancy Scott married 17 March 1796
John Coulter and Margaret McIllroy married 3 November 1796
John Cole and Mary McDonough married 4 February 1797
Richard Collings and Fanny Brown married 8 May 1797
John Clingman and Ann Wise married 17 December 1797
David Chesran and Mary Hanel married 24 December 1797
Henry Courtenay and Isabella Purviance married 10 January 1799

Peter Clopper and Rachel Wells married 1 December 1799
James Chandler and Nancy West married 3 January 1800
Jacob Curtis and Elizabeth Deagan married 13 February 1800
Hezekiah Deane and Rebecca Lowndes married 17 March 1778
Elias Dorsey and Susanna Snowden married 8 June 1779
Andrew Davidson and Anne Stokes married 18 July 1779
Joseph Dorrity and Margaret Carroll married 20 December 1779
Joseph Dorsey and Mille Gillis married 27 July 1780
Josiah Davies and Margaret Hallock married 21 December 1780
John Dumerte and Elizabeth Keeports married 25 June 1782
Moses Davis and Cathrine Dunn married 21 July 1782
John Downey and Emy Stoxall married 15 June 1784
Cornelius Dorman and Anne Casment married 26 October 1784
Cumberland Dugan and Margaret Kelso married 31 October 1786
William Denny and Elizabeth Biays married 12 June 1788
Anthony Daniels and Anna Maria Mincey married 17 March 1793
Thomas Downes and Susannah Marsh married 10 June 1794
John Baptist Godart Delisle and Sophia DeGoff married 15 Sept. 1794
Henry Devonshere and Ariabella Cole married 17 September 1794
---- [blank] DeMongin and Ruth Calwell married 20 November 1794
William Davis and Mary McMahon married 11 December 1794
Robert Davidson and Mary Dance married 20 May 1795
Andrew Davidson and Mary Somerville married 19 November 1795
William Davis and Ruth Owings married 30 June 1796
James Doake and Polly Henry married 15 September 1796
Thomas Dinsmore and Hannah Dodd married 19 January 1798
Hugh Deaver and Darby Holbrook married 18 February 1798
William Davidson and Hidey Cornelius married 29 May 1798
John Downey and Betsy Owings married 11 November 1800
Joseph Evans and Anne Ellicot married 17 June 1776
John Evans and Letitia Ellicot married 23 June 1778
David Ellicot and Martha Evans married 28 September 1778
John Ellicot and Cassandra Hopkins married 8 April 1779
John Ensor and Urith Gorsuch married 13 May 1779
Robert Eden and Minah Coale married 16 March 1781
Thomas Edwards and Mary Adams married 10 June 1787
Nathaniel Ellicott and Elizabeth Ellicott married 5 September 1790
William Ensor and Rachel Conales married 22 November 1791
William Elvans and Elizabeth Rogers married 13 September 1795
Thomas Edwards and Anne Gordon married 13 September 1798

FIRST PRESBYTERIAN CHURCH 75

Thomas Elwert and Susanna Matthews married 11 July 1799
Daniel French and Rachel Wilson married married 3 November 1781
Frederic Folger and Isabella Emmit married 7 March 1782
James Fulton and Anne Christopher married 10 October 1786
John Frost and Sarah Krap married 20 April 1787
Basil Fisher and Sophia Paradise married 29 December 1787
William Lee Forman and Jane Spear married 20 November 1790
William Furlong and Sally Johnson married 5 May 1791
Francis Fraser and Mary Perkins married 3 June 1792
Isaac Forsyth and Frances Brown married 22 December 1792
Joseph Fisher and Elizabeth Cruses married 6 August 1794
Moor Falls and Rebecca Wilson married 24 September 1796
William Fulton and Mary Davidson married 6 November 1800
George Geddis and Isabella Hayes married 11 December 1777
Mordecai Gist and Mary Sterett married 23 January 1778
James Glyn and Elizabeth Roberts married 6 April 1779
Philip Gibbons and Margaret Sinclair married 4 June 1780
William Goslin and Eleanor Western married 14 September 1780
James Gibson and Catherine Ettyburn married 22 June 1784
John Gwin and Grete Stull married 20 September 1785
Samuel Gray and Anne Rice married 22 September 1787
Russell Greene and Peggy Sly married 7 October 1788
Richard Gittings and Mary Sterett married 20 November 1788
Francis Galloway and Margaret Shocknesey married 23 March 1790
York Griffin and Susanna Belt married 6 June 1790
Obed Gardiner and Deborah Gottier married 3 June 1791
James Gittings and Harriet Sterett married 23 April 1793
Henry Green and Elizabeth Walters married 15 January 1794
David ---- [Ed. Note: The rest of the line was blank.]
Michael Gordon and Frances Savage married 7 August 1794
Henry Grass and Elizabeth Isaacks married 2 October 1794
William Gardner and Ann Hahn married 10 May 1795
Peter Gisse and Susannah Decter married 4 June 1795
John Gilmore and Jane Smith married 11 January 1796
Mark Guishard and Catharine McCabe married 22 February 1796
Thomas Gamble and Margaret Collins married 18 September 1796
Francis Godin and Margaret Meek married 17 November 1796
Ebenezer Graves and Mary Anderson married 31 August 1797
Duncan Gordon and Eleanor Mitchell married 23 December 1797
Simon Gross and Ann Job married 25 January 1798

James Glenn and Mary Weaver married 16 May 1799
William ---- [Ed. Note: The rest of the line was blank.]
Isaac Hall and Anne Mease married 28 August 1770
William ---- [Ed. Note: The rest of the line was blank.]
Philip Hopkins and Catharine Evans married 13 March 1775
John Hughes and Agness Graham married 14 March 1775
Robert Jenkins Henry and Martha Stevenson married 18 September 1778
George Hammond and Elizabeth Wells married 12 June 1779
David Harris and Sarah Crocket married 14 September 1780
Daniel Hughes and Susanna Schlater married 26 October 1780
John Hollins and Janet Smith married 31 December 1785
Thomas Hana and Mary Hanward married 15 June 1786
Daniel Howling and Cornelia McMyer married 23 August 1787
David Harris and Frances Halton Moale married 23 January 1788
James Harvey and Anne Farel married 7 February 1790
James Hobbs and Anne Knox married 25 December 1790
James Harris and Susannah Daull married 1 July 1794
Jethro Hathaway and Eleanor Buckley married 7 May 1795
John Hurton and Elizabeth Peck married 9 june 1795
Michael Henray and Rachel Woaden married 18 July 1795
Thomas Hammet and Mariah Rosanna Stine married 13 September 1795
John Holliday and Margaret Rareton married 9 May 1796
William J. Hall and Grace Craig married 26 January 1797
Abraham Hogen and Rebecca Buchanan married 13 June 1797
William Harvey and Elizabeth Eton married 24 August 1797
John Hogan and Eleanor Keaton married 27 October 1797
Edward Hannah and Rebecca McLure married 8 November 1797
Alexander Haslet and Elizabeth Highjah married 15 February 1798
Stephen Hawk and Agness Hamilton married 12 July 1798
Benjamin Haing and Rose Swanwick married 30 October 1798
Israel Hoit and Sarah Megaff married 22 November 1798
Jesse Hammett and Jane Young married 10 July 1799
William Hill and Elizabeth Charleton married -- June 1795
John Ingram and Sarah Hutcheson married 27 April 1779
Silas Ingles and Margaret Harris married 3 December 1786
Clark Ingram and Mary Dorsey married 4 December 1795
James Irvin and Sarah Cunningham married 5 February 1799
John Johnson and Cloe Lainten married 17 June 1801

FIRST PRESBYTERIAN CHURCH 77

Thomas Jones and Elizabeth McLure married 25 November 1779
William James and Susanna Landon married 24 November 1785
Charles Jessop and Mary Gorsuch married 13 April 1786
Elijah Johnson and Margaret Gamble married 14 August 1790
Levin Jones and Mary Jackson married 24 May 1791
Joshua Joyce and Elizabeth Johnson married 30 April 1793
John Jaffries and Sarah Lea married 17 September 1793
Caleb Johnson and Jane Shields married 7 November 1793
Pierce Joice and Mary Cross married 31 July 1794
William James and Janey Hay married 13 November 1794
John Jarvis and Nancy Williams married 4 June 1795
Francis Johnson and Margaret Crocket married 14 September 1795
Edward Johnston and Maria Coffal married 24 November 1795
George Jeffords and Catharine Robinson married 28 January 1796
Collin Jackson and Jane Nicoll married 25 February 1796
William James and Flora Alexandria married 14 February 1797
William James and Elizabeth James married 16 November 1797
William Jones and Margaret Peck married 4 April 1799
Nathaniel Jackson and Nelley Curtis married 14 September 1799
William Jones and Eliza Leary married 9 February 1800
Patrick Keith and Mary Godfrey married 26 June 1780
William Knox and Elizabeth Page married 4 February 1781
John Kitters and Rachel Tawson [Towson?] married 12 July 1791
Richard Kearney and Ann McCaskey married 27 August 1797
Frederick Konicke and Elizabeth Henlon married 5 December 1797
Alexander Knox and Elizabeth Easton married 8 May 1799
John Kilpatrick and Rachel Collet married 18 June 1801
John Lloyd and Anne Ewing married 28 April 1768
Elijah Lewis and Mary Sullivan married 3 April 1775
William Lynch and Elizabeth Regan married 17 June 1779
Robert Lyon and Susanna Hall married 2 December 1783
Robert Long and Sarah Wilson married 4 May 1784
Samuel Liggat and Jane Parker married 15 December 1787
John Lewis and Sarah Kirby married 30 April 1789
John Leahry and Esther Duncan married 25 November 1790
Miles Littlejohn and Sarah Paine married 26 September 1792
John Lidiard and Mary Garty married 26 March 1793
Cornelius Lowe and Elizabeth Bevan married 11 May 1793
John Litzinberger and Martha McClintick married 31 December 1793
William Lyons and Rachel McCoy married 10 March 1795

Christopher Lewthwaite and Agness Carlile married 9 July 1797
James Lyon and Anna Spencer married 16 July 1797
Charles Lawson and Elizabeth Green married 8 April 1798
Anthony Law and Kitty Bausman married 3 December 1799
Charles Leader and Hannah Smith married 3 December 1799
Enoch Levering and Hannah Brown married 28 January 1800
William Leatherberrow and Deborah Thompson md 18 April 1801
David McLellan and Janit Buchanan married 30 April 1768
Balcher Myers and Margaret Wright married 18 April 1770
Samuel Morris and Rebecca Owen married 7 November 1770
Samuel McRea and Janit Weer married 12 December 1770
William McDonnell and Mary Callaghan married 16 June 1772
David McLure and Elizabeth Crone married 25 March 1773
James Morgan and Sarah Bryon married 5 January 1775
James Major and Eve Greathouse married 18 September 1775
John Montgomery and Sarah Relp married 30 January 1777
Thomas McGuire and Mary Stevenson married 15 April 1779
William Martin and Margaret Crawley married 26 April 1779
Richard Mercier and Cassandra Jevis married 9 May 1772? [Ed. Note:
    The year could have been 1779 or 1782, and her last name "Tevis."]
Robert Moore and Ruth Chapman married 23 July 1782
James Morgan and Nancy Travers married 21 November 1782
Thomas Moffat and Hannah Presbury married 30 January 1783
Edward Morris and Sarah Scott married 1 April 1783
Alexander McLean and Kesiah Haslet married 1 November 1785
John McCarty and Elizabeth Sawbright married 24 November 1785
Charles Myers and Elizabeth Garrold married 30 December 1786
Thomas McElderry and Elizabeth Parker married 16 June 1787
Archibald Murray and Mary McFarrin married 23 February 1788
John McNamee and Elizabeth Justice married 3 May 1788
John McCoy and Sarah Wade marrieed 21 July 1790
William McCarty and Margaret Peasely married 5 December 1790
William Marshall and Louisa Brant married 19 December 1790*
[*Ed. Note: The record mistakenly showed the year as "1700".]
Alexander Maclevain and Sarah Poutenay married 28 June 1791
Edward Mitchell and Charlotte Valentine married 17 November 1791
John McKinsee and Ann Strawble married 11 January 1792
William McFeadon and Ann Ellick married 4 August 1792
Cornelius McCarty and Sarah Pitcher married 27 September 1792
Philip Mosher and Johanna Robinson married 11 September 1793

FIRST PRESBYTERIAN CHURCH 79

Joseph McCammon and Sarah Burk married 30 November 1793
Nicholas Ruxton Moore and Sarah Kelso married 25 December 1793
John McMyers and Elizabeth Pit married 16 January 1794
William McElroy and Elizabeth Hagerty married 26 February 1794
Hugh McCurdy and Grace Allison married 17 June 1794
William P. Matthews and Eliza Sterett married 3 October 1794
John Muschert and Hetty Eastburn married 17 January 1795
Robert Myers and Mary James married 14 February 1795
John McKean and Ann Helm married 4 April 1795
George Martin and Ann Jackson married 31 May 1795
Kennedy Morrow and Mary Wilson married 21 July 1795
James McConkey and Agness Nichol married 13 December 1795
Robert Mickle and Eliza Etting married 24 December 1795
Thomas Maholl and Elizabeth Burnside married 13 November 1796
James Milford and Mary Ann Stone married 9 October 1797
Thomas Megarrity and Elizabeth Gray married 27 February 1798
John McLine and Mary Ann Thornburgh married 6 December 1798
John McFaden and Priscilla Wilson married 20 December 1798
Thomas Bell Mix and Anna Maria Hanson married 11 February 1799
Colin McKenzie and Sarah Pinkerton married 25 May 1799
Thomas McDermot and Jane Cunningham married 26 May 1799
John McInnally and Grace Taylor married 7 July 1799
James McElroy and Sarah Winn married 28 September 1799
George McKey and Martha Dillworth married 26 November 1799
Alexander Mitchell and Eliza Torrance married 19 December 1799
Thomas B. McCabe and Constant Love Peacock married 1 January 1800
Alexander McCulloch and Sarah Spicer married 1 January 1801
George Nicholas and Mary Smith married 28 December 1778
William Nayler and Clementina Abercrombie married 22 May 1779
William Newton and Rachel Lawrence married 24 December 1782
James Neill and Susanna Ellicott married 28 September 1784
Wilson Cary Nicholas and Margaret Smith married 29 January 1785
Magness Norquay and Jane Trotmon married 17 July 1795
Stephen Needles and Nancy Martin married 17 April 1796
Philip N. Nicholas and Mary Spear married 18 February 1799
William Norris and Sarah Schaffer married 26 December 1799
John Pugh and Mary Owen married 18 July 1773
Matthew Patton and Rebecca May married 9 May 1775
John Pine and Mary Coats married 16 November 1775

Samuel Purviance and Catherine Stewart married 18 April 1776
William Patterson and Dorcas Spear married 15 May 1779
Thomas Palmer and Margaret English married 21 May 1779
Joseph Perego and Jemima Woodward married 9 May 1783
John Prichard and Elizabeth Whitacar married 25 February 1787
James Patterson and Jane Keath married 13 May 1787
Humphrey Pierce and Anne Williamson married 6 August 1789
James Pogue and Elizabeth McDonough married 24 July 1790
Thomas Pamphilon and Rebecca Weary married 7 October 1790
James Prat and Sarah Shaw married 13 January 1791
James Parker and Mary Pampillion married 22 March 1792
William Peale and Polly Berry married 24 December 1793
Peter Powel and Elizabeth Foster married 7 October 1794
James Price and Elizabeth Lewis married 17 June 1795
Henry Peerson and Mary Childs married 19 October 1795
David Parley and Sarah Wright married 26 June 1796
David Polk and Margaret Cooper married 10 November 1797
James Purviance and Eliza Young married 23 November 1797
David Pearson and Mary Ann Kimbo married 30 January 1798
Levy Pierce and Elizabeth Williamson married 12 September 1798
John Purviance and Abigail Dugan married 3 January 1799
Hugh Patrick and Nancy Gill married 2 June 1799
Robert Pendergrass and Johanna Rogan married 28 December 1800
William Quay and Mary Burk married 7 November 1795
Patrick Quinlon and Mary Graham married 6 January 1799
Aquila Randall and Rebecca Cad married 8 June 1779
William Rogers and Elizabeth Dawson married 19 November 1786
James Reed and Eleanor Unick married 13 April 1790
Robert Reeves and Rachel Shields married 15 August 1790
William Robb and Elizabeth Gartz married 15 April 1791
Robert Lockhart Ross and Elizabeth McLure married 26 January 1792
Allen Rogers and Rebecca Evans married 11 April 1792
Hugh Reed and Mary Elfry married 28 November 1792
Roger Robbins and Rebecca Keeland married 3 October 1793
Samuel Reed and Eleanor Morrison married 26 December 1793
James Riddell and Jane Adams married 10 March 1794
William Russell and Catharine Deagan married 16 December 1795
Hugh Rankin and Margaret Hughes married 2 November 1797
John Roan and Jane Robinson married 23 November 1798
Hezekiah Reese and Eleanor McMullan married 8 December 1798

FIRST PRESBYTERIAN CHURCH 81

Richard Robinett and Mary Shaw married 18 November 1800
David Sutherland and Eleanor Stockdell married 10 September 1776
Benjamin Shipley and Agness Short married 12 December 1776
Caleb Shields and Jane Brown married 17 June 1777
Samuel Smith and Margaret Spear married 31 December 1778
Talbot Shipley and Rachel Chew married 26 August 1779
John Spear and Elizabeth Smith married 14 September 1779
John Stevens and Mary Reardon married 10 October 1779
John Stump and Cassandra Wilson married 17 October 1779
George Salmon and Rebecca Mercer married 21 October 1779
John Stevenson and Sarah Carey married 12 October 1780
John Shepherd and Mary Anne Galloway married 24 February 1781
Peter Sharp and Anne Dickinson married 27 March 1783
Jeremiah Smith and Rebecca Asheton married 21 October 1784
Peter Swindall and Catharine Hisdale married 6 April 1786
George Stiles and Anne Steel married 6 June 1786
James Somervell and Anne Relp married 27 January 1787
Simeon Sixsmith and Mary Groves married 8 August 1789
Robert Smith and Margaret Smith married 7 December 1790
John Scott and Anne Baise married 25 December 1790
John Cowder Stewart and Mary Barnett married 28 December 1790
George P. Stevenson and Esther Smith married 3 February 1791
John Spence and Mary Jaffray married 6 August 1791
Richard Smith and Mary Bevan married 25 September 1791
Archibald Stewart and Sarah Nelson married 26 November 1791
Joseph Slater and Sarah Smith married 15 September 1793
Arthur Smith and Mary Anderson married 30 January 1794
Alexander Scroggs and Nancy McElroy married 20 February 1794
Seth Sanger and Catharine Elkins married 7 August 1794
Obadiah Starr and Ruth Boyd married 8 August 1795
William Simmons and Sarah Dorton married 9 August 1796
John Snides and Ann Parkin married 15 September 1796
John Sinard and Tany Cook married 9 November 1797
William Snuggrass and Catharine Hart married 7 December 1797
Robert Skillman and Hannah Sailors married 24 December 1797
Joseph Spear and Barbara Spear married 10 January 1798
David E. Stewart and Jane Purviance married 16 May 1799
Alexander Sandison and Jane Alexander married 13 July 1799
Thomas Sweeting and Catharine Wineman married 14 November 1799
James Stewart and Elizabeth Hannah married 24 November 1799

Thomas Stewart and Mary McDowell married 16 March 1801
William Tumbleson and Jane Hombledon married 2 March 1778
William Trapnell and Honor Wheeler married 14 October 1779
James Tate and Elizabeth Coulter married 29 January 1782
William Taylor and Hannah Judah married 9 January 1783
Matthews Travers and Jane Biays married 19 September 1784
Herman Triev and Frances West married 22 July 1787
John Turnpaugh and Hannah Macklascey married 20 September 1787
Jacob T. Towson and Jane Boyd married 19 April 1788
James Toole and Susanna Moore married 9 August 1788
John Tagert and Mary Williamson married 12 October 1790
Joseph Totten and Elizabeth Jackson married 28 July 1792
Moses Thompson and Mary Eyres married 1 May 1793
Andrew Turnbull and Hannah Robinson married 26 January 1794
Josias Thompson and Jane Forsyth married 19 November 1795
Matthew Topham and Mary Jacobs married 2 June 1796
Jacob Tennis and Sarah Williams married 26 September 1796
Nathan Tyson and Sally Jackson married 25 January 1798
Jonathan Towser and Mary McAllister married 16 November 1798
Aust Ulery and Sarah Dooley married 8 November 1796
William Weer and Catherine Osborne married 9 March 1769
Thomas Wells and Mary Major married 4 March 1773
William Weer and Elizabeth Blair married 20 May 1776
Thomas Weer and Mary Beerman married 31 October 1776
Benjamin West and Agness Varley married 29 May 1777, P. [sic]
Thomas Williamson and Ruth Hurd married 26 November 1778
Greenberry Wheeler and Susanna Welch married 11 May 1779
Francis Ward and Sarah Goodman married 26 August 1779
Samuel Williamson and Micah Wells married 1 June 1780
Walter Welsh and Eleanor Burk married 8 May 1781
James Welsh and Ruth Vaughn married 15 August 1783
Henry White and Elizabeth Rust married 12 January 1784, P. [sic]
Robert Workman and Jane Dunsheaf married 13 August 1784
Otho Holland Williams and Mary Smith married 18 October 1785
Stephen Wilson and Rebecca Nelson married 13 February 1786
John Williams and Margaret Remmage married 8 April 1790, PA.
John Williams Woodbrough and Elizabeth Leere married 29 July 1790
Henry Willey and Mary Goodridge married 1 January 1791
Samuel Walker and Frances S. Smith married 25 October 1792
John R. Wheaton and Elizabeth Murray married 20 November 1793

FIRST PRESBYTERIAN CHURCH

Levin Wise and Anna Scott married 31 May 1794
Thomas Wagers and Margaret Wooden married 12 September 1794
Frederic Williams and Rachel Smith married 13 November 1794
William Waddle and Nancy Cox married 14 January 1795
John Wilson and Eleanor Ferguson married 12 February 1797
John Wallace and Mary Alexandria married 13 April 1797
John Wright and Nancy Hatch married 15 October 1797
John Williams and Lydia Robinson married 9 November 1797
Joseph Walker and Mary Frasier married 11 July 1798
John Willis and Nancy Hite married 13 December 1798
William Watkins and Peggy McMullen married 13 January 1799
Thomas Wilson and Sarah Robinson married 24 February 1799
Andrew Williams and Elizabeth Duncan married 31 March 1799
John Whitelock and Mary Montgomery married 13 April 1800
Robert Wiley and Mary Weiley married 24 April 1800
Jacob Young and Leah Mason married 16 January 1781
Jesse Young and Jane McDonough married 30 January 1796
William Young and Catharine Minsker married 19 January 1797

RECORD OF MARRIAGES SOLEMNIZED BY JAMES INGLIS, PASTOR OF THE FIRST <u>PRESBYTERIAN CHURCH, BALTIMORE CITY, SINCE HIS ACCESSION, 1802-1819</u>

<u>1802</u>
May 6 - John Etchberger and Ailsey Fulford
May 13 - Nicholas Smith and Martha Caldwell
Jun 7 - Arthur Morgan and Nancy Lacaze
Aug 15 - John Bryson and Margaret Bond
Oct 16 - James McKenzie and Eleanor Burrows
Nov 26 - William Haslet and Isabella McKim
Dec 23 - John Galloway and Ann Locherd
Dec 26 - John Carty and Margaret Elward

"On the 25th day of November in the same year, the Rev. Dr. Muir, of Alexandria, solemnized the rites of marriage between Rev. James Inglis, pastor of this congregation, and Jane Swan Johnston, member of the same."

1803
Jan 1 - William Barns and Elisa Blanch
Jan 4 - Jacob Poe and Bridget Kennedy
Jan 20 - Jesse Levering and Sarah Brown
Feb 1 - James Grimes and Eleanor Dickenson
Feb 24 - Hugh Leckey and Eleanor Carey
Jun 7 - James Kerr and Isabella Wilson
Jul 14 - John Champlin and Fanny Fishwick
Jul 28 - William Porter and Jane Pannel
Aug 13 - William Asher and Eleanor Waller
Sep 20 - Alexander Reinagle and Ann Duport
Oct 6 - John Hunter and Elizabeth Adams
Oct 11 - Ralph Porter and Bethiah Cunningham
Oct 20 - John Shepherd and Elizabeth Barnes
Oct 31 - John Bradenbabugh and Priscilla Few
Nov 3 - John McIntire and Lilly Ann Atmore
Nov 13 - Thomas Forte and Agnes Leuthwaite

1804
Jan 3 - John Light and Mary Pearson
Jan 19 - Isaac Warren and Rosanna Mackmee
Mar 5 - George Ord and Margaret Biays
Apr 10 - Henry Polkinhorn and Catherine Askew
May 1 - William Clemm, Jr. and Harriet Poe
Jul 22 - Lewis Butt and Henrietta Everton
Jul 26 - Rezin White and Ann Neale
Sep 25 - John Miller and Ellen Handling

1805
Jan 3 - Andrew Hazlehurst and Frances Purviance
Mar 16 - Alexander Young and Elizabeth Rowe
May 9 - William Philips and Elizabeth Robinson
Jul 6 - Peter Van Lassel and Catherine Baker
Nov 26 - James Gunn and Elizabeth Robb

1806
Jan 23 - Thomas Finley and Ann Perry Bell
Feb 27 - John Eades and Jane Hogg [?]
Mar 20 - John McNeale and Elizabeth Wilson
Jul 16 - Giles Williams and Elizabeth Fletcher

FIRST PRESBYTERIAN CHURCH 85

Aug 7 - William Coulter and Sarah Humphreys
Aug 25 - John Tennar and Sally Clark
Oct 9 - Charles Young and Eleanor McMan
Oct 30 - Jonathan Meredith and Hannah Haslett
Nov 6 - John Hunter and Rebecca Stephens

1807
Mar 19 - Robert Dickey and Ann Brown
May 27 - Matthias Johnson and Margaret Watson
Jun 9 - Daniel L. Thomas and Jane Olliphont
Jun 9 - William Coulson and Hannah Underwood
Jun 23 - John Buffurn and Jane Keys
Aug 25 - Jesse L. Keene and Janney Bryden
Dec 24 - Alexander Nisbet and Mary C. Owings
Dec 28 - Hector and Sally, slaves (by certificate of consent under the hands of their proprietors respectively).
Dec 31 - Samuel Gardiner and Elizabeth Moren

1808
Jan 14 - John B. Martin and Eliza Flemming
Feb 4 - Jams P. Boyd and Anna Machenry
Mar 21 - Alexander Morton and Martha Mathewson
Apr 8 - Lawrence Keene and Maria Martin
Jun 16 - Elisha Allen and Mary Litchfield
Jun 17 - Thomas Phipps and Elizabeth Ballentine
Jun 28 - James B. McAllister and Sarah Dickey
Sep 1 - Nicholas Murray and Elizabeth Watson
Sep 15 - James McCulloch and Elizabeth White
Oct 29 - William Johnson and Jennet Sinclair

1809
Jan 8 - Robert McConnell and Eleanor Burn
Mar 9 - Joseph Berret and Mary Eliot O'Donnel
Apr 18 - Benjamin Arnold and Margaret Ramsey
Apr 22 - Andrew McGuech and Mary Nelson
Apr 27 - Richard B. Magruder and Maria Stricker
Jul 4 - Charles M. Poor and Elizabeth Roberts
Aug 9 - James Jackson and Bertha Moore
Aug 10 - Thomas Carroll and Ann Cousins
Sep 12 - William Roney and Alice McBlair

Sep 14 - James Sterratt and Maria Harris
Oct 5 - Richard B. Mitchell and Elizabeth Bedford
Nov 28 - Joseph Dowson and Susanna Savage

1810
Jan 18 - George Rogers and Elizabeth Neale Ford
Mar 7 - George J. Brown and Esther Allison
Apr 14 - Henry Cook and Patty Ross, slaves (with the permission of their respective proprietors).
Sep 1 - John Catts and Frances Neal
Sep 13 - Silas Dewey and Elizabeth Dowell
Oct 11 - Samuel Harris and Eliza Story Conkling
Nov 17 - Young Martin and Isabella Carr
Dec 22 - Robert Allison and Eliza Augusta Allender
Dec 27 - Kinsey Mockeboy and Ann Jordan

1811
Feb 20 - Henry Courtney and Elizabeth Isabella Purviance
Apr 14 - Augustine R. Denos and Eleanorra Curry
May 2 - Samuel H. West and Catherine Bantz
May 16 - Reverdy Hayes and Tabothy Fairbairn
May 21 - Benjamin Williams and Sarah Morton
Aug 8 - Henry White and Margaret Elder
Oct 5 - Roswell L. Colt and Margaret Oliver
Nov 19 - John Fisher and Ann Robinson
Dec 26 - John Louis Roy La Reintrie and Catherine Neilson
Dec 29 - Abraham Parkes [Parker?] and Sarah Wright

1812
Jan 9 - David Delacour and Elizabeth Patton
Mar 5 - Aaron Barling and Rebecca Tucker
Apr 8 - John Auchincloss, Jr. and Matilda Inglis
Jun 9 - Benedict William Hall and Mary Calhoun
Jun 23 - Daniel William McHenry and Sophia H. Ramsay
Sep 8 - Robert Purviance and Frances Young
Sep 29 - John Vincent and Nancy Campbell
Nov 17 - Benjamin Wilson and Ann Bates
Nov 19 - William Eaton and Mary Keys
Nov 26 - Edward Dennison and Eliza Wilson

1813

Jan 5 - William Garnons and Catharine Bryan
Jan 5 - Solomon Witney [Whitney] and Margaret Pate
May 2 - Thomas J. Leakin and Mary L. Little
Aug 23 - George McDormet and Sarah Hughes
Sep 28 - Stephen Randall and Harriet Campbell
Sep 30 - Elijah Beam and Charlotte Christiana Robison
Oct 12 - James Ferguson and Catherine Robb
Nov 13 - Shadrach and Hester, slaves of Joseph Steratt with their master's permission)

1814

Mar 1 - William Cowles and Margaret Hall
Mar 1 - William A. Ridgely and Elizabeth Dumeste
Apr 5 - Wells Chase and Amelia Jamison
Apr 10 - George Callender and Drusilla Pocock
Apr 14 - Jacob Heaflick and Charlotte Grant
Apr 21 - Henry Boteler and Priscilla Robinson
Apr 23 - Joseph Clarke and Susannah Silence
May 14 - Dudley Poor and Deborah H. O'Donnell
Jul 6 - John Dougherty and Susan Thompson
Jul 14 - Francis Castine and Elizabeth Linkins
Jul 26 - Moses Bowser and Lydia Russell

1815

Jan 11 - Dr. T. A. Stansbury and Ann Biays
Jan 25 - Charles DeMangin and Elizabeth Caldwell
Mar 14 - Robert Y. Wellford and Louisa Gittings
Mar 29 - Hugh Campbell and Maria S. Death
Apr 1 - Joshua Barton and Mary Lynch
Apr 18 - Robert Watson and Rachel Price
Apr 19 - George Crockett and Mary Ann Fulton
Apr 20 - Edward Patterson and Sidney Smith
Apr 21 - William Briant and Susanna Crea
May 14 - Richard Wilmot Hall and Eliza Taylor
Jun 1 - George Williams and Elizabeth B. Hawkins
Jun 6 - Lemuel Ludden and Margaret McDonough
Jun 8 - John D. Vowell and Margaretta Brown
Aug 7 - John H. Poor and Jane E. Taylor
Aug 7 - James Harwood and Mary Elder

Sep 16 - George Smallwood and Juliet Jarber [Jarboe?]
Sep 26 - Charles Bond and Frances Pindell
Oct 12 - John Revell and Charlotte Frazier Shahanasey
Oct 16 - William Pelloy and Rosally Brown
Nov 14 - Horatio Bevin and Jane Myles
Dec 7 - Henry Smith and Jane McThowen
Dec 14 - John M. Berkley and Mary Stephens

1816
Jan 4 - Robert Thomas and Nelly McClish (colored people)
Jan 10 - Isaac Allen and Hannah Clarke
Jan 11 - William Parish and Elizabeth Ball
Jan 14 - Jonathan Hancock and Sophia Stutson
Jan 25 - George Barger and Elizabeth Hay
Jan 30 - Peregrine Knight and Sarah G. Forrest
Feb 8 - John A. Webster and Rachel Biays
Mar 3 - Gabriel Grenier and Annette Caroline Colim Sutrine
Mar 13 - Henry White and Eliza Gersonderffer
Mar 23 - George F. De La Roche and Ann Maria McNulty
Mar 29 - Robert McCrea and Maria Sterley
Apr 11 - Thomas Despeaux and Ann Stevenson
Apr 21 - James Patton and Rebecca Joiner
Apr 21 - John Jacob Siemsen and Eleanor McConnell
May 1 - James Brooks and Biddy McMahon
May 9 - John Grayson and Martha Wray
May 16 - John Eagan and Jane Sinclair
May 16 - Joseph Caldwell and Mary King
May 22 - Edward Toogood and Nancy Peterson
May 30 - George Johnson and Mary McClain
Jun 16 - Samuel McCoy and Magdalina Heilholtz
Sep 21 - Robert Cochran and Mary Ann Prucy
Sep 29 - J. H. Parmele and Priscilla Horne
Oct 3 - John Yeager and E. M. M. Hanson
Oct 7 - William Th. Fryatt and Susanna Jarboe
Dec 26 - Coffee (slave of Mr. William Conway) and Nancy (slave of Mrs. Ridgley).

1817
Jan 21 - Edward M. Greenway and Maria Taylor
Feb 11 - Alexander L. Boggs and Susan Greer

Mar 24 - John Hoohard and Agness Murray
Mar 27 - Israel P. Thompson and Angelica Robinson
Apr 17 - William Wood and Ann Ghant [Ghent?]
Apr 17 - William Ferguson and Margaret Craig
May 1 - John Redgrave and Elizabeth Hoffman
May 15 - John L. Francis and Jane Johnson (free people of color)
May 20 - James B. Latimer and Catharine H. Lyon
May 26 - Andrew Dulany and Margaret McIntire
May 29 - William Osborn and Elizabeth Coler
Jun 2 - George B. Groves and Isabella Boyd
Jun 5 - Charles Roberts and Hetty Lurnmaux
Jun 19 - Hamilton R. Holston and Sarah Walker
Jun 29 - James Mosher and Elizabeth Nickerson
Jul 3 - Peter Mason and Mary Carpenter
Aug 7 - Robert Elliott and Mary Coffin
Oct 3 - Ellis Barron and Mary Forwood
Oct 13 - John Jamison and Mary Martin
Oct 14 - David Polk and Sophia Smith
Nov 7 - Samuel Smith and Mary Hissey
Nov 17 - Bolton Jackson and Frances Jane Grant
Dec 3 - Philip Thomas and Frances Johnson

1818
Feb 24 - Benjamin C. Howard and Jane Gilmor
Mar 10 - Lewis Wells and Ann Small
Mar 29 - Joseph L. Lord and Fanny Douglass
Apr 14 - John M. Hepburn and Eliza S. Johnston
May 5 - Thomas Dance and Augusta Temple Sterratt
May 20 - James Sutor and Nancy McCaffer
Jun 4 - Jacob Schley and Anna P. Jones
Jun 23 - John Reynolds and Barbara Forney
Jun 25 - John Botts and Ann Miller
Jul 1 - Bayley Keys and Priscilla Taylor
Aug 2 - George Sumwalt and Elizabeth Chisholm
Aug 13 - Nathan S. Beemis and Susanna Ashmore
Aug 18 - Richard Burnett and Elizabeth McCullough
Aug 27 - Ammael Toy and Sarah Gardner
Sep 10 - Charles Lymas and Phoebe Clark
Oct 8 - Samuel Winchester and Frances Mactier
Nov 28 - John Burke and Margaret Nicholson

Dec 4 - Nicholas and Hagar, slaves (the former of Judge Nisbet, the latter of Mrs. Cockey).
Dec 8 - John Bradford and Ann Eliza Stricker

1819
Jan 2 - William Benning and Ann White
Jan 7 - Auzi McTibbals and Susan Gwinn
Jan 18 - William Read and Lydia Maria Fenn
Feb 9 - Daniel Warfield and Ann Mactier
Apr 12 - Daniel Hewes and Mary Jones
May 9 - Isaac C. Atkinson and Amelia Stables [Stabler?]
May 28 - William C. Beck and Sarah Matilda McCoy
Jun 17 - Samuel Rankin and Arianna Bryson

RECORD OF MARRIAGES SOLEMNIZED BY WILLIAM NEVINS, PASTOR OF THE FIRST PRESBYTERIAN CHURCH, IN BALTIMORE CITY, FROM 1820 TO 1835

1820
Oct 19 - Horace W. Waters and Alverda Robinson
Oct 19 - Benedict William Hall and Ann Calhoun
Oct 19 - Robert Wilson and Elizabeth Kelty
Nov 16 - Henry Hall and Charlotte J. Ramsay
Nov 23 - Anthony Bailey and Phillis Cheeseman (free colored)
Dec 24 - James Bailey (slave) and Listy Johnson (free woman)

1821
Feb 6 - David P. Polk and Letitia J. Stewart
Feb 27 - Joseph Cummins and Jane H. Knox
May 15 - Henry Carroll and Mary B. Sterrett
Jun 12 - Edward G. Williams and Ann Gilmor
Sep 25 - George Y. Kelso and Ellen Rich
Oct 18 - Robert Lyon, Jr. and Mary Latimer
Oct 25 - William H. Murray and Isabella Maria Sterling

1822
Jan 8 - William L. Gill and Elizabeth Ann Stewart
Jan 17 - Alexander Stevens and Elizabeth Turner

FIRST PRESBYTERIAN CHURCH

Mar 15 - William Patterson and Elizabeth Ferguson
Apr 25 - James McIlroy and Sarah Myers
Jun 10 - James Yeat and Marion Muir
Nov 12 - Stephen S. Wilson and Ann J. Harris

1823
Jan 23 - Samuel Canhoon and Hester Shaw
Feb 25 - Alexander Rutherford and Agnes Ferguson
Mar 25 - Charles Crook, Jr. and Sarah Ann Brown
May 15 - James Walker and Harriet Shorter (colored)
Jun 5 - George Morrison and Elizabeth Lovell
Jun 19 - Robert Leslie and Ann Downs
Jul 22 - Richard H. Douglass and Letitia McCurdy
Sep 9 - John A. Brown and Grace Brown
Nov 5 - William E. Mayhew and Maria M. Hobby
Nov 20 - Joseph W. Stone and Ann Stone
Nov 25 - William T. Johnson and Dorothea Mactier
Dec 4 - Andrew Ellicott and Emily Ann McFadon

1824
Jan 8 - Philip T. Tyson and Rebecca Webster
Feb 3 - Patrick Macaulay and Sarah Thornburgh
Mar 9 - James H. McCulloh, Jr. and Eliza Mactier
Mar 30 - John A. Bentz and Caroline Jane Henderson
May 13 - Anthony Wood and Julia Ann Williams (colored)
Jun 22 - James J. Atkinson and Mary Virginia Cole
Aug 26 - Robert Bates and Margaret Crocket
Sep 23 - John Hull and Elizabeth Potter (colored)
Sep 26 - Stanislas Andebert and Amelia Fulton
Sep 28 - Thomas Borland and Catharine H. Ogle
Nov 11 - Christopher Rankin and Juliana Stricker
Nov 11 - Jesse Betts and Margaret Jackson (colored)

1825
Jan 27 - Daniel Nathans and Patience Armote (colored)
Feb 19 - James Parker and Ann Mary Baltsell
Feb 24 - James D. Nicholson and Angeline McIlvain
Apr 7 - Robert Neilson and Margaret Wolfenden
May 17 - Thomas Ellicott, Jr. and Louisa McFadon
May 26 - Thomas D. Johnston and A. M. English Elliot

Jun 20 - William Sidney Winder and Ariminta R. Bailey
Jul 19 - James Stewart and Ellen Stewart
Aug 28 - George R. Bodley and Mary Amos
Sep 6 - Robert M. Gibbes and Emily Oliver
Oct 20 - David Stewart and Mary Adelaide Morton
Oct 27 - Alfred Crawford and Eliza Aitken
Nov 15 - Henry Hatton and Elizabeth M. Denton
Nov 22 - William F. Small and Agnes E. Robison
Dec 5 - Andrew Young and Maria McDowlin

1826
Jan 26 - John T. Bartholomew and Julian Stine
Feb 12 - Richard B. Crow and Charlotte A. Franklin
Mar 16 - Adam Barker and Eliza Anderson (colored)
Mar 21 - James Brown (slave) and Charlotte Rice (colored)
May 9 - Samuel O. Hoffman and Louisa A. Gilmor
May 16 - Edmund Didier and Adeline M. Taylor
Jun 22 - Solomon R. Conway and Ann B. McMillan
Jul 4 - John Bowman and Mary Mitchell
Aug 12 - Robert Maltimore and Catharine H. Mattocks
Sep 12 - Anthony Chase and Julia Williams (slaves)
Sep 14 - Alexander Murdock and Susan Turnbull
Nov 7 - John C. Moale and Julia A. Taylor
Nov 13 - John Sappington and Lavinia R. Bagely
Nov 14 - Joseph Branson and Mary Ann Dukehart
Nov 15 - Joseph J. Nicholson and Laura C. Stricker
Nov 23 - Halson Vashon and Harriet A. Lee (colored)
Dec 21 - George Day and Sarah Ann Hennaman
Dec 21 - Michael Knight and Mary Scobey

1827
Jan 16 - Edmund G. Edrington and Ann M. Cochran
Apr 5 - Irvine Turner and Ann McCabe (colored)
Jul 17 - Robert H. Broadnax and Mary Ann T. Love
Dec 18 - Trueman Cross and Isabella Stewart
Dec 18 - John Grant and Mary Ann Wheeler
Dec 20 - Hezekiah Wilkinson and Mary Connor

1828
Jan 1 - John Harrington and Margaret McCormick

Feb 19 - Rezin D. Hewitt and Delia Coulter
Feb 28 - Joseph Drabelle and Maria Isett
Mar 25 - John M. Brien and Rebecca S. Meredith
Jun 12 - John M. Harman and Margaret P. Hanna
Oct 7 - William B. Buchanan and Ellen B. Carr
Oct 23 - Robert Pilson and Mary Jane Ennis
Nov 4 - Garretson Draper and Charlotte Tartar (colored)

1829
Apr 5 - Robert Johnson and Harriet Harris (slaves of J. Swan)
Apr 21 - John Philpot and Susan J. Stewart
Jun 10 - Samuel Manning and Susan Sheppard
Jul 7 - Gardiner Greene Howland and Louisa Sophia Meredith
Jul 9 - George Canvass (slave) and Julian Green (free colored)
Jul 13 - William C. Dawson and Elizabeth Switzer
Jul 14 - Samuel Jones, Jr. and Ann E. Forman
Sep 3 - Lewis Williams and Hannah Evans
Oct 13 - Job Dorsey (slave) and Abigail Hardy (free colored)
Nov 24 - Rezin H. Snowden and Margaret McFadon
Dec 28 - Richard Chenoweth and Mary Ann Brannan

1830
Jan 5 - Orson Kellogg and Eleanor Ann Clark
Jan 7 - Joseph M. Kasson and Mary Dickinson
Jan 10 - Thomas Gifford and Maria Bandel
Jan 28 - Francis Bates and Eleanor Stone
Mar 30 - William Edie and Mary Elder
Apr 5 - Isaac A. Coles and Juliana Rankin
Apr 6 - William Carlock and Matilda Hammond
Apr 22 - James Bates and Sarah Bolton
May 25 - Charles W. Yonce and Margaret Ann Boggus
Jun 3 - John Crerar and Mary Beatty
Jun 8 - Samuel G. Winchester and Grace Mactier
Jun 10 - Isaac Smith Homans and Sarah Ann Sheppard
Jun 16 - Ede V. Menzies and Adeline James
Jul 22 - Pheonix Nicoll Wood and Mary Ann McDowell
Jul 22 - William Crisfield and Ann Martin
Aug 13 - George W. Knowlton and Elizabeth Carroll
Sep 16 - Wilson M. Cary and Jane Margaret Carr
Sep 28 - Joseph Lolson and Elizabeth Gifford

Oct 21 - John Carrere, Jr. and Esther L. Buchanan
Nov 18 - John Williams and Isabella White (free colored)
Nov 20 - William D. Whiteford and Mary Beaty
Nov 30 - John P. R. Stone and Martha Ann Taylor

1831

Feb 20 - Levin H. Dunkin and Isabella J. Myers
Mar 24 - Thomas J. Thompson and Mary Campbell
Mar 29 - James Blake and Eliza Sprole
Mar 31 - James Adams and Margaret Ann Mills
Apr 19 - David S. Courtenay and Elizabeth D. Hawkins
Apr 26 - Joseph Bird and Elizabeth M. Hyde
May 12 - Talbot D. Jones and Harriet Wight
Jun 7 - Robert Davis and Caroline McConky
Jun 15 - Mordecai S. D. Lyon and Eveline Perkins
Jul 17 - James Roach and Caroline Seamon
Jul 17 - Hiram Richardson and Catherine Gilbert
Aug 2 - James Redman and Elizabeth Swann
Oct 4 - James P. Wilson and Margarett Hollins
Oct 25 - Eli Hewitt and Ann Coulter
Nov 1 - Louis M. Goldsborough and Elizabeth G. Wirt
Nov 7 - James F. Carleton and Anne Maria Jones
Nov 10 - Franklin Anderson and Elizabeth Stirling
Dec 13 - William A. Griffith and Jane Kelly
Dec 20 - Alexander Clendinen and Elizabeth Ann Stewart

1832

Mar 15 - James W. Tolley and Mary Brown
Mar 26 - John Wilson and Charlotte Gibson
Apr 7 - John Mayben and Mary Murphy
Apr 10 - Robert Francis and Jane Brooks
Apr 16 - Matthew M. Kevile and Sarah J. Garland
May 1 - David Henning and Mary Ann Hitzelberger
May 23 - Charles H. Winder and Mary H. Sterett
May 27 - Andrew Foot and Henrietta Hynson (free colored)
Jun 14 - John A. Adams and Sophia Hyde
Jun 19 - Nicholas R. Merryman and Clarissa Philpot
Jul 5 - Alexander C. Robinson and Rosa E. Wirt
Jul 12 - Robert Green and Eliza Lockerman
Jul 31 - Henry Varner and Rose Ann Henning

FIRST PRESBYTERIAN CHURCH

Aug 14 - David H. Musser and Ann Jennings
Sep 20 - Matthew Shaw and Sophia Galbach
Oct 30 - Henry A. Griffith and Jane E. Blackner
Oct 30 - Henry Kneeland, Jr. and Margaret S. Barr
Nov 1 - Henry S. Coulter and Esther Coulter

1833
Jan 12 - Robert Benthall and Isabella Freeman Watson
Feb 14 - Edward K. Lafferty and Eliza Legard
Mar 20 - George N. Hollins and Maria R. Sterett
Apr 2 - Samuel Lawrence and Alison Turnbull
Apr 18 - John Mallonee and Rachel Lyon
May 30 - William Shannon and Margaret Ramsay
Jun 12 - Arad B. Newton and Eliza Jane Ives
Jun 21 - John McCarral and Margaret M. Harrison
Aug 4 - David P. Simkins and Adelia Bennet (at Cape May)
Aug 8 - Fenn E. Larrant and Eliza Penrose
Sep 5 - Solomon O'Brien and Margaret Prentice
Sep 17 - William Fitzhugh Turner and Jane Smith Hall
Oct 3 - John L. Allen and Sophia A. Rankin
Oct 20 - Henry James Roberts and Isabella Sitler
Oct 22 - George Powell Woodward and Elizabeth Gelbach
Oct 22 - William A. Pleasants and Elizabeth Clopper
Nov 14 - John Gore and Ann Francis
Dec 12 - Jacob Johns and Nancy Ruark
Dec 17 - Robert W. Allen and Catharine Ferguson

1834
Jan 12 - Isaac Crusey and Sarah Corwine
Jan 21 - Seth S. Summerson and Eliza J. Sitler
Feb 20 - John A. Craig and Sarah J. Armstrong
Feb 26 - William Hanna and Caroline Small
May 6 - Andrew Pearson and Catherine E. Ferguson
Jun 10 - Patrick Gibson and Anna C. Finley
Sep 11 - Flemming Hixon and Elizaebth W. Braden
Sep 11 - Willis L. Williams and Sarah M. Phillips
Oct 7 - James Henry Doughty and Sally Harman Brown
Nov 2 - John Mitchell and Sarah Jane Dameson
Dec 2 - John Spear Nicholas and Mary Ann Gilmor

1835

Jan 1 - John Holty and Margaret Nicoll
Jan 29 - Thomas Murdoch and Mary Campell [Campbell]
Feb 12 - George B. Stevenson and Augusta Virginia Levering
Feb 19 - Philip Rogers Hoffman and Emily Louisa Key

May 12 - William L. Gill and Ann E. U. Ball - "This marriage was celebrated by Rev. John Owen, but recorded by Rev. J. C. Backus subsequently."

RECORD OF MARRIAGES SOLEMNIZED BY JOHN C. BACKUS, PASTOR OF THE FIRST PRESBYTERIAN CHURCH, IN BALTIMORE CITY, FROM 1836 TO 1840

1836
Jul 19 - Ann S. Wilson and ---- [blank] Fulton
Sep 25 - Joshua Butts and Mary R. Tilden
Oct 4 - Moses Shaw and Ann Shephard
Nov 26 - William R. Reade and Mary Ann Cooper

1837
Apr 18 - Andrew H. Long and Marion L. Donaldson
May 11 - William Street and Eliza Albert
May 11 - Moses Grant and Frances Barnes (colored)
May 29 - Joseph E. Trippe and Sarah P. Cross
Jun 12 - Howard Swain and Charlotte M. Banks
Jul 6 - William White and Elizabeth E. Beam
Sep 12 - Thomas Green and Eliza Brown (colored)
Sep 25 - John S. Donnell and Mrs. Ann Gilmor Williams
Oct 10 - Francis Hyde and Melinda Greenwood
Oct 12 - Benjamin Alleyne and Sophia Reidout (colored)
Oct 25 - Robert C. Long and Elizabeth W. Edes
Oct 25 - Thomas Francis and Margaret Brown
Dec 14 - Charles R. Powel and Elizabeth E. Merryman

1838
Jan 6 - Robert H. Archer and Elizabeth M. Archer
Jan 23 - George Guyther and Mary A. Goodrick

May 15 - Jesse Slingluff and Frances E. Cross
May 28 - Ernest A. Hennings and Caroline E. Campbell
May 29 - John E. Massey and Eliza A. League
Oct 4 - Charles W. Pairo and Mary Jane Edes
Oct 16 - Thomas E. Bond and Anne Morris
Nov 1 - James S. Shields and Harriet A. Terrel

1839
Jan 29 - Samuel K. George and Sophia H. Finley
Jun 4 - Charles A. Miltenberger and Henrietta F. Dunbar
Jun 25 - Thomas Sanderson and Hannah A. Pearson
Oct 14 - Joseph G. Armor and Rachel Scobey

1840
Jan 9 - Thomas J. Hendrix and B. R. M. Jackson
Apr 16 - William Davison and Sophia Brown
May 14 - Henry Y. Martin and Mary Ann Hardin
Jul 21 - J. Campbell White and Mary Williams
Jul 21 - Charles McBlair and Fanny Duncan
Nov 18 - Campbell Graham and Elizabeth S. Gilmor

BAPTISMS BY JAMES INGLIS, PASTOR OF THE FIRST PRESBYTERIAN CHURCH IN THE CITY OF BALTIMORE SINCE HIS ACCESSION TO THE CHARGE OF THE SAID CONGREGATION ON THE 25TH DAY OF 1802 [THROUGH THE YEAR 1820]

Jane Inglis, daughter of Alexander and Frances Mactier, born March 3, 1802, baptized April 27, 1802
George Stiles, son of Edward and Mary Stiles, aged between 5 and 6 months, baptized May 2, 1802
William Forman, son of William Lee and Jane Forman, born January 21, 1802, baptized May 16, 1802
William Spear, son of Joseph and Barbara Spear, born December 20, [1801?], baptized May 16, 1802 [Ed. Note: The year of birth was mistakenly recorded as "1804."]
Rebecca Anne Williams, daughter of Andrew and Elizabeth Williams, aged between 4 and 5 months, baptized May 17, 1802

Donald Fraser, son of William and Margaret Fraser, born March 2, 1802, baptized May 9, 1802

Andrew Sandison, son of Alexander Sandison (mother dead), born August --, [1801?], baptized June 11, 1802

Margaret Prentice, daughter of Alexander and Rosanna Prentice, born "----, 1802" [sic], baptized June 11, 1802

Esther Williams, daughter of Jacob and Mary Williams, aged between 4 and 5 months, baptized June 20, 1802

Stephen Wilson, son of Robert and Ann Wilson, born November 7, [1801?], baptized June 29, 1802

William Goldsmith, son of Joseph and Rachel Goldsmith, aged between 11 and 12 months, baptized July 10, 1802

David Caldwell, son of John and Margaret Caldwell, born October 7, 1798, baptized July 7, 1802

Martha Caldwell, daughter of John and Margaret Caldwell, born June 7, 1801, baptized July 7, 1802

George Ogle, son of William and Nelly Ogle, aged between 17 and 18 months, baptized July 19, 1802

John Craig, son of Thomas and Bethiah Craig, born September 26, 1801, baptized July 28, 1802 (twin)

Louisa Craig, daughter of Thomas and Bethiah Craig, born September 26, 1801, baptized July 28, 1802 (twin)

Alverda Robinson, daughter of Alexander and Angelica Robinson, born "30, ----" [sic], baptized July 6, 1802

Robert Purviance, son of John and Abigail Purviance, born February 14, 1802, baptized July 13, 1802

Seth Sanger, son of Seth and Catharine Sanger, born March 15, [1802?], baptized July 15, 1802 [Ed. Note: The year of birth was mistakenly recorded as "1806."]

Charles Jeffrey Mitchell, son of Alexander and Eliza Mitchell, born June 2, 1802, baptized August 1, 1802

Robert Henry Stewart, son of William and Eliza Stewart, born July 7, 1802, baptized August 5, 1802 (twin)

Caroline Matilda Stewart, daughter of William and Eliza Stewart, born July 7, 1802, baptized August 5, 1802 (twin)

John Winning Duke, son of James and Mary Duke, born May 22, 1802, baptized August 11, 1802

James Inglis Tagert, son of John and Mary Tagert, born March 17, 1802, baptized August 12, 1802

FIRST PRESBYTERIAN CHURCH

Ann Somervell Harris, daughter of David and Sally Harris, born ---- [blank], baptized August 12, 1802
John Graham, son of James and Charlotte Graham, born July 15, 1802, baptized September 3, 1802
Maria Pogue, daughter of James and Elizabeth Pogue, born May 2, 1802, baptized September 13, 1802
Jane Hammet, daughter of Jesse and Jane Hammet, born November 14, 1801, baptized September 13, 1802
Mary Gallagher, daughter of Alexander and Betsey Gallagher, born July 9, 1802, baptized September 13, 1802
Thomas Oliver, daughter of Robert and Eliza Oliver, born June 7, 1802, baptized September 15, 1802
James Ready, son of John and Elizabeth Ready, born June 17, 1802, baptized September 19, 1802
Jane Grey, daughter of George and Isabella Grey, born September 12, 1802, baptized September 26, 1802
Charles Vashan Nickerson, son of Lewis and Elizabeth Nickerson, born July 31, 1802, baptized September 27, 1802
Mary Williams Smith, daughter of Robert and Margaret Smith, born December 13, 1801, baptized October 7, 1802
Ann Jane Mehool, daughter of Thomas and Elizabeth Mehool, born September 17, 1802, baptized October 12, 1802
Annasia McDermont, daughter of Thomas and Jane McDermont, born August 29, 1802, baptized October 12, 1802
Rachel Maxwell Neal, daughter of Hugh and Rachel Neal, born March 30, 1802, baptized October 15, 1802
James Angel, son of John and Ann Angel, born October 13, 1802, baptized October 26, 1802
Rebecca Stabler, daughter of William and Margaret Stabler, born September 18, 1802, baptized November 7, 1802
William Thompson, son of William and Eleanor Thompson, born October 28, 1802, baptized November 10, 1802
Mary McIntosh, daughter of Donald and Mary McIntosh, born October 23, 1802, baptized November 19, 1802
Margery Sinclair, daughter of Robert and Nancy Sinclair, born October 29, 1802, baptized November 19, 1802
Josiah McClenachan, son of Elijah and Mary McClenachan, born August 17, 1802, baptized November 21, 1802
Isabella Nicoll, daughter of David and Dorcas Nicoll, born June 24, 1802, baptized November 21, 1802

Joseph Bucher, son of Dewalt and Magdalena Bucher, born October 27, 1802, baptized December 4, 1802

Nancy Bucher, son of Dewalt and Magdalena Bucher, born October 27, 1802, baptized December 4, 1802

Stewart Brown, son of Stewart and Sarah Brown, born January 4, 1802, baptized December 19, 1802

Ann Gilmor, daughter of William and Mary Ann Gilmor, born September 9, 1802, baptized December 29, 1802

Jane Inglis Gettis, daughter of William and Catherine Gettis, born July 26, 1798, baptized January 25, 1803

Mary Maxwell Gettis, daughter of William and Catherine Gettis, born August 20, 1800, baptized January 25, 1803

Sarah Gettis, daughter of William and Catherine Gettis, born August 20, 1800, baptized January 25, 1803

William Gettis, son of William and Catherine Gettis, born November 2, 1802, baptized January 25, 1803

William Auld, son of William and Elizabeth Auld, born December 27, 1802, baptized February 1, 1803

Ann Scott, daughter of Robert and Elizabeth Scott, born February 12, 1802, baptized February 12, 1803

Maria Wheeler, daughter of Jesse and Nancy Wheeler, born January 16, 1803, baptized February 20, 1803

Eleanor Murphy, daughter of John and Eleanor Murphy, born May 10, 1802, baptized April 3, 1803

Mary West, daughter of James and Maria Louisa West, born November 27, 1801, baptized April 8, 1803

Esther Coulter, aged 31 years and upwards, baptized April 27, 1803

Alexander Coulter, son of Alexander and Esther Coulter, born July 12, 1801, baptized April 27, 1803

Esther Smith Buchanan, daughter of James and Elizabeth Buchanan, born December 19, 1802, baptized May 1, 1803

William Bedford Stricker, son of John and Martha Stricker, born January 9, 1803, baptized June 8, 1803

Maria Moore (black), daughter of Matthias and Violet Moore, born October 10, 1799, baptized June 19, 1803

Robert Patterson McCandless, son of Robert and Rachel McCandless, born January 21, 1803, baptized June 30, 1803

Jane Sleppy, daughter of Jacob and Jane Sleppy, born November 4, 1802, baptized June 30, 1803

FIRST PRESBYTERIAN CHURCH 101

Eviline Manson, daughter of William and Catherine Manson, born May 25, 1803, baptized July 7, 1803

Elizabeth McDonald, daughter of Alexander and Mary McDonald, born July 7, 1803, baptized July 11, 1803

John Mosher, son of Philip and Joanna Mosher, born July 5, 1803, baptized July 12, 1803

William Hunter, son of Alexander and Ann Hunter, born June 14, 1803, baptized July 24, 1803

Maria Falls, daughter of Moore and Rebecca Falls, born July 3, 1803, baptized July 25, 1803

Susanna McDowell, daughter of George and Susanna McDowell, born February 16, 1803, baptized August 1, 1803

Caroline Jane Henderson, daughter of Robert and Phebe Henderson, born July 17, 1802, baptized August 9, 1803

Andrew Fulton, son of William and Mary Fulton, born August 10, 1803, baptized August 21, 1803

William Caruthers, son of William Ewing and Elizabeth Caruthers, born December 21, [1802?], baptized August 21, 1803 [Ed. Note: Birth was mistakenly recorded "December 21, 1803."]

Robert Smith, son of Robert and Margaret Smith, born February 13, 1803, baptized October 8, 1803

Jane Irwin, daughter of James and Sarah Irwin, born September 12, 1803, baptized October 10, 1803

John Colhoon, son of Benjamin Chambers and Lilly Kennedy Colhoon, born September 22, 1803, baptized October 31, 1803

Edward Jenner Smith, son of James and Ann Smith, born September 21, 1803, baptized November 1, 1803

George Alexander Brown, son of Stewart and Sarah Brown, born July 25, 1803, baptized November 24, 1803

William Alexander Gordon, son of John and Anna Maria Gordon, born October 25, 1803, baptized December 4, 1803

Rebecca McKeen, daughter of John and Ann McKeen, born September 22, 1803, baptized December 18, 1803

Mary Catharine Behn, daughter of John Herman and Violet Behn, born August 28, 1803, baptized December 25, 1803

William Cowper Inglis, son of James and Jane Inglis, born Oct. 5, 1803, baptized October 23, 1803, by the Rev. John Glendy

Isabella Maria Sterling, daughter of James and Elizabeth Sterling, born September 27, 1803, baptized January 1, 1804

Alexander Mitchell, son of Alexander and Eliza Mitchell, born September 20, 1803, baptized January 15, 1804

Henry Stevenson Coulter, son of John and Mary Coulter, born September 24, 1803, baptized January 26, 1804

Samuel Finley, son of Ebenezer and Jane Finley, born February 1, 1804, baptized February 1, 1804

George Poe, son of Jacob and Bridget Poe, born November 10, 1803, baptized February 2, 1804

Nancy Ann Prentice, daughter of Alexander and Rosanna Prentice, born December 26, 1803, baptized February 5, 1804

Nancy Fraser, daughter of William and Margaret Fraser, born January 28, 1804, baptized March 2, 1804

Rachel Broom Lyon, daughter of Samuel and Hester Lyon, born February 14, 1802, baptized March 6, 1804

Jane Graham, daughter of John and Elizabeth Graham, born December 30, 1803, baptized March 30, 1804

William Gibson, son of James and Elizabeth Gibson, born December 2, 1802, baptized April 11, 1804

James Swan White McConkey, son of James and Agnes McConkey, born December 16, 1803, baptized April 15, 1804

Grace Mactier, daughter of Alexander and Frances Mactier, born January 28, 1804, baptized April 19, 1804

John Cumberland Purviance, son of John and Abigail Purviance, born November 15, 1803, baptized May 3, 1804

Joseph Wilson, son of Robert and Ann Wilson, born March 16, 1804, baptized June 14, 1804

James Broom Lyon, son of Samuel and Hester Lyon, born December 27, 1802, baptized July 20, 1804

John Lyon, son of Samuel and Hester Lyon, born January 21, 1804, baptized July 20, 1804

Mary Mask, daughter of Isaac and Mary Mask, born August 30, 1803, baptized July 22, 1804

Sarah ---- [blank], granddaughter of Amynta, servant of John Swan, the said Amynta being sponsor, born ----, baptized July 22, 1804

William Duffield, aged about 24 years, baptized August 26, 1804

Mary Ann Mosher, daughter of James and Ann Mosher, born July 20, 1804, baptized November 4, 1804

Jeremiah Perry Davis, aged 21 years, 6 months, 18 days, baptized November 22, 1804

FIRST PRESBYTERIAN CHURCH

Eliza Rawlins, aged 10 years, 5 months, 13 days, orphan adopted by William S. and Sarah Davis who voluntarily became her sponsors, baptized November 22, 1804
William Buckler, son of William and Ann Thomas Buckler, born September 2, 1804, baptized November 22, 1804
John McCullough, son of William McCullough (mother dead), born February 14, 1804, baptized November 25, 1804
Alexander Downing, son of William and Catherine Downing, born December 8, 1803, baptized December 30, 1804
Cardiffe Taggart, daughter of John and Mary Taggart, born September 24, 1804, baptized December 31, 1804
Sarah Irwin, daughter of James and Sarah Irwin (father dead), born November 15, 1804, baptized December 2, 1804 [Ed. Note: Date not clear; baptism could have been on January 2, 1805?]
Susan Maria Inglis, daughter of James and Jane Swan Inglis, born October 25, 1804, baptized December 2, 1804,* by the Rev. Dr. Samuel Blair, of Germantown, Pennsylvania. [*Ed. Note: Date not clear; baptism could have been on January 2, 1805?]
Sarah Pannel Porter, daughter of William and Jane Porter, born June 3, 1804, baptized February 21, 1805
Delia Coulter, daughter of Alexander and Esther Coulter, born September 26, 1804, baptized March 10, 1805
Jane Lewis Nickerson, daughter of Lewis and Elizabeth Nickerson, (father dead), born January 14, 1805, baptized March 24, 1805
Henry De Vries, son of Christian and Jannatie De Vries, born February 24, 1805, baptized April 1, 1805
Jane Carson, daughter of Andrew and Jane Carson, born March 30, 1804, baptized April 12, 1805
John Louis Buchanan, son of James A. and Elizabeth Buchanan, born March 9, 1804, baptized April 14, 1805
Sarah Maria McDowell, daughter of George and Sus. McDowell, born December 26, 1804, baptized April 16, 1805
Jane Wheeler, daughter of Jesse and Nancy Wheeler, born December 29, 1804, baptized April 30, 1805
Frances Mary Sterret, daughter of Joseph and Mary Sterret, born August 27, 1804, baptized June 4, 1805
Laura Caroline Stricker, daughter of John and Martha Stricker, born January 23, 1805, baptized June 5, 1805
Lavinia McCandless, daughter of Robert and Rachel McCandless, born November 26, 1804, baptized June 11, 1805

Louisa Lawson, daughter of Robert and Elizabeth Lawson, born
  November 1, 1804, baptized July 4, 1805
Isaac Williams, son of Jacob and Mary Williams, born December 5,
  1804, baptized July 7, 1805
Maria Craig, daughter of Thomas and Bethiah Craig, born March 18,
  1805, baptized July 11, 1805
William Winder, son of William H. and Gertrude Winder, born March
  18, 1805, baptized July 31, 1805
Helena Anne West, daughter of James and Maria Louisa West, born
  February 11, 1803, baptized August 2, 1805
William Henry West, son of James and Maria Louisa West, born April
  18, 1804, baptized August 2, 1805
Benjamin West, son of James and Maria Louisa West, born May 4,
  1805, baptized August 2, 1805
Mary Scott, daughter of Robert and Elizabeth Scott, born June 17,
  1805, baptized August 13, 1805
Caroline McIlvain, daughter of Alexander and Sarah McIlvain, born
  May 17, 1801, baptized August 2, 1805
Sally McIlvain, daughter of Alexander and Sarah McIlvain, born
  September 29, 1803, baptized August 2, 1805
Frances Purviance, daughter of James and Eliza Purviance, born
  August 26, 1802, baptized August 2, 1805
Robert Purviance, son of James and Eliza Purviance, born September
  11, 1804, baptized August 2, 1805
James Elder, son of John and Esther Elder (father dead), born July 26,
  1802, baptized August 20, 1805
John Merriam Stabler, son of William and Margaret Stabler, born May
  6, 1805, baptized August 30, 1805
Margaret Alexander Burt, daughter of Andrew and Isabella Burt, born
  March 14, 1801, baptized October 25, 1805
Jane Jamieson Burt, daughter of Andrew and Isabella Burt, born
  December 1, 1803, baptized October 25, 1805
Andrew Wood Burt, son of Andrew and Isabella Burt, born October 6,
  1805, baptized October 25, 1805
John Davidson Smith, son of James and Ann Smith, born September
  19, 1805, baptized November 5, 1805
Jane Buchanan McKeen, daughter of John and Ann McKeen, born
  August 25, 1805, baptized December 1, 1805
Letitia McCreery Stewart, daughter of Archibald and Sarah Stewart,
  born January 1, 1805, baptized December 8, 1805

FIRST PRESBYTERIAN CHURCH 105

Moore Nielson Falls, son of Moore and Rebecca Falls (mother dead), born November 19, 1804, baptized December 15, 1805
Frances Wickes, daughter of Benjamin and Ann Wickes, born February 23, 1802, baptized December 15, 1805
William Scott Cochran, son of William and Deborah Cochran, born November 22, 1805, baptized December 20, 1805
Charlotte Ramsay Robinson, daughter of Alex. and Aug. Robinson, born February 26, 1805, baptized December 20, 1805
Louisa Airy Gilmor, daughter of William and Mary Ann Gilmor, born June 27, 1804, baptized December 28, 1805
Elizabeth Russel Jackson, daughter of James and Helen Jackson, born November 3, 1805, baptized December 29, 1805
Jane Stewart Purviance, daughter of John and Abigail Purviance, born December 29, 1805, baptized January 19, 1806
John Russel, son of James and Elizabeth Russel, born February 7, 1806, baptized February 11, 1806
Susanna Isabella Stewart, daughter of David and Elizabeth Stewart, born August 2, 1805, baptized February 14, 1806
Lexy Christina McDonald, daughter of Alexander and Mary McDonald, born August 24, 1805, baptized March 24, 1806
Mary Clarke, daughter of Joseph and Mary Clarke (father dead), born October 9, 1805, baptized March 26, 1806
Emily Oliver, daughter of Robert and Eliza Oliver, born April 30, 1805, baptized April 9, 1806
Matthew Wilson, son of John and Susanna Wilson, born February 16, 1806, baptized April 20, 1806
Gilbert Pigot Shaw, son of Pigot and Elizabeth Shaw, born September 26, 1805, baptized June 6, 1806
Henry Jacob Isett, son of John and Elizabeth Isett, born April 25, 1806, baptized June 18, 1806
Charles McCandless, son of Robert and Rachel McCandless, born April 14, 1806, baptized June 26, 1806
Ephraim Robinson Philips, son of William and Elizabeth Philips, born March 27, 1806, baptized July 10, 1806
Nancy Murphy, daughter of Samuel and Ann Murphy, born October 1, 1804, baptized July 14, 1806
Esther Morrison Harris, daughter of David and Sally Harris, born May 13, 1806, baptized July 29, 1806
Adeline Margaret Taylor, daughter of William and Maria Taylor, born April 26, 1806, baptized August 3, 1806

Samuel McKean Mactier, son of Alexander and Frances Mactier, born September 5, 1806, baptized September 14, 1806 (twin)

William McKean Mactier, son of Alexander and Frances Mactier, born September 5, 1806, baptized September 14, 1806 (twin)

Frances Jane Hazlehurst, daughter of Andrew and Frances Hazlehurst, born June 19, 1806, baptized September 25, 1806

Charles Little Man, son of Charles and Isabella Man, born September 11, 1806, baptized September 25, 1806

Angeline McIlvain, daughter of Alexander and Sarah McIlvain, born March 28, 1806, baptized September 27, 1806

Samuel Chew Hall Lyon, son of Robert and Susanna Lyon, born October 31, 1802, baptized October 8, 1806

Elisha James Lyon, son of Robert and Susanna Lyon, born May 24, 1805, baptized October 8, 1806

John Tagart, son of John and Mary Tagart, born August 19, 1806, baptized October 8, 1806

Henry Mosher, son of James and Ann Mosher, born June 13, 1806, baptized October 26, 1806

James Smith Cantwell, son of Thomas and Sarah Cantwell, born March 15, 1800, baptized October 29, 1806

James Christopher Swan, son of James and Jane Swan, born October 11, 1806, baptized December 23, 1806

Jane Eliza Porter, daughter of William and Jane Porter, born August 6, 1806, baptized December 23, 1806

James McElroy, son of James and Mary McElroy, born October 14, 1802, baptized January 23, 1807

Mary McElroy, daughter of James and Mary McElroy, born December 30, 1806, baptized January 23, 1807

Robert Smith Buchanan, son of James A. and Elizabeth Buchanan, born December 28, 1806, baptized March 1, 1807

James Purviance, son of James and Eliza Purviance, born February 19, 1807, baptized March 15, 1807

Jane Ferguson, daughter of Robert and Ann Ferguson, born March 9, 1807, baptized March 22, 1807

Frederick Wilson, son of Robert and Anna Wilson, born January 8, 1807, baptized March 25, 1807

Jane Finley, daughter of Thomas and Ann Perry Finley, born November 19, 1806, baptized March 22, 1807 by Rev. Sam Knox

Elizabeth Sterling, daughter of James and Elizaebth Sterling, born January 4, 1807, baptized April 7, 1807

FIRST PRESBYTERIAN CHURCH

Samuel Barr, son of William and Mary Barr, born September 18, 1806, baptized April 17, 1807

Susan Prentice, daughter of Alexander and Rosanna Prentice, born July 15, 1806, baptized April 28, 1807

George Armstrong Lyon, son of Samuel and Hester Lyon, born March 1, 1805, baptized May 20, 1807

Jacob Broom Lyon, son of Samuel and Hester Lyon, born March 14, 1807, baptized May 20, 1807

James Farwell Gray, son of George Lewis and Juliana Penn Gray, born May 16, 1806, in the parish of Malden, Massachusetts, baptized May 28, 1807, in Baltimore, Maryland

Helen Maria ---- [blank], an infant of the household of James and Jane Swan Inglis, the said master and mistress being sponsors, born September 26, 1806, baptized May 31, 1807

William Ogle, born December 13, 1776, aged 30 years, 5 months, 25 days, baptized June 7, 1807

James Ogle, son of William and Sarah Ogle, born May 7, 1804, baptized June 7, 1807

William Ogle, son of William and Sarah Ogle, born February 9, 1805, baptized June 7, 1807

Michael Van Kuik Ogle, son of William and Sarah Ogle, born February 22, 1807, baptized June 7, 1807

Elizabeth Clopper, daughter of Andrew and Ann Clopper, born April 27, 1806, baptized June 8, 1807

Cornelius Clopper, son of Andrew and Ann Clopper, born April 20, 1807, baptized June 8, 1807

Matty Augusta Lindsay Thomas, daughter of William and Ann Thomas, born December 21, 1806, baptized June 8, 1807

Mary Moore Armstrong, daughter of Matthew and Elizabeth Armstrong, born March 22, 1804, baptized June 13, 1807

James Fraser, son of William and Margaret Fraser, born June 22, 1806, baptized June 15, 1807

Sarah McIntire, daughter of John and Lilly Ann McIntire, born February 9, 1806, baptized June 16, 1807

Christian De Vries, son of Christian and Jannatie De Vries, born March 20, 1807, baptized June 17, 1807

William Alexander Scroggs, son of Alexander and Anna Scroggs, born April 25, 1802, baptized July 8, 1807

Robert Allen Scroggs, son of Alexander and Anna Scroggs, born June 25, 1806, baptized July 8, 1807

Henrietta Donaldson, daughter of Joseph and Catherine Donaldson, born April 5, 1807, baptized July 10, 1807

Eleanor Young, wife of Charles Young, aged 19 years, 3 days, born July 9, 1788, baptized July 12, 1807

Henry Young, son of Charles and Eleanor Young, born May 22, 1807, baptized July 12, 1807

James Wheland Witchell, son of James R. and Jane Ann Witchell, born July 3, 1807, baptized July 26, 1807

John Poe, son of Jacob and Bridget Poe, born March 24, 1805, baptized August 9, 1807

George Poe, son of Jacob and Bridget Poe, born March 20, 1807, baptized August 9, 1807

Robert Scott, son of Robert and Elizabeth Scott, born August 25, 1807, baptized August 26, 1807

Sarah Caroline Sears Sterret, daughter of Samuel and Rebecca Sterret, born November 2, 1806, baptized September 2, 1807

Sally Ann Newman, daughter of Joseph and Ann Newman, born August 31, 1807, baptized October 8, 1807

Rebecca Salmon Meredith, daughter of Jonathan and Hannah Meredith, born August -- [blank], 1807, baptized October 13, 1807

James Irvin, son of John and Margaret Irvin, born October 26, 1806, baptized October 16, 1807

Mary Coulter, daughter of Alexander and Esther Coulter, born August 30, 1807, baptized November 12, 1807

Octavus Patterson, son of William and ---- [blank] Patterson, born August -- [blank], 1802, baptized November 18, 1807

Mary Ann Jeromia Patterson, daughter of William and ---- [blank], Patterson, born October 3, 1804, baptized November 18, 1807

Jane Eliza Thomson, daughter of James and Mary Thomson, born ---- [blank], 1807, baptized November 21, 1807

Dunbar Essex Cochran, son of William G. and Susanna Cochran, born October 30, 1807, baptized December 4, 1807 (twin)

Essex Dunbar Cochran, son of William G. and Susanna Cochran, born October 30, 1807, baptized December 4, 1807 (twin)

John Neave Brown, son of Stewart and Sarah Brown, born May 19, 1807, baptized December 30, 1807

Helen Machenry, daughter of Francis Deane and Frances Machenry, born November 4, 1805, baptized December 31, 1807

Ann Machenry, daughter of Francis Deane and Frances Machenry, born September 9, 1807, baptized December 31, 1807

FIRST PRESBYTERIAN CHURCH 109

Josephine Sterret, daughter of Joseph and Mary Sterret, born November 3, 1806, baptized January 1, 1808
James William Sterret, son of Joseph and Mary Sterret, born January 19, 1807, baptized January 1, 1808
David Stewart Buchanan, son of Lloyd and Catharine Buchanan, born August 10, 1807, baptized January 6, 1808
Mary Stewart, daughter of David and Elizabeth Stewart, born August 21, 1807, baptized January 10, 1808
Sarah Ann Pennington Rutter McInnally, daughter of John and Grace McInnally, born June 12, 1807, baptized January 15, 1808
Edward Johnson Mosher, son of James and Ann Mosher, born December 16, 1807, baptized January 17, 1808
Charles Anderson Morton, son of Nathaniel and Sarah Morton, born March 15, 1800, baptized January 21, 1808
George Copeland Morton, son of Nathaniel and Sarah Morton, born September 7, 1803, baptized January 21, 1808
Mary Adelaide Morton, daughter of Nathaniel and Sarah Morton, born July 21, 1806, baptized January 21, 1808
Washington William Alexander Ross, son of Samuel and Elizabeth Ross "(mother dead), left by her in her last illness with consent of her husband to Ann Jane Newman, wife of Joseph Newman, to be by her presented for baptism and educated - Samuel Ross being of the Society of Friends and the said Ann Newman being sponsor for the child - born January 9, 1808, baptized February 4, 1808."
Samuel McKean Mactier, son of Alexander and Frances Mactier, born December 11, 1807, baptized February 20, 1808
George Hanse McDowell, son of George and Susanna McDowell, born October 13, 1807, baptized February 28, 1808
Ann Jackson, daughter of James and Helen Jackson, born November 29, 1807, baptized March 16, 1808
George Chambers Colhoon, son of Benjamin Chambers and Lilly Kennedy Colhoon, born January 12, 1808, baptized April 4, 1808
Elizabeth Cochran, daughter of William and Deborah Cochran, born March 16, 1808, baptized April 27, 1808
John Montgomery Harris, son of David and Sally Harris, born February 25, 1808, baptized June 13, 1808
Ann Christian McCandless, daughter of Robert and Rachel McCandless, born November 12, 1807, baptized June 14, 1808
Thomas Manning, son of Thomas and Sarah Manning, born September 13, 1807, baptized June 17, 1808

Thomas Williams, son of Jacob and Mary Williams, born November 7, 1807, baptized July 19, 1808

Jenny Margaret McDonald, daughter of Alexander and Mary McDonald, born July 3, 1808, baptized July 12, 1808

Mary Ann Gilmor, daughter of William and Mary Ann Gilmor, born May 31, 1806, baptized July 14, 1808

Robert Gilmor, son of William and Mary Ann Gilmor, born May 30, 1808, baptized July 14, 1808

William Edwin Phillips, son of William and Elizabeth Phillips, born May 24, [1805?], baptized July 15, 1808

John Carns, son of John and Isabella Carns, born June 30, 1808, baptized July 17, 1808

Ann Lyon, daughter of James and Rebecca Lyon, born September 8, 1807, baptized July 18, 1808

James Lyon, son of James and Rebecca Lyon, born June 5, 1808, baptized July 18, 1808

Robert Hamilton Gray, son of George Lewis and Juliana Penn Gray, (father dead), born January 4, 1808, baptized July 28, 1808

Mary McClellan McKean, daughter of John and Ann McKean, born June 13, 1808, baptized August 28, 1808

Flora Caldwell Smith, daughter of James and Ann Smith, born August 26, 1808, baptized August 28, 1808

Louisa McFadon, daughter of John and Priscilla McFadon, born August 9, 1801, baptized September 4, 1808

James Wilson McFadon, son of John and Priscilla McFadon, born June 25, 1803, baptized September 4, 1808

Eliza McFadon, daughter of John and Priscilla McFadon, born June 8, 1805, baptized September 4, 1808

Priscilla McFadon, daughter of John and Priscilla McFadon, born August 13, 1808, baptized September 4, 1808

Alexander Fridge Burt, son of Andrew and Isabella Burt, born July 14, 1808, baptized September 28, 1808

Charles Torrance Clopper, son of Andrew and Ann Clopper, born July 8, 1808, baptized October 16, 1808

Jane Boyd, daughter of Peter and Elizabeth Boyd, born September 27, 1808, baptized October 23, 1808

Mary McKnight Barr, daughter of William and Mary Barr, born July 23, 1808, baptized November 18, 1808

Mary Keys, daughter of James and Jane Keys, born September 8, 1808, baptized November 18, 1808

FIRST PRESBYTERIAN CHURCH 111

Helen Jackson, daughter of James and Helen Jackson (mother dead), born December 17, 1808, baptized December 29, 1808
Margaret Smith Purviance, daughter of John and Abigail Purviance, born May 10, 1808, baptized January 11, 1809
Sarah Ann Winter, daughter of Robert and Sarah Winter, born November 17, 1808, baptized January 22, 1809
Sarah Campbell, daughter of John R. and Margaret Campbell, born July 14, 1808, baptized January 22, 1809
Charles Tilden Appleton, son of Nathaniel Walker & Sarah Appleton, born January 11, 1809, baptized January 30, 1809
Emeline Myers, daughter of Jacob and Susanna Myers, born February 12, 1807, baptized February 12, 1809
Jane Myers, daughter of George and Polly Myers, born November 17, 1808, baptized February 12, 1809
Eveline Blair Martin, daughter of John Blair and Elizabeth Martin, born October 19, 1808, baptized February 12, 1809
John Robertson Ferguson, son of Robert and Ann Ferguson, born December 8, 1808, baptized March 3, 1809
Mary Swan Maxwell, daughter of William and Isabella Maxwell, born June 14, 1808, baptized March 11, 1809
Susanna Greer McDowell, daughter of Maxwell and Ruth McDowell, born December 30, 1808, baptized May 13, 1809
Jacob Harman Brown, son of Stewart and Sarah Brown, born January 14, 1809, baptized June 14, 1809
Maria Donaldson, daughter of Joseph and Catherine Donaldson, born May 10, 1809, baptized June 26, 1809
Mary Ann Porter, daughter of William and Jane Porter, born September 1, 1808, baptized July 25, 1809
Mary De Vries, daughter of Christian and Jannatie De Vries, born March 1, 1809, baptized July 26, 1809
Stephen York Van Lill, son of Henry and Ann Van Lill, born June 12, 1809, baptized July 26, 1809
Ann Elizabeth Forman, daughter of Francis and Ann Elizabeth Forman, born December 6, 1808, baptized August 1, 1809
Emmeline Isett, daughter of John and Elizabeth Isett, born May 30, 1809, baptized August 4, 1809
Amelia Jane Snider, daughter of Nicholas and Margaret Snider, born July 13, 1808, baptized August 6, 1809
Amelia Poe, daughter of Jacob and Bridget Poe, born August 11, 1809, baptized September 6, 1809 (twin)

Neilson Poe, son of Jacob and Bridget Poe, born August 11, 1809,
baptized September 6, 1809 (twin)

Alexander Charles Robinson, son of Alexander and Angelica Robinson,
born August 29, 1808, baptized September 13, 1809

Harriet Murray Stewart, daughter of David and Elizabeth Stewart,
born September 14, 1809, baptized October 1, 1809

Julia Craig, daughter of Thomas and Bethiah Craig, born December 27,
1807, baptized October 6, 1809

George Salmon Meredith, son of Jonathan and Hannah Meredith, born
August 31, 1809, baptized October 6, 1809

George Salmon Inglis, son of James and Jane Swan Inglis, born
September 6, 1809, baptized October 6, 1809

William McKesson Taylor, son of William W. and Maria Taylor, born
June 19, 1809, baptized October 25, 1809

Elisha Boudinot Atterbury, son of Lewis and Catherine Atterbury, born
September 7, 1809, baptized November 2, 1809

Catharine Somervell Wilson, daughter of Robert and Anna Wilson,
born June 25, 1809, baptized November 9, 1809

Keturah Ann Mitchell, daughter of James R. and Jane Ann Mitchell,
born June 7, 1809, baptized November 24, 1809

Anthony Kennedy Colhoon, son of B. C. and L. K. Colhoon, born
[December?] 9, 1809, baptized January 4, 1810

Ann Cochran, daughter of William G. and Susanna Cochran, born
August 27, 1809, baptized February 9, 1810

Maria Louisa West, aged nearly 32 years, born May 12, 1778, baptized
February 28, 1810

James West, son of Maria Louisa West (father being dead), born
December 14, 1809, baptized February 28, 1810

William Robison, son of William and Susan Robison, born November 8,
1807, baptized April 7, 1810

Ann Robison, daughter of William and Susan Robison, born August 27,
1809, baptized April 7, 1810

Hannah Warren Buckler, daughter of William and A. T. Buckler, born
February 23, 1809, baptized April 11, 1810

Robert Winter, son of Robert and Sarah Winter, born March 31, 1810,
baptized April 27, 1810

Mary Boyd, daughter of James P. and Ann Boyd, born March 2, 1810,
baptized April 30, 1810

Nicholas Patterson, son of Andrew and Mary Patterson, born August 1,
1809, baptized May 15, 1810

FIRST PRESBYTERIAN CHURCH 113

Mary Cockey Nisbet, wife of Alexander Nisbet, born ---- [blank], baptized June 5, 1810

Colegate Deye Nisbet, daughter of Alexander and Mary Cockey Nesbit, born March 20, 1809, baptized June 5, 1810

Charles Nisbet, son of Alexander and Mary Cockey Nesbit, born May 21, 1810, baptized June 5, 1810

James Bradford Campbell, son of John R. and Margaret Campbell, born April 13, 1810, baptized June 6, 1810

Peter Williams, son of Jacob and Mary Williams, born November 8, 1809, baptized July 15, 1810

Sarah Jackson, daughter of James and Bethiah Jackson, born April 12, 1810, baptized July 20, 1810

John Lyon, son of James and Rebecca Lyon, born January 21, 1810, baptized August 3, 1810

Martha Murray McClenachan, daughter of James and Ann McClenachan, born March 28, 1803, baptized August 20, 1810

Elizabeth Scott McClenachan, daughter of James and Ann McClenachan, born October 1, 1805, baptized August 20, 1810

James Boyles Murray McClenachan, son of James and Ann McClenachan, born July 26, 1810, baptized August 20, 1810

Elizabeth Coulter, daughter of Alexander and Esther Coulter, born February 18, 1810, baptized August 23, 1810

Mary Ann McDowell, daughter of George and Susanna McDowell, born June 22, 1810, baptized September 9, 1810

Jane Eliza Poor, daughter of Charles M. and Elizabeth Poor, born May 12, 1810, baptized September 20, 1810

David Caldwell Harris, son of David and Sally Harris, born April 27, 1810, baptized October 4, 1810

Frances Susan Purviance, daughter of John and Abigail Purviance, born May 5, 1810, baptized December 12, 1810

James Henrich, son of Jacob and Eliza Henrich, born August 2, 1808, baptized December 18, 1810

Walter Henrich, son of Jacob and Eliza Henrich, born April 11, 1809 and baptized December 18, 1810, (died December 19, 1810, being burnt to death)

Jacob Henrich, son of Jacob and Eliza Henrich, born March 9, 1810, baptized December 18, 1810

Evilina Forman, daughter of Francis and Ann Elizabeth Forman, born September 16, 1810, baptized December 18, 1810

Harriet Neilson, daughter of William and Harriet Neilson (the mother having died the 11th), born November 10, 1810, baptized January 13, 1811

William Barr Keys, son of James and Jane Keys, born May 30, 1810, baptized January 21, 1811

Kitty Maria Gray, daughter of Daniel and Affy Gray, (father dead), born January 7, 1806, baptized January 28, 1811

George Gray, son of Daniel and Affy Gray, (father dead), born June 21, 1808, baptized January 28, 1811

Joanna Gray, daughter of Daniel and Affy Gray, (father dead), born August 29, 1810, baptized January 28, 1811

Samuel Smith Buchanan, son of James A. and Elizabeth Buchanan, born December 14, 1810, baptized March 7, 1811

Mary Buchanan Brown, daughter of George J. and Esther Brown, born January 2, 1811, baptized March 7, 1811

William Thompson, son of James and Mary Thompson, born January 27, 1811, baptized March 10, 1811

Eleanor Carroll, daughter of Thomas and Ann Carroll, born May 20, 1810, baptized March 10, 1811

Robert Hazlehurst, son of Andrew and Frances Hazlehurst, born October 19, 1807, baptized March 12, 1811

Henry Hazlehurst, son of Andrew and Frances Hazlehurst, born March 6, 1809, baptized March 12, 1811

Julianna Hazlehurst, daughter of Andrew and Frances Hazlehurst, born February 27, 1811, baptized March 12, 1811

Isham Randolph Finley, son of Ebenezer and Catharine Finley, born October 1, 1810, baptized March 24, 1811

Louisa Sophia Meredith, daughter of Jonathan and Hannah Meredith, born ---- [blank], baptized March 25, 1811

Henrietta Isett, daughter of John and Elizabeth Isett, born February 13, 1811, baptized March 26, 1811

James Finley, son of Thomas and Ann Perry Finley, born August 31, 1810, baptized April 1, 1811

John Guest Atterbury, son of Lewis and Catherine Atterbury, born February 6, 1811, baptized April 23, 1811

Martha Helen Magruder, daughter of Richard B. and Maria Magruder, born December 27, 1810, baptized May 20, 1811

Edward Parish McKeen, son of John and Ann McKeen, born October 2, 1810, baptized August 8, 1811

Elizabeth Grace Rigby (parents dead), granddaughter of Grace Mimm, born December 6, 1801, baptized August 18, 1811

Margaret Pettingall, daughter of Robert and Margaret Pettingall, (mother died soon after delivery), born August 21, 1811, baptized August 21, 1811

Joshua Stewart, son of Ark and Charlotte Stewart (coloured people), born February 2, 1811, baptized September 6, 1811

Erastus Albert Strong, son of Erastus and Nabby Wright Strong, born August 19, 1809, baptized September 14, 1811

Philip Oler, son of Peter and Margaret Oler, born March 11, 1810, baptized September 24, 1811

Sally Harman Brown, daughter of Stewart and Sarah Brown, (mother dead), born May 6, 1811, baptized September 26, 1811

Alexander Brown Norris, son of John and Nancy Norris, born May 10, 1811, baptized October 1, 1811

James Nicholson Montgomery, son of John and Maria Montgomery, born July 14, 1811, baptized October 14, 1811

Matthew Fraser, son of William and Margaret Fraser, born January 8, 1810, baptized January 4, 1812

Isabella Burt, daughter of Andrew and Isabella Burt, born April 30, 1810, baptized January 10, 1812

Dorothea Margaret Stewart, daughter of David and Elizabeth Stewart, born August 25, 1811, baptized January 28, 1812

Elizabeth Warner, daughter of John and Margaret Warner, born January 24, 1812, baptized March 25, 1812

Lloyd Archibald Buchanan, son of Lloyd and Catharine Isabella Buchanan, born June 18, 1811, baptized March 26, 1812

William John Stewart, son of Adam and Eleanor Stewart, born February 27, 1812, baptized "publick" March 28, 1812

James Stewart, son of James and Ann Stewart, born December 4, 1811, baptized "publick" March 28, 1812

William Gilmor, son of William and Mary Ann Gilmor, born December 23, 1810, baptized "publick" March 28, 1812

James William Sterett, son of Joseph and Mary Sterett, born September 3, 1808, baptized April 6, 1812

Mary Harris Sterett, daughter of Joseph and Mary Sterett, born January 6, 1810, baptized April 6, 1812

Joseph Sterett, son of Joseph and Mary Sterett, born March 6, 1812, baptized April 6, 1812

William Burt, son of Andrew and Isabella Burt, born December 15, 1811, baptized "publick" April 12, 1812

Mary Blaikley Smith, daughter of James and Jane Swan Inglis, born January 28, 1812, baptized "publick" April 12, 1812

Selina Boyd, daughter of Samuel and Agnes Boyd, born March 5, 1812, baptized April 30, 1812

Benjamin Harrison Wilson, son of Robert and Anna Wilson, born January 4, 1812, baptized June 9, 1812

Eliza Maria Thomas White, daughter of Joseph and Deborah White, born May 9, 1812, baptized June 10, 1812

Mary Hazlehurst, daughter of Andrew and Frances Hazlehurst, born May 15, 1812, baptized June 10, 1812

John ----, son of Joseph and Jenny ---- (persons of colour), Jenny being slave of Archibald Stewart, born ---- [blank], baptized June 14, 1812

Martha Eloisa Strong, daughter of Erastus and Nabby Wright Strong, born February 24, 1812, baptized "publick" June 21, 1812

James McHenry Boyd, son of James P. and Anna Boyd, born December 15, 1811, baptized June 23, 1812

Emily Meredith, daughter of Jonathan and Hannah Meredith, born May 25, 1812, baptized June 29, 1812

Susanna May Williams, daughter of Benjamin and Sarah Williams, (father deceased), born April 2, 1812, baptized July 1, 1812

Charles Henry Donaldson, son of Joseph and Catherine Donaldson, born November 15, 1811, baptized July 8, 1812

Thomas Deye Nisbet, son of Alexander and Mary C. Nisbet, born September 21, 1811, baptized July 22, 1812

John Purviance, son of John and Abigail Purviance, born July 6, 1812, baptized August 5, 1812

Mary Williams, daughter of Jacob and Mary Williams, born December 14, 1811, baptized "publick" August 23, 1812

John White, son of Henry and Margaret White, born June 15, 1812, baptized September 6, 1812

Maria McIlvaine, daughter of Alexander and Sarah McIlvaine, born April 12, 1809, baptized October 19, 1812

Thomas Hepbrom Buckler, son of W. and A. F. Buckler, born January 4, 1812, baptized November 16, 1812

Edward Gwinn Hall, son of Washington and Ann Hall, born September 16, 1810, baptized December 1, 1812

George Washington Harris, son of David and Sally Harris, born June 13, 1812, baptized December 8, 1812

FIRST PRESBYTERIAN CHURCH 117

Cornelia Clinton Taylor, daughter of W. W. and Maria Taylor, born June 9, 1812, baptized December 14, 1812
Sarah Ann Campbell, daughter of John R. and Margaret Campbell, born September 8, 1812, baptized December 14, 1812
Catharine Jane McClellan, daughter of Robert and Sarah McClellan, born August 27, 1812, baptized January 12, 1813
Henry Fisher, son of John and Ann Fisher, born October 8, 1812, baptized January 12, 1813
Heziah Harrison, adult, born February 12, 1792, baptized "publick" January 17, 1813
Thomas Finley, son of Thomas and Ann Perry Finley, born June -- [blank], 1813, baptized February 4, 1813
George William Brown, son of George J. and Esther Brown, born October 13, 1812, baptized March 15, 1813
Margaret Oler, daughter of Peter and Margaret Oler, born January 23, 1813, baptized March 22, 1813
John Stricker Magruder, son of R. B. and M. Magruder, born March 6, 1813, baptized April 5, 1813
William Baden, son of William and Elizabeth Baden, born October 18, 1812, baptized "publick" May 30, 1813
James Joseph Carroll, son of Thomas and Ann Carroll, born November 23, 1812, baptized June 6, 1813
Ann Catherine Finley, daughter of Ebenezer and Catherine Finley, born September 7, 1812, baptized June 8, 1813
Ruhannah Colhoon, daughter of B. C. and L. K. Colhoon, born January 9, 1813, baptized June 9, 1813
Ann Mary Snider, daughter of Nicholas and Margaret Snider, born May 28, 1813, baptized June 30, 1813
John McDonogh Cole, son of John and Mary Cole, born October 21, 1810, baptized June 28, 1813
William Cole, son of John and Mary Cole, born July 18, 1812, baptized June 28, 1813
Janet Hall, daughter of Benedict William and Mary Hall, born July -- [blank], 1813, baptized July 18, 1813
Mary Burt, daughter of Andrew and Isabella Burt, born March 25, 1813, baptized July 28, 1813
Mary Jane Forman, daughter of Francis and Ann Elizabeth Forman, born June 20, 1813, baptized August 23, 1813
Thomas Willis, son of William and Ann Willis, born August 15, 1813, baptized August 29, 1813

Francis Asbury Stafford, son of William Josephus and Mary Stafford, born November 1, 1808, baptized September 27, 1813

Elizabeth Stewart Buchanan, daughter of Lloyd and Catherine Isabella Buchanan, born September 16, 1813, baptized October 13, 1813

Frederick James Poor, son of Moses and Charlotte Poor, born July 15, 1812, baptized October 18, 1813

Elizabeth Susannah Thompson, daughter of James and Mary Thompson, born June 9, 1813, baptized November 7, 1813

John Auchincloss Inglis, son of J. and J. S. Inglis, born ---- [not stated, but it could be August 26, 1813, since his name and Agness Auchincloss were bracketed together in the register and she was born that date], baptized "publick" November 7, 1813

Agness Auchincloss, daughter of John and Matilda Auchincloss (father dead), born August 26, 1813, baptized "publick" November 7, 1813

George Harrison Buchanan, son of J. A. and E. Buchanan, born March 10, 1813, baptized November 9, 1813

John Oliver Colt, son of Roswell Lyman and Margaret Colt, born September 11, 1813, baptized November 9, 1813

Benjamin May Clopper, son of Andrew and Ann Clopper, born December 18, 1809, baptized November 14, 1813

Rachel D. Clopper, daughter of Andrew and Ann Clopper, born November 7, 1811, baptized November 14, 1813

Ann Clopper, daughter of Andrew and Ann Clopper, born June 11, 1813, baptized November 14, 1813

Julia Ann May Clopper, daughter of Edward N. and Grace Clopper, born April 22, 1812, baptized November 14, 1813

Moses Poor, born August 26, 1774, baptized November 20, 1813

George Harris Poor, son of Moses and Charlotte Poor, born September 17, 1806, baptized "publick" November 20, 1813

Charles Henry Poor, son of Moses and Charlotte Poor, born June 11, 1808, baptized "publick" November 20, 1813

William Augustus Poor, son of Moses and Charlotte Poor, born July 18, 1809, baptized "publick" November 20, 1813

Rebecca Virginia Neilson, daughter of Oliver H. and Caroline Neilson, born ---- [blank], 1813, baptized December 14, 1813

Catherine Stewart, daughter of David C. and Elizabeth Stewart, born November 20, 1813, baptized December 26, 1813

Rebecca Lyon, daughter of James and Rebecca Lyon, born ---- [blank], baptized December 27, 1813

John Thompson Barr, born Dec. 15, 1786, baptized Dec. 28, 1813

Margaret Sterrett Barr, daughter of J. T. and Jane Barr, born July 13, 1813, baptized December 28, 1813
Richard Keys Eaton, son of William and Mary Eaton, born August 16, 1813, baptized December 28, 1813
William White, son of Henry and Margaret White, born January 7, 1814, baptized "publick" January --, 1814
Emma Hazlehurst, daughter of Andrew and Frances Hazlehurst, born August 11, 1813, baptized January 18, 1814
Ramsay McHenry, son of Daniel and Sophia H. McHenry, born January 15, 1814, baptized February 16, 1814
Henry ----, slave of Mrs. Lydia Calhoun, born July 12, 1794, baptized April 10, 1814
James Williams, son of Jacob and Mary Williams, born October 1, 1813, baptized "publick" June 12, 1814
Mary Deborah Denison, daughter of Edward and Deborah Denison, born December 27, 1806, baptized June 13, 1814. "Eliza ----, the second wife of the said Edward, uniting with him in the presentation of this child."
Robert Miller Denison, son of Edward and Eliza Denison, born November 29, 1813, baptized June 13, 1814
Marguerite Ann Delacour, daughter of David and Elizabeth Delacour, born October 18, 1813, baptized July 13, 1814
Esther Coulter, daughter of Alexander and Esther Coulter, born December 31, 1812, baptized July 13, 1814
William Robinson Beam, son of Elijah and Charlotte Christianna Beam, born June 21, 1814, baptized October 8, 1814
Benjamin Chambers Colhoun, son of B. C. and L. K. Colhoun, born March 1, 1814, baptized October 8, 1814
Maria Ridgeley Sterrett, daughter of Joseph and Mary Sterrett, born April 12, 1814, baptized November 15, 1814
Henry Payson Neilson, son of Oliver Hugh and Caroline Neilson, born ---- [blank], 1814, baptized November 15, 1814
Mary Jane Knippenberg, daughter of Andries and Elizabeth Knippenberg, born July 19, 1814, baptized November 20, 1814
Martha Doran Allen, born March 22, 1789, bapt. November 25, 1814
Sophia Hanson Finley, daughter of Ebenezer and Catharine Finley, born August 26, 1814, baptized November 25, 1814
Samuel Sterrett Barr, son of John Thompson and Jane Barr, born September 9, 1814, baptized November 25, 1814

Alexander Finley [name of parents not stated], born February 19, 1814, baptized January 26, 1815

Francis Keller Forman, son of Francis and Ann Elizabeth Forman, born October 21, 1814, baptized March 10, 1815

Samuel Hazlehurst, son of Alexander and Frances Hazlehurst, born September 2, 1814, baptized March 22, 1815

Lydia Calhoun Hall, daughter of Benedict W. and Mary Hall, born February 20, 1815, baptized April 11, 1815

Anna Mary Wilson, daughter of Robert and Anna Wilson, born December 18, 1814, baptized April 20, 1815

Catharine Eve Fisher, daughter of John and Anne Fisher, born March 29, 1815, baptized May 3, 1815

William Burt, son of Andrew and Isabella Burt, born September 14, 1814, baptized July 2, 1815

Cassandra Owings Nisbet, daughter of Alexander and Mary Nisbet, born August 30, 1813, baptized July 20, 1815

Ann Tweedie Nisbet, daughter of Alexander and Mary Nisbet, born April 1, 1815, baptized July 20, 1815

Elizabeth Jane Ward, daughter of James and Lucretia Ward, born August 13, 1815, baptized August 21, 1815

Margaret Boyd [name of parents not stated], born August 9, 1815, baptized August 27, 1815

Ann Pannell Porter, daughter of William and Jane Porter, born November 2, 1810, baptized October 13, 1815

Isabella Porter, daughter of William and Jane Porter, born November 13, 1813, baptized October 13, 1815

Sarah McCulloh Porter, daughter of William and Jane Porter, born January 22, 1815, baptized October 13, 1815

James Craig Colt, son of Roswell and Margaret Colt, born October 3, 1815, baptized October 18, 1815

William Huber, son of Henry and Ellen Huber, born October 27, 1815, baptized November 10, 1815

William Robb Fergusson, son of James and Catharine Fergusson, born September 28, 1815, baptized December 7, 1815

Sarah Eliza Poor, daughter of Dudley and Deborah Poor, born March 11, 1815, baptized July 6, 1815

Frances Ann Purviance, daughter of William and Jemima Purviance, born June 29, 1815, baptized August 10, 1815

Henry Young, son of Mrs. Mary Young, born November 18, 1812, baptized September 26, 1815

Antoinette McFadon [name of parents not stated], born October 20, 1812, baptized November 28, 1815

John Henry McFadon [name of parents not stated], born November 1, 1815, baptized November 28, 1815

Andrew Hazlehurst, son of Andrew and Frances Hazlehurst, born December 14, 1815, baptized January 11, 1816*

Charles Brown [name of parents not stated], born March 23, 1813, baptized January 16, 1816*

Sarah Ann Brown [name of parents not stated], born October 31, 1815, baptized January 16, 1816*

[* Ed. Note: The previous three entries in the register indicated baptisms in July, but they were actually in January. The error is clear as subsequent entries were made in February, March, etc.]

Richard William Keys, son of John F. and Margaret Keys, born October 15, 1815, baptized February 3, 1816

Louisa Sherlock Sterrett [name of parents not stated], born January 12, ---- [1816?], baptized February 3, 1816

John Kirkland Poor, son of Moses and Charlotte Poor, born June 18, 1814, baptized February 12, 1816

Samuel Wagner McClellan, son of Samuel and Eliza McClellan, born March 26, 1815, baptized February 26, 1816

Jacob Poe, born October 11, 1776, baptized March 3, 1816

James Mosher Poe [name of parents not stated], born January 3, 1812, baptized March 3, 1816 [Ed. Note: Father was probably Jacob Poe since they were both baptized on the same day.]

Susan Maria Inglis, daughter of Andrew [Andries?] and Elizabeth Knippenberg, born September 30, 1815, baptized March 10, 1816

Benjamin Edes, son of Benjamin and Mary Ann Edes, born September 30, 1812, baptized March 26, 1816

Mary Jane Edes, daughter of Benjamin and Mary Ann Edes, born April 8, 1815, baptized March 26, 1816

William Gwynn Neilson, son of Oliver and Caroline Neilson, born March 31, 1816, baptized April 26, 1816

Jane Swan Johnston, daughter of James and Jane Swan Johnston, born April 25, 1816, baptized June -- [blank], 1816

Samuel Finley, son of Thomas and Ann P. Finley, born August 27, 1815, baptized September 28, 1816

Jane Huber, daughter of Henry and Ellen Huber, born September 26, 1816, baptized October 1, 1816

Juliet Pierpont, daughter of John and Mary Pierpont, born July 30, 1816, baptized October 9, 1816

Zebulon Rudulph, born June 28, 1794, bapt. "publick" Oct. 30, 1816

Martha Jane Ricaud [name of parents not stated], born October 1, 1816, baptized November 3, 1816

Elizabeth Sarah Colt, daughter of Roswell and Margaret Colt, born September 2, 1816, baptized December 2, 1816

Margaret Patterson [name of parents not stated], born February 11, 1816, baptized December 9, 1816

Delia Woodward Adams, daughter of Eli and Sarah D. Adams, born November 19, 1815, baptized June 30, 1816

James Philips Delacour, son of David and Elizabeth Delacour, born May 23, 1816, baptized October 27, 1816

Sarah Walker, born November 24, 1780, baptized November 24, 1816

Anna Gardner, born July 11, 1784, baptized November 24, 1816

"These [last two] names were omitted in their respective months."

Ann Scobey, born November 7, 1794, baptized January 15, 1817

Mary Ann Scobey, daughter of John and Ann Scobey, born September 7, 1810, baptized January 17, 1817

Elizabeth Scobey, daughter of John and Ann Scobey, born March 18, 1812, baptized January 17, 1817

Emma Scobey, daughter of John and Ann Scobey, born June 19, 1816, baptized January 17, 1817

Lauretta Hazlehurst, daughter of Andrew and Frances Hazlehurst, born February 8, 1817, baptized February 8, 1817

Eliza Gwynn, wife of Charles Gwynn, born December 3, 1793, baptized March 5, 1817

Elizabeth Maria Gwynn, daughter of Charles and Eliza Gwynn, born June 20, 1815, baptized March 5, 1817

Sarah Matilda Gwynn, daughter of Charles and Eliza Gwynn, born January 9[?], 1817, baptized March 5, 1817

George Ward, son of Ebenezer and Margaret Ward, born March 4, 1817, baptized March 6, 1817

Mary Finley, daughter of John M. and Mary V. L. Finley, born December 17, 1817, baptized March 27, 1817

Mary Jane Barr, daughter of John T. and Jane S. Barr, born December 14, 1817, baptized March 27, 1817

William Wellington Meredith, son of Jonathan and Hannah Meredith, born May 3, 1814, baptized May 22, 1817

FIRST PRESBYTERIAN CHURCH 123

Elizabeth Sarah Meredith, daughter of Jonathan and Hannah Meredith, born October 24, 1816, baptized May 24, 1817
Elizabeth Buchanan Hall [name of parents not stated], born January 17, 1817, baptized May 24, 1817
Edward ---- [last name not stated], son of William and Elizabeth ---- [blank], born March 22, 1817, baptized May 29, 1817
Edward Pannell Porter, son of William and Jane Porter, born March 24, 1817, baptized June 11, 1817
Thomas William Magruder, son of Richard B. and Maria Magruder, born January 23, 1815, baptized June 17, 1817
Laura Maria Magruder, daughter of Richard B. and Maria Magruder, born May 21, 1817, baptized June 17, 1817
Sophia Rogers [name of parents not stated], born May 27, 1817, baptized June 23, 1817
David Hyde, son of Francis and Mahitabel Hyde, born June 14, 1817, baptized June 23, 1817
Allison Clopper [name of parents not stated], born May 19, 1815, baptized June 28, 1817
Samuel Evans McElderry, son of John and Ann McElderry, born September 26, 1816, baptized July 2, 1817
Catharine Elizabeth Fergusson, daughter of James and Catharine Fergusson, born April 25, 1817, baptized July 2, 1817
Sophia Margaretta Charlotte Schminke, daughter of George and Anna Schminke, born November 11, 1816, baptized July 14, 1817
James Stirling, son of William and Mary Stirling, born June 10, 1817, baptized August 27, 1817
Elliott O'Donnell Poor, son of Dudley and Deboran Poor, born April 10, 1817, baptized September 3, 1817
Elizabeth Williams, daughter of Jacob and Mary Williams, born April 26, 1817, baptized "publick" September 21, 1817
Samuel Hall Taggart, son of John and Mary Taggart, born August 1, 1811, baptized September 26, 1817
John Steward Wilson, son of Robert and Anna Wilson, born September 25, 1817, baptized October 20, 1817
James Smith Mackenzie, son of Colin and Sarah Mackenzie, born September 24, 1817, baptized October 24, 1817
Martha Jane Winchester, daughter of William and Hannah Winchester, born October 21, 1817, baptized November 13, 1817
Agness Salome Beam [name of parents not stated], born October 20, 1816, baptized January 1, 1818

Henry Robinson, son of Thomas and Louisa Robinson, born April 4, 1816, baptized January 12, 1818

Isabella Despeaux, daughter of Thomas and Hannah Despeaux, born February 6, 1817, baptized May 11, 1818

"These [last 3] names were omitted from their respective months."

Elizabeth Carruthers, daughter of Samuel and Elizabeth Carruthers, (mother dead), born December 20, 1817, baptized January 17, 1818

Hannah Doak, daughter of John and Hannah Doak, born January 5, 1818, baptized January 23, 1818

James Morrison Harris, son of David and Sarah Harris, born November 20, 1817, baptized January 26, 1818

James Barkley, son of John and Ann Barkley, born February 19, 1818, baptized February 19, 1818

Sidney Buchanan Brown, daughter of George and Esther Brown, born January 15, 1818, baptized February 27, 1818

Robert Henry Mills, son of Thomas and Eliza D. Mills, born December 5, 1817, baptized March 2, 1818

Andrew B. McConnell, son of John D. and Euphemia McConnell, born March 1, 1818, baptized March 13, 1818

Thomas Way Grayson, son of John and Martha Grayson, born October 25, 1817, baptized April 7, 1818

Augusta Temple Sterrett [name of parents not stated], born March 4, 1818, baptized April 7, 1818

Fanny Owings Nisbet, daughter of Alexander and Mary Nisbet, born April 10, 1818, baptized April 30, 1818

Mary Devereux Colt, daughter of Roswell and Margaret Colt, born December 10, 1817, baptized May 26, 1818

Catharine Ann Donaldson, daughter of Joseph Donaldson [name of her mother not stated], born January 13, 1818, baptized June 8, 1818

William Wellington McClellan, son of Samuel and Eliza McClellan, born March 27, 1817, baptized June 18, 1818

Benjamin Sterrett Barr, son of John T. and Jane S. Barr, born June 15, 1818, baptized June 23, 1818

John Greer Boggs, son of Alexander L. and Susan G. Boggs, born November 24, 1817, baptized June 26, 1818

Maria Huber, daughter of Henry and Ellen Huber, born June 16, 1818, baptized June 27, 1818

Oliver Hamilton, son of William and Rebecca Hamilton, born July 5, 1818, baptized July 20, 1818

FIRST PRESBYTERIAN CHURCH 125

Rebecca Barkley, daughter of John and Mary Barkley, born November 2, 1816, baptized July 31, 1818

Sarah Jane Barkley, daughter of John and Mary Barkley, born December 3, 1817, baptized July 31, 1818

Elizabeth Knippenberg, daughter of Andries and Elizabeth Knippenberg, born May 9, 1817, baptized July 31, 1818

William Morehead, son of John and Mary Morehead, born December 25, 1817, baptized August 1, 1818

Elizabeth Jane Sutherland, daughter of William and Isabella Sutherland, born July 20[?], 1818, baptized August 9, 1818

Mary ----, slave of George Poe, born May 1, 1791, baptized August 13, 1818

Elizabeth Edes, daughter of Benjamin and Mary Edes, born July 31, 1817, baptized September 5, 1818

Rachel Scobey, daughter of John and Ann Scobey, born February 9, 1818, baptized September 13, 1818

Alexander McTaggart, son of James and Mary McTaggart, born February 23, 1818, baptized September 14, 1818

Catharine Bearhosse, daughter of Thomas and Margaret Bearhosse, born September 28, 1818, baptized November 9, 1818

Emily Jane Purviance, daughter of William Y. and Jemima Purviance, born December 9, 1818, baptized January 26, 1819

James Ross Burt, son of Andrew and Isabella Burt, born February 11, 1818, baptized February 11, 1819

John David Delacour, son of David and Eliza Delacour, born October 15, 1818, baptized February 11, 1819

Marietta Camilla Haskell, daughter of John and Polly Haskell, (father not baptized), born Aug. 4, 1814, baptized Feb. 28, 1819

William Dame, son of Thomas and Augusta Temple Dame, born February 11, 1819, baptized March 9, 1819

Rosalber Ludden, daughter of Lemuel and Margaret Ludden, born August 18, 1816, baptized March 16, 1819

Elizabeth Eve Beam [name of parents not stated], born March 30, 1819, baptized April 19, 1819

Caroline Helena Neilson, daughter of Oliver Hugh and Caroline Neilson, born February 9, 1819, baptized May 28, 1819

Elizabeth Ward, daughter of Ebenezer and Margaret Ward, born May 20, 1818, baptized January 17, 1820

Mary Calhoun Hall, daughter of Benedict William and Mary Hall, (mother deceased), born June 4, 1818, baptized May --, 1820

Charles Smith Gilmor, son of William and Mary Ann Gilmor, born April 22, 1817, baptized May 21, 1820

Elizabeth Sherlock Gilmor, daughter of William and Mary Ann Gilmor, born November 5, 1818, baptized May 21, 1820

Emilie Wilhelmine Schminke, daughter of George and Anna Schminke, born December 13, 1818, baptized June 8, 1820

George Washington Spies, son of John Peter and M. Spies, born April 26, 1818, baptized June 8, 1820

Emily Ann Gwinn, daughter of Charles and Eliza Gwinn [Gwynn], born June 17, 1819, baptized July 13, 1820

FIRST PRESBYTERIAN CHURCH

RECORD OF PERSONS BAPTIZED BY WILLIAM NEVINS, PASTOR OF THE FIRST PRESBYTERIAN CHURCH, BALTIMORE, SINCE HIS ACCESSION OCT. 19, 1820

Ann Rebekah Finley, daughter of Thomas and A. P. Finley, born January 26, 1817, baptized November 7, 1820
Mary Jane Finley, daughter of Thomas and A. P. Finley, born April 13, 1818, baptized November 7, 1820
Sylvester Larned Finley, son of Thomas and A. P. Finley, born December 3, 1819, baptized November 19, 1820
Eliza O'Donnell Finley, daughter of Eben L. and Eliza W. Finley, born October 16, 1820, baptized November 19, 1820
Augusta Jemima Purviance, daughter of William T. and Jemima Purviance, born October 25, 1820, baptized November 21, 1820
Adelaide Morton Hyde, daughter of Francis and Mehitabel Hyde, born August 18, 1819, baptized November 26, 1820
Mary Eliza Schley, daughter of Jacob and Ann B. Schley, born January 10, 1820, baptized December 6, 1820
Eliza Lee, an adult [no age given], baptized February 3, 1821
James Muncaster Brown, son of Stewart and Sarah Brown, born December 8, 1820, baptized February 13, 1821
Robert Bigham, son of Gordon and Candace Bigham, born November 17, 1820, baptized February 13, 1821
Caroline Forman, daughter of Francis and Ann Elizabeth Forman, born October 24, 1817, baptized March 12, 1821
William Raymond Forman, son of Francis and Ann Elizabeth Forman, born July 28, 1819, baptized March 12, 1821
Roswell Lyman Colt, son of Roswell and Margaret Colt, born January 25, 1821, baptized March 20, 1821
Ann Ruth Boggs, daughter of Alexander L. and Susan Boggs, born November 23, 1820, baptized April 10, 1821
John Owings Nisbet, son of Alexander and Mary Nisbet, born September 9, 1819, baptized April 16, 1821
Ann Hathaway, daughter of Ebenezer and Sarah W. Hathaway, born October 23, 1820, baptized June 3, 1821
Elizabeth Brown, daughter of George and Isabella Brown, born May 15, 1821, baptized June 5, 1821
John Swan, son of James and Elizabeth Swan, born January 27, 1821, baptized June 14, 1821

Jane Neilson, daughter of Oliver H. and Caroline Neilson, born May 25, 1821, baptized June 18, 1821

Emma Claudine Meredith, daughter of Jonathan and Hannah Meredith, born March 3, 1818, baptized June 19, 1821

Charlotte Aurelia Winder, daughter of William H. and Gertrude Winder, born May 14, 1820, baptized July 3, 1821

Susan Jourdan, an adult [no age given], baptized July 22, 1821

Charles Alfred Jourdan, son of Jonathan and Susan Jourdan, born January 30, 1815, baptized July 22, 1821

Mary Ann Delacour Jourdan, daughter of Jonathan and Susan Jourdan, born July 22, 1816, baptized July 22, 1821

George Edwin Jourdan, son of Jonathan and Susan Jourdan, born October 17, 1818, baptized July 22, 1821

John Matthew Walker, son of John Wesley and Rachel Walker, born November 30, 1820, baptized July 22, 1821 (twin)

Mary Jane Elizabeth Walker, daughter of John Wesley and Rachel Walker, born November 30, 1820, baptized July 22, 1821 (twin)

John Robert Quimby, son of Benjamin and Magaretta Quimby, born February 19, 1821, baptized July 25, 1821

Georgina Maria Mills, daughter of Thomas and Eliza D. Mills, born January 23, 1820, baptized July 27, 1821

Mary Ann Bixby, daughter of Nathaniel P. and Margaret Bixby, born December 20, 1819, baptized August 6, 1821

Robert Thomas, son of Robert and Ellen Thomas, born November 18, 1818, baptized August 6, 1821

John Thomas, son of Robert and Ellen Thomas, born April 1, 1821, baptized August 6, 1821

Catharine Maria McClellan, daughter of Samuel and Eliza McClellan, born December 24, 1818, baptized August 7, 1821

Rachel Wagner McClellan, daughter of Samuel and Eliza McClellan, born September 6, 1820, baptized August 7, 1821

Henrietta Frances Dunbar, daughter of George L. and Frances Dunbar, born December 8, 1815, baptized August 7, 1821

Maria Louisa Dunbar, daughter of George L. and Frances Dunbar, born March 29, 1821, baptized August 7, 1821

William Ford Jourdan, son of Jonathan and Susan Jourdan, born August 14, 1821, baptized September 17, 1821

Robert Gilmor Howard, son of Benjamin C. and Jane G. Howard, born May 11, 1821, baptized September 25, 1821, "on the fiftieth anniversary of his great-grandparents marriage, at Beach Hill. Died 20th December 1821."

Grace Davison Brown, daughter of James and Louisa K. Brown, born August 25, 182, baptized September 28, 1821

George Jacob Schley, son of Jacob and Anna B. Schley, born June 29, 1821, baptized October 16, 1821

James Howard McHenry, son of John and Juliana McHenry, born October 11, 1820, baptized November 11, 1821

Jacob Williams, son of Jacob and Mary Williams, born May 29, 1821, baptized November 16, 1821

Benjamin Dove Hyde, son of Francis and Mehitabel Hyde, born August 24, 1821, baptized November 25, 1821

William Wallace Taylor, son of Robert A. and Mary Ann Taylor, born June 29, 1821, baptized December 20, 1821

Andrew Clopper, son of Andrew and Ann B. Clopper, born march 24, 1815, baptized March 10, 1822

George Washington Clopper, son of Andrew and Ann B. Clopper, born February 19, 1817, baptized March 10, 1822

Amelia Clopper, daughter of Andrew and Ann B. Clopper, born April 1, 1819, baptized March 10, 1822

John Pillar Boyd, son of James and Ann Boyd, born August 3, 1816, baptized March 15, 1822

Elizabeth Ferguson, daughter of John and Elizabeth Ferguson, born September 15, 1821, baptized March 18, 1822

Benjamin Caldwell Edes, son of Benjamin and Mary Ann Edes, born March 26, 1819, baptized April 29, 1822

Agnes Maria Edes, daughter of Benjamin and Mary Ann Edes, born September 16, 1821, baptized April 29, 1822

John Petticore, an adult [no age given], baptized May 3, 1822

Susan Smith Gilmore, daughter of William and Mary Ann Gilmore, born January 20, 1822, baptized May 7, 1822

Mary Smith Williams, daughter of Edward T. and Ann Williams, born March 17, 1822, baptized May 7, 1822

Samuel Burns, son of Francis and Elizabeth Burns, born March 2, 1822, baptized June 19, 1822

Rosalie O'Donnell Finley, daughter of E. L. and Eliza W. Finley, born July 1, 1822, baptized July 22, 1822

John McElderry, son of John and Ann W. McElderry, born October 25, 1818, baptized July 30, 1822

Mary Jane Boggs, daughter of Alexander L. and Susan Boggs, born April 17, 1822, baptized July 30, 1822

Ann Thornton, daughter of Sam and Rose Thornton, born June 28, 1822, baptized September 7, 1822

Henry Broughton Bromwell, an adult, baptized November 1, 1822

Henrietta Melinda Bromwell, daughter of H. B. and Henrietta Bromwell, born July 29, 1820, baptized November 1, 1822

William Edward Ogle, son of James and Mary Ogle, born August 18, 1822, baptized November 1, 1822

Jane Craig Cobb, son of R. L. and Margaret Cobb, born October 26, 1822, baptized November 12, 1822

Robert Smith, son of Joseph and Jane Smith, born August 30, 1822, baptized November 12, 1822

Thomas Montgomery Harris, son of David and Sarah Thomas, born September 5, 1822, baptized December 5, 1822

William Gifford, son of Alexander and Mary Gifford, born March 7, 1811, baptized December 17, 1822

James Gifford, son of Alexander and Mary Gifford, born March 2, 1813, baptized December 17, 1822

Hugh Gifford, son of Alexander and Mary Gifford, born June 25, 1817, baptized December 17, 1822

Robert Gifford, son of Alexander and Mary Gifford, born October 13, 1819, baptized December 17, 1822

John William Finley, son of Thomas and Ann P. Finley, born March 31, 1822, baptized December 17, 1822

Elizabeth Robinson Phillips, daughter of William and Elizabeth Phillips, born November 19, 1822, baptized December 17, 1822

Hope Margaret Moncrieff Pattison, daughter of John and Rebecca Pattison, born November 5, 1822, baptized January 17, 1823

Charles Meredith, son of Jonathan and Hannah Meredith, born ---- "date not given," baptized March 10, 1823

Margaret Jane Ferguson, daughter of James and Catherine Ferguson, born January 15, 1823, baptized April 3, 1823

John Grant Jackson, son of Bolton and Frances Jane Jackson, born February 18, 1823, baptized April 7, 1823

Charles Degen Purviance, son of William Y. and Jemima Purviance, born February 17, 1823, baptized April 10, 1823

Henry Langdon Butler, son of William and Alice M. Butler, born December 9, 1822, baptized May 1, 1823

Olivia Lowry Gill, daughter of William L. and Elizabeth A. Gill, born
February 21, 1823, baptized May 2, 1823
Mary Lucy White, daughter of Samuel K. and ---- [blank] White, born --
-- [blank], baptized May 2, 1823
William Lewis Delacour, son of David and Eliza Delacour, born
February -- [blank], 1823, baptized May 5, 1823
Sophia Howard, daughter of Benjamin C. and Jane Howard, born
September 3, 1822, baptized May 8, 1823
William Lorman Clopper, son of Andrew and Ann B. Clopper, born
April 28, 1823, baptized May 25, 1823
Julianna Jackson, daughter of James and Bethiah Jackson, born
December 12, 1822, baptized June 25, 1823
---- [blank] Buckler, baptized July 3, 1823
Thomas Buchanan Gamble, son of Thomas and Margaret Gamble, born
September 5, 1818, baptized July 14, 1823
George Reed Gamble, daughter of Thomas and Margaret Gamble, born
August 7, 1821, baptized July 14, 1823
Alexander Davison Brown, son of George and Isabella Brown, born
May 30, 1823, baptized July 18, 1823
William Price, son of Mrs. Watson - Col. Mosher, sponsor, born ---- [no
date given], baptized September 25, 1823
---- [blank] Petticore, baptized October 1, 1823
Mary Randolph Finley, daughter of E. L. and E. W. Finley, born
October 4, 1823, baptized November 17, 1823
William McFadon, son of John and ---- [blank] McFadon, born ---- [no
date given], baptized December 4, 1823
Benjamin Sterrett, son of John Y. and ---- [blank] Sterrett, born ---- [no
date given], baptized December 11, 1823
Sydney Calhoun Hall, daughter of B. W. and Ann Hall, born ---- [no
date given], baptized December 22, 1823
Mary Immell Forman, daughter of Francis and Ann E. Forman, born
April 23, 1822, baptized January 23, 1824
John Wallace Barkley, son of John M. and Mary Barkley, born October
14, 1819, baptized February 22, 1824
Mary McCullough Barkley, daughter of John M. and Mary Barkley,
born August 28, 1821, baptized February 22, 1824
Ann Eliza Barkley, daughter of John M. and Mary Barkley, born
January 4, 1824, baptized February 22, 1824
Sarah Stephens, daughter of Alexander and Elizabeth Stephens, born
September 26, 1822, baptized February 22, 1824

Sally Rebecca Chambers, a colored child of Philip and Lucy Ann
  Chambers, born ---- [no date given], baptized March 11, 1824
Philip Barton Key Nevins, son of William and Mary Nevins, born
  February 3, 1824, bapt. June 13, 1824, by Rev. J. J. Davis
Ann Catharine Hyde, daughter of Francis and Mehitable Hyde, born ----
  [no date given], baptized June 13, 1824
Ellen Stewart Boyd, daughter of Alexander and ---- [blank] Boyd,
  born ---- [no date given], baptized June 14, 1824
Janet Russell, daughter of Walter and Elizabeth Russell, born June 19,
  1824, baptized July 16, 1824
Eliza Johnson, wife of C. Johnson, baptized July 21, 1824
Melinda Greenwood, baptized July 21, 1823
Lucy Johnson, a colored woman, baptized July 23, 1824
Marian Gilmor Howard, daughter of Benjamin C. and Jane Howard,
  born ---- [no date given], baptized July 23, 1824
Mary Carroll Dance, daughter of Thomas and Augusta Dance, born
  February 11, 1822, baptized September 3, 1824
---- [blank] Baltzell, baptized September 22, 1824
James Jarratt, son of ---- and Harriet Jarratt (colored), born July 26,
  1824, baptized October 26, 1824
Mary Ann Murdoch, daughter of William F. and Mary E. Murdoch born
  November 16, 1824, baptized December 1, 1824
John Thompson, son of John T. and ---- [blank], born ---- [blank],
  baptized December 24, 1824 [Ed. Note: This name could be John
  Thompson Barr, and thus a son of John T. and Jane S. Barr.]
Christopher Johnson, son of Christopher and Eliza Johnson, born
  September 27, 1822, baptized January 4, 1825
Mary Stith Johnson, daughter of Christopher and Eliza Johnson, born
  December 1, 1823, baptized January 4, 1825
Henry Clay McClellan, son of Samuel and Eliza McClellan, born ---- [no
  date given], baptized January 5, 1825
William Harmaney Boggs, son of Alexander and Susan Boggs, born
  October 3, 1824, baptized January 7, 1825
Mary Eliza Dunken, daughter of G. L. and F. Dunken, born Dec. 4,
  1823, baptized January 10, 1825, by Mr. Summerfield
Mary Butler, daughter of William and Alice M. Butler, born February
  13, 1825, baptized March 7, 1825
Gilmor Meredith, son of Jonathan and Hannah Meredith, born ---- [no
  date given], baptized April 4, 1825

FIRST PRESBYTERIAN CHURCH 133

Charles John Morris Gwynn, son of Charles and Elizabeth Gwynn, born October 21, 1822, baptized April 20, 1825
Rebecca Angelica Waters, daughter of Horace W. and Alverda Waters, born December 21, 1824, baptized April 23, 1825
Emily Oliver Colt, daughter of Roswell L. and Margaret Colt, born February 21, 1825, baptized April 26, 1825
Grace Ann Brown, daughter of George and Isabella Brown, born January 5, 1825, baptized April 30, 1825
John Haskill, an adult [no age given], baptized April 30, 1825
Susan McCullough Lyon, daughter of Robert and Mary C. Lyon, born January 9, 1823, baptized June 8, 1825
Elizabeth Russell Lyon, daughter of Robert and Mary C. Lyon, born August 9, 1824, baptized June 8, 1825
James Smith Ferguson, son of James and Catherine Ferguson, born April 12, 1825, baptized June 25, 1825
Theodore Joseph Haskill, son of John and Mary Haskill, born ---- [no date given], baptized July 16, 1825
William Benedict Brown, son of James and Louisa K. Brown, born April 23, 1825, baptized July 16, 1825
Samuel Ridout, son of John and Prudence G. Ridout, born September 15, 1824, baptized July 17, 1825
John Purviance Gill, son of William L. and Elizabeth A. Gill, born January 23, 1825, baptized September 18, 1825
Ellen Cross Edes, daughter of Benjamin and Mary Ann Edes, born August 26, 1823, baptized September 26, 1825
Richard Andrew Edes, son of Benjamin and Mary Ann Edes, born August 28, 1825, baptized September 26, 1825
Alexander Fridge Murdoch, son of William F. and Mary E. Murdoch, born September 18, 1825, baptized October 14, 1825
James Stephens, son of Alexander and Elizabeth Stephens, born July 2, 1824, baptized October 16, 1825
Lawrence Hitchcock Terrill, son of ---- Terrill, born ---- [no date given], baptized October 16, 1825
Harriet Abigail Terrill, daughter of ---- Terrill, born ---- [no date given], baptized October 16, 1825
Elliot Buckingham Terrill, son of ---- Terrill, born ---- [no date given], baptized October 16, 1825
Virginia Caroline LaFayette Terrill, daughter of ---- Terrill, born ---- [no date given], baptized October 16, 1825

Sophia McHenry Hall, daughter of Henry and Charlotte J. Hall, born August 15, 1824, baptized October 25, 1825

Sarah Jane Boggs, daughter of William and Caroline Boggs, born September 26, 1824, baptized November 12, 1825

Ann Smith, daughter of Samuel W. and Eleanor Smith, born January 14, 1825, baptized November 18, 1825

Andrew Aitken, son of Robert and ---- [blank] Aitken, born ---- [no date given], baptized November 27, 1825; "dead" [no date]

John Stricker Bradford, son of John and Ann E. Bradford, born February 19, 1820, baptized November 28, 1825

George Patterson Bradford, son of John and Ann E. Bradford, born January 12, 1822, baptized November 28, 1825

Julia Rankin Bradford, daughter of John and Ann E. Bradford, born December 20, 1823, baptized November 28, 1825

Richard Magruder Bradford, son of John and Ann E. Bradford, born November 2, 1825, baptized November 28, 1825

Margaret Louisa Hall, daughter of B. W. and Ann Hall, born October 20, 1825, baptized November 29, 1825

William Hyde de Venville Johnston, son of Christopher and Eliza Johnston, born Feb. 13, 1825, baptized Dec. 1, 1825; "dead"

John O'Donnell, son of John and Mary O'Donnell, born September 5, 1825, baptized December 3, 1825

Eleanor Swan, daughter of James and Elizabeth Swan, born ---- [no date given], baptized January 16, 1826

John Craig Stapler, son of John and Margaret Stapler, born December 3, 1825, baptized January 28, 1826 (twin)

William Taylor Stapler, son of John and Margaret Stapler, born December 3, 1825, baptized January 28, 1826 (twin)

Mary Robinson, an adult [no date given], baptized February 4, 1826

Elizabeth Wallington Morrison, daughter of George and Elizabeth Morrison, born ----, bapt. February 4, 1826; "dead" [no date]

Jane Young Kelso, daughter of George Y. and Ellen Kelso, born May 6, 1825, baptized February 6, 1826

Henrietta Veron Bird, daughter of Henry and Eleanor Bird, born April 1, 1825, baptized February 23, 1826

Mary Tyson Gibson, daughter of George S. and Maria Gibson, born January 3, 1826, baptized May 3, 1826; "dead" [no date]

William Hamelton, son of William and Mary Hamelton, born ---- [no date given], baptized May 6, 1826

John Lambie, son of James and Mary Lambie, born December 28, 1825, baptized June 14, 1826; "dead" [no date given]
Abraham Dubois Edgerton, son of Charles and Jane Edgerton, born June 23, 1821, baptized June 14, 1826
Mary Susan Edgerton, daughter of Charles and Jane Edgerton, born May 16, 1826, baptized June 14, 1826
John Archibald Stewart, son of James and Ellen Stewart, born May 28, 1826, baptized June 19, 1826; "dead" [no date]
Julianna Walker, daughter of James and Harriet Walker (colored), born May 13, 1826, baptized July 10, 1826
Morgan Gibbes Colt, son of Roswell L. and Margaret Colt, born March 10, 1826, baptized August 5, 1826 [Ed. Note: Although the record gave his name as Proswell, it was actually Roswell.]
Robert Oliver Gibbes, son of Robert M. and Emily Gibbes, born July 19, 1826, baptized August 5, 1826
William Russell Nevins, son of William and Mary D. Nevins, born April 24, 1826, baptized October 15, 1826, by the Rev. Dr. Miller, of Princeton.
Mary Gausson Coward, daughter of Thomas and Margaret Coward, born May 22, 1823, baptized November 6, 1826
Thomas Richard Coward, son of Thomas and Margaret Coward, born November 1, 1824, baptized November 6, 1826
Sarah Jane Coward, daughter of Thomas and Margaret Coward, born August 16, 1826, baptized November 6, 1826
Rebecca Rich Kelso, daughter of George Y. and Ellen Kelso, born July 14, 1826, baptized November 14, 1826
Mary Murdoch, daughter of William F. and Mary E. Murdoch, born ---- [no date given], baptized January 30, 1827
James Stephen Barkley, son of John M. and Mary Barkley, born April 29, 1826, baptized February 1, 1827
James Perry Walker, a colored adult, baptized February 3, 1827
Elliot Johnson, son of Thomas D. and A. M. Elizabeth Johnson, born May 2, 1826, baptized February 14, 1827
Benjamin Wood Foster, son of B. W. and Hannah Foster, born July 16, 1810, baptized February 27, 1827
Hannah Maria Foster, daughter of B. W. and Hannah Foster, born April 20, 1813, baptized February 27, 1827
David Wood Foster, son of B. W. and Hannah Foster, born March 13, 1816, baptized February 27, 1827

Ann Swift Foster, daughter of B. W. and Hannah Foster, born June 25, 1819, baptized February 27, 1827
Elizabeth Allen Foster, daughter of B. W. and Hannah Foster, born May 11, 1825, baptized February 27, 1827
Henry Bird [no date of birth given], baptized May 5, 1827
John H. Haskill [no date of birth given], baptized May 5, 1827
Sarah Y. Edes [no date of birth given], baptized May 5, 1827
Mary Ann Levering [no date of birth given], baptized May 5, 1827
Eliza B. Levering [no date of birth given], baptized May 5, 1827
Caroline Mitilda Bird, daughter of Henry and Eleanor Bird, born ---- [no date given], baptized May 5, 1827
Agnes Gibson, daughter of William and Mary Gibson, born February 16, 1820, baptized May 5, 1827
Mary Gibson, daughter of William and Mary Gibson, born February 21, 1822, baptized May 5, 1827
William Francis Gibson, son of William and Mary Gibson, born March 28, 1825, baptized May 5, 1827
Laura Ann Schley, daughter of Jacob and Anna B. Schley, born June 12, 1824, baptized May 5, 1827
Bazel Barker, son of Adam and Eliza Barker (colored), born ---- [no date given], baptized May 5, 1827
Maxwell McDowell Boggs, son of Alexander L. and Susan Boggs, born November 13, 1826, baptized June 6, 1827
Amanda Virginia Delacour, daughter of David and Eliza Delacour, born July 21, 1825, baptized June 7, 1827
Eliza Stary Harris [no date of birth given], baptized July 28, 1827
Eliza Wilson [no date of birth given], baptized July 28, 1827
John Americus Scarborough [no date of birth], bapt. July 28, 1827
Nesbit Hawthorn Gill, son of William L. and Elizabeth Gill, born ---- [no date given], baptized July 28, 1827
Alexander Boggs, son of William and Caroline Boggs, born ---- [no date given], baptized July 28, 1827
Ann Williams Howard, daughter of Benjamin C. and Jane Howard, born ---- [no date given], baptized September 19, 1827
Jane Gilmor Howard, daughter of Benjamin C. and Jane Howard, born ---- [no date given], baptized September 19, 1827
John Ridout, son of John and Prudence G. Ridout, born July 15, 1827, baptized October 10, 1827
Emily Monroe Butler, daughter of William and Alice M. Butler, born July 18, 1827, baptized October 12, 1827

FIRST PRESBYTERIAN CHURCH 137

Charles Henry Conway, son of Solomon R. and Ann B. Conway, born July 3, 1827, baptized November 3, 1827
Maria Ann Semon, daughter of David and Harriet Semon, born July 10, 1827, baptized November 4, 1827
William Turnbull Murdock, son of Alexander and Susan Murdock, born August 13, 1827, baptized November 7, 1827
Catherine Petticore [no age given], baptized November 10, 1827
George Gibson, son of George S. and Maria Gibson, born May 27, 1827, baptized November 20, 1827
Eudocia Gelston Hills, daughter of Samuel and Eudocia Hills, born December 8, 1826, baptized December 26, 1827
Mrs. Elizabeth Boyd, wife of Jeremiah Boyd, baptized Feb. 2, 1828
William Nevins Bird, son of Henry and Eleanor Bird, born ---- [no date given], baptized February 3, 1828
Fanny Dunbar, daughter of George T. and Frances Dunbar, born ---- [no date given], baptized February 15, 1828,
James Stewart, son of James and Ellen Stewart, born November 10, 1827, baptized February 19, 1828
James Boyd, son of Jeremiah and Elizabeth Boyd, born March 29, 1821, baptized March 25, 1828
Alexander Hamilton Boyd, son of Jeremiah and Elizabeth Boyd, born April 30, 1823, baptized March 25, 1828
Isabella Boyd, daughter of Jeremiah and Elizabeth Boyd, born April 3, 1825, baptized March 25, 1828
George Washington Boyd, son of Jeremiah and Elizabeth Boyd, born February 22, 1827, baptized March 25, 1828
William Taylor Moale, son of John C. and Julia A. Moale, born September 12, 1827, baptized April 16, 1828
Alice Murdoch, daughter of William F. and Mary E. Murdoch, born March 22, 1828, baptized April 19, 1828
William Howard Neff, son of Peter and Isabella L. Neff, born March 29, 1828, baptized April 22, 1828
Isabella Brown, daughter of George and Isabella Brown, born October 11, 1827, baptized April 22, 1828
---- [blank] Small, baptized May 3, 1828
---- [blank] Moody, baptized May 3, 1828
---- [blank] Spriggs, baptized May 3, 1828
Alexander Oscar Ferguson, son of John and Elizabeth Ferguson, born March 12, 1827, baptized July 12, 1828

Joseph Hopkinson Smith, son of Francis H. and Susan T. Smith, born August 24, 1826, baptized July 17, 1828

James William Geddes, son of James and Sarah Geddes, born June 10, 1824, baptized July 26, 1828

Ann Eliza Geddes, daughter of James and Sarah Geddes, born April 1, 1826, baptized July 26, 1828

Margaret Ann Geddes, daughter of James and Sarah Geddes, born February 6, 1828, baptized July 26, 1828

Ellen Weld Riddle, daughter of John and Mary Ann Riddle, born March 20, 1825, baptized July 28, 1828

Elizabeth Amelia Riddle, daughter of John and Mary Ann Riddle, born January 21, 1827, baptized July 28, 1828

Jane Margaret Carr, baptized October 31, 1828

Deveraux Colt, son of Roswell L. and Margaret Colt, born ---- [no date given], baptized November 26, 1828

Thomas Oliver Colt, son of Roswell L. and Margaret Colt, born January 28, 1829, baptized February 19, 1829

William Gilmor Howard, son of B. C. and J. G. Howard, born February 20, 1829, baptized March 15, 1829

Mary Stoughton Winder, daughter of W. S. and Araminta R. Winder, born May 3, 1826, baptized April 8, 1829

Charlotte Evans [no age given], baptized May 1, 1829

Anna Key Nevins, daughter of William and M. U. Nevins, born Sept. 29, 1828, bapt. May 2, 1829, by Rev. J. Breckinridge

Susan Greer Boggs, daughter of Alexander L. and Susan Boggs, born January 26, 1829, baptized May 7, 1829

William Jefferies Boggs, son of William and Caroline Boggs, born October 14, 1828, baptized May 7, 1829

Sarah Chew Finley, daughter of Eben L. and Eliza W. Finley, born May 5, 1829, baptized May 31, 1829

Thomas Fridge Murdock, son of Alexander and Susan Murdock, born May 9, 1829, baptized July 5, 1829

Francis Hopkinson Smith, son of F. H. and Susan T. Smith, born August 21, 1828, baptized July 26, 1829

Lydia Hall, daughter of B. W. and Ann Hall, born June 11, 1829, baptized August 30, 1829

John Rodolph Neff, son of Peter and Isabella L. Neff, born August 25, 1829, baptized September 1, 1829

Ann Maria Draper, daughter of Garretson and Charlotte Draper, born August 21, 1829, baptized September 28, 1829

FIRST PRESBYTERIAN CHURCH 139

James Eddy, son of James and Letitia Eddy, born September 4, 1829, baptized October 9, 1829

John Cole Murdoch, son of William F. and Mary E. Murdoch, born October 22, 1829, baptized December 6, 1829

Richard Henry Moale, son of John C. and Julia A. Moale, born December 3, 1829, baptized December 29, 1829

Charles Huffman Armour, son of John and Mary Armour, born August 7, 1827, baptized January 1, 1830

Alexander Martin Morrison, son of George and Elizabeth Morrison, born May 10, 1829, baptized January 7, 1830

George Read Hollins Walker, son of James and Harriet Walker, born September 23, 1829, baptized February 6, 1830

Mary Stephens, daughter of Alexander and Elizabeth Stephens, born July 12, 1826, baptized March 23, 1830

Rebecca Baptist Stephens, daughter of Alexander and Elizabeth Stephens, born February 10, 1828, baptized March 23, 1830

Lucinda Baptist Stephens, daughter of Alexander and Elizabeth Stephens, born November 6, 1829, baptized March 23, 1830

Amelia Frasier Finley, daughter of Thomas and Ann P. Finley, born September 6, 1824, baptized March 24, 1830

Robert Smith Finley, son of Thomas and Ann P. Finley, born August 9, 1826, baptized March 24, 1830

William Reynolds Finley, son of Thomas and Ann P. Finley, born July 10, 1828, baptized March 24, 1830

Elizabeth Margaret Didier Finley, daughter of Thomas and Ann P. Finley, born February 21, 1830, baptized March 24, 1830

James Moir Stewart, son of John and Elizabeth Stewart, born September 16, 1829, baptized April 6, 1830

Ann Eliza Hall, daughter of Henry and Charlotte S. Hall, born October 28, 1828, baptized April 10, 1830

Frances Ann Conway, daughter of Solomon R. and Ann B. Conway, born November 1, 1829, baptized April 10, 1830

Christiana Everitt, daughter of G. W. and ---- [blank] Everitt, born ---- [no date], baptized April 22, 1830; "dead" [no date]

Mary Ann Talbot [no age given], baptized April 30, 1830

Sarah Jane Geddes, daughter of James and Sarah Geddes, born ---- [no date], baptized May 9, 1830

Elizabeth Jane Spence, daughter of John and Tracy Spence, born ---- [no date], baptized May 9, 1830

Mary Catharine Spence, daughter of John and Tracy Spence, born ---- [no date], baptized May 9, 1830

Robert Nelson Stewart, son of James and Ellen Stewart, born February 26, 1829, baptized May 14, 1830

Margaret Oliver Colt, daughter of R. L. and Margaret Colt, born April 25, 1830, baptized May 23, 1830

Henry Arthur Bird, son of Henry and Eleanor Bird, born ---- [no date], baptized August 7, 1830

Albert Boyd, son of Jerermiah and Elizabeth Bird, born ---- [no date], baptized August 7, 1830

Mary Cecilia Sands, daughter of John and Bethiah Sands, born October 28, 1828, baptized August 11, 1830

Ellen Sands, daughter of John and Bethiah Sands, born October 28, 1828, baptized August 11, 1830

Samuel Ruark, son of ---- [blank] and Mary Ruark, born December 25, 1818, baptized September 14, 1830

Robert Henry Maxwell Carroll, son of Henry and Mary B. Carroll, born December 20, 1823, baptized September 29, 1830

Samuel Sterrett Carroll, son of Henry and Mary B. Carroll, born December 15, 1825, baptized September 29, 1830

Elizabeth Maxwell Carroll, daughter of Henry and Mary B. Carroll, born August 19, 1827, baptized September 29, 1830

Elizabeth Colhoon, daughter of Benjamin C. and Lilly K. Colhoon, born ---- [blank], baptized October 13, 1830

Phebe Downing Clarke, baptized October 22, 1830

Juliana McHenry Howard, daughter of Benjamin C. and Jane Howard, born ---- [blank], baptized October 23, 1830

John Litzinger, son of John and Elizabeth Litzinger, born November 10, 1820, baptized October 23, 1830

John Henry Osborn, son of John and Sarah Osborn, born January 20, 1830, baptized October 23, 1830

Legh [sic] Richmond Smith, son of Francis H. and Susan T. Smith, born ---- [blank], baptized December 3, 1830

Henry Kellogg, son of Orson and Eleanor Ann Kellogg, born ---- [blank], baptized December 26, 1830

Sarah Ann Shaw, daughter of Thomas and Esther Shaw, born ---- [blank], baptized February 20, 1831

Mary Catharine Knight, daughter of Michael and Mary Knight, born August 22, 1830, baptized March 22, 1831

FIRST PRESBYTERIAN CHURCH 141

Joseph Dunbar, son of George L. and Frances Dunbar, born ----
[blank], baptized March 22, 1831

Julia Isaetta Coles, daughter of Isaac A. and Juliana Coles, born
January 13, 1831, baptized April 3, 1831

Ann Maria Hall, daughter of B. W. and Ann Hall, born February 21,
1831, baptized April 3, 1831

John Boggs, son of William and Caroline Boggs, born November 23,
1830, baptized April 23, 1931

Elizabeth Ann Knight, daughter of Michael and Mary Knight, born
October 3, 1827, baptized April 23, 1831

Isabella Robinson Small, daughter of William F. and Agnes E. Small,
born September 26, 1830, baptized April 23, 1831

Sydenham Rush Clarke, son of Susannah [sic] and Phebe D. Clarke,
born May 1, 1824, baptized May 3, 1831*

Ann Eliza Downing, daughter of Susannah [sic] and Phebe D. Clarke,
born February 20, 1830, baptized May 3, 1831. [*Ed. Note:
"Susannah" apparently was transcribed in error by the clerk. An
entry in 1830 shows the communion of Phebe D. Clarke and
another in 1831 shows the communion of "Mr. Shammah Clarke"
who are most likely the "Susannah and Phebe D. Clarke" referred to
above.]

Jane Brown, an adult [no age given], baptized May 4, 1831

James Calhoun Buchanan, son of W. B. and Ellen B. Buchanan, born
May 12, 1831, baptized June 18, 1831

Anna Mary Lyon [no age given], baptized July 16, 1831

Hannah Jamieson [no age given], baptized July 16, 1831

Esther Ann Barney [no age given], baptized July 16, 1831

Louisa Emily Nevins, daughter of William and Mary L. Nevins, born
January 27, 1831, baptized July 16, 1831, by Rev. Mr. Post

John Amos Worley, son of John and Sarah M. Worley, born October
31, 1829, baptized July 16, 1831

Ellen Craig Colt, daughter of R. L. and Margaret Colt, born July 22,
1831, baptized August 5, 1831

James Wilson, son of James and Catharine Wilson, born May 23, 1818,
baptized August 14, 1831

Ann Eliza Wilson, daughter of James and Catharine Wilson, born
January 3, 1821, baptized August 14, 1831

John Wilson, son of James and Catharine Wilson, born May 17, 1823,
baptized August 14, 1831

Thomas Wilson, son of James and Catharine Wilson, born September 7, 1827, baptized August 14, 1831

George Morrison, son of George and Elizabeth Morrison, born January 31, 1831, baptized August 22, 1831

Thomas Dance, son of Thomas and Augusta T. Dance, born February 12, 1826, baptized October 21, 1831

William Barker, son of Adam and Eliza Barker (colored), born ---- [blank], baptized October 21, 1831

John Kelso, son of George Y. and Ellen Kelso, born April 3, 1831, baptized December 2, 1831

William Morris Murdoch, son of W. F. and Mary E. Murdoch, born June 30, 1831, baptized January 19, 1832

Charles Nisbet Murdock, son of Alexander and Susan Murdock, born July 23, 1831, baptized January 23, 1832

Margaretta Hutton Brown, daughter of Harman and Margaretta Brown, born November 6, 1831, baptized February 4, 1832

Jane Boggs, daughter of Alexander L. and Susan Boggs, born June 17, 1831, baptized March 6, 1832

Harriet Robinson, daughter of James S. and Mary Robinson, born October 6, 1827, baptized March 20, 1832

Laura Robinson, daughter of James S. and Mary Robinson, born February 22, 1832, baptized March 20, 1832

Archibald Stirling, son of Archibald and Elizabeth Ann Stirling, born ---- [blank], baptized May 12, 1832

Benjamin Chambers Colhoon, son of Benjamin C. and Lilly K. Colhoon, born May 7, 1820 [sic], baptized May 17, 1832

Henry Hill Carroll, son of Henry and Mary B. Carroll, born December 7, 1830, baptized June 2, 1832

Mary Bordien Carroll, daughter of Henry and Mary B. Carroll, born January 30, 1832, baptized June 2, 1832

George Robb Ferguson, son of James and Catharine Ferguson, born March 11, 1832, baptized July 10, 1832

Alexander William Stephens, son of Alex and Elizabeth Stephens, born October 2, 1831, baptized August 3, 1832

Charlotte Ann Draper, daughter of Garretson and Charlotte Draper, born March 1, 1832, baptized September 12, 1832

John Riddle, son of John and Mary Ann Riddle, born November 21, 1832, baptized November 23, 1832

Sarah Carter [no age given], baptized December 5, 1832

Maria Mathers [no age given], baptized December 5, 1832

FIRST PRESBYTERIAN CHURCH 143

George Whitmarsh [no age given], baptized December 8, 1832
Mary Whitmarsh [no age given], baptized December 8, 1832
James Shaw, son of Thomas and Esther Shaw, born September 29, 1832, baptized December 8, 1832
Martha Richards, daughter of ---- [blank] and Margaret Richards, born November 5, 1820, baptized December 8, 1832
Pierce Ann Richards, daughter of ---- [blank] and Margaret Richards, born October 28, 1822, baptized December 8, 1832
William Penn Richards, son of ---- [blank] and Margaret Richards, born September 23, 1824, baptized December 8, 1832
Elias Zachariah Richards, son of ---- [blank] & Margaret Richards, born December 16, 1826, baptized December 8, 1832
Mary Richards, daughter of ---- [blank] and Margaret Richards, born July 28, 1830, baptized December 8, 1832
Samuel Smith Carr, son of Dabney S. and Sydney S. Carr, born August 10, 1831, baptized December 13, 1832
Mary Jane Hollins, daughter of James P. and Margaret Wilson, born August 21, 1832, baptized December 13, 1832
Charles Osborn, son of John and Sarah Osborn, born May 4, 1832, baptized December 20, 1832
Elizabeth Johnson Brown, daughter of George and Isabella Brown, born August 24, 1832, baptized January 1, 1833
Alexander Geddes, son of James and Sarah Geddes, born April 22, 1832, baptized January 23, 1833
Marshall Pike Smith, son of Francis H. and Susan T. Smith, born December 23, 1832, baptized January 31, 1833
George Trull Coulter, son of Alexander and Eliza Coulter, born November 21, 1831, baptized February 5, 1833
Anna Catharine Stricker Bradford, daughter of John and Ann E. Bradford, born March 22, 1831, baptized February 11, 1833
John Stricker Coles, son of Isaac A. and Juliana Coles, born February 8, 1832, baptized February 11, 1833
Elizabeth Turner, daughter of Asa and Martha Turner, born January 5, 1833, baptized April 15, 1833
Sarah Rogers Winder, daughter of W. S. and Araminta R. Winder, born September 23, 1832, baptized April 28, 1833
William Carvel Hall, son of B. W. and Ann Hall, born May 10, 1833, baptized May 13, 1833
William Henry Spence, son of John and Tracy Spence, born ---- [blank], baptized June 8, 1833

William Carmichael Nicholson, son of Joseph J. and Laura C.
Nicholson, born August 13, 1832, baptized June 14, 1833
Mary Armistead Moale, daughter of John C. and Juliet A. Moale, born
April 30, 1832, baptized June 27, 1833
Ann Maria Worley, daughter of John and Sarah M. Worley, born
January 23, 1832, baptized July 6, 1833
Peter Carr Buchanan, son of W. B. and Ellen B. Buchanan, born April
12, 1833, baptized July 16, 1833
Virginia Cary, daughter of Wilson M. and Jane M. Cary, born May 13,
1833, baptized July 16, 1833
Mary Louisa Coakley, daughter of P. H. and Sarah Coakley, born
March 11, 1833, baptized July 18, 1833
Elizabeth Mooney, daughter of Daniel and Sarah Mooney, born July 7,
1832, baptized August 7, 1833
Alexander Fridge Murdoch, son of Alexander and Susan Murdoch, born
July 3, 1833, baptized October 13, 1833
Mary Richard Kellogg, daughter of Orson and Eleanor Ann Kellogg,
born July 31, 1832, baptized October 28, 1833
William Wirt Goldsborough, son of Louis M. and Elizabeth G.
Goldsborough, born June 7, 1833, baptized November 10, 1833
William John Francis, son of Robert and Jane Francis, born August 8,
1833, baptized November 14, 1833
Mary Ann Gore, daughter of William and Sarah Gore, born September
30, 1833, baptized November 14, 1833
Henry Alexander Elliot, son of John and Catharine Elliot, born May 1,
1831, baptized November 21, 1833
Eliza Ann Stewart Leslie, daughter of Robert and Ann Leslie, born ---
[no date given], baptized November 23, 1833
William Wirt Robinson, son of Alexander C. and Rosa E. Robinson,
born August 2, 1833, baptized November 25, 1833
Marion Murdoch, daughter of W. F. and Mary E. Murdoch, born July 8,
1832, baptized January 5, 1834
Helen Murdoch, daughter of W. F. and Mary E. Murdoch, born
December 12, 1833, baptized January 5, 1834
Eliza Ann Geddes, daughter of James and Sarah Geddes, born
September 17, 1833, baptized January 16, 1834
Deborah Hopkins Parsons [no age given], baptized March 8, 1834
Isabella Courtenay, daughter of David T. and Elizabeth D. Courtenay,
born April 15, 1832, baptized March 8, 1834

Thomas Henry Austin Hardester, son of Jacob and Mary Ann
Hardester, born December 10, 1826, baptized March 8, 1834
Sarah Jane Carroll Hardester, daughter of Jacob and Mary Ann
Hardester, born January 27, 1830, baptized March 8, 1834
Grafton Hayne Wilcox, son of James and Ann B. Wilcox, born April 30,
1827, baptized March 8, 1834
Wesley Banningson Wilcox, son of James and Ann B. Wilcox, born
December 25, 1829, baptized March 8, 1834
Ellen Rich Kelso, daughter of George L. and Ellen Kelso, born
February 6, 1833, baptized March 18, 1834
Helen Tiernan Nicholson, daughter of Joseph J. and Laura C.
Nicholson, born August 15, 1834, baptized September 9, 1834
Ellen Howard, daughter of Benjamin C. and Jane G. Howard, born ----
[blank], baptized September 13, 1834
Margaret Yates Stirling, daughter of Archibald and Elizabeth Ann
Stirling, born ---- [blank], baptized September 13, 1834
Mary Jane Bell, daughter of George and Mary Bell, born May 22, 1834,
baptized November 3, 1834
John Owen, son of John and ---- [blank] Owen, born ---- [blank],
baptized December 13, 1834
Christopher James Francis, son of ---- [blank], born January 11, 1835,
baptized February 28, 1835
Athelander Fosson Coakley, child of ---- [blank], born January 18, 1835,
baptized February 28, 1835, by the Rev. Mr. Owens
Julia Catharine Colt, daughter of R. L. and ---- [blank] Colt, born May
22, 1835, baptized May --, 1835
William White Ramsey Hall, son of H. Y. and Churl [sic] J. Hall, born
June 15, 1835, baptized June 30, 1835, by Rev. Mr. Owens
Ann Eliza Knight, daughter of ---- [blank], born February 23, 1834,
baptized July 22, 1835
Sarah Ann T. Seward, daughter of ---- [blank], born September 18,
1834, baptized July 31, 1835
Susan Murdoch, daughter of W. F. and Mary Murdoch, born June 22,
1835, baptized July 31, 1835

RECORD OF PERSONS BAPTIZED BY JOHN C. BACKUS, PASTOR OF THE FIRST PRESBYTERIAN CHURCH IN BALTIMORE CITY, BEGINNING IN 1836 [TO 1840]

John Murdoch, son of Alexander and Susan Murdoch, born March 23, 1836, baptized ---- [no date], 1836

Rebecca Campbell Murdoch, daughter of Thomas and Mary Murdoch, born October 25, 1835, baptized ---- [no date], 1836

Laura Wirt Robinson, daughter of Alexander and Rosa Robinson, born May 31, 1835, baptized ---- [no date], 1836

Thomas Barklie Coulter, son of Alexander and Eliza Coulter, born October --, 1833, baptized ---- [no date], 1836

Mifflin Coulter, son of Alexander and Eliza Coulter, born March 30, 1836, baptized ---- [no date], 1836

David Courtnay, son of David S. and Elizabeth D. Courtnay, born November 30, 1833, baptized October --, 1836

Henry Courtnay, son of David S. and Elizabeth D. Courtnay, born August 22, 1835, baptized October --, 1836

Mary Catharine Rodgers, adopted daughter of Catharine Latimer, born December 15, 1829, baptized October --, 1836

Emily Louisa Moale, daughter of John C. and Juliet Ann Moale, aged 2 years, baptized December --, 1836

Ellen Geddes, daughter of ---- [blank] and Sarah Geddes, born April 23, 1836, baptized December --, 1836

James Towson Coakley, son of P. P. and S. Coakley, born April 11, 1837 [sic], baptized January --, 1837

---- [blank] Stirling, son of Archibald and Elizabeth Stirling, born ---- [blank], baptized April --, 1837

---- [blank] Francis, son of Robert Francis [sic], born ---- [blank], baptized April --, 1837

Annie Murdoch, daughter of William and Mary Murdoch, born ---- [blank], baptized October --, 1837

Thomas Shirley Turner, son of William F. and Jane Turner, born August 4, 1837, baptized November 26[?], 1837

Ann Cleves Pleasants, daughter of W. A. and Elizabeth Pleasants, born December 3, 1836, baptized November 7, 1837

Lucy Grey Owen, daughter of ---- [George] and Mary Owen, born January 5, 1831, baptized November --, 1837

Henry Duning Owen, son of George and Mary Owen, born October 19, 1833, baptized November --, 1837

---- [blank] Robinson, child of Alexander and Rosa Robinson, born ---- [blank], baptized November --, 1837

George Henry Rodgers, son of John and Agnes Rodgers, born March 3, 1828, baptized December --, 1837

FIRST PRESBYTERIAN CHURCH

Martha Ann Rodgers, daughter of John and Agnes Rodgers, born May 8, 1830, baptized December --, 1837

---- [blank] Courtnay, child of David and Elizabeth Courtnay, born ---- [blank], baptized December --, 1837

Ann Fridge Murdoch, daughter of William F. and Mary Murdoch, born June 2, 1837, baptized December --, 1837

Catherine Garland, daughter of James and Sarah Garland, born August 6, 1830, baptized December --, 1837*

James Garland, son of James and Sarah Garland, born April 4, 1834, baptized December --, 1837*

Eliza Jane Garland, daughter of James and Sarah Garland, born March 29, 1837, baptized December --, 1837*

[*Ed. Note: The baptism of the above Garland children could have been in January, 1838, since the record is not clearly written. However, they were subsequently recorded as baptized in 1839.]

William Sterret Carroll, son of Henry and Mary B. Carroll, born November 5, 1837, baptized February --, 1838

Antoinette Harris, "adult S," baptized March --, 1838

Rachel Muncaster, "adult M," baptized March --, 1838

Mrs. ---- Clara, "adult W," baptized June --, 1838

Archibald Coulter, son of Alexander and Eliza Coulter, born October 3, 1837, baptized June 18, 1838

William Wirt Clarke, son of Susannah [sic] and ---- [blank] Clarke, born June 28, 1833, baptized June 18, 1838*

Charles Chauncey Clarke, son of Susannah and ---- [blank] Clarke, September 17, 1836, baptized June 18, 1838*

[*Ed. Note: Probably the children of Shammah and Phebe D. Clarke.]

Caroline Rebecca Clarke, daughter of A. and ---- [blank] Clarke, born November 17, 1835, baptized June 18, 1838

Mary Nisbet Murdock, daughter of Alexander and Susan Murdock, born ---- [blank], 1838, baptized July 1, 1838

Frederick Wilson Hollins, son of George and Maria Hollins, born June 22, 1838, baptized October 7, 1838

Margaret Murdoch, daughter of William and Mary Murdoch, born April 2, 1838, baptized ---- [blank], 1838

Francis Nicholson, son of Joseph and Laura Nicholson, born ---- [blank], baptized ---- [blank], 1838

William Gilmor Howard, son of Benjamin C. and Jane Howard, born ---- [blank], baptized ---- [blank], 1838

Lydia H. Winder, daughter of Sidney and Arminta Winder, born March 18, 1838, baptized ---- [blank], 1838
Harriet Muncaster, daughter of ---- [blank] Muncaster, born ---- [blank], baptized ---- [blank], 1838
Sarah Smith, adult, baptized ---- [blank], 1838
Mary Allen Haskell, daughter of John and Minerva Haskell, born July 2, 1838, baptized January 5, 1839
David Stewart, son of David and ---- [blank] Stewart, born ---- [blank], baptized February 28, 1839
Cary Ann Carr, daughter of Dabney and Sidney Carr, born October 31, 1833, baptized May --, 1839
John Smith, son of ---- [blank] Smith, born December 6, 1836, baptized ---- [blank], 1839
Hetty C. Cary, daughter of Wilson and Jane M. Cary, born May 15, 1835, baptized ---- [blank], 1839
Wilson Cary, son of Wilson and Jane M. Cary, born December 11, 1839 [sic], baptized ---- [blank], 1839
---- [blank] Coakley, son of ---- [blank] Coakley, born ---- [blank], baptized September --, 1839
William Tell Adreon, son of William T. and Susanne Adreon, born June 11, 1832, baptized October --, 1839*
Henry Clay Adreon, son of William T. and Susanne Adreon, born April 15, 1839, baptized October --, 1839. [*Ed. Note: The name of the parents of the above two Adreon boys was subsequently entered in register in a different handwriting.]
Mary Catherine Powell, daughter of Charles and ---- [blank] Powell, born November 27, 1838, baptized ---- [blank], 1839*
Catherine G. Garland, daughter of James and Sarah Garland, born August 6, 1830, baptized ---- [blank], 1839*
James Garland, son of James and Sarah Garland, born April 4, 1834, baptized ---- [blank], 1839*
Eliza Jane Garland, daughter of James and Sarah Garland, born March 29, 1837, baptized ---- [blank], 1839. [Ed. Note: The above Garland children were recorded earlier in the register as having been baptized in December, 1837, or Jan., 1838?]
Lucy Gray Owen, daughter of Capt. ---- [blank] Owen, born January 15, 1831, baptized ---- [blank], 1839
Henry Dunning Owen, son of Capt. ---- [blank] Owen, born October 19, 1833, baptized ---- [blank], 1839

Grame Turnbull, son of Henry C. and Ann Turnbull, born March 14, 1839, baptized ---- [blank], 1839

Edward Courtnay, son of David S. and Elizabeth Courtnay, born March 23, 1839, baptized ---- [blank], 1839

Eleanor Fulford Torrance, daughter of George and Eleanor Torrance, born May 18, 1839, baptized ---- [blank], 1839

Russel Murdoch, son of William and Mary Murdoch, born February 12, 1839, baptized ---- [blank], 1839

Lydia Calhoun Turner, daughter of W. F. and Jane Turner, born July 22, 1839, baptized ---- [blank], 1839

Edward Ingle Hyde, son of Moses and Anna Maria Hyde, born July 10, 1839, baptized ---- [blank], 1839

Caroline Augusta Davis, daughter of Robert and Caroline Davis, born November 25, 1833, baptized ---- [blank], 1840

Eliza Jane Davis, daughter of Robert and Caroline Davis, born November 15, 1835, baptized ---- [blank], 1840

Margaret Matilda Davis, daughter of Robert and Caroline Davis, born May 9, 1838, baptized ---- [blank], 1840

Mary Davis, daughter of Robert and Caroline Davis, born September 5, 1840, baptized ---- [blank], 1840, and written in the left margin: "Died December 31, 1845."

Elizabeth Turnbull, daughter of Henry C. and Ann G. Turnbull, born April 30, 1840, baptized ---- [blank], 1840, and written in the left margin: "Died [22?] June 1843."

James Campbell Murdoch, son of Thomas and Mary C. Murdoch, born May 14, 1840, baptized ---- [blank], 1840

Josephine Armor, daughter of James G. and Rachel Armor, born August 30, 1840, baptized ---- [blank], 1840

Louisa Cole Murdoch, daughter of William F. and Mary Murdoch, born May 28, 1840, baptized ---- [blank], 1840

LIST OF PERSONS WHO WERE BORN PRIOR TO 1840 AND BAPTIZED AFTER 1840
[Names gleaned from the First Presbyterian Church baptism records.]

John B. Lynch, son of ---- [blank] and Jane Lynch, born December 26, 1836

James Lynch, son of ---- [blank] and Jane Lynch, born Jan. 9, 1839

Sophia Finley Gibson, daughter of Patrick and Anna Gibson, born March 8, 1835

Mary Elizabeth Gibson, daughter of Patrick and Anna Gibson, born January 13, 1837

George Sanderson Gibson, son of Patrick and Anna Gibson, born September 13, 1839

William Henry Lovejoy, son of Amos and ---- Lovejoy, born October 7, 1836

Ann Isabella Lovejoy, daughter of Amos and ---- Lovejoy, born January 29, 1838

Rosabella Sutton Lovejoy, daughter of Amos and ---- Lovejoy, born September 3, 1839

Ellen Harvey Harvey [sic], daughter of Henry D. and Harriet Harvey, born October --, 1840

Margaret Seth, colored child belonging to Mr. Jacobs, born May 1, 1837

Henry Holt, son of Daniel and Ann E. Holt, born January 3, 1840

RECORD OF BURIALS ATTENDED BY WILLIAM NEVINS, PASTOR OF THE FIRST <u>PRESBYTERIAN CONGREGATION, BALTIMORE, SINCE HIS ACCESSION IN 1820</u>

<u>1820 BURIALS:</u>
Aug 24 - A child of Mr. Rusk
Sep 2 - Robert Bigland
Oct 5 - Mr. Biass
Oct 12 - A child of Mr. Ross
Nov 7 - Mr. Maxwell
Nov 16 - Asa Dykes
Nov 17 - Mrs. Catherine Isabella Buchanan
Dec 10 - Mrs. John Caldwell
Dec 19 - Capt. Matthias Rich

<u>1821 BURIALS:</u>
Jan 20 - Gen. Joseph Sterrett, aged 48
Jan 22 - Ann Hyde, aged 18
Feb 12 - A child of Mr. Thomas, aged 1
Feb 27 - William Bowden, Esq., of Petersburg, Virginia
Mar 3 - Francis Purviance, aged 82

FIRST PRESBYTERIAN CHURCH 151

Jun 3 - Mrs. Anderson
Jun 22 - Oliver H. Neilson, age 27
Jul 2 - Robert Watson, age 37
Aug 1 - A child of Thomas Mills, aged 1 1/2
Aug 1 - Mrs. Cochran
[n.d.] - Gen. John Swan and Mrs. Vonkapff - died in my absence
Sep 17 - Eli Munn, aged 30
Sep 24 - Thomas H. Conkling, aged 29
Sep 25 - Mrs. Thomas
Oct 18 - A child of Alexander Boyd, aged 3
Nov 20 - A child of Robert Thomas (coloured)
Nov 22 - A daughter of Thomas Dinsmore, aged 12
Dec 21 - Robert Gilmore Howard, aged 7 months

1822 BURIALS:
Jan 15 - Robert Gilmor, Sr., aged 74
Feb 24 - A child of Andrew Clopper, aged 1
Apr 13 - John Scobey
[n.d.] - Mrs. Dysart died in my absence
May 20 - William Brown died in my absence, aged 23
May 27 - Mrs. Dumest, aged 61
Jun 13 - A child of Mr. Kendall, aged 1
Jun 30 - Mr. Costin
Jul 24 - Mrs. Cashan, aged 57
Jul 24 - Mr. Charles Torrance, aged 77
Jul 24 - Mrs. Edward Clopper - died at Cape May
Jul 26 - Mr. William Turnbull, aged 72
Aug 14 - Miss Burnside of Mr. Duncan's congregation
Aug 23 - A child of Mr. Bromwell, aged 3 months
Aug 24 - A child of Mr. Thorndick Chase, Dr. Glendy's congregation
Aug 25 - Dr. George Brown, aged 68
Sep 8 - Mr. Andrew Agnew
Sep 14 - Mr. Ebenezer Finley
Sep 24 - Mrs. Frances J. Wicks, aged 21
Oct 7 - Died - John McHenry at Mercersburg, PA, aged 32
Oct 11 - Mrs. Maxwell
Oct 26 - Mr. Robert Patterson
Dec 6 - Mr. William Winchester, aged 35
Dec 9 - A child of David Harris, aged 3 months
Dec 4 - Died at sea, James Decalour, aged 50

Dec 30 - Mrs. Woods, aged 73

1823 BURIALS:
Feb 26 - A child of Mr. R. L. Colt, aged 6 1/2
Feb 26 - James C. Buchanan, aged 24
Mar 12 - A child of Mr. Meredith, aged 1
Mar 15 - Mr. Messonier, aged 73
Mar 29 - Miss Mary Stewart
Apr 4 - Miss Clarissa Pierce
Apr 11 - Died - Henry Lamson at St. Thomas
May 7 - Mrs. Frink, aged 62
May 26 - Dr. Coulter of Dr. Glendy's congregation
Jun 6 - Mr. John Oliver
Jul 6 - A child of Mr. Walker
Jul 25 - Mrs. Esther Elder
Sep 3 - Died - Mrs. Chapman & the Sunday before Mr. Chapman
Sep 19 - Mrs. Oliver
Sep 25 - William Harris
Sep 26 - Mrs. Allen of Dr. Glendy's congregation
Sep 28 - Mr. Robinson of Dr. Glendy's congregation
Oct 5 - A child of Mrs. Watson, aged 5
Oct 7 - Mrs. Courtenay
Oct 9 - Mr. Thornhill
Oct 23 - Mr. G. Lawson, aged 53
Dec 2 - A child of Alexander L. Boggs, aged 1
Dec 12 - A child of John T. Barr, aged 1
Dec 17 - Mr. Lloyd Buchanan
Dec 18 - A child of Alexander L. Boggs, aged 2
Dec 30 - Miss Hester Dysart of Mr. Duncan's congregation

1824 BURIALS:
Jan 24 - A child of Samuel McClellan, aged 1 1/2
Jan 28 - A child of J. W. McCullough, aged 2
Feb 7 - Shorter, a colored girl, aged 15
Mar 9 - Mr. John Rich, aged 30
Mar 13 - Mr. Anderson, a stranger
Mar 28 - Mr. Johnson, aged 56
May 24 - Died - Gen. William H. Winder, aged 49
May 24 - A child of Ebenezer Finley, aged 2
Jun 20 - A Mr. Ripple

Jun 24 - Mr. Andrew Clopper
Jun 28 - Mrs. Humphrey Pierce
Jul 4 - Died - P. B. K. N. [sic]
Jul 25 - A child of E. L. Finley, aged 1
Aug 21 - Mrs. Jane McKinley
Sep 2 - A child of Mr. Dance, aged 5
Sep 3 - Miss Isabella Patterson
Sep 17 - Mr. Thomas Dinsmore
Sep 19 - Mr. Benjamin Sterett
Oct 18 - Mr. Butterfield of Jacketts Harbour
Oct 19 - Mrs. Millar of Mr. Duncan's congregation
Dec 6 - Lucy Johnson, a colored woman

1825 BURIALS:
Jan 5 - A child of Samuel ---- [blank], aged 5
Jan 6 - A child of Christopher Johnson, aged 1
Jan 11 - Henry J. Isett, aged 19
Jan 16 - Robert G. Harper, aged 61
Feb 10 - Mrs. Murray, a colored woman, age 16
Feb 12 - A child of Mr. McGibbon, aged 5 months
Mar 4 - Mr. A. A. McGibbon, aged 28
Apr 16 - Mr. Penniman of 1st Independent Church, aged 44
Jun 24 - Gen. John Stricker, aged 66
Jun 23 - Died at Boston, Francis Hyde, Jr., aged 20
Sep 13 - Mr. George McIlvain
Sep 26 - Mrs. Mayhew of 1st Independent Church
Sep 21 - Died - Mrs. Guthrie in Cecil County, aged 65
Nov 12 - A child of Samuel Harris, aged 1 1/2
Nov 17 - Mr. Elder
Nov 29 - A child of Robert Aitken of Dr. Glendy's congreg., aged 1
Dec 9 - Mrs. Charlotte C. Beam, aged 30
Dec 26 - Robert M. Henderson, aged 26

1826 BURIALS:
Jan 4 - Dr. Nathaniel Andrews, aged 67
Jan 17 - Mr. Felty Nelson, aged 86
Jan 26 - Mrs. Frances McTier, aged 59
Feb 9 - Mr. James Inglis, aged 88
Mar 18 - A child of the Rev. Mr. Duncan, aged 3
Mar 22 - John P. Boyd, aged 9

[n.d.] - Died in my absence, Isabella Porter, aged 14
[n.d.] - Died in my absence, Miss Grace Rose
Jun 7 - William Inglis, aged 23
Jun 20 - A child of Mr. James Stewart, aged 3 weeks
Jun 23 - A child of Dr. G. S. Gibson, aged 5 1/2 months
Jul 19 - Died in my absence, Josephine Sterret, aged 20
[n.d.] - A child of Mr. William Butler, aged 1 1/2
Aug 1 - Died in my absence, a child of Chris. Johnson, age 1 1/2
Aug 9 - Henry L. Williams, aged 35
Aug 12 - Mrs. Ludden
Sep 11 - A child of Mr. Jas. Bain, aged 1 1/2
Sep 15 - A daughter of Mr. Dance, aged 4 1/2
Sep 20 - A Mr. McLean
Oct 3 - Buried by Mr. Duncan, a child of William Hamilton
Oct 15 - Miss ---- [blank], aged 20
Oct 30 - Mr. Mills

1827 BURIALS:
Feb 6 - John M. Barkley, aged 35
[n.d.] - James Barkley, son of J. M. Barkley, aged 10 months
Feb 26 - A child of Mr. Bain, aged 3 years
Feb 28 - Mr. Jacob Schley, aged 45
Apr 3 - A child of Mr. Benty, aged 6 months
Apr 14 - A child of Mr. Stout, aged 9 days
May 9 - Died in my absence, Mrs. C. C. Edgerton
Jun 1 - Mr. Ralph Smith of the 2nd Church
Apr 24 - Mr. John Hollins of the 2nd Church
Jun 15 - Mrs. White, wife of Henry White
Aug 15 - Carvil Kelly, aged 17
Sep 15 - Mr. C. Blodget, aged 17
Sep 22 - A child of Mr. Bird - Mr. Breckinridge attended, aged 1
Oct 8 - A child of Mr. C. C. Edgerton, aged 1 1/2
Oct 13 - A son of Mr. P. Oller, age 16
Oct 21 - Mr. Jacob Williams, aged 62
Nov 2 - Miss Perkins from the Eastern Shore
Nov 21 - Miss Frances Purviance, aged 25
Nov 26 - Mrs. Blayney, aged 65
Dec 12 - Mr. Alexander H. Boyd (service by Mr. Williams)

1828 BURIALS:

FIRST PRESBYTERIAN CHURCH 155

Jan 27 - Edward P. Moody, aged 9
Feb 2 - John Nisbet, aged 8
Mar 5 - Mr. Sinton, aged 45
Mar 7 - Ephraim Hammond, aged 19
Mar 28 - A child of Mrs. Wood, aged 6 months
Jun 6 - Mr. Dougherty of St. Paul's Church, aged 79
Jun 7 - Miss Chaffee of Mr. Duncan's congregation, aged 37
Jun 12 - Mr. John Barron of 2nd Presbyterian Church, aged 47
Jun 18 - Mr. Gilbert of 3rd Presbyterian Church, aged 42
Jul 1 - Died - Mrs. McGibbon (Mr. Morrison attended the funeral)
Jul 7 - A child of Dr. G. S. Gibson, aged 1
Jul 12 - A child of Mrs. Coonrod, aged 1
Jul 14 - Mr. Whitelock
Jul 18 - Mr. John Montgomery of Duncan's congregation, aged 66
Jul 27 - A child of Mr. George Y. Kelso, aged 2 months
Aug 1 - Mrs. Elizth. A. Gill (Mr. Breckinridge attended), aged 27
Aug 14 - A child of Mrs. Scott, aged 1
Aug 24 - Charlotte Stricker (Mr. Breckinridge attended), aged 29
Sep 23 - Mr. William Butler, aged 34
Oct 2 - Mr. William Barksdale (a stranger), aged 76
Oct 2 - E. R. Phillips, aged 23
Oct 4 - Mr. Alexander Coulter, aged 67
Oct 14 - Miss Mary Ann Mosher, aged 24
Oct 17 - A child of Mr. Wilkinson of 2nd Pres. Ch., aged 2 months
Nov 6 - Mr. West from the infirmary, aged 45
Nov 24 - Mrs. Rich, aged 69
Nov 26 - A child of Mr Crawford of 2nd Pres. Ch., aged 1
Nov 28 - A child of Mr. R. L. Colt, aged 1 1/4
Nov 29 - Mr. George Gray, aged 88

<u>1829 BURIALS:</u>
Jan 20 - A daughter of Mr. Mark of 3rd Pres. Ch., aged 12
Jan 29 - Mr. Andrew Boyd, aged 50
Feb 7 - Died - Mr. Edward G. Williams at Williamsport, aged 39
Feb 16 - Mr. George Sterret, aged 32
Mar 5 - Mr. Peachim, of Norfolk, aged 70
Mar 17 - A child of Mr. B. C. Howard, aged 1 month
Mar 18 - Mr. Edward Toogood, a colored man, aged 78
Mar 21 - A child of Mrs. Ruark, aged 6
May 25 - A child of Elizabeth Haggerty, aged 1

May 25 - Mrs. Torrance, aged 71
Jun 15 - A child of Mrs. Bayard, aged 6
Jun 26 - A child of Mrs. Johnson, aged 1
Jul 19 - A child of Mr. Mopps, aged 7
Aug 9 - Died at Hagerstown, Mrs. Inglis, aged 85
Aug 9 - Died in my absence, Mrs. Dinsmore, aged 80
[n.d.] - Robert Thomas, aged 43
Sep 2 - A child of Mr. P. Neff, aged 1 week
Sep 8 - Mr. William Gilmor, aged 54
Sep 12 - A child of D. Cunningham, Jr., aged 5 weeks
Sep 14 - Mr. Thomas Francis, aged 23
Oct 22 - Mrs. ---- [blank]
Nov -- - Died - Mrs. Joanna Delacour
Nov 24 - Miss Sarah Carroll, aged 21
Dec 17 - Mr. John Swan, aged 39
Dec 17 - Mrs. Mary Young, aged 71
Dec 30 - Died at Montgomery, Alabama, Mr. James Inglis, aged 23

1830 BURIALS:
Mar 20 - Margaret McMillan
Apr 6 - Mr. White
Apr 22 - Alexander Boggs, son of A. L. Boggs, aged 10
Apr 23 - A child of G. W. Everitt, aged 5 months
May 13 - A child of Capt. William Owen, aged 2
May 17 - A child of Mr. Clarke, aged 3
May 24 - Mr. John McElderry, of 2nd Pres. Ch., aged 42
Jun 13 - A son of Mr. Petticore
Jul 26 - Mrs. Rebecca S. Brien, aged 23
Jun -- - Died in my absence, a child of Adam Barker, aged 1 week
Aug 1 - A child of Mr. W. Barr of Duncan's congreg., aged 9 months
Aug 6 - Mr. Hatch (a stranger)
Aug 6 - A child of Mr. Kaufman of the 3rd Pres. Ch., aged 3 months
Aug 12 - Mr. Samuel Keep, of Washington, D.C., aged 26
Aug 14 - A child of Mr. John Sands, aged 2
Aug 20 - Eliza S. Buchanan, aged 30
Aug 21 - Emily G. McKim (attended with Mr. Breckinridge), aged 22
Aug 25 - A child of Mr. Dabney Carr, aged 2
Aug 26 - A child of Mr. W. L. Gill, aged 4
Aug 30 - A child of Mr. W. F. Murdoch, aged 1
Sep 10 - A child of Mr. Barret, aged 4

Sep 22 - Elizabeth Brown, daughter of George Brown, aged 10
Sep 29 - John P. Gill, son of Mr. W. L. Gill, aged 6
Oct 1 - Eben LaFayette Finley, son of S. L. Finley, aged 5
Oct 15 - A child of Mr. James Stewart, aged 20
Oct 19 - Mr. John McKay
Oct 20 - Elizabeth Colhoon, aged 13
Nov 23 - Attended with Mr. Henshaw the funeral of Harriet Murray and on November 27 the funeral of James E. B. Murray, children of Mr. W. H. Murray.
Dec 7 - Mrs. Mary ---- [blank]
Dec 10 - Leah Blue, a slave of Mrs. Finley, aged 50
Dec 31 - Agnes C. Wirt, aged 16

1831 BURIALS:
Jan 8 - A child of Mr. Akn. [Alex.?] Coulter, aged 4 months
Jan 13 - A daughter of Mr. Geddes, aged 4 1/2 years
Jan 14 - A daughter of Mr. G. T. Dunbar, aged 3
Jan 17 - Mr. Hollins Carr, aged 19
Jan 31 - Mr. Peter Edes, aged 45
Feb 10 - A son of Mr. Henry Carroll, aged 7
Feb 25 - Mr. W. Gardner, aged 18
Mar 19 - A son of Mr. Westerman (of Sunday School), aged 15
Mar 24 - A child of Mr. M. Knight, aged 7 months
Apr 22 - Mr. James Stewart, aged 44
May 25 - A Miss Jackson of the 3rd Pres. Ch.
Jun 3 - A child of Mr. Sullivan of 3rd Pres. Ch., aged 10 months
Jun 8 - Mrs. Hannah Winchester
Jun 18 - Mr. McDonald
Jul 3 - A child of Mr. Riddle, aged 4
Jul 6 - A child of Mr. Gardner, aged 1
Jul 12 - Elizabeth Ann Amey
Aug 2 - W. H. Poe
Aug 18 - A child of Mr. Geddes, aged 4 months
Sep 3 - Mrs. J. P. Thompson, aged 32
Sep 10 - Mr. James Ramsay, of 2nd Pres. Ch., aged 54
Sep 10 - Died in my absence, Mrs. Sarah Y. Edes, aged 29
Oct 11 - J. Adrian Dumest, aged 32
Oct 17 - Mrs. McIlhenny, of 3rd Church
Oct 24 - Mrs. Elizabeth M. Hopkins
Nov 8 - A son of John McFadon, aged 13

Nov 15 - Mrs. Nathaniel Smith, aged 82
Nov 27 - A child of Mr. F. H. Smith, aged 1
Dec 4 - Mr. Alexander Mactier, aged 73
Dec 12 - Mr. James P. Boyd
Dec 18 - Catharine Taggart (Mr. Bain attended)
Dec 25 - Died - Mrs. Catharine Stockton (Mr. Henshaw attended)
Dec 30 - A child of J. W. C. Conine, aged 4

1832 BURIALS:
Jan 14 - Mrs. Elizabeth Isett, aged 62
Jan 27 - A child of J. W. Conine, aged 2
Jan 31 - Mrs. Ruth McDowell (Mr. Musgrave attended), aged 59
Feb 22 - A child of Mr. Parker, aged 3
Mar 14 - A child of Mr. Alex Forsyth, aged 2
Mar 15 - Mr. John Torrance, aged 38
Apr 3 - Mr. George Aikin, aged 66
May 18 - Mr. William F. Small, aged 35
May 19 - A child of William Crawford, Jr., of 2nd Ch., aged 1
Jun 6 - A child of Mr. Bolton, of 2nd Ch., aged 6
Jun 30 - Miss Rachel Graham, of 2nd Ch.
Jul 15 - Miss Leahy, of Frederick, aged 35
Jul 19 - Mr. Humphrey Buckler, of 2nd Ch., aged 72
Jul 26 - Mrs. Lyon in the country, aged 67
Aug 13 - Mr. William W. Taylor, aged 63
Aug 14 - Mr. Donaldson (of cholera)
Aug 15 - A child of Mr. Carlock, aged 2
Aug 24 - Mrs. Dr. Allison, aged 74
Aug 27 - Mrs. McNeal (of cholera)
Aug 28 - Mr. Chambers (of cholera)
Aug 31 - Mr. Elliot, aged 72
Sep 2 - Mrs. Edes (of cholera, Mr. Williams attended), aged 75
Sep 3 - Mr. William Stewart, of 2nd Church (of cholera), aged 21
Sep 4 - Mrs. Mayer (of cholera), aged 42
Sep 4 - Mr. James Nicholson (of cholera), aged 30
Sep 4 - Mr. William Phillips, aged 54
Sep 5 - Mr. Benjamin Edes (of cholera)
Sep 7 - Mrs. Sarah Brown (of cholera), aged 81
Sep 19 - Mrs. Capt. Myers, aged 52
Sep 10 - Miss Anna M. Lyon (of cholera), aged 22
Sep 22 - Mrs. John Spear Smith, aged 42

FIRST PRESBYTERIAN CHURCH 159

Oct -- - Died - Mrs. Jane Hollins, aged 70
Oct -- - A child of M. Knight, aged 5
Nov -- - Mr. Stewart Brown, aged 63
Dec 15 - Miss Zelah Carvan
Dec 29 - Mrs. Selvige, of 3rd Church
Dec 10 - Died at New Orleans, Mrs. Dance

<u>1833 BURIALS:</u>
Jan 24 - Mrs. N. B. Woodward, aged 20
Jan 26 - Mrs. Rosanna Prentice, aged 72
Feb 4 - A child of Mr. Waite, aged 4
Feb 13 - Mr. Edward Pannel, Jr., aged 40
Feb 22 - Mrs. Ellen Kelso, aged 32
Apr 5 - Dr. Duncan, aged 72
Apr 7 - Mr. Stephen S. Wilson, aged 31
Apr 9 - Mrs. Turnbull
Apr 15 - Andrew Hazlehurst, aged 17
Apr 20 - Thomas O. Kean, aged 28
Apr 29 - Died - A child of F. H. Smith, aged 5
May 12 - Mr. Isaac Caustin, aged 75
Jun 7 - A child of William Lemmon, of Christ's Church, aged 1
Jun 14 - A child of W. C. Conine, aged 1
Jun 24 - Mr. Archibald Stewart, aged 76
Jun 30 - Mr. James Sloan, aged 84
Jul 2 - A child of Mr. John Spence, aged 3 months
May 14 - Died - Mr. C. C. Egerton
Jul 7 - Mr. Dubois Martin, aged 91
Jul 9 - A child of Mr. Perry, aged 1/2 year
Jul 9 - A child of Mr. Warley, aged 1 1/2 years
Jul 11 - A child of Mr. J. C. Moale, aged 1/4 year
Jul 13 - Mr. Samuel Sterett, aged 77
Jul 19 - A child of Mr. Elisha Lee, aged 1 year
Jul 24 - A child of Mr. Frederick Dugan, aged 1/4 year
Oct 18 - A child of Mr. Armourer, aged 6
Oct 18 - A child of Mr. Hardesty, aged 1
Oct 23 - Susan Kelly, aged 24
Nov 10 - A Mr. Hutchinson, of New York, aged 27
Nov 11 - Benj. May Clopper, aged 24
Nov 22 - Mrs. Margaret McHenry, aged 72
Nov 27 - Mrs. Mary Rogers

Dec 4 - Mr. Selvage, of 3rd Church

1834 BURIALS:
Jan 17 - Mrs. Eliza Barker (colored), aged 33
Jan 21 - Mary S. Inglis, aged 21
Jan 23 - A child of Mr. Thomas Johnston, aged 1 1/2
Jan 28 - Mr. David Polk (colored)
Feb 18 - Died at Washington, D. C., William Wirt, aged 62
Mar 12 - Miss Mary Walker
Mar 18 - A child of David Stewart, Esq., aged 1
Mar 20 - A child of Mr. O. Kellog, aged 2
Mar 22 - Died - Dr. Moor Falls, aged 80
Mar 31 - Miss Jane Stirling, aged 50
Apr 5 - J. W. Barkley, aged 14
Apr 6 - Alexander Brown, Esq., aged 70
Apr 6 - Died - A child of James Ferguson, aged 2
May 8 - Mrs. David Stewart (Harris officiated), aged 27
May 11 - Mr. Robert Miller (Harris officiated), aged 67
May 25 - A child of William Egerton (Mr. Stone attended), aged 3
Jun 8 - A child of James Geddes (Mr. Musgrave attended), aged 1
[n.d.] - Died in my absence, Mr. William Moody
[n.d.] - Died in my absence, Mrs. Hardester
Sep 30 - A child of Mr. Dungan (Mr. Owen attended)
Oct 1 - A child of Mr. Dungan (Mr. Owen attended)
Oct 1 - Frederick Wilson (Mr. Williams attended)
Nov 3 - Mrs. McKonkey
Nov 8 - Died - Mrs. M. H. Nevins, aged 33
[n.d.] - Miss Agnes Bryson
Dec 18 - Mrs. Ann Key, aged 62
Dec 27 - Mrs. Elizabeth Pearson, aged 86
Dec 29 - Mrs. Robert Watson, aged 34
Dec 31 - Robert Oliver, Esq., aged 77

1835 BURIALS:
Jan 15 - Miss Jane S. Purviance, aged 29
Jan 22 - A child of R. L. Colt, aged 3
[n.d.] - A child of P. Neff, aged 1
Feb 9 - William Patterson, aged 83
Feb 10 - William Buckler, aged 73
Feb 24 - Edward Pannell, aged 83

[n.d.] - ---- [blank] Thornhill
[n.d.] - ---- [blank] Stockton
May 24 - A child of Dr. Robinson, aged 21 months

RECORD OF BURIALS ATTENDED BY JOHN C. BACKUS, PASTOR OF THE FIRST PRESBYTERIAN CHURCH OF BALTIMORE [BEGINNING IN 1836 THROUGH 1838]

1836 BURIALS:
Oct -- ---- [blank] Holstein
Oct 14 - Susan Anderson, A. E.[sic], aged 31
Dec 4 - A child of Mr. Parker, A. E.[sic], aged 11 months
[n.d.] - Mary Copeland
[n.d.] - Lawrence Tyrrel
[n.d.] - Julia A. Foxwell, A. E.[sic], aged 41 years

1837 BURIALS:
[n.d.] - ---- [blank] Finley
[n.d.] - ---- [blank] Jackson
Mar 17 - Ehalynda Towson Coakley, daughter of P. H. and S. C. Coakley, aged 2 years and 2 months
Apr 8 - Ann P. Boyd, W.[sic]
Apr 18 - Mary M. Williamson, W., A. E. [sic] from hospital

1838 BURIALS:
Feb -- - A child of Mr. A. Clarke
[n.d.] - Susannah M. Dowell [McDowell?], A. E.[sic], aged 6
Mar -- - Child of Mr. Geddes
Apr 2 - Mr. Christopher Johnson, W., Mr. Musgrave [sic]
May 5 - Janetta Sophia Scrivener, orphan asylum, age 11 yrs. 1 mo.
Jul 13 - Mr. Jos. Sterret, aged 57

[Ed. Note: There were no entries (?) for burials in 1839 and 1840.]

RECORD OF THE COMMUNICANTS OF THE FIRST PRESBYTERIAN CHURCH AND THE RECORD OF PERSONS RECEIVED IN COMMUNION WITH THE FIRST PRESBYTERIAN CHURCH IN THE CITY OF BALTIMORE SINCE THE ACCESSION OF JAMES INGLIS TO THE PASTORAL CHARGE OF THE SAME. SUBMITTED TO, AND ACKNOWLEDGED <u>BY, THE SESSION OF THE SAME IN THE MANNER, FORM AND ORDER FOLLOWING</u>

[Ed. Note: Two lists of communicants between 1802 and 1806 were found in the register and have been combined below into one list. They began with the date April 25, 1802, but few additional dates were recorded. It appeared that several were members prior to 1802 and many were indicated as "dead," but there were few dates given. After 1806 there was only one list of names found in the register.]

<u>1802</u> [and possibly earlier]
William Smith
William Buchanan (died September 19, 1804, aged 77)
Robert Purviance
James Calhoun
David Stewart
Robert Gilmor
Dr. George Brown
Christopher Johnston
James McHenry
George Salmon
Margaret Galbraith
Mary Allison
Grizzel Taggart
Mary Taggart, wife of John Taggart
Frances Purviance, wife of Robert Purviance
Ruhannah Colhoon
Mary Graham
Rose Brown, wife of Dr. George Brown
Ann Brown
Jane Brown
Susannah Johnston, wife of Christopher Johnston, dead
Maria Stith Johnston
Jane Swan Inglis, wife of Rev. James Inglis, dead

Anna Maria Inglis
Sydney Buchanan
Margaret Buchanan
John Martin and Elizabeth his wife
Alexander Brown and Grace his wife
Jane Finley, wife of Ebenezer Finley
Joseph Swan (died ----)
Ann Swan
Dr. John Crawford (since become a member of 2nd Church)
Jane Hunter
James Sterling (dead) and Elizabeth his wife (dead)
James Martin (since become a member of the 2nd Church)
Mary Inglis, wife of James Inglis (dead), received on certificate from the Rev. Samuel Miller, one of the ministers of the United Presbyterian Churches in the City of New York)
James Priestley
James Mosher
Ann Clayton Kennedy, wife of John Kennedy
James H. McCulloch
Dr. John Campbell White (since become a member of 2nd Church)
Hugh Young
Charles Torrance
Eliza Purviance, wife of James Purviance, dead
Frances Young, dead
Ann Ferguson, wife of Robert Ferguson, dead
Elizabeth Robb, wife of William Robb (died October 10, 1806)
Robson Barnes (died ----)
Elizabeth Isabella Purviance
Letitia Purviance (died ----)
Margaret McHenry, wife of James McHenry
---- Shedden, wife of J. Shedden
Mary Lawder, wife of Alexander Lawder
Ellen Moore
Sylvanus Bourne (by certificate from the Rev. James Low, Pastor of the English Reformed Church at Amsterdam)
Jane McComb
Esther Coulter, wife of Alexander Coulter
Catherine Atterbury (dead), wife of Lewis Atterbury, dead (received on certificate from the church of Newark)

Julia Boudinot (received on certificate from the Rev. Dr. Alexander McWhorter and Rev. E. D. Griffin, Pastors of the 1st Presbyterian Church of Newark, New Jersey)
Robert Gilmor, Jr. [one list stated "Robert Gilmor the Younger"]
Hannah Taylor, wife of William Taylor, died January 23, 1812
Margaret Caldwell, wife of John Caldwell
Ellen McMillan
Ann Perry Bell
Elizabeth Stewart, wife of David Stewart
Sarah Brown
Ruth Disert
Sarah Smith, widow of Nathaniel Smith
Eliza Anderson
Rebecca Bourne, wife of Sylvanus Bourne (died ----)
Margaret Smith, wife of Samuel Smith
Margaret Smith, wife of Robert Smith
Jane Hall, wife of Josias Carvil Hall (died March 1, 1812)
Jane Forman, wife of William Lee Forman
Ann Somervell, wife of James Somervell
Sally Harris, wife of David Harris
Jane Harris
Sarah Smith, widow of James Smith (received by certificate from the church of Upper Octorora)
James Inglis, dead
Martha Stricker, wife of John Stricker, dead
Mary Ann Gilmor, wife of William Gilmor
William Downing and Catherine his wife (received on certificates from the Rev. Robert Cathcart, Pastor of the Congregation of Round Hill and the Rev. Samuel Martin, Pastor of Congregation of Chanceford)
Helena Stewart (gone to St. Paul, stricken off - see minutes September 22, 1839)
Grace Mimm (received on certificate from the Rev. Robert Cathcart), dismissed by certificate August 18, 1811
John Elder and Esther his wife (John Elder since dead), received on certificate from the church at Chanceford under the hand of the Rev. John Slemons)
John Elder, died May 10, 1805 (was drowned)
Isabella Marr, wife of Charles Marr, from ---- [blank]
Betsey Fromentin, wife of Elegins Fromentin, from --- [blank], dead
Gertrude Winder, wife of W. H. Winder

FIRST PRESBYTERIAN CHURCH 165

Esther Winder
Alexander Prentice and Rosanna his wife
William W. Taylor and Maria his wife

1806-1808
April - John McLellan
April - Elizabeth Torrance, wife of Charles Torrance
Margaret McDonogh, died
Sarah Cantwell
Ann Thomas Buckler, wife of William Buckler
Jane McClellan
Elizabeth Isett, wife of John Isett, by certificate from the Rev. Dr. Davidson, Pastor of Carlisle
Jane Ann Mitchell, wife of James Mitchell
Lucia Taylor
John McKeen
Mary Young
Susanna Buckman, wife of John Buckman, by certificate from the Rev. Dr. Green, Senior Pastor, 2nd Church, Philadelphia, dead
Hannah Meredith, wife of Jonathan Meredith
James Coxe
William Wilson
Jane Sterling, dead
Joseph C. Yeates
Elizabeth Pearson and William Harrison - "These names should have been entered before, but it was not known that either had communicated. E. P. joined the communion of April, 1806, and W. H. that of October 1806."
Magnus Norquay (died May 11, 1807)
Mary Stewart, dead
Dr. James Smith and Ann his wife - Unitarian
Angelica Robinson, wife of Alexander Robinson
Mary Barr, wife of William Barr, removed
Stewart Brown (dead) and Sarah his wife (died August 23, 1811)
David Harris
Elizabeth Hall, wife of Alexander Hall, died
Eleanor Thompson
William Maxwell (by certificate from the Rev. Dr. Miller, one of the ministers of the United Presbyterian Churches in New York)

Anna Wilson, wife of Robert Wilson (stricken off - see minutes September 23, 1839)
Deborah Cochran, wife of William Cochran
Ann Eliza Stricker, dead
Matilda Inglis
David C. Stewart, dead
Flora Caldwell - Unitarian

1809
April 3 - Esther Allison, dead
Josias Carvil Hall
Nathaniel Walker Appleton and Sarah his wife, removed
Mary Appleton, removed
Nancy Holmes, removed
Isabella Maxwell, wife of William Maxwell, and their daughter Isabella Maxwell
Eliza Finlater
Mary McClellan
Robert Winter, dismissed by certificate October 12, 1811
Charles M. Poor
Rachel McCandless, wife of Robert McCandless
Mary Hartshorne, wife of William Hartshorne, Jr., removed
John Tagart
Mary Stewart, dead
Lilly Kennedy Colhoon, wife of Benjamin Chambers Colhoon
Elizabeth Colhoon
Dr. Maxwell McDonald and Ruth his wife, and Margaret Bayly, by certificate from the Rev. Robert Cathcart

1810-1812
John R. Campbell and Margaret his wife
Elizabeth Baden wife of William Baden
May - Rebecca Rich, wife of Matthias Rich, dead
Catharine Finley, wife of Ebenezer Finley
Ann Elizabeth Forman, wife of Francis Forman
Eliza Oliver, wife of Robert Oliver, dead
Peggy Oliver, dead
Hetty Dawes, wife of James Dawes, dead

FIRST PRESBYTERIAN CHURCH 167

James Wilson and Bethiah his wife (from the congregation of Sinking Valley, Pennsyslvania)
Jane Thornhill
Maria Louisa West
Hope Bain (died November 24, 1812) and Elizabeth his wife, died
Nathaniel Ramsay, died
Molly Sterret, wife of Joseph Sterret, dead

Thomas Vose (omitted in communion of May, 1811, to be added to the next), received on certificate from the church of Rev. Thaddeus Mason Harris, of Dorchester, Massachusetts
Charlotte Poor, wife of Moses Poor
Maria Montgomery, wife of John Montgomery, by certificate of the Rev. Dr. J. Livingston, minister of the Reformed Dutch Church in the City of New York, dead
David W. Boisseau, dead
Lydia Calhoun
Jane Mosher, died July 10, 1812
Elizabeth Buchanan, wife of James A. Buchanan
Mary Way or Wray, wife of John Wray or Way, by certificate of Rev. Dr. Davidson, Carlisle
Ann Boyd, wife of James P. Boyd
Ann Allison, heretofore a communicant in the Lutheran Church
James Ward, a coloured man
Elizabeth McLellan
Eleanor Bond, heretofore a communicant in the Presbyterian Church of Ireland
Hannah Bayly, wife of H. E. Bayly, on certificate from Rev. Robert Cathcart
James H. Parmele, dismissed November 12, 1812
Sergeant Hall, by certificate from 1st Cong., Pennsylvania
Eliza Bond
Maria Isett
Grace McInnally
Sarah Donovan, wife of Jeremiah Donovan, a communicant heretofore in Ireland
Erastus Strong
Maria Buel, wife of Isaac Buel, by certificate from the church in Elizabethtown, New Jersey, died
William Gilmor

Sarah Reeve Gilmor, wife of Robert Gilmor, Jr., St. Pauls
Mary Hall, wife of Benedict William Hall, dead
Ruth Wallace

1813-1814
November - Moses Poor
Thomas Finley
Mary Cope, wife of ---- [blank] Cope, by certificate from Rev. Robert Cathcart
May - Eliza Dennison, wife of Edward Dennison
Eliza Dawson, wife of Richard Dawson
Hugh Thompson, dead
---- Dumest, dead
---- French, dead
Roswell L. Colt, removed
Martha Doram Allen
John Thomson Barr
Elijah P. Barrows, dismissed
Margaretta Brown
Mary Cole, wife of John Cole
Eliza Johnston
Henry Martin, a freeman of colour
Caroline Neilson, wife of H. Neilson
Deborah Hibernia Poor, wife of Dudley Poor
Martha Guthrie, by certificate from the congregation of Greensburg
John Maund, by certificate from Rev. Dr. Janeway
Sophia McHenry
Garretson Draper, a freeman of colour, brother of Riley Draper
Riley Draper, a freeman of colour, brother of Garretson Draper
Dorcas A. McCoy, wife of Henry McCoy
Rebecca Maria McCoy
Charlotte Gilburg, a woman of colour, owned by Harriet Hammond
John Coulter, dead
Elizabeth Hunter, wife of John Hunter

1815
Eliza Hall, wife of Dr. R. W. Hall
Elizabeth Conklin

FIRST PRESBYTERIAN CHURCH

Matilda Irwin, by certificate from Gettysburg Congregation
Lucy Ward, wife of James Ward, free person of colour
John F. Keyes and wife, by certificate
Eli Adams and wife, by certificate
S. M. McCoy
William R. Swift, dead
Jacob Williams and wife
Letitia McCreery
Margaret Saunderson
William Lovell and wife

1816
Richard W. Polkinson
Mary Keys, wife of Richard Keys
David McLellan
William Brown, person of colour
Thomas Jones, person of colour
Samuel Douglas, person of colour
Robert Thomas, person of colour
Charlotte White, person of colour
Mary Pierpont, wife of John Pierpont, by certificate
J. D. Delacour and Joanna his wife, by certificate, dead
Mary Cox
Mrs. Margaret Eaton
Mary Swift, wife of William R. Swift
Edward and Nancy Toogood, blacks, dead
Mary Mason, coloured
Cossy Lewis, coloured
Benjamin Lane, coloured
Aaron Cockshaw, St. Peters
William Taylor, dead
Joshua T. Russell and Mary Ann his wife, by certificate
Francis Hyde and Mehitabel, by certificate
Zebulon Rudulph
Joseph A. Wallace, Mr. Duncan's
Andrew Wallace
Elizabeth Ann Lovell
Betsey Saunderson, coloured
Diana Jackson, coloured
Maria Smith, coloured

Henry Brown, coloured

1817
Harriet Moody
Mrs. Shaw with Ann and Elizabeth her daughters, on certificate
Catharine Stricker
Sarah R. Rich
Samuel McCulloch
Juliana Howden, coloured
Hannah Purl, coloured
Nancy and Sydney, of Mrs. Ridgeley's household
Patience, of Jno. McKeen's household
Maria McLellan, wife of David McLellan, on certificate
Ann Scobey, wife of John Scobey
Alexander McTier, dead
Ann Eliza Cox
Oliver H. Nielson
Eliza Gwynn, wife of Charles Gwynn
Joseph Taylor and Jane his wife
Ann McKeen, wife of John McKeen
Paris Howden, coloured
Ann Wood, wife of John Wood
Susan ----, of Thomas Finley's household
Jno. Williams, of Richard W. Hall's household
Anne Buckler
Flora Turner, slave of John Cole
Patience Holmes, wife of Samuel Holmes
Maria Nichols, slave of George Heide
Ann Fisher, wife of John Fisher
Charlotte Ream [Beam?], wife of Elijah Ream [Beam?], dead
Ann White, free coloured woman
Elizabeth DeMangin
William Winchester and Hannah his wife
Benjamin Sterrett and Margaret his wife, dead
Jane S. Barr, wife of John T. Barr, dismissed
Mary McClenaghan
Charlotte Ramsay
Eliza Harper, by certificate from Rev. E. S. Ely
Nancy McCrea, by certificate from Piney Cree Church
David Pole, free coloured

FIRST PRESBYTERIAN CHURCH 171

Mrs. C. Stockton, by certificate from Dr. Griffin and Wilson

1818
James Jootle [Tootle?]
Louisa Torrance, died May 5, 1878 [sic]
William McGray, by certificate from Church of Gettysburg

1819
Thomas Beenhope and wife, from Scotland
Mary Ann Miller
Richard Mills

RECORD OF PERSONS RECEIVED INTO COMMUNION IN THE FIRST PRESBYTERIAN CHURCH IN THE CITY OF BALTIMORE SINCE THE ACCESSION OF REV. WILLIAM NEVINS TO THE PASTORAL CHARGE OF THE SAME [BEGINNING IN YEAR 1821]

1821
February - Lemuel Holmes, Jr., by certificate, dismissed
Mrs. Turnbull, by certificate, dead
Frances Dunbar
John McKay
Eliza Lee
Grace Brown
Rebecca C. Bell
Ellen Rich, dead
Agnes Robison
Ann McMullan
May - Margaret Mills
Malinda Holmes
Letitia McCurdy, dismissed
August - Susan Jourdan, became a baptiste [sic]
Harriet Bibby, Mr. Seymour dismissed to 4th Church, 1858
November - Ann Turnbull
Betsey Turnbull
Catharine Ferguson
Eliza McTier, dead
Mary Ann Muir

Rebecca Rich
Jane Howard
Harriet West
George Brown and Isabella his wife, certificate 2nd church

1822

February - John McHenry, dead
Susan Boggs, 2nd Church
May - Catharine Hammond, dismissed by certificate
Eleanor Dugan, by certificate, deceased
Alverda Waters, by certificate, deceased
Sidney McLaughlin, dead
Ann Hall
Elizabeth Claggett
Malvina McClellan
John Petticore
August - Mary Ann Edes, by certificate
Maria McClellan, by certificate
Sarah Williams
Margaret McMillan
Mary R. Edes, dead
November - Susan McDowell
Elizabeth McDowell
Sarah M. McDowell
Eleanor Scott
Juliet Ann Taylor
Susan Inglis
Henrietta Bromwell, removed
Henry B. Bromwell, removed
Henry Lamson, dead

1823

February - Elizabeth Linton
Martha Edes
Mary J. McCurdy, dismissed
Susan Turnbull
Rebecca Eddy, by certificate
May - Sarah Dorrence, by certificate, dismissed
Margaret Edgerton

FIRST PRESBYTERIAN CHURCH 173

Anna Downs

Alice M. Butler
Ann Williams
Dorothy MacTier
July - John Stricker, dead
Eliza Buchanan
Jane Smith

1824
February - Mary Gifford
Catherine Petticon [Petticore?]
Phebe Smith, coloured
July - James Brown, dismissed
Louisa K. Brown
David Delacour
Elizabeth Delacour
Eliza Johnson
Melinda Greenwood
Ellen Stewart
Ann Maria McKeen
Margaret Prentiss
Mary Prentiss
Lucy Johnson, coloured, dead
Phebe Lennas, coloured

1825
February - Matilda Graham
Charlotte Ford
Susannah McDowell
Louisa Godman
May - Catharine DeBartholdt, by certificate, dismissed
George Weir
Mary Weir
Elizabeth Mosher
Ann S. Wilmer
John Hamilton
John Haskill
Mary Haskill

July - Benedict William Hall
Margaret Waddell
October - Bethiah Jackson
John P. Reid

1826
February - Mary Robinson, dead
Lucinda Hodges, dismissed
John D. Schick, a Lutheran
Adam Barker, coloured
May - William Hamilton, dismissed
Mary Hamilton
Sarah DeBartholdt, dismissed October 3, 1827, to join 2nd P. Church
Alexander Nisbet
Eliza Barker, coloured
August - Harriet Terrill [Ferrill?]
November - Ellen Thompson
Andrew Gregg - Duncan's
William F. Small, dead

1827
Esther Harris
William Egerton, dead
James P. Walker, coloured
May - Elizabeth Pogue
Eliza W. Finley
Eleanor Bird, dimissed
Henry Bird, dismissed
Sophia Hyde, dismissed
Eliza M. Hyde, dismissed
Elizabeth Scobey
David Courtenay
Mary Torrance
Julianna Rankin
Susan Kelly, dead
Eliza Kelly, dead
Clarissa Philpot
Susan J. Stewart
Elvin B. Levering
Mary Ann McDowell

Randolph J. Finley, Methodist
Mary Gibson
Nancy Hammond, dismissed
Anna B. Schley
Hope Bain, dismissed
Mary A. Henderson
Sarah T. Edes
Jane Brown
Mary Stewart
Francis Purviance (dead)
Charlotte Dinsmore
Mary McDowell
John N. Brown
Henry Turnbull
Caroline Turnbull
Mary Nisbet
Henrietta Lovell
William L. Gill
Mary Inglis
Samuel G. Winchester, dismissed
John McKeen, Jr.
John H. Haskill
George P. Woodward
Elvin M. Dinsmore
Sally Brown
Ann Clopper
Elizabeth Clopper
Rachel Clopper
Jane J. McTier
Grace McTier
July - Mrs. Jane Porter
Mrs. Eliza S. Harris
Mrs. Sarah Holstein, dead
Mrs. Caroline Boggs, removed
William Boggs
George S. Gibson
John A. Scarborough
Ann Pannel
Sydney Calhoun
Esther Buchanan

Ann Foreman, dismissed
Hannah Evans
Elvin Wilson
Elizabeth Henderson
Ann Warfield
November - Mrs. Mary Ann Riddle
Mrs. Catherine Petticore
Mrs. Mary Murdock
Charles C. Egerton, dead
Francis Foreman
Ephraim Hammond, dead
George S. Inglis, dismissed
Samuel H. Scarborough, removed
Letitia M. Stewart
Elizabeth Stirling
Elizabeth Ann Amey
Ann Compton
Rebecca Falls
Sarah M. Smith
Jane J. Buckler
Sarah Jackson
Agnes Dykes, by certificate, Sermahagon [?] Church, Scotland

1828
February - Mrs. Mary Chapman
Mrs. Sarah Brown, wife of Stewart Brown
Mrs. Elizabeth Boyd, wife of Jeremiah Boyd
Mrs. Betsey Spriggs, a slave of Joseph Taylor
Evelina Foreman
April - John C. Smith, dismissed
William F. Sprole
May - Mrs. Dorothea Falls, dismissed May, 1828
Mrs. Sarah Geddes
Margaret P. Hanna
Eleanor Ann Clark
July - Robert Francis, by certificate
Mary D. Nevins, by certificate, dead
John M. Harris, by certificate
Mary Jane Edes (stricken from the list - see minutes 22 Sept 1839)

Leah Blue, colored
November - Jane Margaret Carr
Samuel M. Wilson
William Moody, by certificate
Thomas Philbrook, by certificate

1829
February - George Morris
Mrs. Ann Morris
David Stewart
Peter Williams, dead
Mrs. Hannah Kneeland
Sarah E. Nicholas
May - James Armstrong, Jr.
Mary Armstrong
Margaret McConky
Ann Redgrace
Arminta R. Winder
Jane Shipley
Elizabeth Wallender
Susannah Adreon
Charlotte Evans
Sarah Frank
Frances Ida Downer
Jane Presbury, colored
Rebecca Burke, colored
July - John Armour, dismissed to join western church of C. B. [sic]
    November 21, 1835
James Clarkson, by certificate
Edward G. Fisher
Elizabeth D. Hawkins
Andrew Simund
Ann Simund
Elizabeth Ann Simund
November - Sarah M. Courtenay
Benjamin Williams
Michael Knight, dismissed to join the western church of City Balt. [sic],
    November 21, 1835

1830

February - Harriet Sterret
May - Mrs. Ann Anderson, dismissed
Mrs. Mary Armour, dismissed to join western church, Nov. 21, 1835
Mrs. Mary B. Carroll
Mrs. Catharine Murray
Mrs. Sarah Osborn, by certificate dismissed
Miss Catharine Hamilton
Miss Mary Ann Talbot
Mr. Andrew Francis
Mr. John C. Reid, dismissed
Mr. James Jackosn
August - Mrs. Rhoda Clarkin, dismissed April, 1837, to 5th Church
Mrs. Mary Ruark, dead
Mrs. Augusta T. Dance
Mrs. Sydney Smith Carr
Miss Catharine G. Wirt, removed
Mr. Robert Golder, by certificate from Zanesville, Ohio
Mr. William M. Francis
October - Mrs. Elizabeth Litzinger
Mrs. Phebe D. Clarke
Mrs. Ellen B. Buchanan, dismissed
Mrs. Elizabeth M. Decker, dismissed to join church at New Castle
Miss Margaret S. Purviance
Miss Ann C. Finley
Miss Sophia H. Finley
Miss Ann Jennings
Miss Mary Jackson
Mr. Andrew Dinsmore, by certificate from Chesnut Level

1831

January - Mrs. Catharine Wilson
Mr. Thomas Shaw
March - Mr. Francis H. Smith
Mrs. Susan F. Smith
April - Miss Jane J. Purviance, dead
Mr. John Rodgers
Mr. Joshua Butts
Mr. Moses Hyde
Mr. George D. Purviance

Mrs. Mary Pilkington
Mrs. Catharine Carr
Mr. Alexander Coulter
Mrs. Margaret Coulter
July - Mrs. Margaret Gamble, cert. from Scotch P. Church, Montreal
Mr. William Hogg, by certificate from Charlestown P. Church
Mrs. Jane Hogg, by certificate from Rock Church
Mrs. Hannah Jamieson
Mrs. Mary Knight, dismissed, western church
Mrs. Mary Robinson
Miss Alison M. Turnbull
Miss Rosa E. Wirt
Miss Esther Anne Barney
Miss Sarah C. Elliot, dismissed
Miss Sarah Carson
Miss Ann E. W. Ball - Mrs. William Gill
Miss Jane Brown
Miss Anna Mary Lyon, dead
Miss Sarah McCullough
Mr. William F. Murdoch
Mr. Archibald Stirling
Mr. Cornelius Clopper
Mr. Shammah Clarke
Mr. William Wirt, dead
November - Mrs. Mary Wannall, by cert. from 1st Church, Washington
Mrs. Ann Waters, dismissed from 1st Church, Washington
Mrs. Elizabeth N. Barney, by certificate from St. Peters Episcopal Church, Baltimore
Mrs. Sarah Coakley, by certificate from 2nd Church, Washington
Miss Maria Jane Scott, by certificate from Hanover Ch., Wilmington
Miss Agnes Bryron [sic], decd., by certificate from 2nd Ch., Balt.
Mr. Edward M. Vandervoort, dead, by certificate from 1st Ch., Wash.
Mr. Joseph Perkins, dismissed, by certificate from Upper Octarara
Mr. Joseph L. Sanford, removed, by cert. from 1st Ch., Alexandria
Mrs. Elizabeth G. Goldsborough
Mrs. Elizabeth Ann Stirling
Miss Mary B. Armistead
Miss Maria Falls

1832

February - Miss Catharine Irwing
Miss Ellen T. Wirt
Miss Mary Ann Scott
Miss Elizabeth Buchanan, by cert. from Union Church, Urbana, Ohio
Mrs. Mary Ann Patterson
Patrick Gibson
James Purviance, Jr.
May - Stephen Collins, by certificate from 2nd Church, Wash. D.C.
Mrs. Betsey Crook, by cert. from Circleville Ch., Ohio, dismissed
Jane Gregg, by certificate from Cornwallis Church, Nova Scotia,
    dismissed to join 5th Presbyterian Ch., Baltimore, Jan. 20, 1836
John B. McDowell
George McDowell
Joseph Pearson
Mrs. Mary Pearson
Mrs. Margaret Richards
Mrs. Elizabeth Jane Stafford
Mrs. Jane Easton
Mrs. Eleanor Torrance
Mary C. Torrance
Maria McIlvain
July - Mrs. Mary Owen
Mrs. Elizabeth Smith
Mary Campbell
Helen A. West
Esther Gregg, dismissed to join 5th Presbyterian Church, Baltimore
Elizabeth W. Edes (stricken from list - see minutes 23 Sept 1839)
Maria L. Weems
Alexander Murdoch
Jeremiah Boyd
December - Mrs. Margaret Whitney, dismissed to join western church,
    November 25, 1835
Pamelia Ann Nickerson
Lucretia Emory
Sarah Carter
Maria Mathers
Ann Ballintine
Margaret M. Taggart
Mary Whitmarsh

George Whitmarsh
Anna Wilson (colored), by certificate from 2nd Church, Wash., D.C.

1833
March - Mrs. Ann Brobston, by certificate from 3rd Ch. Philadelphia
Mrs. Ruth E. D. Clarke, by cert. from Cong. Ch. of Rutland, Mass.
Mrs. Cath. Newcomb, by certificate from Independent Presbyterian
   Church, Savannah, dismissed March 24, 1835
Mary Palmer, by certificate from Hanover St. Ch., Wilmington, Del.
Mary Ann Cole
Rebecca Rooker
Harriet Rooker, dismissed
Rachel Scobey
Joseph Hyde
June - Alexander Park, dismissed
John Elliott
Moor Falls, dead
September - William Skilling, by certificate from Belfast, Ireland
David Owen, from Wales
Jane Owen, from Wales
Caleb Owen, from Wales
Ann Maria Matthews
November - Harriet Park, by cert. from 2nd Ch., Alex., dismissed
Beverly C. Sanders, by certificate from 1st Church, Washington
Charlotte Sanders, by certificate frm 1st Church, Washington
Ann Sanders, by certificate from 1st Church, Washington, dismissed to
   go to Nashville, March 3, 1835
John W. Hamilton, by certificate from Poplen Pres. Church, N. C.
Sarah Ann Hamilton, by certificate from Poplen Pres. Church, N. C.
Margaret S. Duncan, by certificate from 1st Church, Carlisle
Maria Lowry Donaldson

1834
March - James Campbell
Ann B. Wilcox
Deborah H. Parsons
Mary Ann Hardester, dead
Catharine H. Latimer
Mary Ann Gilmor

Martha E. Robinson
Jane E. Biscoe
Catharine DeBartholt, by certificate, dismissed, 5th Church
Frances Barnes (colored)
June - Emily Cumming, dismissed to join Princeton, New Jersey
September - Lucy Ann Robertson
Margaret Hollingshead, by certificate from 1st Ch., Washington
Emma Cumming, by certificate from 2nd Church, Newark
Sarah DeBartholt, by certificate from Northampton, Pennsylvania, dismissed to 5th Church
Joseph F. Peters, by certificate from 2nd Church, Pittsburgh, dismissed March 30, 1835
William H. Fowler, by certificate from 1st Ch., Washington, dead
December - Mrs. Mary Ann Griffith
Miss Ann Clopper
Miss Amanda Reisinger
Mr. Robert W. Pendleton, by certificate from Presbyterian Church, Winchester, VA (stricken off - see minutes September 23, 1839)

1835
March - Maria Jane Scott, by certificate from Pres. Ch., Elkton
Mary Ann Scott, by certificate from Presbyterian Church, Elkton
Mrs. Sarah Gilmor
June 6 - Mrs. Anna Seward
James Watson
John McKeen, Jr., by certificate from 5th Presbyterian Church, Baltimore, dismissed November 21 to join western church

RECORD OF PERSONS RECEIVED INTO COMMUNION IN THE FIRST PRESBYTERIAN CHURCH, IN BALTIMORE, SINCE THE ACCESSION OF JOHN C. BACKUS TO THE <u>PASTORAL CHARGE OF THE SAME [BEGINNING WITH THE COMMUNIONS IN 1836]</u>
[Ed. Note: Many of the following names have M, S, or W after them. It has been assumed that meant "married," "single," or "widowed."]

1836
October - Jane Turner, deceased, M.
Elizabeth Jarvis, dismissed, S.
Mary Fisher, certificate from 3rd Ch.
Charles Powell, certificate from Pres. Ch., dismissed

1837
January - Amos Lovejoy, certificate from Bowdoin St. Ch., Boston
Minerva S. Haskell, cert. from Pres. Ch., N. Granville, N.Y., dead
William R. Stuart, cert. from Pres. Ch., Princess Ann, MD, removed
April - Luther Terry, cert. from 1st Ch., Hartford, Conn., removed
Eliza Grayson, W., cert. from Pres. Ch., Bardstown, KY, removed
John Rodgers, M., an Elder formerly connected with Mr. Duncan's church, deceased
Maria Hollins, M., deceased
---- [blank] Gould, M., removed
---- [blank] Riegart, S., deceased
July - John Ridout and Pru T. Ridout, formerly of the Presbyterian Church, Hagerstown, certificate past time for recd., dismissed
Mary Mathers, S., certificate from Pres. Ch., Baltimore, deceased
John Gore, M., admitted upon examination, removed
Ann Gore, M., admitted upon examination
Isabella Morris, S., admitted upon examination
Lavinia Smith, S., admitted upon examination
---- [blank] Page, W., admitted upon examination
---- [blank] McDonald, W., colored, admitted upon examination
October - Margaret Harwood, S., admitted upon examination, deceased
---- [blank] Saunders, W., admitted upon examination, dismissed
---- [blank] Parker, M., admitted upon examination, deceased
John Watts (colored), examined, formerly Methodist, no certificate
Benjamin Alleyre [Allegre?], admitted upon examination, dead
Mr. A. Crawford, C. [sic]

1838 - Admissions
John C. Ely, certificate from the Congregational Church
Eunice Ely, M., certificate from the Congregational Church
Catherine Stewart, W., cert. from 2nd Pres. Ch., Balt., deceased
Angelica Gill, W., certificate from 7th Pres. Ch., New York
Julius A. Fay, cert. from Cong. Ch., Waltham, Mass., dismissed
Aaron L. Chaprn [Chapin?], cert. from Yale College, New Haven, Ct.

---- [blank] Levering, W., on profession of faith, dead
Sarah Garland, M., on profession of faith
Isabella Mosher, M., on profession of faith
Gertrude Winder, S., on profession of faith, dead
Mrs. Bond, M., on profession of faith
Anna Morris, S., on profession of faith
Jane Porter, S., on profession of faith
Elizabeth Gwinn, S., on profession of faith
April - ---- [blank] Warfield, M., on profession of faith
---- [blank] Muncaster, M., on profession of faith, dismissed
Antoinette Harris, S., on profession of faith
Elizabeth S. Gilmor, S., on profession of faith
Margaret Armstrong, S., on profession of faith
Louisa Dunbar, S., on profession of faith
Nancy Bailey, S., on profession of faith, dismissed
Frances Jane Hazlehurst, S., on profession of faith
Amanda Stratton, M., by certificate, dismissed
July - ---- [blank] Taylor, M., on profession of faith
July - ---- [blank] Clara, W., on profession of faith
Mary Jane Finley, S., on profession of faith, deceased
Aurelia Winder, S., on profession of faith, dismissed
Margaret Armstrong, S., on profession of faith
Mary Foreman, S., on profession of faith
Mary McKeen, S., on profession of faith
Martha Richards, S., on profession of faith
Harriet Tyrrell, S., on profession of faith, deceased
Elizabeth Swearer, S., on profession of faith, dismissed
Willowby Lewis, M., on certificate or rather from Mr. Gibson's church without
Anna G. Turnbull, M., on certificate from 1st Church, Philadelphia
October - Eloisa Michard, M., on certificate from Central Presby. Church in New York
---- [blank] Whitmarsh, M., on profession of faith, dismissed
Dr. Sidney Buchanan, S., on profession of faith, dismissed
Susanna G. McDowell, S., on profession of faith
Mary Flanagan, S., on profession of faith, dismissed
Sarah Smith, S., on profession of faith, removed
Percy Richards, S., on profession of faith
Charlotte Robinson, S., on profession of faith, dismissed
Margaret Fay, M., certificate from 2nd Pres. Ch., Balt., dismissed

1839
January - Dr. Alexander Robinson, M., on profession of faith
Susanna Atkinson, W., on profession of faith
Ann Porter, S., on profession of faith, dismissed
April - Louisa Rodgers, S., on profession of faith
Caroline Bentz, W., on profession of faith
Eliza Clarke, W., on certificate from 2nd Ch., Washington, deceased
Frances Clarke, S., certificate from 2nd Ch., Washington, dismissed
Elizabeth Clarke, S., certificate from 2 Ch., Washington, dismissed
Letitia Clarke, S., certificate from 2nd Ch., Washington, dismissed
July - James Imbrie, S., certificate from 6th Ch., Phila, dismissed

Maria Jones, S., colored, admitted upon examination, and dismissed
October - Jane Parkhill, M., admitted by certificate

1840
January - Jane Jones, certificate from 1st Ch., Washington DC, dead
Matilda Otterson, certificate from 1st Ch. Washington DC, dismissed
---- [blank] Davis, M., on profession of faith, dismissed
Mary Harwood, M., on profession of faith
Mary Harwood, S., on profession of faith
Mary Hall, S., on profession of faith, deceased 1848
Mary Roberts, S., on profession of faith
Margaret Bridner, S., on profession of faith
Susannah Bridner, S., on profession of faith
Margaret Irwing, S., on profession of faith
John B. Fulton, M., on profession of faith, dismissed
James Childs, M., on profession of faith, dismissed
April - James Whitmarsh, S., on profession of faith, dismissed
Jane Senseny, W., on profession of faith, dismissed
Mrs. Edward Taylor, M., on profession of faith, dismissed
Louisa Howard Hoffman, M., on profession of faith, dismissed
Mary Williams, M., on profession of faith, dismissed by discipline
Mary Keller, S., on profession of faith, dismissed by discipline
Mary Bridner, S., on profession of faith, dismissed
Ann Whiteman, S., on profession of faith, dismissed
---- [blank] Lestie, S., on profession of faith, dismissed
Elizabeth Arnold, S., on profession of faith, dismissed

July - Letitia C. Backus, W., certificate from 1st Pres. Ch. Phila.
Grace Brown, S., on profession of faith, dismissed
October - M. S. Baer, on certificate from 5th Church, Baltimore
Matilda C. Baer, on certificate from 5th Church, Baltimore
Lydia R. Baer, on certificate from 5th Church, Baltimore
Isabella Caldwell, on certificate from 5th Church, Baltimore, dismissed to South Carolina
Sophia Howard, on profession of faith, dismissed
Elizabeth Phillips, on profession of faith
J. H. Stickney, on profession of faith, dismissed

LIST OF THE OFFICERS OF THE FIRST PRESBYTERIAN CHURCH OF BALTIMORE (MINISTERS, ELDERS, DEACONS, TRUSTEES, SEXTONS) FROM 1763 TO 1840

[Information gleaned from *A Brief History of the First Presbyterian Church of Baltimore*, by William Reynolds, Session Member, in 1913; *The First Presbyterian Church of Baltimore: A Two-Century Chronicle* by Rev. John Hamish Gardner, Jr., D. D. (Pastor, 1936-1962), 1962].

Rev. Patrick Allison, D. D., Minister, 1763-1802
Rev. James Inglis, D. D., Minister, 1802-1819
Rev. William Nevins, D. D., Minister, 1820-1835
Rev. John C. Backus, D. D., Minister, 1836-1879
William Lyon, M. D., Elder, 1763/1781?-before 1797
John Smith, Elder, 1763/1781?-before 1797
Col. William Buchanan, Elder, 1763/1781?-before 1804
James Sterrett, Elder, 1763/1781?-before 1797
William Smith, Elder, 1797 - before 1804
Robert Purviance, Elder, 1797-1806 (died)
James Calhoun, Elder, 1797-before 1804
Robert Gilmor, Elder, 1797-before 1804
David Stewart, Elder, 1797-1817
Christopher Johnston, Elder, 1797-1817
George Salmon, Elder, 1804-1807
Ebenezer Finley, Elder, 1804-1817
John McKeen, Elder, 1809-1818
Stewart Brown, Elder, 1809-1818
Maxwell McDowell, M. D., Elder, 1814-1817, 1829-1848

FIRST PRESBYTERIAN CHURCH 187

Col. James Mosher, Elder, 1814-1817, 1818-1840
Thomas Finley, Elder, 1814-1818
David W. Boisseau, Elder, 1814-1818
John F. Keys, Elder, 1816-1817
William W. Taylor, Elder, 1818-1829
James Delacour, Elder, 1819-1822
George Morris, Elder, 1829-1846
David S. Courtenay, Elder, 1833-1840
John N. Brown, Elder, 1833-1852
William L. Gill, Elder, 1833-1880
John Rogders, Elder, 1840-1861
David Stewart, M. D., Elder, 1840-1847
John Falconer, Elder, 1840-1847
James Stirling, Deacon, 1804-?
John McKeen, Deacon, 1804-1809
John Taggart, Deacon, 1804-?
Henry C. Turnbull, Deacon, 1840-1847
John H. Haskell, Deacon, 1840-1847
Moses Hyde, Deacon, 1840-1847
Lancaster Ould, Deacon, 1840-1847
John Smith, Trustee, 1764-1781
William Lyon, M. D., Trustee, 1764-1781
Col. William Buchanan, Trustee, 1764-1781
William Smith, Trustee, 1764-1814
William Spear, Trustee, 1764-1789
James Sterrett, Trustee, 1764-1781
Jonathan Plowman, Trustee, 1764-1774
Alexander Stenhouse, M. D., Trustee, 1765-1775
John Boyd, M. D., Trustee, 1765-1789
Robert Purviance, Trustee, 1765-1806 (died)
Samuel Purviance, Trustee, 1770-1787
John Little, Trustee, 1770-1773
Samuel Brown, Trustee, 1771
James Calhoun, Trustee, 1771-1816
William Neill, Trustee, 1773-1785
Hugh Young, Trustee, 1779-1783
John Sterrett, Trustee, 1779-1785
David Stewart, Trustee, 1779-1818
Nathaniel Smith, Trustee, 1779-1787
Joseph Donaldson, Trustee, 1782-1783

Robert Gilmor, Trustee, 1782-1822
Gen. Samuel Smith, Trustee, 1782-1835
William Patterson, Trustee, 1785-1811
Christopher Johnston, Trustee, 1787-1819
George Brown, M. D., Trustee, 1787-1821
Stephen Wilson, Trustee, 1789-1794
Gen. John Swann, Trustee, 1790-1818
William Robb, Trustee, 1792-1804
J. A. Buchanan, Trustee, 1796-1810
George Salmon, Trustee, 1804-1807
Gen. John Stricker, Trustee, 1807-1822
Stewart Brown, Trustee, 1807-1832
Col. James McHenry, Trustee, 1810-1816
Amos A. Williams, Trustee, 1812-1822
Alexander Fridge, Trustee, 1814-1839
Alexander McDonald, Trustee, 1816-1836
James Cox, Trustee, 1817-1844
Robert Purviance, Jr., Trustee, 1818-1825
James Calhoun, Jr., Trustee, 1818-1819
Judge Alexander Nisbet, Trustee, 1819-1854
Robert Smith, Trustee, 1822-1828
Robert Gilmor, Jr., Trustee, 1822-1840
Judge John Purviance, Trustee, 1822-1854
John McHenry, Trustee, 1822
Jonathan Meredith, Trustee, 1822-1825
George Brown, Trustee, 1825-1859
Roswell L. Colt, Trustee, 1828-1836
John T. Barr, Trustee, 1828-1832
Henry Bird, Trustee, 1831-1832
James Armstrong, Trustee, 1832-1839
Archibald Stirling, Trustee, 1832-1835, 1839-1888
James Swann, Trustee, 1832-1854
Alexander Murdoch, Trustee, 1835-1856, 1858-1879
James Campbell, Trustee, 1835-1838
Francis T. Hyde, Trustee, 1836-1855
Francis Forman, Trustee, 1836-1854
Thomas Finley, Trustee, 1838-1846
Christian A. Schaefer, Trustee, 1839-1846
---- [blank] Morris, Sexton, 1767-?
William Flahaven, Sexton, ?-1772

Henry Cain, Sexton, 1784-?
Charles Young, Sexton, 1805-1810
John Hasselbaugh, Sexton, 1811-1814
John Spence, Sexton, 1826-1845

SECOND PRESBYTERIAN CHURCH, BALTIMORE CITY - NAMES OF MEMBERS AND OTHERS CONTAINED IN THE CHURCH COMMITTEE'S MINUTES AND TREASURER'S ACCOUNTS, 1803-1830, FROM AN INDEX BY V. B. BARNES, c1939. [A COPY OF THIS RECORD BOOK IS MAINTAINED AT MARYLAND HISTORICAL SOCIETY.]

H. Abbott, Robert C. Aisquith, A. Aitken, Andrew Aitken (Aiken), Robert Aitken (Aiken), Dr. Patrick Allison, Rev. Dr. Alexander, James Alexander, James W. Alexander, H. Alricks, Harmanus Alricks, H. Anderson, Henry Anderson, N. Andrews, Nat. Andrews, Nathaniel Andrews, Dr. Annan, S. Annan, Samuel Annan, David Armour, James Armstrong, James Armstrong and son, J. Armstrong, Robert Armstrong, Robert C. Armstrong, John Arnold, William Ashmead, Hugh Auther.

Jno. Bailey, John Bankson, John Bannimon, William Bantz, Joseph Barker, P. Barker, William Barker, Mrs. Barnes, Samuel Barnes, Mrs. James Barnes, Mr. Barney, J. H. Barney, John H. Barney, Joshua Barney, ---- Barrett, John Barron, ---- Beatty, James Beatty, W. T. Beatty, William Beatty, William H. Beatty, James Beers, Leonard Belt, Rev. Dr. Bend, Col. Biays (Byas), James Biays, George Bier, John Bishop, Mrs. Blair, Elizabeth Blair, Judge Bland, Theodorick Bland, Harmanus Boggs, John G. Boggs, Hugh Bonner, John Borland, J. Boulding, Jehu Boulding, James Bowie, Peter Boyd, John Breckenridge (Brackenridge), The Rev. Mr. Breckenridge, Robert J. Breckenridge, Thomas Bramley, B. Bromer, William Bromwell, Capt. Brown, Alexander Brown, ---- Bryson, John Bryson, N. Bryson, N. G. Bryson, Nathan G. Bryson, Nathaniel G. Bryson, Mr. Buchanan, R. Buchanan, Robert Buchanan, Humphrey Buckler, David Burke, Richard Burnett, Samuel Burns, G. Butler, W. H. Byrne.

James Caldwell, Thomas Caldwell, ---- Caldwell, B. C. Calhoun, Thomas Calwell, Mr. Camp, William Camp, Mrs. Campbell, Archibald Campbell, D. Cannon, Dennis Cannon (Canon), W. F. Carey, John Carnes, James Carnighan, Patrick Caughey, Captain Chase (Chace), Bissel Chase, T. Chase, Thomas Chase, Thorndike Chase, Daniel Cheston, Mons. Chevaliery, William Childs, Adam Clackner, James Clark, Mrs. Clem, Dr. Clendenen (Clendening), A. Clendenen, William H. Clendenen, Andrew Clopper, Edward N. Clopper, Peter Clopper, David Cochran,

SECOND PRESBYTERIAN CHURCH 191

William Cochran and brothers, John Cole, ---- Cole, Thomas Cole, William Cole, John Cook, Henry S. Coulter, Dr. John Coulter, Mrs. Craggs, ---- Craggs, Mr. Craig, J. Craig, John Craig, John D. Craig, John Crawford, Jno. Creaton, Hans J. Creery, J. Creery, Jonathan Creery. Walter Crook, Mr. Cross, A. Cross, Andrew Cross, Robert Cross, William Cross, William S. Cross and Company, Captain Cunningham (Cunnyngham), H. Cunningham, John Cunningham.

Abraham Davidson, Daniel Davidson, James Davidson, Christopher Deshen (Deshon), Thomas Dewit, George S. Dickey, ---- Dickson (Dixon), Thomas Dickson, John Diffenderffer, Mr. Dinsmore, Patrick Dinsmore, George Dobbin, Thomas Dobbin, Mrs. Doddy, James Donnelly, Joshua Dorsey, John Dougherty, Cumberland Dugan, Henry Dukehart, John Duncan, R. Dunwoody, Robert Dunwoody, P. Durkee.

N. W. Easton, Mrs. Easton, Mr. Edwards, ---- Edwards, Samuel Elberger, Mr. Elliot (Elliott), John Elliott, Jos. Ennis, W. Evans.

Peter Fenby, Robert Ferguson, Thomas Finley, Henry M. Fisher, William Lee Foreman, Alexander Forsyth, John Frail, Mr. Fransiscus, J. Fransiscus, John Fransiscus, William H. Freeman, A. & J. Fulton, David Fulton, William Fulton.

Alexander Gallagher, James Galloway, Mr. Gable, R. Gamble (Gambal), Mr. Gamble, T. Gamble, Thomas Gamble, John Gardner, Captain Gibson, James Gibson, James Gibson Jr., William Gibson, J. H. Giese, W. H. Giese, W. Hy. Giese, Archibald George, Alexander Gifford, George Gilbreath, J. S. Gilman (Gillman), Jacob Glaser, Misses Glendy, Rev. Mr. John Glendy, John W. Glenn and Company, John Gordon, William Gordon, Dr. Graham, David Graham, H. Graham, Hamilton Graham, James Graham, Robert Graham, William Graham, William T. Graham, Mrs. Grant, H. W. Gray, Walton Gray, Thomas Greer, Mr. Gregg, James Grieves, Rev. Mr. Guiteau, James Gunn.

Charles Hall, James Hall, Levin Hall, Mr. Hall, ---- Halleck, Alexander Hamilton, J. Hamilton, James Hamilton, John A. Hamilton, Charles Hammill, ---- Hanna, A. B. Hanna, Alexander B. Hanna, Andrew Hanna, James Hanna, John Hanna, Charles C. Harper, Hall Harrison, William G. Harrison, Jos. Haskins Jr., James Haslett, William Haslett, John Hasloop (Heslip), Mr. Haynes, D. F. Haynes, William Hays, Hugh

Hazelton, James Herron (Heron), R. B. Herron, A. Hill, T. G. Hill,
Thomas G. Hill, ---- Hiss, George Hobson, Joseph Hodges, John
Hoffman, Jos. Holbrook, Josh. Holbrook, ---- Hollins, Mr. Hollins, John
Hollins, J. Smith Hollins, J. S. Hollins, John Smith Hollins, Mr. Hook,
William Hooper, John E. Howard, Robert Howard, William Hubberd, J.
Hudgins, Christopher Hughes, William Hughes, John Hutson, Mr.
Hutton, J. Hutton, James Hutton.

Rev. Dr. Inglis, Andrew Ingram, J. Jackson, James Jackson, George
Jacobs, John James, Joseph Jamison, P. Janvier, Rev. Dr. Johns,
James Johnson, Mrs. Jones, Talbot Jones.

Captain Kane, John M. Kane, John Kearns, Daniel Keho, Luke
Kiersted (Keirsted), Henry Kelsy, J. Kennedy (Kenedy), John Kennedy,
Henry Kerl, Archibald Kerr, R. J. Kerr, David Kirkland, Jer.
Kirkpatrick, Samuel Knox, R. Kribs, William Kribs (Krebs), ---- Kyle,
Adam B. Kyle, Adam E. Kyle.

Richard Landy (Lundy), Jacob Laudenslayer (Laudenslager), A. Law,
James Law, Robert Lawson, Thomas Layman, Mr. Leache, Thomas
Leaman, R. Lemmon, ---- Lemmon, ---- Liggett, Thomas M. Linnard, K.
Long, Kennedy Long, Robert Carey Long, Henry Long, John
Loughridge, Colonel Loury, Samuel Loury, Miss Love, Mr. Lovell, Mr.
Lyon.

John McAllister, Michael McBlair, John McCabe, John McCalister, Mr.
McClanahan, William M. McCleary, Robert McCleery, M. McClellan,
Samuel McClellan, R. McClelland, ---- McClernan, William McCleve, Mr.
McConkey, ---- McConkey, Mrs. McConkey, James McConkey, John
McConkey, W. McConkey, William McConkey, William McCormick,
Mrs. McCurdy, ---- McCurdy, Hugh McCurdy, Mr. McDonald, Col.
McDonald, Gen. McDonald, Jn. McDonald, P. McDonald, William
McDonald, Dr. McDowel, ---- McElderry, Hugh McElderry, Thomas
McElderry, Mr. McEldin, John McElivee, P. McGuire (McGuyer),
Patrick McGuire, John McIlroy, John McIntire, Rev. Mr. McKay, C.
McKenzie, T.M. McKenzie, Mrs. McKim, John McKim, John McKim
Jr., Samuel McKim, W. D. McKim, William D. McKim, John McKinnell,
Mr. McKonkey, Mr. McLaughlin, Major and Colonel McLaughlin,
Matthew McLaughlin, M. McLaughlin, Robert McLaughlin, Charles
McLean, James McNeil, John McWilliam.

SECOND PRESBYTERIAN CHURCH 193

Thomas Marean, J. Martin, James Martin, Moses Maxwell, Alexander Maydwell, Charles H. Mercer, --- Mezick, B. Mezick, Babtist Mezick, George Miles, Rev. Dr. Miller, G. W. Miller, Jacob Miller, James Miller, Robert Miller, Samuel Miller, Mr. Millimon (Milleman), George Millimon, Alexander Mitchell, Edward Mitchell, Francis J. Mitchell, ---- Mitchell, Samuel Moale, J. Monroe, John Monteith, Mr. Moody, John Moore (Moor), John Lee Moore, R. Moore and sons, Robert Moore, Samuel Moore, Thomas Moore, J. Morrow, James Morrow, John Morrow, A. B. Morton, James Moshier, George Meyers (Moyers), Mr. Monroe (Munroe), Isaac Monroe, Joel Munson, Mr. Murphy, Thomas Murphy, ---- Murray (Murry).

Hugh Neilson, Mrs. Neilson, John Nelson, Robert Nesbit, Rev. Mr. Nevins, William Nevins, Lawson (Lason) Newman, Mrs. Norris, William Norris, N. Oliver, Mr. Oston.

Dr. Page, James Page, J. Pannell, James Pannell, A. Parks, Andrew Parks, John Parks, Elisha Parr, ---- Patterson, Rev. Mr. Patterson, A. Patterson, Andrew Patterson, Walter Patterson, Walter Patterson Jr., ---- Payson, Henry Payson, William Pechin, H. Pennington, Mrs. Perry, D. Peters, Daniel Peters, George Philips, William Pinkerton, W. Pinckney, Mr. Plowman, ---- Poe, Mr. Poe, David Poe, Jacob Poe, ---- Purviance, James Purviance.

Christopher Raborg, C. Raborg and son, Mrs. Ramsay, James Ramsay, Mrs. Rankin, John Readell, V. Reynolds, W. Rickey, Captain Ridgely, Thomas Ring, J.O. Rodgers, Richard Rodgers, J.C. Rogers, R. Rogers, Richard Rogers, Mr. Rogers, William Roney, Mr. Ross, B. C. Ross, Benjamin C. Ross, R. Ross, William Ross, Js. Rouse, Thomas Ryan.

Mrs. Sabby, Nathaniel Saltonstall, William Sankey, James Sears, Jeffry Dillon Shanley, Mr. and Mrs. Shaw, John Shaw, John Shedden, Thomas Sheppard (Shepperd), Joseph Shore, John Silvers, Thomas Sinclair, Samuel Slater, ---- Slemmer (Slimmer), C. Slemmer, Christian Slemmer, ---- Sloan, J. Sloan, James Sloan, Jacob Small, Mr. Smith, Dr. Smith, A. Smith, Arnold Smith, J. S. Smith, John Smith, Joseph Smith, Mrs. Joseph Smith, Ralph Smith, Samuel Smith, Dr. Smull, D. B. Smull, Mr. Solomon, Elkin Solomon, L. Solomon, James Somervill, Captain Southward (Southard), William Southward, Mr. Spear, Jos. Spear, Mrs. Spence, Robert Spencer, William T. Spurrier, ----

Stansbury, Joshua Stapleton, Henry Star (Starr), Matthew Steene, Mr. Sterett, Dr. Sterling, W. Sterling, Dr. W. Sterling, William Sterling, J. Stevens, Mr. Stevenson, Mr. Stewart (Stuart), Colonel Stewart, A. Stewart. D. C. Stewart, David C. Stewart, James Stewart. Mrs. James Stewart, John Stewart, Robert Stewart, R. Stewart, Richardson Stewart, Thomas Stewart, William Stewart, W. Stewart, John Stickney, T. Stiff, E. Stiles, Edward Stiles, G. Stiles, George Stiles, Mr. Stiles, Mary Stiles, W. Stirling Jr., William Stirling, Mrs. Stockden, ---- Swan, J. E. Swan, John Swan, John E. Swan, P. Swartz, Thomas Sweeting.

---- Tagart, L. S. Tarr (Terr), Levin S. Tarr, Levin Tarr and Company, John B. Taylor, William Taylor, Walter Thecker, P. E. Thomas, James Thompson, N. Thompson, Nathaniel Thompson, William Thompson, A. Thornton, George Tower, ---- Trimble, William Trimble, Jas. Trippe, Mr. Tutton.

---- Usher, William Van Wyck, Jno. Vance, William Vance, J. B. Varnum, Steven Vickery.

S. Walker, J. Wallace, Joseph Wallace, George Warner, Thomas Warner, General Washington, Mr. Waters, Samuel Weeks, J. West, William Whann, ---- White, Dr. White, J. C. White, John C. White and son, John Campbell White, Thomas White, Charles Whitely, Alexander Wiley, Mr. Williams, Amos A. Williams, N. F. Williams, Nathaniel Williams Jr., Sam Williams, Thomas Willis, W. and T. Willis, ---- Wilson, J. Wilson, John Wilson, William Wilson, H. Wright, Vincent Wyle, David Yerkess, J. Young.

SECOND PRESBYTERIAN CHURCH, BALTIMORE, MEMBERSHIP ROLLS, 1826-1840

[Note: These church membership rolls begin in 1826, but they do not give dates of admission until 1833. Therefore, it is assumed that those names without dates were admitted between 1826 and 1833, so the phrase "admitted before 1833" is used in the following list. Also, a name in parenthesis after the member's name may indicate either the person the member lived with, or their married name. It is not clear from the ledger unless it actually said they married.] A copy of the ledger is in the Maryland Historical Society

SECOND PRESBYTERIAN CHURCH 195

Library, with the following introductory note written by J. H. Brown, clerk: "This record book contains the names of all the persons who were admitted to the church during the ministry of the several pastors commencing with that of the Rev. Dr. John Breckenridge up to the present time. Dr. John Breckenridge commenced his labours in the autumn of 1826. There are also recorded the names of such as were members before that time [and] they are designated in the book by the following =." [Ed. Note: Here the recorder put a double line that resembled an equals (=) sign]. "Baltimore, June 11, 1853."

Aitken, Mrs., admitted before 1833, died [no dates given]
Andrews, Mrs., admitted before 1833, died [no dates given]
Anderson, Christiana, admitted before 1833 [no date given]
Annan, Samuel, admitted before 1833 [no date given], dismissed 1834
Armour, Ann Eliza, admitted before 1833 [no date], dismissed 1834
Andrews, Miss Jane W.[?], admitted before 1833 [no date given]
Andrews, Miss Hannah Buckler, admitted before 1833 [no date given]
Archer, John T., admitted before 1833 [no date given], struck off by order of session September 20, 1847
Alberger, Lavinia, admitted before 1833 [no date given], struck off by order of session September 20, 1847
Aitken, Rebecca, admitted before 1833, dismissed [no dates given]
Armour, Miss Elizabeth, admitted December, 1833, died October, 1842
Armour, Joseph G., admitted July, 1835
Alricks, Miss Harriet, admitted July, 1838
Alricks, Miss Jane, admitted, October, 1839
Alnutt, Mrs. Margaret, admitted March, 1840, baptized [no date]
Armour, James, admitted January, 1834
Alberger, Mrs. Job, admitted October, 1834, dismissed 1839
Abbott, Mrs. Lydia, admitted November, 1838
Anspeck, Mrs., admitted November, 1838
Biays, Mrs. James, admitted before 1833 [no date given]
Beatty, William H., admitted before 1833 [no date given]
Bankson, Mrs., admitted before 1833 [no date given]
Beatty, James, admitted before 1833, died October 5, 1851
Beatty, Mrs. James, admitted before 1833 [no date], died June, 1851
Bryson, Nathan G., admitted before 1833 [no date], died June, 1851
Barney, J. H., admitted before 1833 [no date], died June, 1851
Byrne, Mrs., admitted before 1833 [no date], died February, 1848
Brown, Mrs. Mary, admitted before 1833 [no date given]

Barrier, Miss Ann, (Mrs. Moore), admitted by 1833 [no date given]
Barrickman, Hannah, admitted before 1833 [no date], died Feb., 1848
Burke, Mrs., admitted before 1833 [no date given], dismissed 1847
Barklie, Mrs. Jane, admitted before 1833 [no date], dismissed 1847
Barklie, Anna, admitted before 1833 [no date given], dismissed 1847
Barklie, Jane, admitted before 1833 [no date given], dismissed 1847
Barklie, Hester, admitted before 1833 [no date], dismissed 1847
Beattie, Sarah, (Mrs. David McKim), admitted before 1833 [no date]
Bigham, John, deacon, admitted by 1833 [no date], dismissed 1847
Baker, Mrs. Elizabeth, admitted before 1833 [no date given], struck off by order of session September 20, 1847
Barrier, Rebecca, (Mrs. Thomas), admitted by 1833, dismissed 1846
Barklie, Emily, admitted before 1833, dismissed September, 1846
Barrier, Mrs. Jane, admitted before 1833 [no date given]
Brown, Mrs. Susan, admitted before 1833 [no date given], struck off by order of session November 8, 1847
Brooks, Nathan C., admitted before 1833 [no date], dropped 1840
Bolton, Mrs. Hannah, admitted before 1833, and "left" [no dates]
Beatty, Mrs. Mary N., admitted before 1833 [no date given]
Byrne, Miss Anne, admitted before 1833 [no date given]
Beatty, Mrs. Elizabeth, (Mrs. Hugh Purviance), admitted before 1833
Brown, Jacob Harman, ruling elder, admitted before 1833 [no date]
Brown, Mrs. Margarette, admitted before 1833 [no date given]
Boggs, Mrs. A. J., admitted before 1833 [no date given]
Belt, Miss Mary, admitted February, 1833
Breckinridge, Mrs. Sophoniste, admitted Feb. 1833, died Dec. 1844
Bickly, Samuel, admitted February, 1833
Buck, Miss Maria, (Mrs. Cooth), admitted February, 1833, baptized
Bowie, Miss Maria, admitted February, 1833
Byrne, Miss Isabella, admitted December, 1833
Black, Mrs. Eliza, admitted December, 1833, dismissed 1838
Bowen, Miss Hannah, admitted December, 1833, struck off by order of session [no date, probably September 20, 1847]
Brown, Thomas, admitted December, 1833
Bowie, Mrs. Ann, admitted December, 1833
Bolton, Mrs. Marie, admitted December, 1833, struck off by order of session September 20, 1847
Barnes, James G., admitted November, 1834, struck off by order of session September 20, 1847
Blakey, Mrs. Mary, admitted March, 1835, excommunicated [no date]

SECOND PRESBYTERIAN CHURCH 197

Brown, Robert, admitted March, 1836, dismissed 1863
Brown, Sarah A., admitted March, 1836, died 1841
Barrier, Eliza, admitted December, 1839, died July, 1883
Boggs, William, admitted December, 1839, dismissed 1862
Boggs, Mrs. Caroline, admitted December, 1839, died March, 1847
Bannerman, Miss, admitted April, 1834, died August 12, 1856
Baldwin, Mrs. Sophia, admitted March, 1836, dismissed March, 1846
Bright, Edward, admitted March, 1836, struck off by order of session November 8, 1847
Cross, Mrs. Rachel, admitted before 1833, died 1843
Cross, Miss Eliza, admitted before 1833, died March, 1846
Cross, Miss Martha, admitted before 1833, died February 8, 1855
Cross, Miss Phillis, admitted before 1833, died in 1855
Crawford, Mrs. Rachel, admitted before 1833, died in 1855
Caldwell, Caroline (Mrs. Norris, Abingdon), admitted before 1826 =
Carson, George, ruling elder, admitted before 1826, died 1841 =
Chase, Miss Elizabeth, admitted before 1833, and "left" [no date]
Clem, Mrs. Maria, admitted before 1833, struck off by order of session September 20, 1847
Childs, Mary, admitted before 1833, and "left" [no dates given]
Conkling, Mrs. Elizabeth, admitted before 1833 [no date given]
Cross, Richard J., ruling elder, admitted before 1833 [no date given], died November 19, 1856
Cross, Andrew Boyd, admitted before 1833 [no date given], licensed to preach [no date given]
Champlain, Eliza P., admitted before 1833 [no date given], married Mr. Trippe, and turned Methodist [no date given]
Creary, Miss Catharine, admitted before 1833 [no date given]
Cross, Miss Margaret, (Mrs. Boyd), admitted by 1833, dismissed 1846
Carson, Mrs. Eliza, admitted before 1833, dismissed March, 1847
Cummins, Thomas, admitted before 1833 [no date], died 1835
Cummins, Mrs. Jane, admitted before 1833 [no date], died 1841
Cox, John, admitted before 1833 [no date given], dropped 1841
Crawford, Mrs. Eliza, admitted before 1833 [no date], dropped 1841
Coulson, Miss Georg. [sic], admitted before 1833, and dropped 1851
Crawford, Anna Maria, admitted by 1833, "gone to New Orleans," 1847
Coward, Mrs. Margaret, admitted before 1833 [no date given], struck off by order of session September 20, 1847
Carroll, William H., admitted before 1833, dropped September, 1847
Carroll, Mrs. Mary A., admitted before 1833, dropped Sept., 1847

Coulter, Mrs. Mary Ann, admitted before 1833 [no date given]
Cockey, Mrs. Eliza, admitted before 1833, dismissed July 27, 1846
Cross, Sarah Patterson, admitted before 1833 [no date given], married Capt. Trippe, died October 3, 1853
Coulston, Miss Margta. [sic], admitted before 1833, dismissed 1852
Cross. Richard J., admitted November, 1832, died September 20, 1849
Chapman, Mrs. Ann, admitted April, 1833, died September 20, 1849
Cross, Miss Elizabeth, (Mrs. Webster), admitted May 1833, dismissed
Cross, Miss Jane, (Mrs. Moore), admitted Dec., 1833, dismissed 1853
Carothers, Miss Jane, admitted December, 1833, dismissed [no date]
Cook, John, admitted December, 1833, struck off by order of session September 20, 1847
Carson, Samuel K., admitted December, 1833, struck off by order of session September 20, 1847
Carson, Miss Elizabeth, admitted December, 1833, died January, 1834
Carson, George Jr., admitted December, 1833, struck off by order of session [no date, probably September 20, 1847]
Carter, John P., minister, admitted January, 1834, and licensed to preach [no date given]
Carter, Mrs. Martha, admitted January, 1834
Carter, Sophia Ann, admitted November, 1834
Carter, Miss Matilda, admitted November, 1834, baptized [no date]
Carter, Miss Maria, admitted November, 1834, baptized [no date]
Cooper, George E., admitted March, 1835, dismissed 1844
Cummings, Miss Jane, admitted October, 1839, dismissed 1845
Clendinin, W. A., admitted December, 1833, struck off by order of session September 20, 1847
Carroll, Miss Louisa, admitted Dec., 1833, dismissed March 18, 1846
Cooper, Sarah A., now Mrs. Carey, admitted Mar., 1835, died [date?]
Carey, W. F., ruling elder, admitted March, 1835, dismissed [died?]
Cockrill, Sophia, admitted January, 1839, dismissed May, 1846
Dinsmore, Patrick, admitted before 1833, died December 28, 1851
Dickson, Mr. J., admitted before 1833 [no date given]
Dickson, Mr. W., admitted before 1833 [no date given]
Dobbin, Mrs., admitted before 1833 [no date given]
Duff, Mrs., admitted before 1833 [no date given], died 1846
Davidson, Mrs., admitted before 1833, died December 21, 1852
Dinsmore, Mrs., admitted before 1833 [no date given], struck off by order of session September 20, 1847
Doherty, Mrs., admitted before 1833 [no date given], died 1863

SECOND PRESBYTERIAN CHURCH 199

De La Roche, Mrs. Jane, admitted before 1833, and "left" [1847?]
Dunn, Mrs. Elizabeth, admitted before 1833 [no date], died 1841
Debarthall, Miss Sarah, admitted before 1833 [no date given]
Dunn, Miss Jane, admitted before 1833 [no date], died May, 1855
Dubois, Mrs. Jane Elliott, admitted 1833, died July, 1848
Davidson, Miss Mary Ann, (Mrs. McCormick), admitted before 1833
Dorrance, James, admitted before 1833 [no date given], struck off by order of session September 20, 1847
Dinsmore, John M., admitted before 1828, died 1828
Dale, Samuel, admitted before 1833 [no date given], struck off by order of session September 20, 1847
Dugent, Francis, admitted before 1833 [no date given], struck off by order of session November 8, 1847
Dinsmore, Miss Margaret, admitted before 1833, dismissed 1851
Dailey, William F., admitted December, 1833, dismissed 1843
Deaver, Miss Honora, admitted January, 1834, struck off by order of session September 20, 1847
Dougherty, Jane, admitted December, 1833 [name scratched off list]
Dubois, Edmund C., elder, admitted Mar., 1840, dismissed June, 1847
Dorsey, Mrs. Rebecca, admitted March, 1840, dismissed June, 1840
Dorsey, Dr. Lloyd, admitted March, 1840, dismissed June, 1840
Dukehart, Elizabeth, admitted March, 1837, dismissed 1841
Davis, Miss Phoebe, admitted March, 1838, married Capt. Gray, dismissed [no date given]
Drew, Capt. Joseph, admitted April, 1839, struck off by order of session September 20, 1847
Downs, Dr. Dion, admitted April, 1840, died August 2, 1857
Dailey, Ann Jane, admitted April, 1840, dismissed 1844
Dougherty, Jane, admitted September, 1840, dismissed [no date]
Elder, Miss Mary, "married and gone," circa 1833 [no date given]
Entniggle, John Joseph, admitted December 1833, died June, 1846
Everhart, Ester, admitted June, 1840, dismissed 1841
Fransiscus, J. M., admitted before 1833, dismissed March, 1846
Fransiscus, Mrs. J. M., admitted before 1833, dismissed March, 1846
Fenby, Peter, ruling elder, admitted before 1826, dismissed 1846 =
Fenby, Samuel, admitted before 1833 [no date given], died 1834
Fenby, Mrs. Alley, admitted before 1833, dismissed March, 1846
Fenby, Miss Theodosia, admitted before 1833 [no date], died 1866
Fenby, Peter Jr., admitted before 1833 [no date given], died 1834

Farnham, Catharine, admitted before 1833 [no date given], struck off by order of session September 20, 1847
Freyer, Miss Eleanor, admitted February, 1833, dismissed [no date]
Fenby, Miss Ann, admitted December, 1833, dismissed March, 1846
Fenby, Miss Sarah, now Mrs. Baggs [Boggs?], admitted December, 1833 and dismissed in 1848
Fenby, Miss Theodosia, admitted December, 1833, dismissed [no date]
Fenby, Ann Jane, admitted December, 1833, dismissed [no date]
Fenby, Richard D., admitted December, 1838, dismissed Mar. 18, 1846
Francis, Mary A., colored,, admitted April, 1833
Gallager, Mrs. A., admitted before 1833 [no date given]
Graham, Mrs. Hamilton, admitted before 1833 [no date], died 1849
Graham, Miss Rachel, admitted before 1833 [no date], died 1849
Graham, Miss Rach. J., admitted before 1833, dismissed Jan., 1849
Graham, Miss Mary, admitted before 1833, dismissed January, 1849
Gamble, Mr., admitted before 1833 [no date given], died 1844
Gibson, Mrs., admitted before 1833 [no date], died January, 1849
Giles, Mrs. Ann, admitted before 1826 = [no date given]
Giles, Jacob, admitted before 1833 [no date], died November 7, 1851
Graham, Jane, admitted before 1833, and "left" [no dates given]
George, Archibald Sr., admitted before 1833 [no date], died 1840
George, Archibald Jr., admitted before 1833 [no date], died 1862
George, Mrs. Isabella, admitted before 1833 [no date given]
George, William, admitted before 1832 [no date], dismissed 1832
George, Mrs. Jane, admitted before 1833 [no date given]
Gould, Mrs. Jane, admitted before 1833 [no date given], died 1835
Gordon, Edward, admitted before 1833 [no date given]
Gordon, Jane, admitted before 1833 [no date given]
Gold [Gould?], Sarah Ann, admitted before 1833 [no date given]
Gray, James, admitted before 1833, and "left" [no date given]
Gray, Mrs. Mary, admitted before 1833, and "left" [no date given]
Gilbert, Miss Mary S., admitted before 1833 [no date], died 1835
Giles, W. F., admitted December, 1833, dismissed [no date]
George, Samuel K., admitted December, 1833, dismissed 1842
George, Mrs. Elizabeth, admitted December, 1833
George, Isabella, admitted December, 1833, married W. Wilson, died February 15, 1857
George, Miss Sarah, admitted December, 1833, married D. C. Harris, struck off by order of session September 20, 1847

George, Miss Eliza, admitted November, 1834, married S. Fenby, died September, 1847
Gambrill, Mrs. Mary A., admitted November, 1837
Gray, Mrs. Mary, admitted November, 1837, died September, 1838
Gray, Mrs. Phoebe, admitted November, 1837, married Mr. Kelsey, died January 2, 1859
George, Mrs. Sophia, admitted June, 1839, dismissed 1841
Gillespie, Miss Catharine, admitted June, 1840, died 1856
Groton, Mrs. Phoebe, admitted January, 1834, struck off by order of session September 20, 1847
Gridley, Mrs., admitted March, 1835, dismissed 1844
Hamilton, Mr., admitted before 1833 [no date given]
Hamilton, Mrs., admitted before 1833 [no date given]
Hutton, Miss, admitted before 1833 [no date given]
Hannah, Mrs., admitted before 1833 [no date given], struck off by order of session September 20, 1847
Humes, Mrs., admitted before 1833 [no date given], died 1844
Hays, William, admitted before 1833 [no date given], died 1842
Hall, Mrs., admitted before 1833 [no date given]
Hutton, Mrs. Margaret, admitted before 1833 [no date], died 1834
Hamilton, Ellen, admitted before 1826 [no date given], died 1840
Hamilton, Jane, admitted before 1833 [no date given]
Hasson, John, admitted before 1833 [no date given], died 1861
Hasson, Mrs. Mary, admitted before 1833 [no date given], died 1861
Hasson, Mary Jr., admitted before 1833 [no date], dismissed 1865
Hasson, Maria (now Forsythe), admitted before 1833 [no date given], dismissed to Aisquith Street, May, 1851
Hall, Mrs. Ann, admitted before 1833 [no date given], struck off by order of session September 20, 1847
Hollins, Miss Georgiana S., admitted before 1833, died 1840
Hammill, Alex, admitted before 1833 [no date], dismissed 1844
Hammill, Mrs. Olivia, admitted before 1833, dismissed 1844
Hassan, Miss Rebecca, (married J. Hassan), admitted before 1833 [no date given], and noted as "died" [no date given]
Hollins, Mrs. Cordelia, admitted before 1833 [no date], died 1848
Hollins, Marsha (Mrs. Wilson), admitted before 1833, died 1834
Hill, Miss Susan, admitted December, 1833
Hantszche, John S., admitted December, 1833, struck off by order of session September 20, 1847
Hantszche, Mrs., admitted December, 1833, died [no date given]

Hutchins, Susan, admitted December, 1833, struck off by order of session September 20, 1847
Hurdevant [Sturdevant?], Miss, admitted Dec., 1833, dismissed 1835
Hollins, Robert S., deacon, admitted January, 1834, dismissed 1848
Herring, Miss Barb., admitted July, 1834, dismissed [no date]
Hill, Mrs. Margaret, admitted March, 1834, died 1844
Hill, Miss Ann, admitted January, 1834, baptized [no date given]
Hill, Miss Eliz., admitted January, 1834, dismissed [no date given]
Holland, Miss M., admitted November, 1835, struck off by order of session September 20, 1847
Habersett, Mrs. Phoebe, admitted December, 1837, dismissed 1844
Habersett, Henry, admitted December, 1837, dismissed 1844
Howard, Mrs. Rob., admitted December, 1837, died 1839
Hall, Miss Jane, admitted December, 1837, dismissed [no date given]
Hamilton, William, admitted December, 1839, died 1839
Hamilton, Mrs. Rebecca, admitted December, 1839, died 1856
Hazelthorpe, Elizabeth, admitted December, 1839, baptized, "left"
Hazelthorpe, Edward, admitted December, 1839, baptized papist, "in California" [no date given]
Haman, Miss Martha (Mrs. Gourley), admitted September, 1840 [Ed. Note: Baltimore marriage licenses show that Martha "Heman" married George Gourley on May 6, 1844. *Baltimore Sun.*]
Haman, Miss Isabella (Mrs. Magee), admitted September, 1840 [Ed. Note: Baltimore marriage licenses show that Isabella "Heman" married John C. "Megee" on September 11, 1851. *Baltimore Sun.*]
Haman, Miss Margaret (Mrs. Hunraman?), admitted September, 1840
Henderson, Miss J., admitted December, 1833, married [name not given], and struck off by order of session September 20, 1847
Herring, James, admitted July, 1834, struck off by order of session September 20, 1847
Hill, Catharine, admitted September, 1834, died [no date given]
Janvier, Perigo, admitted before 1833, dismissed 1840
Janvier, Mrs. Catharine, admitted before 1826, dismissed 1840 =
Johnson, J., admitted before 1833 [no date given], struck off by order of session September 20, 1847
Johnson, Mrs., admitted before 1833 [no date given], struck off by order of session September 20, 1847
Johnson, Miss Jane, admitted December, 1833, married to ---- Tyson
Jones, Miss Eleanor, admitted December, 1833, married Rev. G. Owen
Johnson, Mrs. Nancy, admitted January, 1835, dismissed 1844

Johnson, Mrs. Ann M., admitted January, 1838
Johnson, Mrs. Margaret, admitted June, 1840, dismissed 1844
Johnson, Isaac, admitted December, 1833, dismissed 1844 [elder]
Kerr, Archibald, deacon, admitted before 1833, died 1834
Kinstead, Mrs. Luke, admitted before 1833, removed [no date given]
Kyle, Adam B., admitted before 1833, dismissed March 30, 1852
Kelso, Mrs. Ellen, admitted before 1833, died 1862
Kelso, Miss Elizabeth Augusta, admitted before 1826, married [no name or date given], dismissed [no date given] =
Kyle, Mrs. A. B., admitted before 1833, dismissed March 30, 1852
Kelzo [sic], Miss Jane, admitted in 1833, married Rev. S. Guiteau
King, Mrs. M. A., admitted November, 1835, baptized papist [no date given], dismissed September, 1849
King, Susan Jane, admitted March, 1836, baptized [no date given]
King, Miss Jane, admitted March, 1838
Kyle, Isabella M., admitted December, 1839, died June, 1849
Low, Mrs., admitted before 1833 [no date given]
Lightbody, Mrs., admitted before 1833 [no date given]
Lively, ----, colored man, preacher, admitted before 1833
Lewis, Ann, admitted before 1833 [no date given]
Long, Emmaline, admitted before 1833 [no date given]
Lightbody, John, admitted by 1833, dismissed in 1835 to go to Texas
Lyford, Mrs. Margaret, admitted before 1833, dismissed July, 1852
Lyford, Mary Ann (now Mrs. Baker), admitted by 1833, dismissed 1852
Lewis, Willoughby, admitted before 1832 [no date given], died 1832
Lightner, Mrs. Eliz., admitted February, 1833
Lord, Miss Lydia, admitted February, 1833
Livingston, John, admitted July, 1833, dismissed [no date given]
Lightbody, John, admitted July, 1836, dismissed [no date given]
Logan, James, admitted July, 1836, dismissed 1844
Logan, Mrs. Mary, admitted September, 1840, dismissed 1844
Love, William, admitted September, 1839, licensed to preach [date not given], struck off by order of session September 20, 1847
Mitchell, Mrs. A., admitted before 1833, died November 7, 1848
Mundell, Mrs., admitted before 1833 [no date given], died 1848[?]
McCabe, Mrs., admitted before 1833 [no date given]
McDonald, Genl. Wm., ruling elder, admitted before 1833, died 1845
McNeal, Mrs., admitted before 1833 [no date given]
McKonkey, William, admitted before 1833, died [no date given]
McKonkey, Mrs., admitted before 1833 [no date given], died 1851

Mathers, Catharine, admitted by 1833, married and removed, "dropt"
Mathers, Mary, admitted before 1833, dismissed 1837, "dropt"
McKim, Mrs., admitted before 1833 [no date given], died 1842
McKim, Miss, admitted by 1833, now Mrs. Williamson, died [no date]
McKim, Miss Martha, admitted before 1833, died [no date given]
McAlister, Mr. Jno., admitted before 1833, died [no date given]
McAlister, Mrs., admitted before 1833 [no date given]
McWilliams, Miss, admitted before 1833, died February 20, 1851
McKonkey, Jont.[?], admitted before 1830 [no date], died 1830
McKonkey, Mrs., admitted before 1830, died June 18, 1852
McClellan, Dr. Daniel, admitted before 1833, dismissed 1841
Moffitt, Elizabeth, admitted before 1826, struck off by order of session November 8, 1847 =
Mahool, Emily, admitted before 1833, married A. Baxter [no date]
McKonkey, Margaret, admitted before 1833, dismissed [no date given]
McNulty, Eliz., admitted before 1833, dismissed [no date given]
Maffitt, Mary, admitted before 1833 [no date given], struck off by order of session September 20, 1847
Mitchell, Miss J. A., admitted before 1833 [no date given]
Monk, Mrs. Ann, admitted before 1833 [no date given], died 1841
Mahool, Mrs. Isabella, admitted before 1833, dismissed [no date]
McKonkey, Miss Maria L., admitted before 1833, married [no date]
McDermott, Miss Jane, admitted before 1833 [no date given]
Mitchell, Margaret, admitted before 1833, married Mr. Aitken and withdrew from the church, dismissed at her own request
Myers, George, admitted before 1833, suspended but was restored subsequently, later dismissed [no date given]
McIntire, David, admitted by 1833, dismissed by request [no date]
McElderry, John, admitted before 1833 [no date given]
Morton, Mrs., admitted before 1833 [no date given]
McDonough, Lavinia, admitted before 1833 [no date given], struck off by order of session September 20, 1847
McKee, Joseph L., admitted before 1833 [no date given], student of theology, dismissed 1842
McIntire, Catharine, admitted before 1833, dismissed 1842
McIntire, Sarah Ann, admitted before 1833, dismissed 1842
McElderry, Mrs. Ann, admitted before 1833 [no date given]
McDermott, Miss Ann, admitted before 1833 [no date given]
McElwae [?], Mary, admitted before 1833 [no date given], died 1834
McNulty, ----, admitted November 24, 1832, dismissed 1841

SECOND PRESBYTERIAN CHURCH

Myers, Mrs. Louisa, admitted February 13, 1833, dismissed [no date]
McKim, Mary Ann, admitted February 15, 1833, died [no date given]
McKenzie, Mrs. Ruhamah, admitted December 3, 1833, died [no date]
McCorkel, William, admitted December 3, 1833, dismissed 1845
McLanahan, Ann M., admitted December 7, 1833
Moore, Robert, admitted December 3, 1833, dismissed 1835
McDonald, Martha, admitted December 19, 1833, dismissed 1863
Millholland, Sarah, (Mrs. Know), adm. Dec. 17, 1833, dismissed 1834
Moore, Mrs. Eleanor, admitted December 23, 1833, "left" [no date]
Myers, George Jr., admitted January 27, 1834
McLanahan, Ann, admitted May 5, 1834 [name scratched off the list]
Maxwell [?], J. W., admitted November 7, 1834, dismissed 1846
Maxwell [?], Elizabeth, admitted November 7, 1834, dismissed 1846
McGuirk, Margaret, admitted November 25, 1834, "papist rebaptized"
Mooney, Daniel, admitted 1838
Mackenzie, Henrietta, admitted 1838, dismissed 1838
Mahool, Sarah, admitted 1838, dismissed 1838
McEldery, Henry, admitted 1838, dismissed [no date given]
McEldery, Sarah, admitted 1838, dismissed [no date given]
Montell, Mary G., admitted September 30, 1839, dismissed [no date]
Morrison, Rosina, admitted September 30, 1839, dismissed 1844
Morris, Catharine, admitted April 7, 1840, dismissed March 18, 1846
Murphy, W. J., admitted May 8, 1833, dismissed 1834
Matchett [Malchell?], Jane, admitted December, 1833, dismissed 1862
Mahool, Eliza, admitted January, 1834, dismissed March 18, 1846
McCann, Mrs. Mary, admitted June, 1834, struck off by order of
    session [no date given, probably September 20, 1847]
McJilton, Phillis, admitted May, 1834, dismissed [no date given]
McFall, Mrs., admitted March, 1836, dismissed [no date given]
Mittoner [Miltoner?], Dr., admitted Mar., 1836, dismissed [no date]
Norris, Mrs. Mary, admitted December, 1834, dismissed 1851
Norris, Miss Margaret, admitted July, 1835, baptized [no date]
Newell, Charles, admitted December, 1839, dismissed 1843
Newell, Sarah, admitted December, 1839, dismissed 1843
Owen, Joshua, admitted December, 1833, dismissed March 18, 1846
Perry, Mrs., admitted before 1833 [no date given], died 1850
Porter, Mr., admitted before 1833 [no date given], died 1850[?]
Porter, Mrs., admitted before 1833 [no date], died July 23, 1859
Porter, Miss, admitted before 1833 [no date given]
Pawson, Mrs. Mary, admitted before 1833, dismissed January, 1849

Peabody, James A., admitted by 1826, license to preach [no date]
Pue, Margaret Rutter, admitted before 1833, now Mrs. Cornelius Beatty, dismissed March, 1847
Parker, William S., admitted before 1833, struck off by order of session September 20, 1847
Pettit, Obediah, admitted before 1833, dismissed 1838
Pettit, Mrs. E. M., admitted before 1833, "dropt" 1838
Porter, Miss Margaret, admitted December 6, 1833
Pogue, Arthur, admitted December 2, 1833, "dropt" 1838
Perry, Susan, admitted January 5, 1834, struck off by order of session September 20, 1847
Pogue, Sarah, admitted January 5, 1834, dismissed 1840
Perry, Albert, admitted March 25, 1835
Potcher [?], Walter, admitted March 11, 1836, "dropt" 1838
Patterson, Eliza A., admitted June 9, 1839, dismissed May, 1846
Porter, Margareta, admitted June 22, 1840 [name scratched off list]
Ramsay, Mrs., admitted before 1833, dismissed March 18, 1846
Ramsay, Miss Letty, admitted before 1833 [no date given], died 1838
Ramsay, Miss Elizabeth, admitted before 1833 [no date], died 1863
Ramsay, Miss, admitted before 1833 [no date given], died 1866
Ramsay, Miss Amanda, admitted before 1826 [no date given], struck off by order of session September 20, 1847 =
Rutter, Anna Alethia, (Mrs. Archibald Kerr), admitted before 1833 [no date given], died March 26, 1850
Ramsay, Jefferson, admitted before 1833 [no date], dismissed 1841
Robinson, Mrs. Elizabeth, admitted before 1833, dismissed 1841
Reeder, Mrs. Ann W., admitted before 1833 [no date], died 1835
Robinson, Ann, admitted before 1833, dismissed [no date given]
Russel, Miss Margaret, admitted February, 1833, was apparently removed [no date] and then admitted again in November, 1841
Ramsey, Joseph, admitted February, 1833, dismissed 1845
Roney, Mrs. Alice, admitted December, 1833, died November, 1846
Roney, John, admitted December, 1833, struck off by order of session September 20, 1847
Ramsay, Miss Sarah, admitted December, 1833, married and dismissed
Ramsay, Agnes V. (Mrs. Barnes), admitted December, 1833, and "left"
Spear, Mrs., admitted before 1833 [no date given]
Spillman, James, deacon, admitted before 1833 [no date], died 1848
Stewart, Mrs., admitted before 1833 [no date given], died 1853
Starr, ----, admitted before 1833 [no date given], died 1853[?]

Shuter, Mr., admitted before 1833 [no date given], died [no date]
Shuter, Mrs., admitted before 1833 [no date given]
Stansbery [Stansbury], Mrs. Ann, admitted before 1826, died 1834 = Spillman, Mrs. Maria Ann, admitted before 1833 [no date], died 1843
Searley, Miss Sophia, admitted before 1833, suspended [no date]
Storr [Starr?], Catharine, admitted before 1833, died [no date]
Spencer, Miss, admitted before 1833, and "left" [no date given]
Stewart, James, admitted before 1833 [no date given], struck off by order of session September 20, 1847
Stephins, Elizabeth, admitted 1829, struck off by order of session September 20, 1847
Smith, Mrs., admitted before 1833 [no date given], struck off by order of session September 20, 1847
Stirling, William, admitted before 1832 [no date given], died 1832
Stirling, Mrs. William, admitted before 1832 [no date], died 1843
Scott, Mrs., admitted before 1833 [no date given], died 1843[?]
Scott, Jane, admitted before 1833, dismissed at her request [date?]
Stewart, Catharine, admitted before 1833 [no date given], dismissed 1838
Smith, Mary Ann, admitted before 1831 [no date given], died 1831
Smith, Miss Susan, admitted 1832, dismissed December, 1849
Show, Mrs. Mary (now Mrs. Cooke), admitted 1833, struck off by order of session September 20, 1847
Spencer, Mrs. Susan, admitted 1833, dismissed 1835
Smith, Miss Eleanor (now Mrs. Morrison), adm. 1833, dismissed 1849
Scott, Miss Catharine A., admitted 1833, dismissed 1839
Stewart, Joseph, admitted 1833, dismissed 1844
Stewart, James, admitted 1834, struck off by order of session November 8, 1847
Stewart, Mrs. Ellen, admitted 1834, dismissed [no date given]
Smith, William, admitted March, 1835, died 1839
Stewart, Mrs. Isabella, admitted March, 1837, dismissed 1867
Stewart, Joseph O., admitted September, 1839, dismissed 1844
Springer, David C., admitted March, 1840
Sommerville, Caroline O., admitted September, 1840
Southgate, Mrs. Ursula, admitted 1840, dismissed 1841
Sprekleson, Mrs. Jane, admitted May, 1833, dismissed April, 1851
Sherwood, Miss Ann, admitted May, 1833, struck off by order of session September 20, 1847
Shuster, Eliza, admitted December, 1833, struck off by order of session September 20, 1847

Stewart, Mrs. Eleanor, admitted January, 1834, struck off by order of session [no date, probably September 20, 1847]
Surrell [Sewell?], Mrs. E., admitted March, 1835, dismissed 1862
Stowe, Jeremiah, admitted March, 1838, struck off by order of session September 20, 1847
Stowe, Harvey, admitted ---- [blank, probably March, 1838], struck off by order of session September 20, 1847
Trimble, Mrs., admitted before 1833 [no date], died July 18, 1853
Trott, Mrs., admitted before 1833, dismissed [no dates given]
Trimble, Rebecca B., admitted before 1833, dismissed April 2, 1833
Thomas, Caleb, admitted before 1833 [no date given]
Taylor, Mrs. Catharine, admitted before 1833 [no date given], struck off by order of session September 20, 1847
Taylor, Mrs. S. Dr. [sic], admitted before 1833 [no date given], removed to Florida [no date given]
Troxel, Miss Isabella, (Mrs. Stephen Williams), admitted before 1833 [no date given], dismissed [no gate given]
Trippe, Joseph E., ruling elder, admitted December, 1839, dismissed
Tennant, Miss H., admitted March, 1840, struck off by order of session November 8, 1847
Torrance, Miss Eliz. R. (Mrs. Simmons), admitted June, 1840, struck off by order of session November 8, 1847
Torrance, Mary S., admitted June, 1840, dismissed 1840
Todd, Mrs. Ann, admitted June, 1840
Tyson, Jonathan, admitted July, 1840, dismissed 1841
Wilson, John, ruling elder, admitted by 1833, died January 29, 1855
Wilson, Mrs. Isabella, admitted by 1833, died October 6[?], 1852
Willis, Thomas, admitted before 1833 [no date given], struck off by order of session September 20, 1847
Willis, Mrs., admitted before 1833 [no date given], struck off by order of session September 20, 1847
White, J. C., admitted before 1833 [no date given]
White, Mrs., admitted before 1833 [no date given]
Wilson, Mrs. Cold [sic], admitted before 1833 [no date given]
Wallace, Elizabeth, admitted before 1826 [no date given], married and removed October 30, 1833 =
Wilkinson, James, admitted before 1833 [no date given], died 1842
Wilkinson, Mrs. Anna, admitted before 1833 [no date given]
Williams, Elizabeth (Mrs. Robinson), admitted before 1833 [no date]
Weir, Joseph, admitted before 1833 [no date given], dismissed 1834

SECOND PRESBYTERIAN CHURCH 209

Webb, Miss Hannah, admitted before 1833 [no date given], married to Mr. Pendexter [no date given], dismissed 1862

Weir, Sarah, admitted before 1833 [no date given], struck off by order of session September 20, 1847

Wilson, James, admitted before 1833 [no date], dismissed Mar., 1847

Wilson, Mrs. Maria, admitted before 1833 [no date], dismissed 1847

Wilson, Margaret, admitted before 1833 [no date given], married to J. Herman Brown [no date given]

Wolfe, Maria, admitted before 1833 [no date given], struck off by order of session November 8, 1847

Weems, Mrs. Mary Ann, admitted before 1833 [no date given]

Wilson, Sarah (now Mrs. W. F. Giles), admitted before 1833 [no date given], died 1845

Warden, James E., admitted February, 1833, dismissed 1862

Wilson, William H., admitted December, 1833, died November 16, 1857

Wilson, John E., admitted December, 1833

West, Mrs. Catharine, admitted December, 1833, died 1834

Warden, Robert M., admitted January, 1834, died 1841

Warden, James B., admitted March, 1840, died 1840

Weaver, Miss Catharine, admitted March, 1838, dismissed 1844

White, Mrs. Sarah J., admitted March, 1838, dismissed 1844

Winchester, Miss Caroline, admitted April, 1839, baptized, married, and dismissed 1841

Wedge, Mrs. Ann M., admitted December, 1833, died [no date given]

Wilson, Dinah, colored, admitted December, 1833, removed [no date]

Webb, George, admitted December, 1833, suspended 1840

Williams, Mrs. S., admitted July, 1834, dismissed [no date given]

Whiteman, Mrs. A., admitted July, 1836, struck off by order of session November 8, 1847

Wells, Robert K., admitted September, 1840, dismissed 1843

Yerkis, Stephen, admitted November, 1838, licensed to preach [no date given], struck off by order of session [no date given]

Ed. Note: In the back of the aforementioned book are 22 pages of baptism records (over 100 names) between 1844 and 1865, noting: "The names of the children here recorded are all that the stated clerk has been able to obtain. If there was any list kept previous to the books coming into his hands, he has not been able to find it. Signed: J. H. Brown, June 11, 1853." However, review of these entries revealed one baptism prior to 1840 that was subsequently recorded among the later baptisms:

"John Wilson Brown, son of J. H. and Margaretta Brown, baptized December 10, 1836, by Rev. S. Gitteau."

SECOND PRESBYTERIAN CHURCH 211

MEMBERSHIP INFORMATION GLEANED FROM THE SESSIONAL RECORDS OF THE FIFTH PRESBYTERIAN CHURCH IN THE CITY OF BALTIMORE, 1833 TO 1840 [THE ORIGINAL RECORD BOOK ENDS IN 1858, AND IS MAINTAINED BY THE MANUSCRIPT DIVISION (M.362) OF THE MARYLAND HISTORICAL SOCIETY.]

[Briefly] Rev. James G. Hamner began preaching in the summer of 1833 in the southern section of Baltimore where the desire for a new church soon arose. A committee chaired by the Rev. Mr. Nevins organized the Fifth Presbyterian Church on October 17, 1833: John McKeen, Jr., Ruling Elder; Hope Bain, Ruling Elder; Robert Golder, Benjamin Williams, David Owen, Caleb Owen, Catharine Ferguson, Jane Hamner, Mary L. Hamner, Jane Owen, Ruth McFerran, Ann Burroughs, Phebe Armstrong, Ann Armstrong, Elizabeth Davis, Elizabeth Evans.

October 25, 1833
John M. Butler, examined and received into membership
John Creery, examined and received into membership
Dr. M. S. Baer, examined and received into membership
Mrs. Margaret Butler, examined and received into membership
Mrs. Wealthy Ann Creery, examined and received into membership
Mrs. M. C. Baer, examined and received into membership

December 13, 1833
Miss Hannah Ring, examined and received into membership
Miss Elizabeth A. Tepler, examined and received into membership
Mrs. Menie R. Brown, examined and received into membership
Mr. Samuel Law, received by certificate
Mr. John Butler, baptized

February 1, 1834
Miss Hanna M. Ellicott, examined and received into membership
Miss Harriet Griffith, examined and received into membership
Mrs. Cecilia Roche, examined and received into membership
Mrs. Elizabeth Bukree, examined and received into membership
Mr. Ephraim Carrington, examined and received into membership
Mr. Thomas Davis, examined and received into membership
Absalom Owen, examined and received into membership
Joshua Owen, examined and received into membership

Miss H. M. Ellicott, baptized

May 24, 1834
John Morrow, received by certificate from 2nd Ch., Wilmington, Del.
Mrs. Ann Morrow, received by certificate from 2nd Ch., Wilmington
Mrs. Christiana Carrington, examined and received in membership
Mrs. Hannah Hennyman, examined and received into membership
Mr. Samuel Sutherland, examined and received into membership
John Frederick Morrow [Murrow?], infant, baptized

June 13, 1834 - June 30, 1834
Miss Elizabeth Jewry and Mrs. Ruth McFerran testified in the case of Mrs. H. Hennyman who had been charged with "intemperance in the use of ardent spirits" (intoxication). After careful deliberation, the church admonished her and exhorted her not to touch, taste or handle ardent spirits again.

September 27, 1834
Mr. Robert Cockrane, examined and received into membership
Mr. James Patterson, examined and received into membership
Mrs. Ann Margaretta Cunningham, examined and received in
    membership
Mrs. Henrietta Eliza Sewell, examined and received into membership
Miss Elizabeth P. Hooper, examined and received into membership

January 10, 1835
Mrs. Sarah Gulley, examined and received into membership
Miss Sarah Foster, examined and received into membership

January 12, 1835
Mr. John F. Cassell, examined and received into membership

February 1, 1835
Mr. John F. Cassell, baptized
Catharine Gulley, infant of Mr. and Mrs. Gulley, baptized
William Gulley, infant of Mr. and Mrs. Gulley, baptized

April 25, 1835 - September 12, 1835
Hope Bain was brought up on charges "of highly censurable and offensive intercourse with a girl of acknowledged bad character" (a prostitute named Theresa) and "of telling a known untruth with the

SECOND PRESBYTERIAN CHURCH

intent to deceive" (lying). John F. Cassell and William Leeche testified. Hope Bain, once a Ruling Elder, was then excommunicated.

September 12, 1835
Mrs. Mary Ann Monroe, examined and received into membership
Mrs. Elizabeth Stewart, examined and received into membership
Miss Maria Elizabeth Randall, examined and received into membership
Miss Rebeka B. Barkley, examined and received into membership
Miss Elizabeth Barbine, examined and received into membership
Mr. A. C. Gibbs, received on certificate
Mrs. Eliza L. Gibbs, received on certificate
Mr. Andrew C. Gibbs, received on certificate
Mrs. Mary Ann Monroe, baptized

March 12, 1836
Mr. Robert Taylor, examined and received into membership
Mrs. Isabella Taylor, examined and received into membership
Mrs. ---- Cassell, examined and received into membership
Miss Eliza Roche, examined and received into membership
Mary Eliza Monroe, daughter of Mrs. Monroe, baptized
Jane Hastings Monroe, daughter of Mrs. Monroe, baptized
Emily Frances Monroe, daughter of Mrs. Monroe, baptized
Hannah Russell Taylor, daughter of Mr. and Mrs. Taylor, baptized
Mary Patterson Taylor, daughter of Mr. and Mrs. Taylor, baptized
Isabella Norris Taylor, daughter of Mr. and Mrs. Taylor, baptized

May 7, 1836
Miss Esther Gregg, received on certificate from 1st Church

July 8, 1836
Mr. Phillip Gulley, examined and received into membership
Mr. Josiah Richardson, received on certificate from 3rd Church
Reliance C. Richardson, wife of Josiah, received on certificate
Mrs. Jane Thomas, received on certificate from 2nd Church

September 10, 1836
Miss Arabella Needham, examined and received into membership
Mrs. Jane Bunting, examined and received into membership
Mr. William T. Johnson, examined and received into membership
Mrs. Susan Smith, received on certificate
Miss Elizabeth T. Smith, daughter of Susan, received on certificate

Miss Catharine DeBarthalt, received on certificate
Miss Sarah DeBarthalt, received on certificate
Maria Ellen Gibbs, daughter of Mr. and Mrs. A. C. Gibbs, baptized
Miss A. Needham, baptized

November 12, 1836
Mr. Brandy Green and wife Mary Green, received on certificate
Mrs. Samantha Williams, received on certificate
Mrs. Pheobe McJilton, received on certificate
Mrs. Mary Robinson, received on certificate
Mrs. Priscilla Keys, received on certificate

January 7, 1837
M. S. Baer, Ruling Elder
A. C. Gibbs, Riling Elder
John C. Backus, Moderator
Mr. Robert Cockran, received on certificate
Mrs. Mahany [Maharry?], received on certificate

April 21, 1837
John Norcom, M. D., received on certificate
Ann Eunice Norcom, wife of John, received on certificate
Mrs. Dorothea Falls, received on certificate

May 6, 1837
Mrs. Ann Raborg, examined and received into membership
Mrs. Rebecca Patton, examined and received into membership
Miss Mary Ann Wright, examined and received into membership
Mrs. ---- [blank] Claskins, received on certificate

June 5, 1837
William Henry Thomas, son of Mr. and Mrs. Thomas, baptized

July 5, 1837
Emilia Keys, infant daughter of Mr. and Mrs. Bayly Keys, baptized

July 8, 1837
Miss Ann Butler, examined and received into membership
Mr. Beverly C. Sanders, received on certificate
Mrs. Charlotte Sanders, received on certificate

SECOND PRESBYTERIAN CHURCH 215

Mrs. William B. Davies, received on certificate
Miss Ellenor Clendennen, received on certificate

November 4, 1837
Miss Sarah Elizabeth Goldsborough, received into membership
Mrs. Elizabeth Haden, examined and received into membership
Mrs. Delia Davidson, examined and received into membership
Miss Susan Foxwall, examined and received into membership
Miss Rebecca Staples, examined and received into membership
Mr. John F. McJilton, received on certificate
Mr. Richard Cockrane, received on certificate
Mrs. Elizabeth Cockrane, received on certificate
Miss Mary Cockrane, received on certificate
Miss Jane Cockrane, received on certificate
Mrs. Eliza Crawford, received on certificate

January 6, 1838
Mr. and Mrs. Brett, received on certificate
Mr. Nathaniel C. Dare, examined and received into membership
Mr. Edward W. Dukehart, examined and received into membership
Mrs. Sarah Ann Dukehart, examined and received into membership
Miss Mary Livinia Bayly, examined and received into membership
Mrs. Frances M. Chadwick, examined and received into membership
Miss Anna Maria Goldsborough, examined and received into membership
Miss Henrietta Eugenia Goldsborough, received into membership
Mrs. Amanda Tyson, examined and received into membership
Mrs. Samuel White, examined and received into membership
Mrs. Margaret White, examined and received into membership

March 1, 1838
Mrs. Sarah McElderry, received into membership and to be baptized
Mrs. Mary LeCompte, examined and received into membership

March 3, 1838
Mr. and Mrs. Josh Crosby, received on certificate
Miss Geraldine Sarah Vickers, examined and received into membership
Miss Margaret Randall, examined and received into membership
Mrs. Sarah Ann Messiter, examined and received into membership

May 3, 1838

Miss Mary Jane Spedden, received into membership and to be baptized
Miss Eliza Jane Bayly, received into membership and to be baptized
Mr. Josiah Richardson, suitable to be an Elder, ordained May 5th
Mr. Jonathan Crerry, suitable to be an Elder, ordained May 5th

May 5, 1838
Mrs. Elizabeth Dare, examined and received into membership
Miss Catharine Butler, examined and received into membership

June 30, 1838
Mr. James Cockrane, received on certificate

September 1, 1838
Mrs. Mary Alricks, examined and received into membership
Mrs. Margaret Derickson, examined and received into membership
Mr. Spencer Rowe, received on certificate
Mr. Joseph Grascup [Groscup?], received on certificate

November 3, 1838
Mr. George W. Granger, examined and received into membership
Mrs. Mary Granger, wife of George W., received into membership
Mrs. Henrietta Graham, examined and received into membership
Mrs. Margaret Morton, examined and received into membership
Miss Marietta Eliza Harris, examined and received into membership

January 4, 1839
Mr. Robert Morton, examined and received into membership

February 27, 1839
Miss Mary Jane Keys, examined and received into membership
Miss Ruth Maria Griffith, examined and received into membership

March 1, 1839
Mrs. Amelia Sophia Kane, examined and received into membership

May 1, 1839
Mrs. Ann Jane Chase, examined and received into membership
Mrs. Elenora Wilson, examined and received into membership
Mr. ---- [blank] McCabe, received on certificate from 2nd Church

SECOND PRESBYTERIAN CHURCH

July 6, 1839
Mrs. Ann Rea, examined and received into membership
Mrs. Mary Monahan, examined and received into membership

August 29, 1839
Miss Mary McCulloch Barkley, examined and received into membership

October 25, 1839 - November 6, 1839
George Granger was charged with having "eloped with another man's wife, left this city, and left his wife in a destitute situation." Mr. Stewart and Mr. Dukehart testified. Granger was excommunicated.

November 1, 1839
Miss Mary Ann Levering, received on certificate
Miss Eliza B. Levering, received on certificate
Mrs. Maria Nibler [?], received on certificate

November 2, 1839
Mrs.[?] D. H. Blanchard, examined and received into membership

December 7, 1839
Mr. Lemuel E. Duvall, examined and received in membership
Mrs. Mary Jane Duvall, examined and received into membership
Mr. Gorge M. Uhler, examined and received into membership
Mr. Jonathan Tyson, baptized
Col. Thomas Sheppard, examined and received into membership
Capt. Joel Vickers, examined and received into membership
Mr. Joseph Stubbs, baptized
Mrs. Margaret McElderry, examined and received into membership
Mr. John Littlejohn, examined and received into membership
Mrs. Ellenora Littlejohn, examined and received into membership
Miss Sally Ann Dorsey, examined and received into membership
Miss Rebecca A. Wilmer, examined and received into membership
Mrs. Jane R. Dull, examined and received into membership
Miss Elizabeth Ann Dull, examined and received into membership
Mr. Robert Hooper, examined and received into membership
Mrs. Ellen C. Hooper, examined and received into membership
Mrs. Mary McKinnon, examined and received into membership
Miss Charlotte C. Baer, examined and received into membership
Miss Lydia R. Baer, examined and received into membership

Miss Rebecca P. Gregory, examined and received into membership
Mr. Joshua Harvey, received into membership and baptized
Mrs. Catharine Harvey, received into membership and baptized
Mr. B. Albert Vickers, examined and received into membership
Mr. John Jackson, examined and received into membership
Mr. William Davison, examined and received into membership
Mrs. Sarah Davison, examined and received into membership
Mrs. Catharine Jordan, examined and received into membership
Miss Sarah Pope, received into membership and baptized
Mr. Peter Pendleton, examined and received into membership
Mr. Joseph Keys, examined and received into membership
Mr. William McCabe, examined and received into membership
Mr. Samuel Pattison, examined and received into membership
Miss Mary E. Needham, received into membership and baptized

January 1, 1840
Capt. Asa Needham, received into membership and baptized
Mr. Alexander Mason Rogers, examined and received into membership
Miss Julia Ann Warfield, examined and received into membership
Miss Mary Ann Henderson, received into membership and baptized
Miss Mary Bayless, examined and received into membership
Miss Jane Taylor, examined and received into membership
Miss Ann Maria Wolford, received into membership and baptized
Miss Mary Jane Atchison, examined and received into membership
Mrs. Juliana Middlemore, examined and received into membership
Mrs. Frances M. Lucas, examined and received into membership
Mrs. Regina Maria Sperry, examined and received into membership
Mrs. Eliza Rogers, examined and received into membership

January 3, 1840
Mr. William C. Keener, examined and received into membership
Mrs. Elizabeth H. Keener, examined and received into membership
Mrs. Elizabeth W. Vickers, examined and received into membership
Mr. Thomas B. Hungerford, received into membership and baptized
Mrs. Eliza J. Frazer, examined and received into membership
Mr. Forbes Redman, examined and received into membership
Mrs. Ellonora Spedden, received into membership and baptized
Miss Mary S. Tyson, received into membership and baptized
Mrs. Margaretta Trayser, examined and received into membership
Miss Sarah Ann Hammond, examined and received into membership

SECOND PRESBYTERIAN CHURCH

Mr. Alexander M. Carter, received on certificate
Mrs. Elizabeth B. Dukehart, baptized

February 25, 1840
Mr. Albert Trego, received into membership and baptized
Miss Maria L. Wellins, examined and received into membership
Mr. Aquilla D. Hughes, examined and received into membership
Mrs. Mary Brocchins [?], examined and received into membership
Mr. George L.[T.?] Stubbs, examined and received into membership
Miss Margaret J. Fergusson, examined and received into membership
Mr. Robert McKinnon, examined and received into membership
Mrs. Mary Foulks, examined and received into membership
Mrs. Isabella West, examined and received into membership
Mrs. Adeline Trego, received into membership and baptized
Mrs. Ann Graham, examined and received into membership
Miss Robanie [?] Brown, examined and received into membership

February 28, 1840
Mr. Jonathan S. Eastman, examined and received into membership
Mrs. Mary Milnor, received into membership and baptized
Miss Elizabeth R. Frazer, examined and received into membership

April 29, 1840
Dr. A. H. Briscoe, examined and received into membership
Mr. Abraham Buckwalter, examined and received into membership
Mrs. Margaret Buckwalter, examined and received into membership

May 2, 1840
Mr. F. N.[?] Alricks, examined and received into membership
Miss Sarah Ziglar, examined and received into membership

July 3, 1840
Mr. George Coss, examined and received into membership
Mrs. Rebecca McCreight, examined and received into membership
Mrs. Jane Hamilton, examined and received into membership
Mrs. Margaret Darrach, received on certificate
Miss Hannah Espy, received on certificate

July 4, 1840

Mr. Joel Thomas, examined and received into membership
Mrs. Amanda Murray, examined and received into membership

November 5, 1840
Mrs. Margaret Taylor, received on certificate from Rutgers Street
 Presbyterian Church in New York

December 29, 1840
Mr. J. R. Snethers, received on certificate
Mrs. Maria Snethers, received on certificate
Mr. Henry Nolen, examined and received into membership
Mr. Alexander Morton, examined and received into membership
Mr. John Legg, examined and received into membership
Mrs. Ann Armitage, examined and received into membership
Miss Rebecca B. Talbott, examined and received into membership
Miss Emily F. Keener, examined and received into membership

SECOND PRESBYTERIAN CHURCH 221

LIST OF NAMES TAKEN FROM TABLET AT WESTMINSTER GRAVEYARD, FAYETTE AND GREEN STREETS, BALTIMORE [TYPED PAGE INSERTED IN THE REGISTER]

Gen. John Spear Smith, 1786-1866
Gen. Joseph Sterett, 1771-1821
Brig. Gen. Benjamin Edes, --- -1832
A.D.C. George Pitt Stevenson, 1791-1819
Col. James A. Buchanan, 1768-1840
Col. David Harris, 1770-1841
Col. Samuel McClellan, 1787-1858
Col. James Mosher, 1761-1843
Capt. John Smith Hollins, 1787-1858
Capt. Mathias Rich, --- -1820
Corporal Joseph Pearson, 1783-1860
Corporal John Hollins, 1760-1827
Elijah Porter Barrows, 1768-1854
Cumberland Dugan, 1747-1836
Hammond Dugan, 1797-1841
William McClellan, 1771-1814
James R. McCulloh,   -1836
Jonathan Meredith, 1785-1872
Dr. Maxwell McDowell, 1771-1848
Dr. John Boyd, 1746-1790
Isaac Caustin, 1758-1833
Robert Gilmor, 1748-1822
Mayberry Helm, 1710-1790
James Jaffray, --- -1820
Christopher Johnston, 1751-1819
John McDonough, 1737-1809
Robert Purviance, 1734-1806
Christopher Raborg, 1750-1815
John Smith, 1722-1794
Robert Smith, 1758-1842
William Smith, 1728-1814
John Spear, --- -1796
David Stewart, 1746-1795
James Stirling, 1751-1820
Matthew Swan, 1743-1795
William W. Taylor, 1769-1832

Dr. Abraham VanBibber, 1743-1805

In War of 1812 and Revolution:
Commodore Joseph James Nicholson 1791-1858
Gen. Samuel Smith, 1752-1839
Gen. John Stricker, 1759-1825
Gen. David Poe, 1743-1816
Col. Paul Bentalou, 1735-1826
Maj. Samuel Sterett, 1756-1833

In Revolution:
Gen. William Buchanan, 1732-1804
Gen. John Swan, 1750-1821
Col. David McClellan, 1741-1790
Col. James McHenry, 1755-1816
Col. Nathanial Ramsay, 1741-1817
Maj. Nathaniel Smith, --- -1793
Capt. Frederick Folger, --- -1820
Capt. David Harris, 1753-1809
Capt. George P. Keeports, 1753-1817
Capt. John McClellan, 1738-1820
Capt. David Porter, 1754-1808
Capt. Joseph Smith, --- -1817
Capt. John Sterett, --- -1805
Lt. John McClure, --- -1825
Lt. Andrew Aitken, 1757-1809
James Calhoun, 1743-1817 [First Mayor of Baltimore]

Other Names:
James Purviance, 1772-1836
Jacob Schley, 1783-1827
John Torrence, 1794-1832

Colonel John Stuart Skinner, 1788-1851, assisted Francis Scott Key (1780-1843) to obtain the release of Dr. William Beanes from the British Fleet in 1814 whose rescue led to the writing of the National Anthem. (Erected by the National Star Spangled Banner Centennial Committee on the centenary of the signing of the Treaty of Ghent, December 24th, 1814).

"Herein are deposited the remains of Katharine Bentalou, daughter of Jacob Keeports, who was born in this city Gay Street, on the 8th of April, 1759, married at the house in which she was born in the 20th of December 1780, to Paul Bentalou, died the 11th of January 1813, at half past 3 in the morning, expired in the arms of her tender and disconsolate husband at the age of 53 years, 9 months, 3 days, the last 32 years and 22 days of which passed in a most endearing and reciprocal connubial happiness. Her death was as calm and resigned as her life was pure and virtuous!"----"A true copy of the epitaph or inscription in the upright marble slab on the right hand side facing the brick and stone mausoleum under the extreme southeastern corner of the Westminster Presbyterian Church as the southeast corner of Fayette and Green Streets, Baltimore, Maryland. Copied by Mr. Joseph Aloysius Weber, of Philadelphia, on Thursday, December 22, 1921, at 2:30 p.m. From these dates Mrs. Bentalou was in her 54th year when she died, in her 21st year when she married Paul Bentalou, and in her 33rd year of her wedded life." [typed]

WESTMINSTER PRESBYTERIAN CHURCH CEMETERY RECORDS IN BALTIMORE CITY

[Ed. Note: These tombstones were copied by Mary White Mann in 1942 and are very incomplete. This church was not built until 1852, but the cemetery surrounding the church was originally on the grounds of the First Presbyterian Church. The land was purchased from Col. John Eager Howard (1787), now located at the corner of Green and Fayette Streets in west Baltimore. A complete listing of burials (and other information) was published in 1984 by Mary Ellen Hayward and R. Kent Lancaster, of the Westminster Preservation Trust, Inc., and was entitled *Baltimore's Westminster Cemetery and Westminster Presbyterian Church: A Guide to the Markers and Burials, 1775-1943*. This 63-page book should certainly be consulted for more details.]

James Calhoun (1743-1816), First Mayor of Baltimore, Jan. 16, 1797
Capt. John Cunyngham (1761, Scotland - 1817, Baltimore, Maryland)
John Cunyngham, died 1791, aged 4 months
Joseph Mather (1793-1857)
Arabella Mather, died 1836, age 87
Jane Augusta Byer (1797-1888), wife of John G. Byer, and daughter of John and Margaret Cunyngham
Stirling vault
J. Armstrong vault
Stewart vault
A. Fridge vault
G. Kelson vault
R. Watson vault
William Nevins vault, 1820
Philip Hunter Key vault, 1821
Young vault
Davies and Gilmore vault
G. M. Dowell vault
G. C. Morton vault
Buckler and Andrews vault
Lorriance vault
J. Taylor vault
W. W. Taylor vault
J. F. Barr vault
Von Kapff vault
Robinson vault

SECOND PRESBYTERIAN CHURCH

Samuel Smith (1693-1784)
John Smith (1722-1791)
Gen. Samuel Smith (1752-1839)
Rev. John Chester Backus (1810-1884), 4th Pastor of 1st Presb. Ch.
E. Pannell vault
Stricker vault
Torrance vault
Didier vault
Cumberland Dugan, died 1856, aged 90
Margaret Dugan (1782?-1852), wife of Cumberland Dugan
Frederick J. Dugan (1804-1853)
Graham and Barklie vault
Col. Nathanial Ramsay (died 1817, aged 76)
Tyson Irvin Gibson vault
Christian J. Baum (1825-1862)
Edgar Allan Poe (January 20, 1809 - October 7, 1849) Stone Monument
Esther Coulter, relict of the late Alexander, died 1857, age 86
Alexander Coulter, died 1828, aged 68
Mary Coulter, died 1817, aged 8 years, second daughter of Alexander
    Esther Coulter
Alexander Coulter, died 1795, aged 1 month, second son of Alexander
    Esther Coulter
Elizabeth Coulter, died 1817, aged 6 years, third daughter of Alexander
    and Esther Coulter
Jacob Schley, died 1827, aged 46
Anna Barbara Jones (1794-1846)
Mary Eliza Schley (1820-1902), daughter of Jacob and Eliza Schley
Eunice Schley [?], no dates
Mary A. Prentice (1803-1878)
Alexander Prentice, died 1812, aged 82
Maria Louisa ---- [West?], (1778-1862)
Helena Anna Tucker (1803-1843), daughter of James and Louisa West
John Donogh (1737-1809)
Ann Helm, died 1706 [1796?], aged 80, wife of Abraham Mayberry
    Helm
George Pollock, died 1769 [sic], aged 58
Martha Jane Winchester, died 1818, aged 11 months, daughter of
    William and Hannah Winchester (others illegible)
Rosalie O'Donnell Finley, age 25 months [date?], (others illegible)
James Davidson, 1800-

Andrew ---- (illegible)
Jane McKnight Finley, died 1800, aged 15 years
John McClellan (1769-1856)
Mary McClellan, died 1811, aged 69, consort of John McClellan
Anna McClellan (1761-1849)
Andrew Carson, died 1816, aged 67
Jane Carson, died 1819, aged 55
Jane Sindall, age 86 [no date], daughter of the late Andrew and Jane Carson
Mary Jane Carr Nicholas (1801-1830), daughter of John and Jane Hollins and wife of John Smith Nicholas
Sarah Lennox, died 1818, aged 78
Ann Holmes, died 1792, aged 36, wife of John Holmes
Robert Biddel, died 1809, aged 18
Mary Biddel, died 1787, aged 45
Louise Biddel (11 months), no date?
Amelia Biddel (8 months), no date?
Sarah Matilda Biddel (age 12 years), no date?
George Pitts Stevenson, died 1791, aged 27
John Hollins (1760, England - 1827, Baltimore)
John Hollins Nicholas (died 1828), grandson of John Hollins
Henry Courtenay (1776-1854)
Robert McClellan (1771-1811)
William and Janet Olo, Lelia, [sic]
Sarah McClellan, died 1861, aged 76 (other dates illegible)
Mary Barkley, wife of John M. Barkley, and daughter of James and Rebecca Stevens, died 1862, aged 70
James Stevens, died 1808, age 48, son of James and Rebecca Stevens
Robert Purviance (aged 73), no date?
Mrs. Frances Purviance, died 1821, aged 82
Broadnax Atkinson (1831-1880)
Janet Dugan (1783-1839)
Robert Davidson, died 1891, aged 81
Jane S. Needles, died 1876, aged 76
Ann Walter (1777-1818), wife of James L. Walker and daughter of James Martin, Sr.
James Martin, died 1888, aged 87
Susan Martin, died 1862, aged 75
Sally Bradish (December 17, 1792, aged 18 years)
William Bradish (January, 1793, aged 6 years)

John M. Barkley (died 1827, aged 55)
Rebecca Stevens, died 1856, aged 80
Rose Ross (died 1803), consort of James Ross, merchant of this city
Jane Caustin (1802, no age?)
Isaac Caustin, age 55 [no date?], (Mausoleum of children illegible)
Henry Payson, died 1815 [no age], (Mausoleum)
Eunice Payson, died 1818 [no age?]
Abigail Payson, died 1811, aged 13
William Hutton, died 1789, aged 33
Sophie Anderson, died 1861, aged 8[?] years
Elizabeth Ramsay (tablet), aged 63, died November 11, 1850[?]
Jane Ramsay, died November 27, 1864
Arabella Ramsay, died May 24, 1866
Thomas W. Ramsay, died April 1, 1798, aged 46
Elizabeth Ramsay, died July 16, 1826, aged 76, wife of Thomas W.
    Ramsay and daughter of Michael and Jane Erskine
Debor (?) Cochran (1770-1821), (other names illegible)
R. Henderson (died 1825, aged 27)
Capt. William Bryden (1767, Scotland - 1840, Baltimore, Maryland)
Elizabeth G. Bryden (1789, London, England - 1839, Baltimore, MD)
John Crawford (1746, Ireland - 1813, Baltimore, Maryland),
    Grandmaster of Mason's, State of Maryland
John Brown, died 1791, aged 19
Sarah Brown, died 1832, aged 82
Jessie Brown, 1790, aged 20 months
Anne Bennett, died 1800, aged 81
Elizabeth Hill, died 1812, aged 4 months, daughter of Washington and
    Anne Hill
Elizabeth Gallagher, died 1852, aged 70
Dr. John Boyd (dates illegible)
Patrick Allison, Doctor of Theology, died 1802, aged 62
Mary Allison, wife of Rev. Dr. Patrick Allison, died 1832
Robert E. Henderson, died 1827 [no age?], (other names illegible)
Georgiana Hollins (1813-1840), daughter of John Smith Hollins and
    Rebecca Hollins
C. Dugan Hollins (1833-1858)
Rebecca Hollins (1788-1869), relict of John Smith Hollins
Joseph Pearson - Robert Smith, vault
E. Robinson - Henry Dickson Dawes (1859-1934), vault
William E. Phillips (1808-1890)

Francis N. Dawes (1853-1891)
Agnes B. Dawes (1857-1932)
Henry Dawes (1820-1873)
Elizabeth P. Dawes (1832-1899?)
Josias Rutter Bodley - no dates
Mary Bodley, wife of Thomas Bodley - dates illegible
Alexander Lander, died 1803, aged 40 years
David Poe, Sr. (1743, Londonderry, Ireland - 1816, Baltimore), patriot of the Revolution and grandfather of Edgar Allan Poe

[Ed. Note: The copyist (in 1942) noted there were others buried in the early years, but many of these tombstone dates were illegible. Therefore, it would be wise for researchers to consult the book by Hayward & Lancaster (noted above) as it appears there are several mistakes and omissions in this 1942 list of vaults and burials.]

SECOND PRESBYTERIAN CHURCH 229

GLENDY GRAVEYARD TOMBSTONE INSCRIPTIONS (FAITH PRESBYTERIAN CHURCH) BALTIMORE CITY, BROADWAY AND GAY STREETS (CHURCH ORGANIZED IN 1850)
[Ed. Note: Obviously, the following burials pre-date the formation of Faith Presbyterian Church. The church register did not indicate who copied the tombstones or when they copied them. Caution should be exercised as to accuracy and completeness of the information.]

John and Alexander Gregg, vault
J. Gibson and W. H. Conkling, vault
L. H. Dunkin, vault
A. George, vault
Davis Hays, vault
James George, vault, 1836
Gen. William McDonald, vault, 1855
Dr. Alexander Clendinen, vault
---- Swan, vault
Mrs. Jane James, departed this life October 23, 1827, aged 51 years
John James, departed this life August 28, 1841, aged 76 years
Silas Post, died in "Buenas Ayers," January 6, 1831, aged 26 years
Isabella Post, daughter of Russell and Electa M. Post, died March 8, 1830, aged 6 months and 1 day
David Knox, a native of County Antrim, Ireland, departed this life September 2, 1826, aged 47 years
Mary Jane McKeown (April 17, 1815 - June 15, 1885), wife of Henry M. McKeown and eldest daughter of Thomas and Rachel Barrett
Henry M. McKeown (September 25, 1837 - December 3, 1902), eldest son of Henry M. and Mary J. McKeown
Eleanor Murphy, wife of Capt. John Murphy, of Baltimore, died August 12, 1820, in the 49th year of her age, after a severe illness of several weeks; also, her daughter Anne Hunt [Murphy?]
Frances Amelia Smull, infant daughter of D. B. and Eliza Smull, died January 12, 1842, aged 21 days
Mary M. Dugdale, daughter of George and Ellen M. Dugdale, died September 11, 1857, aged 1 year, 7 months, and 15 days
Joseph McKeldin, died January 3, 1855, aged 55 years
Edwin Rodgers, departed this life August 10, 1856, aged 1 year, 10 months, and 2 days
Mary Rodgers, on December 15, ----, aged 3 weeks and 4 days

Elizabeth Jane Stevenson, wife of James Stevenson, departed this life December 11, 1849, aged 27 years, and also her three infant children [no names or dates given]

William Lormar departed this life January 8, 1832, aged 45 years

James M. Lormar, born March 10, 1817, died August 8, 1819, son of William and Amelia Lormar

David Lormar (December 30, 1815 - March 13, 1857), son of William and Amelia Lormar

Jacob King, a native of County Derry, Ireland, died July 25, 1858, aged 55 years

James McNeal, Jr., a native of Ireland, departed this life December 22, 1831, in his 45th year

Elizabeth McNeal, wife of James, Jr., departed this life October 5, 1831, in her 18th year, a native of Baltimore County, Maryland

Mary Ann Myers, wife of Capt. Nicholas Myers, departed this life September 18, 1832, in her 52nd year

Myer Myers, son of Nicholas and Susan Myers, died August 30, 1837, aged 20 months and 13 days

Peter Fenby, Sr., a native of Yorkshire, England, died January 27, 1827, aged 71 years

John Breckenridge Fenby died December 13, 1830, aged 3 years

Elizabeth Daily died December 6, 1832, aged 41 years

Elizabeth Fenby died in 1833, aged 84 years

Peter Fletcher Fenby, died January 17, 1844, aged 25 years

Theodosia Fenby, died February 18, 1846, aged 25 years

Mary Jane Fenby, died December 16, 1846, aged 22 years

William Ross, a native of Ireland, departed this life July 1, 1820, in his 60th year

John C. White, vault (removed to Greenmount Cemetery in 1873)

Bettie Mark Stiles (October 11, 1842 - June 10, 1899), wife of Mr. Lee Stiles

Nannie Lisle Stiles, daughter of Mr. Lee and Bettie M. Stiles, died April 15, 1887, aged 10 years

Mr. Lee Stiles (May 27, 1821 - June 7, 1878)

John K. Kane (November 25, 1804 - December 30, 1840)

John M. Kane died May 8, 1822

Ann Kane died August 29, 1833

Samuel K. Kane died in March, 1837

Amelia S. Kane (November 1, 1812 - November 21, 1891), wife of John K. Kane

SECOND PRESBYTERIAN CHURCH 231

Arianna Bouldin (May 10, 1816 - May 24, 1879), wife of Alexander J. Bouldin
Alexander J. Bouldin, died June 12, 1855, aged 56 years
Edwin Bouldin, departed this life July 20, 1844, in his 19th year
Susanna Bouldin, consort of Alexander J. Bouldin, departed this life April 19, 1854, in her 36th year
Col. John Bouldin, departed this life May 5, 1850, in his 70th year
Samuel McKim, who was for many years a highly respected citizen and merchant of Baltimore, was born in Delaware on May 9, 1768, and departed this life on October 1, 1834.
John Cross, a native of Clones, Ireland, and 35 years a citizen of America, departed this life on September 29, 1807, aged 77 years
Jane Cross, consort of John Cross, departed this life on March 6, 1826, aged 85, a native of Guardhill, County Monaghan, Ireland
Andrew Cross, a native of Cecil County, Maryland, and for many years a citizen of Baltimore, departed this life September 23, 1815, aged 43
Jane Young Cross, daughter of Andrew Cross, departed this life on May 26, 1816, aged 1 year and 24 days
Rachel Cross, relict of Andrew Cross and daughter of Thomas and Esther Wallace of Cecil County, Maryland, was born December 15, 1780, and died March 12, 1843
Garvin Crawford died October 9, 1818, in his 21st year
Hugh Crawford, died November 16, 1856, in his 20th year
Maria Louisa Crawford, in little vault
Benjamin Bradford Crawford, in little vault
Jane Ormsby Crawford, in little vault
Sarah Eliza Grey (October 18, 1794 - February 8, 1840)
Robert Ormsby died September 15, 1833
William Crawford Ormsby, died July 16, 1853, aged 18 months
Jane Dunn [?]

Capt. John Kennedy, a native of Ireland, emigrated to this his adopted country in early manhood, and at the Battle of North Point on September 12, 1814, he was Commander of the 2nd Company in 17th Regt. M.M., and for his gallant and soldierly conduct in that action he received the approbation of his superior officers, was born in [County] Monaghan and died in this City [Baltimore] on December 10, 1822, in his 57th year.

Ann Kennedy, wife of Capt. John Kennedy, died November 17, 1851, aged 54 years and 5 months

Thomas Dickson, Esq., departed this life July 8, 1810, aged 52

Sarah Terry (July 24, 1800/1 [sic] - 1816, died in her 16th year) "Sarah Terry was my name, America was my nation, Fells Point my dwelling place, and Christ is my salvation."

William Terry died September 15, 1812, aged 31 years

Alfred Bouldin, son of Alexander and Susan Bouldin, departed this life July 21, 1829, aged 11 months

James Wilson, departed this life June 28, 1845, in his 61st year

FIRST UNITED PRESBYTERIAN CHURCH OF BALTIMORE CITY (NOW CALLED THE MONTEBELLO PRESBYTERIAN CHURCH), RECORD OF COMMUNICANTS, 1826-1840

[Record is available on microfilm M534 at Maryland State Archives.]

William Morris, from Scotland, November 28, 1826, elected Elder
James McIntire, from Ireland, November 28, 1826, "died 1878 or 9"
Elizabeth Dunn, from Dr. Duncan's church, November 28, 1826
Margaret Dunn, November 28, 1826, left, died April 2, 1880
Eliza McIntire, wife of Dr. James McIntire, November 28, 1826
Alexander Orr, November 28, 1826
Ann Orr, wife of Alexander Orr, November 28, 1826
Catherine Munroe, from Glascow [Glasgow], November 28, 1826
Sloan McIntire, brother of Dr. James McIntire, November 28, 1826
John Murdoch, from Presbyterian Church, Ireland, November 28, 1826
Mary Ann Murdoch, wife of John, from Ireland, November 28, 1826
James Thompson, from Est. Church, Scotland, November 28, 1826
Elizabeth Thompson, wife of James, from Scotland, November 28, 1826
Thomas Elliott, from Dr. Duncan's church, November 28, 1826
Mary Elliott, wife of Thomas, from Dr. Duncan's, November 28, 1826
Isabella White, from Dr. Duncan's church, November 28, 1826
Andrew Carothers, from Dr. Duncan's church, November 28, 1826
Isabella Carothers, wife of Andrew Carothers, November 28, 1826
Peter Malcom, from Dr. Duncan's church, November 28, 1826
Jenny Malcom, wife of Peter Malcom, November 28, 1826
John Smith, from Dr. Duncan's, Nov. 28, 1826, Elder 1837, died 1847
Isabella Darling, from Dr. Duncan's church, November 28, 1826
James Wilson, from Reformed Presbyterian Church, November 29, 1826
Agnes Wilson, wife of James, from Ref. Presb. Church, Nov, 29, 1826
James Davidson, from Dr. Duncan's church, June 21, 1827
Isaac McOreden [?], from Dr. Duncan's church, December 6, 1827
Ann Mathison, December 6, 1827
Rachel Forbes, from E. Scroggs, December 6, 1827
Gilbert McCollum, from Dr. Duncan's church, December 6, 1827
Mary McCollum, wife of Gilbert, from Lower Chanceford, Dec. 6, 1827
John Moiles, from Scotland, December 6, 1827
Alexander Dunce, December 6, 1827
Catherine Dunce, wife of Alexander Dunce, December 6, 1827

Jane Dunce, daughter of Alexander Dunce, December 6, 1827 [After her name is written "Brown," indicating she married.]
Margaret Dunce, daughter of Alexander Dunce, December 6, 1827
Agnes Greig, from Glascow [Glasgow], Scotland, December 6, 1827 [After her name is written "McKochnie," indicating she married.]
Will McGill, from Scotland, December 6, 1827
Christiana McGill, wife of Will, from Scotland, December 6, 1827
Samuel Taylor, from Stewartstown, Ireland, May 7, 1828
Isabella Taylor, wife of Samuel, May 7, 1828, died March, 1870
Mary Frizzell, sister of Mrs. Taylor, May 7, 1828, "married William Huston and after his death she married Henry Butt"
Sarah Ann Haliday, from Dunganon, Ireland, May 7, 1828 [After her name is written "McElderry," indicating she married.]
Eliza Cooper, sister of Rev. Dr. J. T. Cooper, from Dr. Duncan's church, May 7, 1828, died ---- [no date given]
Robert Forester, from Scotland, May 8, 1828
Archibald Shaw, from Guinston, and with Dr. Duncan's, May 10, 1828
Elizabeth Shaw, wife of Archibald Shaw, May 10, 1828
James Shepperd, from Richmond County, Virginia, but originally from Scotland, May 10, 1828
Alexander Kinear, from Rev. Heron's church, May 13, 1829
Sarah Kinear, wife of Alexander Kinear, from Rev. A. Stark, New York, May 13, 1829
James Maughlin, from Lower Chanceford, Pennsylvania, May 13, 1829
Ann Maughlin, wife of James, from Lower Chanceford, May 13, 1829
Jane Cooper, mother of Dr. Joseph T. Cooper, May 13, 1829
Janet Thompson, profession of faith, May 13, 1829
Anna Milliken, daughter of Robert Milliken [Millikin], formerly of Philadelphia, November 4, 1829
John Caldwell, from Paisley, Scotland, November 5, 1829
Jean Caldwell, wife of John Caldwell, from Paisley, Scotland, November 5, 1829
Margaret Graham, from Paisley, Scotland, November 5, 1829
Gilbert Barton, of Thistle Factory [sic], November 5, 1829
Andrew Graham, Jr., from Paisley, Scotland, November 7, 1829
Mary Holmes, profession of faith, May 19, 1830
John Arnold, from Ref. Presby. Church, Baltimore, May 19, 1829
Jane Russel, from Scotland, May 19, 1830
George Fullarton, from County Antrim, Ireland, May 19, 1830
Susanna Fullarton, wife of George, from Ireland, May 19, 1830

SECOND PRESBYTERIAN CHURCH 235

William Sherer, from Ireland, May 19, 1830
Andrew Graham, from Rev. Smart of Paisley, Scotland, May 19, 1830
Mary Graham, wife of Andrew, Sr., from Scotland, May 19, 1830
Mary Graham, daughter of Andrew, Sr., from Scotland, May 19, 1830, "married John Smith, Elder, and afterwards Rev. J. H. Andrews"
Nelly Graham, wife of Andrew, Jr., from Scotland, May 19, 1830
John Gabby, from Lower Chanceford, Pennsylvania, May 20, 1830
Jane McFerran, from Dr. Duncan's church, October 27, 1830
James Taylor, from Scotland, October 27, 1830
Elizabeth Taylor, wife of James, from Scotland, October 27, 1830
Agnes Arnold, profession of faith, October 27, 1830
Ann Pedan (Mrs.), profession of faith, October 28, 1830
Susan N. Whyte, wife of Rev. A. Whyte, from A. Ch. [sic], North Carolina, June 2, 1831
Margaret Greig, of Thistle Factory, prof. of faith, June 2, 1831
James McCurdy, from Ireland, November 16, 1831
James Leaky, from Ireland, November 16, 1831
Margaret Patten, from Ireland, November 16, 1831
Margaret Darling, daughter of Isabella Darling, November 17, 1831
Sarah Leaky, wife of James Leaky, profession of faith, May 16, 1832
John Workman, from Lower Chanceford, Pennsylvania, May 17, 1832
Rebecca Workman, wife of John, from Lower Chanceford, May 19, 1832
Esther Russel (Miss), from Ireland, November 8, 1832, died March 8, 1880
Robert Sherer, profession of faith, November 9, 1832
Martha Wilson, profession of faith, November 29, 1833
William Caldwell, from Scotland, November 29, 1833
Margaret Caldwell, wife of William, from Scotland, Nov. 29, 1833
Robert Milliken, from Philadelphia, November 29, 1833
Mary Kinnier, daughter of Alexander, prof. of faith, May 25, 1834
  [After her name is written "Montgomery," indicating she married.]
Mary Wilson, from Ref. Presby. Church, Baltimore, May 25, 1834
  [After her name is written "formerly Mary Landsborough."]
Hugh Graham, certificate from ---- [blank], May 25, 1834
Eliza Russel, wife of Samuel Russel, October 30, 1834
Letitia McCormick, October 30, 1834, "married ---- Barr"
Isabella Graham, profession of faith, October 30, 1834
Robert Stewart, formerly of Ref. Presby. Church, January 4, 1838
Mathew Cowan, formerly of Ref. Presby. Church, January 4, 1838

John Mortimer, from 4th Presbyterian Church, January 4, 1838
Tamerine Mortimer, wife of John, from 4th Church, January 4, 1838
William W. Maughlin, from Lower Chanceford, Pennsylvania, January 4, 1838, died October 6, 1885
Thomas D. Anderson, son of Rev. Anderson, of Scotland, profession of faith, died March 21, 1893
James Fauquenier, profession of faith, January 4, 1838
Agnes Wilson, having left and joined the 4th Presbyterian Church, re-admitted January 4, 1838
Robert Willson, certificate from ---- [blank], January 4, 1838
Anna Maria Smart, wife of Rev. J. G. Smart, certificate from ---- [blank], January 4, 1838, died at Coilo [?], N. Y. ---- [date?]
Mary Ann Maughlin, wife of William W., from 4th Presbyterian Ch., August 22, 1838
Sarah Robinson, from 4th Presbyterian Church, October 4, 1838
Robert Laughlin, from 4th Presbyterian Church, October 4, 1838
Jane Laughlin, from 4th Presbyterian Church, October 4, 1838
Mary Smiley, from 4th Presbyterian Church, October 4, 1838
Margaret Smiley, from 4th Presbyterian Church, October 4, 1838
Helen DeSelding, from Reformed Presby. Ch., N. Y., October 4, 1838
Samuel Garroway, from Scotland, October 4, 1838
Jane [June?] Garroway, wife of Samuel, from Scotland, Oct. 4, 1838
John Laughlin, from Ireland, May 2, 1839
Maria Laughlin, wife of John, from Ireland, May 2, 1839
Mary Jane Cooper, sister of Rev. Dr. Cooper, profession of faith, May 2, 1839, and [later] married Rev. Logue
Thomas Robinson, May 2, 1839
Elizabeth Robinson, wife of Thomas Robinson, May 2, 1839
John Morehead, May 2, 1839
Margaret Yates, profession of faith, May 2, 1839
William Houston, from County Kilbrought, Ireland, May 2, 1839
Rebecca Anderson, sister of Mrs. W. W. McLaughlin, May 2, 1839, profession of faith, and [later] married Mr. Reid of York Co., PA
William Rogers, from 4th Presby. Church, May 2, 1839, died 1892[?]
Eliza Russell, formerly of this congregation, received May 2, 1839 on certificate from Dr. Hanna in Cadiz, Ohio
Matilda Brown (Mrs.), from Larne, Ireland, May 4, 1839
Mary Houston (Miss), sister of William and James, November 14, 1839
Stewart Montgomery, November 14, 1839

SECOND PRESBYTERIAN CHURCH

Jane Kinnier, daughter of Alexander Kinnier, November 14, 1839, and [later] married Samuel F. Wiley
Mary Anderson, widow of Rev. D. Anderson, Nov. 14, 1839, died 1867
Jane Anderson, daughter of Dr. D. Anderson and sister of Thomas D. Anderson, November 14, 1839, died February 6, 1895
Maria N. McCormick, profession of faith, April 30, 1840
Elizabeth Taylor (Miss), profession of faith, April 30, 1840
Thomas Hunter, from County Antrim, Ireland, April 30, 1840
Sarah Jane Hunter, wife of Thomas, from Ireland, April 30, 1840
Isabella Cady, from the 4th Presbyterian Church, April 30, 1840
Hannah Cummings (Mrs.), profession of faith, April 30, 1840
John Smith, certificate from the A. Ch. [sic], Albany, New York, April 30, 1840, later removed to California [no date given]
James Laughlin, certificate from Donegon, Ireland, November 5, 1840, died May 5, 1887
Mary Laughlin, wife of James, from Ireland, November 5, 1840
Alexander Kinnier, Jr., from Manchester, England, November 5, 1840

FIRST UNITED PRESBYTERIAN CHURCH OF BALTIMORE CITY (NOW CALLED THE MONTEBELLO PRESBYTERIAN CHURCH), REGISTER OF BAPTISMS, 1826-1840

Elizabeth McIntire, daughter of James McIntire, baptized August 11, 1825 [sic], by Dr. J. Banks
William Morris Orr, son of Alexander Orr, baptized October 12, 1826 by Rev. James White
Elizabeth Jane Murdoch, daughter of John Murdoch, baptized November 30, 1826, by Rev. Andrew Heron
Edward Elliott, son of Thomas Elliott, baptized November 30, 1826, by Rev. Andrew Heron
Isabella Carothers, daughter of Andrew Carothers, baptized December 4, 1826, by Rev. Andrew Heron
Thomas Elliott, son of Thomas Elliott, baptized October 25, 1827, by Rev. Andrew Heron
George Whyte McIntire, son of James McIntire, baptized December 10, 1827, by Rev. Archibald Whyte
Elizabeth Wilson, daughter of James Wilson, baptized March 9, 1828, by Rev. Archibald Whyte
Daniel Munroe, son of Catharine Munroe, baptized June 18, 1828, by Rev. Archibald Whyte

Janet Russell Orr, daughter of Alexander Orr, baptized August 10, 1828, by Rev. Archibald Whyte

Agnes McGill, daughter of Will McGill, baptized October 8, 1828, by Rev. Archibald Whyte

Martha Crawford Murdoch, daughter of John Murdoch, baptized November 24, 1828, by Rev. Archibald Whyte

Samuel George Taylor, son of Samuel Taylor, baptized March 29, 1829 by Rev. Archibald Whyte, died March 31, 1888

Catherine Brown, daughter of Jane (Dunce) Brown, baptized May 3, 1829, by Rev. Archibald Whyte

Margaret Elliott, daughter of Thomas Elliott, baptized August 23, 1829, by Rev. Archibald Whyte

Mary Ann McIntire, daughter of James McIntire, baptized November 9, 1829, by Rev. Archibald Whyte

William Miles, son of John Miles, baptized May 24, 1830, by Rev. A. Heron

Sarah Jane Russell, daughter of Jane Russell, baptized May 24, 1830 by Rev. A. Heron

Agnes Munroe, daughter of Catharine Munroe, baptized June --, 1830, by Rev. A. Heron

Christiana McGill, daughter of William McGill, baptized October 10, 1830, by Rev. A. Whyte

Mary Jane Fullerton, daughter of George Fullerton, baptized Nov. 1, 1830, by Rev. F. W. McNaughton

Samuel Fullerton, son of George Fullerton, baptized November 1, 1830, by Rev. F. W. McNaughton

Alexander Brown, son of Jane Brown, baptized November 1, 1830, by Rev. F. W. McNaughton

Jane M. Orr, daughter of Alexander Orr, baptized December 5, 1830, by Rev. A. Whyte

Hugh Taylor, son of James Taylor, baptized March 16, 1831, by Rev. A. Whyte

Janet Malcom Bell Graham, daughter of Andrew Graham, baptized March 27, 1831, by Rev. A. Whyte

Martha Elliott, daughter of Thomas Elliott, baptized May 25, 1831, by Rev. A. Whyte

William Caldwell, son of John Caldwell, baptized May 29, 1831, by Rev. A. Whyte

Margaret A. B. Caldwell, daughter of John Caldwell, baptized May 29, 1831, by Rev. A. Whyte

Margaret McIntire, daughter of James McIntire, baptized September 4, 1831, by Rev. A. Whyte
Mary Ann Taylor, daughter of Samuel Taylor, baptized September 4, 1831, by Rev. A. Whyte
Catharine Munroe, daughter of Catharine Munroe, baptized November 20, 1831, by Rev. F. W. McNaughton
Margaret Elizabeth Russell, daughter of Jane Russell, baptized May 21, 1832, by Rev. Anderson
Margaret Ann Workman, daughter of John Workman, baptized June 17, 1832, by Rev. A. Whyte
Anne Orr, daughter of Alexander Orr, baptized November 12, 1832, by Rev. F. W. McNaughton
Mary Anne Miles, daughter of John Miles, baptized November 12, 1832 by Rev. F. W. McNaughton
Richard Henry Leakey [Leaky], son of James Leakey [Leaky], baptized January 5, 1833, by Rev. A. Whyte
Janey McCaghney, daughter of Agnes McCaghney, baptized February 24, 1833, by Rev. A. Whyte
Mary Ann Maughlin, daughter of James Maughlin, baptized March 24, 1832, by Rev. A. Whyte
Andrew Graham, son of Andrew Graham, Jr., baptized March 24, 1832, by Rev. A. Whyte
Eliza Graham, daughter of Andrew Graham, Jr., baptized March 24, 1833, by Rev. A. Whyte
Elizabeth Darling Caldwell, daughter of John Caldwell, baptized March 24, 1833, by Rev. A. Whyte
Esther Ann Russell, daughter of Jane Russell, baptized July 21, 1833, by Rev. A. Whyte
Laetitia McIntire, daughter of James McIntire, baptized September 23, 1833, by Rev. A. Whyte
William James Whyte Taylor, son of Samuel Taylor, baptized September 23, 1833, by Rev. A. Whyte
Agnes Jane Brown, daughter of Jane Brown, baptized September 23, 1833, by Rev. A. Whyte
Margaret Ann Fullerton, daughter of George Fullerton, baptized November 30, 1833, by Rev. T. Beveridge
Elizabeth Sherer, daughter of Robert Sherer, baptized May 22, 1834, by Rev. John Walker
Ellen Taylor, daughter of James Taylor, baptized June 1, 1834, by Rev. John Walker

William George Sherer, son of William Sherer, baptized October 5, 1834, by Rev. Adams
Mary Fleming Caldwell, daughter of William Caldwell, baptized October 12, 1834, by Rev. John Walker
Margaret Miles, daughter of John Miles, baptized December 28, 1834, by Rev. Adams
John Walker Russell, daughter of Jane Russell, baptized December 28, 1834, by Rev. Adams
James Workman, son of John Workman, baptized June 14, 1835, by Rev. Adams
Sarah Jane Leaky, daughter of James Leaky, baptized June 14, 1835, by Rev. Adams
James Holmes Arnold, son of Mary (Holmes) Arnold, baptized September 13, 1835, by Rev. A. Whyte
Agnes McIntire, daughter of James McIntire, baptized January 24, 1836, by Rev. John Adams
Jean Isabella Caldwell, daughter of John Caldwell, baptized January 24, 1836, by Rev. John Adams
Laura Graham, daughter of Andrew Graham, baptized May 22, 1836, by Rev. A. Heron
Mary Ann Sherer, daughter of Robert Sherer [Sheerer], baptized June 12, 1836, by Rev. A. Heron
Elizabeth Fullerton, daughter of George Fullerton, baptized July 17, 1836, by Rev. A. T. McGill
William McGill Caldwell, son of William Caldwell, baptized July 24, 1836, by Rev. A. T. McGill
Augusta McIntire, daughter of James McIntire, baptized October 13, 1837, by Rev. John G. Smart
Elizabeth Stewart, daughter of Robert Stewart, baptized July 3, 1838, by Rev. John G. Smart
John Anderson Caldwell, son of William Caldwell, baptized July 8, 1838, by Rev. John G. Smart
Joseph Elliott, son of Thomas Elliott, baptized July 17, 1838, by Rev. John G. Smart
James Maughlin, son of William W. Maughlin, baptized September 2, 1838, by Rev. John G. Smart
Susanna Fullerton, daughter of George Fullerton, baptized October 14, 1838, by Rev. John G. Smart
Ann Garroway, daughter of Samuel Garroway, baptized December 23, 1838, by Rev. John G. Smart

SECOND PRESBYTERIAN CHURCH

John Laughlin, son of Robert Laughlin, baptized March 17, 1839, by Rev. John G. Smart

Margaret Smart, daughter of Rev. John G. Smart, baptized May 2, 1839, by Rev. C. Webster

Mary Catherine Russell, daughter of Jane Russell, baptized May 2, 1839, by Rev. C. Webster

Elizabeth Ann Robinson, daughter of Thomas Robinson, baptized May 2, 1839, by Rev. C. Webster

Mary Elizabeth Brown, daughter of Matilda Brown, baptized May 12, 1839, by Rev. John G. Smart

Sarah Jane Laughlin, daughter of John Laughlin, baptized June 16, 1839, by Rev. John G. Smart

Robert Brown, son of Matilda Brown, baptized October 13, 1839, by Rev. John G. Smart

Sarah Jane Montgomery, daughter of Stewart Montgomery, baptized November 17, 1839, by Rev. John G. Smart

Sarah Jane McIntire, daughter of James McIntire, baptized May 4, 1840, by Rev. John G. Smart

Rebecca Maughlin, daughter of W. W. Maughlin, baptized May 4, 1840, by Rev. John G. Smart

---- [blank] Hunter, child of Thomas Hunter, baptized May 4, 1840, by Rev. John G. Smart

Agnes Mary Workman, daughter of John Workman, baptized May 14, 1840 by Rev. John G. Smart

Mary Jane McCormick, daughter of Maria N. McCormick, baptized July 5, 1840, by Rev. John G. Smart

James Duncan McCaghney, son of Agnes McCaghney, baptized August 16, 1840, by Rev. John G. Smart

James Laughlin, son of John Laughlin, baptized August 16, 1840, by Rev. John G. Smart

John Gardiner Smart, son of Rev. John G. Smart, baptized November 9, 1840, by Rev. Joseph T. Cooper

John Gib Laughlin, son of James Laughlin, baptized November 9, 1840 by Rev. Joseph T. Cooper

INDEX

-A-
ABBOTT, H., 190
　Lydia, 195
ABERCROMBIE,
　Clementina, 79
ADAMS, Delia
　Woodward, 122
　Eli, 122, 169
　Elizabeth, 84
　James, 94
　Jane, 80
　John, 240
　John A., 94
　Mary, 74
　Sarah D., 122
ADREON, Henry
　Clay, 148
　Susannah, 177
　Susanne, 148
　William T., 148
　William Tell, 148
AGNELL, James, 2
　Joshua Barney, 2
　Mary, 2
AGNEW, Andrew,
　151
AIKEN, Andrew, 190
　George, 158
　Robert, 190
AISQUITH, Robert
　C., 190
AITKEN, A., 190
　Andrew, 1, 2, 3,
　134, 190, 222
　Anne, 1
　Eliza, 2, 92
　Elizabeth, 1, 2, 3
　George, 2

James, 2
Maria, 2
Mrs., 195
Rebecca, 3, 195
Robert, 1, 134, 153,
　190
ALBERGER, Job,
　195
　Lavinia, 195
ALBERT, Eliza, 96
ALBRIGHT, Andrew,
　72
ALDRIDGE, Anne,
　73
ALEXANDER, Betty,
　2
　James, 190
　James W., 190
　Jane, 2, 81
　Rev. Dr., 190
　William, 2
ALEXANDERIA,
　Mary, 83
ALEXANDRIA,
　Flora, 77
ALLEGRE,
　Benjamin, 183
ALLEN, Catharine, 1
　Catherine, 1, 2
　Elisha, 85
　Eliza, 1
　Isaac, 88
　James, 1, 2
　James Williams, 1
　John, 2
　John L., 95
　John William, 1
　Martha Doram, 168

Martha Doran, 119
Mary, 1
Mrs., 152
Robert W., 95
Samuel, 1
Solomon, 1
Thomas, 72
ALLENDER, Eliza
　Augusta, 86
　Joseph, 3, 72
　Joseph Biays, 3
　Mary, 3
ALLEYNE,
　Benjamin, 96
ALLEYRE, Benjamin,
　183
ALLISON, Ann, 167
　Esther, 2, 86, 166
　Grace, 79
　John, 71
　Mary, 2, 162, 227
　Mrs., 158
　Patrick, 2, 71, 186,
　190, 227
　Robert, 71, 86
ALLRIDGE, John, 71
ALNUTT, Margaret,
　195
ALRICKS, F. N., 219
　H., 190
　Harmanus, 190
　Harriet, 195
　Jane, 195
　Mary, 216
AMDERSON, Rev.,
　236
AMEY, Elizabeth
　Ann, 157, 176

AMOS, Mary, 92
AMOUR, Elizabeth, 195
  Mary, 178
ANDEBERT, Stanislas, 91
ANDERSON, Agness, 2
  Andrew, 2
  Ann, 1, 178
  Christiana, 195
  D., 237
  Eliza, 3, 92, 164
  Eliza Polly, 3
  Franklin, 94
  H., 190
  Henry, 3, 72, 190
  James, 1, 71
  Jane, 237
  John, 1, 3
  Mary, 1, 2, 3, 75, 81, 237
  Mr., 152
  Mrs., 151
  Rebecca, 236
  Sophia, 227
  Susan, 161
  Thomas, 1
  Thomas D., 236
  William, 2, 3, 71
ANDREWS, ---, 224
  Cornelia, 2, 3
  Fanny Hughes, 3
  Hannah Buckler, 2, 195
  Isabella, 2
  J. H., 235
  Jane W., 195
  John, 2
  Mrs., 195
  N., 190
  Nat., 190
  Nathaniel, 2, 3, 153, 190
  Thomas, 2
  William, 2
ANGEL, Ann, 99
  James, 99
  John, 99
ANGELL, James, 1, 71
  John Barney Sweeting, 2
  Mary, 1
  William Henry, 1
ANNAN, Dr., 190
  S., 190
  Samuel, 190, 195
ANSPECK, Mrs., 195
APPLETON, Charles Tilden, 111
  Mary, 166
  Nathaniel Walker, 111, 166
  Sarah, 111, 166
ARCHER, Elizabeth M., 96
  John T., 195
  Robert H., 96
ARMISTEAD, Mary B., 179
ARMITAGE, Ann, 220
ARMOR, James G., 149
  Joseph G., 97
  Josephine, 149
  Rachel, 149
ARMOTE, Patience, 91
ARMOUR, Ann Eliza, 195
  Charles Huffman, 139
  David, 190
  James, 195
  John, 139, 177
  Joseph G., 195
  Mary, 139
ARMOURER, Mr., 159
ARMSTRONG, Ann, 211
  Elizabeth, 2, 107
  Francis, 2
  J., 190, 224
  James, 2, 3, 177, 188, 190
  Jane, 2, 3
  John, 2, 71
  Margaret, 184
  Mary, 177
  Mary Moore, 107
  Matthew, 107
  Phebe, 211
  Robert, 190
  Robert C., 190
  Sarah J., 95
  Thomas, 2
  William, 71
ARNOLD, Agnes, 235
  Benjamin, 85
  Elizabeth, 186
  James Holmes, 240
  John, 190, 234
  Mary Holmes, 240
ARRISON, Mary, 1
  Syme, 1
  Thomas Cox, 1
ASHER, William, 84

INDEX

ASHETON, Rebecca, 81
ASHMEAD, William, 190
ASHMORE, Susanna, 89
ASKEW, Catherine, 84
ATCHISON, Mary Jane, 218
ATKINSON, Amelia Elizabeth, 73
Broadnax, 226
Isaac C., 90
James J., 91
Susanna, 185
ATMORE, Lilly Ann, 84
ATTERBURY, Catherine, 112, 114, 163
Elisha Boudinot, 112
John Guest, 114
Lewis, 112, 114, 163
AUCHINCLOSS, Agness, 118
John, 86, 118
Matilda, 118
AULD, Elizabeth, 100
William, 100
AUTHER, Hugh, 190

-B-

BACKUS, J. C., 96
John C., 146, 161, 183, 186, 214
John c., 96
John Chester, 225
Letitia C., 186
BADEN, Elizabeth, 117, 166
William, 117, 166
BAER, Charlotte C., 217
Lydia R., 186, 217
M. C., 211
M. S., 186, 211, 214
Matilda C., 186
BAGELY, Lavinia R., 92
BAGGS, Mrs., 200
BAIL, Robert P., 72
BAILEY, Anthony, 90
Ariminta R., 92
Elizabeth, 4
Hannah, 4
James, 4, 90
John, 190
Margaret, 4
Nancy, 184
Robert, 4
Thomas, 4
William, 4
BAIN, Catharine, 3
Daniel, 3
Elizabeth, 167
Hope, 167, 175, 211, 212, 213
James, 154
Margaret, 3
Mr., 154, 158
BAISE, Anne, 81
BAKER, Catherine, 84
Elizabeth, 196
Jennis Helming, 72
Mrs., 203

BALDWIN, Sophia, 197
BALL, Ann E. U., 96
Ann E. W., 179
Elizabeth, 88
BALLENTINE, Elizbeth, 85
BALLINTINE, Ann, 180
BALTSELL, Ann Mary, 91
BALTZELL, ---, 132
BANDEL, Maria, 93
BANKS, Charlotte M., 96
BANKSON, John, 190
Mrs., 195
BANNERMAN, Miss, 197
BANNIMON, John, 190
BANRES, V. B., 190
BANTZ, Catherine, 86
William, 190
BARBINE, Elizabeth, 213
BARGER, George, 88
BARKER, Adam, 92, 136, 142, 156, 174
Bazel, 136
Eliza, 136, 142, 160, 174
Joseph, 190
P., 190
William, 142, 190
BARKLEY, Ann, 124
Ann Eliza, 131
J. M., 154

J. W., 160
James, 124, 154
James Stephen, 135
John, 124, 125
John M., 131, 135, 154, 226, 227
John Wallace, 131
Mary, 125, 131, 135, 226
Mary McCulloch, 217
Mary McCullough, 131
Rebecca, 125
Rebeka B., 213
Sarah Jane, 125
BARKLIE, ---, 225
Anna, 196
Emily, 196
Hester, 196
Jane, 196
Thomas, 72
BARKSDALE, William, 155
BARLING, Aaron, 86
BARNARD, John, 4
Prisilla, 4
William, 4
BARNES, Elizabeth, 84
Frances, 96, 182
James G., 196
James, Mrs., 190
Mrs., 190, 206
Robson, 163
Samuel, 190
BARNETT, Mary, 81
BARNEY, Anne, 6
Caroline, 6
Elizabeth N., 179

Esther Ann, 141
Esther Anne, 179
Henry, 6
J. H., 190, 195
John, 6
John H., 190
Joshua, 6, 190
Louis, 6
Mary, 71
Mr., 190
William, 6
BARNHELL, David, 3
Jane, 3
Robert, 3
BARNS, William, 84
BARR, Benjamin Sterrett, 124
J. F., 224
J. T., 119
Jane, 119
Jane S., 122, 124, 132, 170
John T., 122, 124, 132, 152, 170, 188
John Thompson, 118, 119, 132
John Thomson, 168
Margaret S., 95
Margaret Sterrett, 119
Mary, 107, 110, 165
Mary Jane, 122
Mary McKnight, 110
Samuel, 107
Samuel Sterrett, 119
W., 156

William, 107, 110, 165
BARRET, Mr., 156
BARRETT, ---, 190
Rachel, 229
Thomas, 229
BARRICKMAN, Hannah, 196
BARRIER, Ann, 196
Eliza, 197
Jane, 196
Rebecca, 196
BARRON, Ellis, 89
John, 155, 190
BARROWS, Elijah P., 168
Elijah Porter, 221
BARRY, Agness, 7, 8
George, 7
John L., 8
Maria, 7
Standish, 7, 8
BARTHOLOMEW, John T., 92
BARTON, Gilbert, 234
Joshua, 87
BATES, Ann, 86
Francis, 93
James, 93
Robert, 91
BAUM, Christian J., 225
BAUSMAN, Kitty, 78
BAYARD, Mrs., 156
BAYDEN, Ann Vetch, 8
Elizabeth, 8
John, 8
BAYLESS, Mary, 218

INDEX

BAYLY, Eliza Jane, 216
  H. E., 167
  Hannah, 167
  Margaret, 166
  Mary Livinia, 215
BAYSON, Airy Ann, 8
  Elizabeth, 8
  John, 8
BEACH, John, 72
BEAM, Agness
  Salome, 123
  Charlotte, 170
  Charlotte C., 153
  Charlotte
    Christianna, 119
  Elijah, 87, 119, 170
  Elizabeth E., 96
  Elizabeth Eve, 125
  William Robinson, 119
BEANES, William, 222
BEARHOSSE,
  Catharine, 125
  Margaret, 125
  Thomas, 125
BEARING, James, 72
BEATTIE, Sarah, 196
BEATTY, ---, 190
  Arthur, 3
  Bateman, 8
  Cornelius, 206
  Eleanor, 3
  Elizabeth, 196
  James, 190, 195
  John, 8, 9
  Mary, 3, 8, 9, 93
  Mary N., 196

W. T., 190
William, 190
William H., 190, 195
BEATY, Mary, 94
BECK, William C., 90
BEDFORD,
  Elizabeth, 86
  Mary, 9
  Mary Cook, 9
  Peter, 9
BEEMIS, Nathan S., 89
BEENHOPE,
  Thomas, 171
BEERS, James, 190
  Mary, 7
  Susanna, 7
  William, 7
BEHN, Henry
  Karclaw, 9
  John H., 9, 72
  John Herman, 101
  Mary Catharine, 101
  Violet, 9, 101
BELL, Ann Perry, 84, 164
  George, 145
  Mary, 145
  Mary Jane, 145
  Rebecca C., 171
BELT, Joseph, 72
  Leonard, 190
  Mary, 196
  Susanna, 75
BEND, Rev. Dr., 190
BENNET, Adelia, 95
  James, 3, 4
  Jane, 3, 4
  John, 3

Samuel, 4
William, 4
BENNETT, Anne, 227
  James, 72
  Joseph, 72
BENNING, William, 90
BENTALOU,
  Katharine, 223
  Paul, 222, 223
BENTHALL, Robert, 95
BENTY, Mr., 154
BENTZ, Caroline, 185
  John A., 91
BERKLEY, John M., 88
BERRET, Joseph, 85
BERRMAN, Mary, 82
BERRY, Polly, 80
BETTS, Jesse, 91
BEVAN, Elizabeth, 77
  Mary, 81
BEVIN, Horatio, 88
BIASS, Mr., 150
BIAYS, Abraham, 5
  Agness, 5
  Ann, 87
  Anne, 6, 7, 8
  Col., 190
  Eliza, 9
  Elizabeth, 4, 9
  Elizbeth, 74
  James, 5, 6, 8, 9, 72, 190, 195
  James A., 7
  Jane, 82

John, 5, 7
Joseph, 4, 5, 6, 7, 8, 9, 72
Margaret, 5, 84
Mary, 4, 5, 6, 7, 8, 9, 72
Matthew, 5
Philip, 8
Rachel, 9, 88
Samuel Smith, 9
Sarah, 5, 6, 7, 8, 9
Susanna, 5
William, 8
BIBBY, Harriet, 171
BICKLEY, Samuel, 196
BIDDEL, Amelia, 226
  Louise, 226
  Mary, 226
  Robert, 226
  Sarah Matilda, 226
BIER, George, 190
BIGGAR, Margaret, 8
  Martha, 8
  Samuel, 8
BIGGES, Gilbert, 72
BIGHAM, Candance, 127
  Gordon, 127
  John, 196
  Robert, 127
BIGLAND, Robert, 150
BIOSHO, Nicholas, 72
BIRD, Caroline Mitilda, 136
  Eleanor, 136, 137, 140, 174

Henry, 136, 137, 140, 174, 188
Henry Arthur, 140
Joseph, 94
Mr., 154
William Nevins, 137
BISCOE, Jane E., 182
BISHOP, John, 190
BIXBY, Margaret, 128
  Mary Ann, 128
  Nathaniel P., 128
BLACK, Eliza, 196
BLACKNER, Jane E., 95
BLAIR, Elizabeth, 82, 190
  Mrs., 190
  Samuel, 103
BLAKE, James, 94
BLAKEY, Mary, 196
BLANCH, Elisa, 84
BLANCHARD, D. H., 217
BLAND, Judge, 190
  Theodorick, 190
BLANEY, Elizabeth, 5
  Nathanel, 5
  Teresa, 5
BLAYNEY, Mrs., 154
BLODGET, C., 154
BLUE, Leah, 157, 177
BODLEY, George R., 92
  Josias Rutter, 228
  Mary, 228
  Thomas, 228
BOGGS, A. J., 196

A. L., 156
Alexander, 132, 136, 156
Alexander L., 88, 124, 127, 130, 136, 138, 142, 152
Ann Ruth, 127
Caroline, 134, 136, 138, 141, 175, 197
Harmanus, 190
Jane, 142
John, 141
John C., 190
John Greer, 124
Mary Jane, 130
Maxwell McDowell, 136
Mrs., 200
Sarah Jane, 134
Susan, 127, 130, 132, 136, 138, 142, 172
Susan G., 124
Susan Greer, 138
William, 134, 136, 138, 141, 175, 197
William Harmaney, 132
William Jefferies, 138
BOGGUS, Margaret Ann, 93
BOISSEAU, David W., 167, 187
BOLTON, Hannah, 196
  Marie, 196
  Mr., 158
  Sarah, 93
BOND, Charles, 88

INDEX

Eleanor, 167
Eliza, 167
James, 72
Margaret, 83
Mrs., 183
Thomas E., 97
BONNER, Hugh, 190
BONSELL, Jesse, 72
BORLAND, John, 190
Thomas, 91
BOSLER, Honor, 3
Jacob, 3
Mary, 3
Rachel, 3
Rebecca, 3
BOTELER, Henry, 87
BOTTS, John, 89
BOUDINOT, Julia, 164
BOULDIN,
Alexander, 232
Alexander J., 231
Alfred, 232
Arianna, 231
Edwin, 231
John, 231
Susan, 232
Susanna, 231
BOULDING, J., 190
Jehu, 190
BOURNE, Rebecca, 164
Sylvanus, 72, 163, 164
BOWDEN, William, 150
BOWEN, Hannah, 196

BOWERING, John, 72
BOWIE, Ann, 196
James, 190
Maria, 196
BOWMAN, John, 92
BOWSER, Moses, 87
BOYD, Agnes, 116
Albert, 140
Alexander, 5, 132, 151
Alexander H., 154
Alexander Hamilton, 137
Andrew, 5, 155
Ann, 112, 129, 167
Ann P., 161
Anna, 116
Elizabeth, 110, 137, 140, 176
Ellen Stewart, 132
George Washington, 137
Isabella, 89, 137
James, 129, 137
James McHenry, 116
James P., 85, 112, 116, 158, 167
Jane, 82, 110
Jeremiah, 137, 140, 176, 180
John, 72, 187, 221, 227
John P., 153
John Pillar, 129
Margaret, 120
Mary, 5, 112
Mrs., 197
Peter, 110, 190

Ruth, 81
Samuel, 116
Selina, 116
BOYER, Agness, 6
Eleanor, 6
John, 6
BOYLE, William, 72
BRACKENRIDGE, John, 190
BRADEN, Elizabeth W., 95
BRADENBABUGH, John, 84
BRADFORD, Ann E., 134, 143
Anna Catharine Stricker, 143
George Patterson, 134
John, 90, 134, 143
John Stricker, 134
Julia Rankin, 134
Richard Magruder, 134
BRADISH, Sally, 227
William, 227
BRAMLEY, Thomas, 190
BRANNAN, Mary Ann, 93
BRANSON, Joseph, 92
BRANT, Louisa, 78
BRECKENRIDGE,
John, 190, 195
Mr., 155
Rev. Mr., 190
Robert J., 190
BRECKINRIDGE,
Mr., 154, 155, 156

Sophoniste, 196
BRETT, Mr., 215
  Mrs., 215
BRIANT, William, 87
BRIDNER, Margaret, 185
  Mary, 185
  Susannah, 185
BRIEN, John M., 93
  Rebecca S., 156
BRIGGS, James, 9, 72
  Rebecca Ensor, 9
  Temperance, 9
BRIGHT, Edward, 197
BRISCOE, A. H., 219
BROADNAX, Robert H., 92
BROBSTON, Ann, 181
BROCCHINS, Mary, 219
BROKE, Ferdinand, 72
BROMER, B., 190
BROMWELL, H. B., 130
  Henrietta, 130, 172
  Henrietta Melinda, 130
  Henry B., 172
  Henry Broughton, 130
  Mr., 151
  William, 190
BROOKS, James, 88
  Jane, 94
  Nathan C., 196
BROWN, Agnes Jane, 239

Alexander, 4, 7, 72, 160, 163, 190, 238
Alexander Davison, 131
Alice, 12
Ann, 85, 162
Capt., 190
Catherine, 238
Charles, 121
David, 8
Edward, 12
Eliza, 96
Elizabeth, 5, 127, 157
Elizabeth Johnson, 143
Esther, 114, 117, 124
Fanny, 73
Frances, 75
George, 5, 6, 7, 8, 9, 124, 127, 131, 133, 137, 143, 151, 157, 162, 172, 188
George Alexander, 101
George J., 86, 114, 117
George John, 6
George William, 117
Grace, 4, 5, 6, 8, 91, 163, 171, 186
Grace Ann, 133
Grace Davison, 129
H., 210
Hannah, 4, 78
Harman, 142
Henry, 170
Hugh Edward, 12

Isabella, 127, 131, 133, 137, 143, 172
J. H., 195, 209
J. Herman, 209
Jacob Harman, 111, 196
James, 3, 92, 129, 133, 173
James Muncaster, 127
James Syme, 3
Jane, 3, 5, 81, 141, 162, 175, 179, 238, 239
Jane Dunce, 238
Jesse, 6
Jessie, 227
John, 3, 4, 5, 6, 7, 72, 227
John N., 175, 187
John Neave, 108
John Wilson, 210
JoOhn A., 91
Joseph Mather, 7
Josiah, 72
Justus, 4, 5, 6
Louisa K., 129, 133, 173
Margaret, 4, 7, 96
Margaretta, 9, 87, 142, 168, 196, 210
Margaretta Hutton, 142
Mary, 94, 195
Mary Ann, 8
Mary Buchanan, 114
Mary Elizabeth, 241
Matilda, 236
Menie R., 211

INDEX

Nancy, 8
Robanie, 219
Robert, 197, 241
Robert Patterson, 9
Rosally, 88
Rose, 5, 6, 7, 8, 9, 162
Sally, 175
Sally Harman, 95, 115
Samuel, 3, 187
Sarah, 3, 4, 5, 6, 7, 9, 84, 100, 101, 108, 111, 115, 127, 158, 164, 165, 176, 227
Sarah A., 197
Sarah Ann, 91, 121
Sidney Buchanan, 124
Sophia, 97
Stewart, 9, 100, 101, 108, 111, 115, 127, 159, 165, 176, 186, 188
Susan, 196
Susanna, 4
Thomas, 6, 72, 196, 241
Thomas Jameson, 5
William, 4, 151, 169
William Benedict, 133
William Harman, 9
BRYAN, Catharine, 87
BRYDEN, Agness, 7
Ann, 8
Ann Vetch, 8
Elizabeth, 6
Elizabeth G., 227

James, 5, 6, 7, 8
Janit, 7
Janney, 85
John, 5
Mary, 5, 6, 7, 8
Violet, 72
William, 8, 227
BRYON, Sarah, 78
BRYRON, Agnes, 179
BRYSON, ---, 190
Agnes, 160
Agness, 7, 9
Airy Ann, 8
Arianna, 90
Edward, 9
Elizabeth, 4, 5, 8, 9
James, 4, 8
John, 4, 5, 8, 9, 83, 190
John Stevenson, 8
N., 190
N. G., 190
Nathan G., 190, 195
Nathan Gregg, 72
Nathaniel G., 190
Robert, 7
William, 5, 7, 8
Winifred, 7, 8
BUCHANAN, Anne
Lydia, 9
Anne Maria, 7
Boyd, 3
Catharine, 109
Catharine Isabella, 115
Catherine Isabella, 118, 150
David Stewart, 109
E., 118
Eliza, 173

Eliza S., 156
Elizabeth, 3, 7, 8, 9, 100, 103, 106, 114, 167, 180
Elizabeth Esther, 4
Elizabeth Sidney, 9
Elizabeth Stewart, 118
Ellen B., 141, 144, 178
Esther, 3, 4, 175
Esther L., 94
Esther Smith, 7, 100
George Harrison, 118
J. A., 118, 188
James, 3, 72, 100
James A., 7, 8, 9, 72, 103, 106, 114, 167, 221
James C., 152
James Calhoun, 9, 141
Jane, 3
Janit, 78
John, 3
John Louis, 103
John Smith, 3
Lloyd, 109, 115, 118, 152
Lloyd Archibald, 115
Margaret, 163
Mary, 71
Mr., 190
Peter Carr, 144
R., 190
Rebecca, 76
Robert, 190

Robert Smith, 106
Samuel Smith, 114
Sidney, 184
Sydney, 163
W. B., 141, 144
William, 3, 4, 162, 186, 187, 222
William B., 93
William Boyd, 8
BUCHER, Dewalt, 100
  Joseph, 100
  Magdalena, 100
  Nancy, 100
BUCK, Maria, 196
BUCKLER, ---, 131, 224
  A. F., 116
  A. T., 112
  Ann, 9
  Ann Hepburn, 9
  Ann Thomas, 103, 165
  Anne, 7, 8, 9, 170
  Elizabeth, 7
  Hannah Warren, 112
  Humphrey, 158, 190
  Jane J., 176
  Jane Johnson, 9
  John, 8
  Thomas Hepbrom, 116
  W., 116
  William, 7, 8, 9, 103, 112, 160, 165
BUCKLEY, Eleanor, 76
BUCKMAN, John, 165

Susanna, 165
BUCKWALTER,
  Abraham, 219
  Margaret, 219
BUD, Eleanor, 134
  Henrietta Vernon, 134
  Henry, 134
BUEL, Isaac, 167
  Maria, 167
BUFFURN, John, 85
BUKREE, Elizabeth, 211
BULDGE, Henry, 72
BULL, Elizabeth, 5
  John, 4, 5, 6
  Judien, 5
  Rachel, 4, 5, 6
  Susanna, 4
BUMRIDES, James, 72
BUNKER, Elizabeth, 9
  George, 9
  Mary, 9
  Moses, 72
BUNTING, Jane, 213
BURGOINE, Jacob, 72
BURK, Eleanor, 82
  Mary, 80
  Sarah, 79
  Thomas, 72
BURKE, Arrabella, 7
  Callendar Randal, 5
  David, 6, 7, 8, 9, 190
  Elizabeth, 6, 7, 8, 9
  George Washington, 9

Harriot, 7
James, 4
Janit, 4
Jefferson, 9
John, 4, 6, 89
Margaret, 5
Mrs., 196
Rebecca, 177
Thomas, 5
BURN, Eleanor, 8, 85
  Hannah, 6, 8
  James, 6, 8
  Jane, 8
  William, 6
BURNETT, Richard, 89, 190
BURNEY, James, 6
  John, 6, 7
  Margaret, 6
  Martha, 7
  Mary, 6, 7
BURNS, Elizabeth, 129
  Francis, 129
  Samuel, 129, 190
BURNSIDE,
  Elizabeth, 5
  James, 5
  Miss, 151
BURROUGHS, Ann, 211
BURROWS, Eleanor, 83
BURT, Alexander Fridge, 110
  Andrew, 104, 110, 115, 116, 117, 120, 125
  Andrew Wood, 104

INDEX

Isabella, 104, 110, 115, 116, 117, 120, 125
James Ross, 125
Jane Jamieson, 104
Margaret Alexander, 104
Mary, 117
William, 116, 120
BURTES, John, 72
BURTON, Margaret, 5
Mary, 5
Richard, 5
BUTLER, Alice M., 130, 132, 136, 173
Ann, 214
Catharine, 216
Emily Monroe, 136
G., 190
Henry Langdon, 130
John, 211
John M., 211
Margaret, 211
Mary, 132
William, 130, 132, 136, 154, 155
BUTT, Henry, 234
Lewis, 84
BUTTERFIELD, Mr., 153
BUTTS, Joshua, 96, 178
BYAS, Col., 190
BYER, Jane Augusta, 224
John G., 224
BYRNE, Anne, 196
Isabella, 196

Mrs., 195
W. H., 190

-C-

CAD, Rebecca, 80
CADY, Isabella, 237
CAIN, Henry, 189
CALDWELL, ---, 190
Caroline, 197
David, 98
Elizabeth, 10, 87
Flora, 166
Isabella, 186
James, 10, 190
Jane, 10
Jean, 234
Jean Isabella, 240
John, 14, 98, 150, 164, 234, 238, 239
John Anderson, 240
Joseph, 88
Margaret, 98, 164, 235
Margaret A. B., 238
Martha, 83, 98
Mary, 14
Mary Fleming, 240
Samuel, 10
Susanna, 10
Thomas, 190
William, 14, 235, 238, 240, 242
William McGill, 240
CALHOUN, Agness, 11
Alexander, 73
Alexander John, 13
Ann, 90
B. C., 190
Elizabeth, 11, 72

James, 11, 162, 186, 187, 188, 222, 224
John, 11
Lydia, 119, 167
Margaret, 11
Mary, 86
Priscilla, 11
Sarah, 13
Sydney, 175
CALLAGHAN, Mary, 78
CALLENDER, George, 87
CALWELL, Elizabeth Darling, 239
John, 73
Ruth, 74
Thomas, 190
CAMERON, Elizabeth, 11
Hugh, 11
James, 11
CAMP, Archibald, 190
CAMPBELL, Caroline E., 97
Catherine, 13
Harriet, 87
Henry, 13
Hugh, 87
James, 73, 181, 188
James Bradford, 113
John, 13
John R., 111, 113, 117, 166
Margaret, 111, 113, 117, 166
Mary, 94, 96, 180
Mr., 190

Mrs., 190
Nancy, 86
Robert, 13
Sarah, 111
Sarah Ann, 117
William, 190
CANHOON, Samuel, 91
CANNON, D., 190
Dennis, 190
Isaac, 11
Jehu, 11
Mary, 11
CANON, Dennis, 190
CANTLE, Barnett, 73
CANTWELL,
  Catharine Gough, 14
  James Smith, 106
  Sarah, 14, 106, 165
  Thomas, 14, 73, 106
CANVASS, George, 93
CAPOOT, Jeremiah, 73
CARELTON, James F., 94
CAREY, Eleanor, 84
  Mrs., 198
  Sarah, 81
  W. F., 190, 198
CARLILE, Agness, 12, 13, 78
  James, 12, 13
  Samuel, 12
CARLOCK, Mr., 158
  William, 93
CARLYLE, John, 73

CARMAN, Achsah, 73
CARMICHAEL,
  Agness, 10
  Alexander, 11
  Anne, 11
  Archibald, 10
  Daniel, 11
  Duncan, 10
  James, 11
  John, 10
  Margaret, 11
  Mary, 11
CARNES, John, 190
CARNIGHAN,
  James, 190
CARNS, Isabella, 110
  John, 110
CAROTHERS,
  Andrew, 233, 237
  Isabella, 233, 237
  Jane, 198
CARPENTER, Mary, 89
CARR, Cary Ann, 148
  Catharine, 179
  Dabney, 148, 156
  Dabney S., 143
  Ellen B., 93
  Hollins, 157
  Hugh, 73
  Isabella, 86
  Jane Margaret, 93, 138, 177
  Samuel Smith, 143
  Sidney, 148
  Sydney S., 143
  Sydney Smith, 178
CARRERE, John, 94

CARRINGTON,
  Christiana, 212
  Ephraim, 211
CARROLL, Ann, 114, 117
  Eleanor, 114
  Elizabeth, 93
  Elizabeth Maxwell, 140
  Henry, 90, 140, 142, 147, 157
  Henry Hill, 142
  James Joseph, 117
  Louisa, 198
  Margaret, 74
  Mary A., 197
  Mary B., 140, 142, 147, 178
  Mary Borden, 142
  Robert Henry
    Maxwell, 140
  Samuel Sterrett, 140
  Sarah, 156
  Thomas, 85, 114, 117
  William H., 197
  William Sterret, 147
CARRON, William, 73
CARRUTHERS,
  Elizabeth, 124
  Samuel, 124
CARSON, Andrew, 12, 13, 14, 103, 226
  Ann, 14
  Eliza, 197
  Elizabeth, 198
  George, 197, 198
  Jane, 12, 13, 14, 103, 226

INDEX

John, 12
Samuel K., 198
Sarah, 13, 179
William, 12
CARTEE, Daniel, 73
CARTER, Alexander M., 219
John P., 198
Maria, 198
Martha, 198
Matilda, 198
Sarah, 142, 180
Sophia Ann, 198
CARTY, John, 83
CARUTHERS,
Elizabeth, 101
William, 101
William Ewing, 101
CARVAN, Zelah, 159
CARY, Hetty C., 148
Jane M., 144, 148
Virginia, 144
Wilson, 148
Wilson M., 93, 144
CASHAN, Mrs., 151
CASMENT, Anne, 74
CASSELL, John F., 212, 213
Mrs., 213
CASTINE, Francis, 87
CASWELL, Josiah, 73
CATHCART, Robert, 164, 166, 167, 168
CATTS, John, 86
CAUGHEY, Patrick, 190
CAULFIELD, Robert, 73

CAUSTEN, Isaac, 11, 12
James, 12
Jane, 11, 12
Joseph, 11, 12
CAUSTIN, Isaac, 159, 221, 227
Jane, 227
CHACE, Captain, 190
CHADWICK,
Frances M., 215
CHAFFEE, Miss, 155
CHAMBERS, Arthur, 11, 12
Elizabeth, 12
John, 12
Lucy Ann, 132
Matilda, 12
Mr., 158
Philip, 132
Sally Rebecca, 132
Samuel, 11
Sarah, 11, 12
William Cooper, 12
CHAMIER, Daniel, 73
CHAMPLAIN, Eliza P., 197
CHAMPLIN, John, 84
CHANDLER, James, 74
CHAPIN, Aaron L., 183
CHAPMAN, Ann, 198
Mary, 176
Mr., 152
Mrs., 152

Ruth, 78
CHAPRN, Aaron L., 183
CHARLETON,
Elizabeth, 76
CHASE, Ann Jane, 216
Anthony, 92
Bissel, 190
Captain, 190
Elizabeth, 197
T., 190
Thomas, 190
Thorndick, 151
Thorndike, 190
Wells, 87
CHEESEMAN,
Phillis, 90
CHENOWETH,
Richard, 93
CHESNUT, James, 13
John, 13
Lydia, 13
CHESRAN, David, 73
CHESTON, Daniel, 190
CHEVALIERY,
Mons., 190
CHEW, Rachel, 81
CHILDS, James, 185
Mary, 80, 197
William, 190
CHISELEY, John, 73
CHISHOLM,
Elizabeth, 89
CHRISTOPHER,
Anne, 75
CHURCH, Samuel, 73

CLACKNER, Adam, 190
CLAGGETT,
  Elizabeth, 172
CLAQUHAUN,
  Elizabeth, 12
  Janit, 12
  Lamont, 12
CLARA, ---, 184
  Mrs., 147
CLARK, Ann, 12
  Ann Eliza Downing, 141
  Eleanor Ann, 93, 176
  Hannah, 88
  James, 190
  Janit, 12
  John, 10, 11
  Mary, 71
  Matthew, 12
  Oliver, 73
  Peter, 12
  Phoebe, 89
  Rachel, 11
  Rebecca, 10, 11
  Robert, 10
  Sally, 85
  Sarah, 11
  Shammah, 141
  Thomas, 12
CLARKE, A., 147, 161
  Caroline Rebecca, 147
  Charles Chauncey, 147
  Eliza, 185
  Elizabeth, 185
  Frances, 185
  Janit, 13
  John, 13
  Joseph, 87, 105
  Letitia, 185
  Margaret, 13
  Mary, 105
  Matthew, 13
  Mr., 156
  Phebe D., 141, 147, 178
  Phebe Downing, 140
  Ruth E. D., 181
  Shammah, 147, 179
  Suannah, 147
  Susannah, 141
  Sydenham Rush, 141
  William Wirt, 147
CLARKIN, Rhoda, 178
CLARKSON, James, 177
CLASKINS, Mrs., 214
CLEM, Maria, 197
  Mrs., 190
CLEMENT, James, 10
  Jane, 10, 11
  John, 10, 11
  Nicholas, 10
  Sarah, 11
  Sidney, 11
CLEMM, William, 84
CLEMMENTS,
  Sarah, 73
CLENDENEN, A., 190
  Dr., 190
  William H., 190
CLENDENING, Dr., 190
CLENDENNEN,
  Ellenor, 215
CLENDINEN,
  Alexander, 94, 229
CLENDININ, W. A., 198
CLIFTON, Thomas, 73
CLINGMAN, John, 73
CLINTON, Elizabeth, 12
  Isaac, 12
  Rachel, 12
CLOPPER, Abraham Duryee, 11
  Allison, 123
  Amelia, 129
  Andrew, 107, 110, 118, 129, 131, 151, 153, 190
  Ann, 107, 110, 118, 175, 182
  Ann B., 129, 131
  Benjamin May, 118, 159
  Charles Torrance, 110
  Cornelius, 10, 11, 107, 179
  Edward N., 118, 190
  Edward Nicol, 10
  Edward Nicols, 14
  Edward, Mrs., 151
  Elizabeth, 12, 95, 107, 175

INDEX

George Washington, 129
Grace, 118
Jane Williams, 13
John, 12
Julia Ann, 118
Leah, 12
Mary, 13, 14
Peter, 13, 14, 73, 74, 190
Rachel, 10, 11, 175
Rachel D., 118
William Lorman, 131
COAKLEY, ---, 148
Athelander Fosson, 145
Ehalynda Towson, 161
James Towson, 146
Mary Louisa, 144
P. H., 144, 161
P. P., 146
S., 146
S. C., 161
Sarah, 144, 179
COALE, John, 73
Minah, 74
COALH, Mrs., 196
COATS, Mary, 79
COBB, Jane Craig, 130
Margaret, 130
R. L., 130
COBENHEIFER, Elizabeth, 72
COCHRAN, Ann, 112
Ann M., 92
David, 190
Debor, 227

Deborah, 105, 109, 166
Dunbar Essex, 108
Elizabeth, 109
Essex Dunbar, 108
Mrs., 151
Robert, 88
Susanna, 108, 112
William, 105, 109, 166, 191
William G., 108, 112
William Scott, 105
COCKEY, Eliza, 198
Mrs., 90
COCKRAN, Robert, 214
COCKRANE, Elizabeth, 215
James, 216
Jane, 215
Mary, 215
Richard, 215
Robert, 212
COCKRILL, Sophia, 198
COCKSHAW, Aaron, 169
COFFAL, Maria, 77
COFFIN, Mary, 89
COHOUN, Moses, 73
COLE, ---, 191
Ann, 14
Ariabella, 74
John, 14, 73, 117, 168, 170, 191
John McDonogh, 117
Mary, 14, 117, 168
Mary Ann, 181
Mary Virginia, 91

Thomas, 191
William, 117, 191
COLEMAN, William, 73
COLER, Elizabeth, 89
COLES, Isaac A., 93, 141, 143
John Stricker, 143
Julia Isaetta, 141
Juliana, 141, 143
COLHOON, Anthony Kennedy, 112
B. C., 112, 117
Benjamin, 109
Benjamin C., 140, 142
Benjamin Chambers, 101, 142, 166
Elizabeth, 140, 157, 166
George Chambers, 109
John, 101
L. K., 112, 117
Lilly K., 140, 142
Lilly Kennedy, 101, 109, 166
Ruhannah, 117, 162
COLHOUN, B. C., 119
Benjamin Chambers, 119
L. K., 119
COLLET, Rachel, 77
COLLINGS, Richard, 73
COLLINS, Janit, 25
John, 25

John Smith, 25
Margaret, 75
Stephen, 180
COLT, Deveraux, 138
Elizabeth Sarah, 122
Ellen Craig, 141
Emily Oliver, 133
James Craig, 120
John Oliver, 118
Julia Catharine, 145
Margaret, 118, 120, 122, 124, 127, 133, 135, 138, 140, 141
Margaret Oliver, 140
Mary Devereux, 124
Morgan Gibbes, 135
Proswell, 135
R. L., 140, 141, 145, 152, 155, 160
Roswell, 120, 122, 124, 127
Roswell L., 86, 133, 135, 138, 168, 188
Roswell Lyman, 118, 127
Thomas Oliver, 138
COMPTON, Ann, 176
CONALES, Rachel, 74
CONINE, J. W., 158
J. W. C., 158
W. C., 159
CONKLIN, Elizabeth, 168
CONKLING, Eliza Story, 86

Elizabeth, 197
Thomas H., 151
W. H., 229
CONN, Alice, 12
Edward, 12
James, 73
Mary Anne, 12
CONNOR, Mary, 92
CONWAY, Ann B., 137, 139
Charles Henry, 137
Frances Ann, 139
James, 73
Solomon R., 92, 137, 139
William, 88
COOK, Henry, 86
John, 191, 198
Tany, 81
COOKE, Mrs., 207
COONROD, Mrs., 155
COOPER, Agness, 12
Andrew, 12
Eliza, 234
George E., 198
J. T., 234
Jane, 234
John, 12
Joseph, 12
Joseph T., 234, 241
Mary Ann, 96
Mary Jane, 236
Rev., 236
Sarah A., 198
COPE, Mary, 168
COPELAND, Mary, 161
COPER, Margaret, 80

CORNELIUS, Hidey, 74
CORNWALL, Hananh, 72
CORWINE, Sarah, 95
COSS, George, 219
COSTIN, Mr., 151
COULSON, George, 197
William, 85
COULSTON, Margta., 198
COULTER, Akn., 157
Alex, 157
Alexander, 13, 14, 73, 100, 103, 108, 113, 119, 143, 146, 147, 155, 163, 179, 225
Andrew, 14
Ann, 94
Archibald, 147
Delia, 93, 103
Dr., 152
Eliza, 143, 146, 147
Elizabeth, 13, 82, 113, 225
Ester, 13
Esther, 14, 95, 100, 103, 108, 113, 119, 163, 225
George Trull, 143
Hannah, 12, 13
Henry S., 95, 191
Henry Stevenson, 102
Hetty, 13

INDEX

John, 12, 13, 14, 73, 102, 168, 191
John Alexander, 12
John Parks, 13
Louisa, 12, 14
Margaret, 14, 179
Mary, 12, 13, 14, 102, 108, 225
Mary Ann, 198
Mifflin, 14, 146
Susan, 14
Thomas Barklie, 146
COUNCILMAN, John, 73
COURTENAY, David, 174
David S., 94, 187
David T., 144
Elizabeth D., 144
Henry, 73, 226
Isabella, 144
James, 73
Sarah M., 177
COURTNAY, David, 146, 147
David S., 146, 149
Edward, 149
Elizabeth, 147, 149
Elizabeth D., 146
Henry, 146
COURTNEY, Henry, 86
COUSINS, Ann, 85
COUTENAY, Mrs., 152
COUTLER, William, 85
COWAN, Mathew, 235

COWARD, Margaret, 135, 197
Mary Gausson, 135
Sarah Jane, 135
Thomas, 135
Thomas Richard, 135
COWLES, William, 87
COX, Ann Eliza, 170
Catharine, 14
James, 14, 188
John, 197
Macdonald, 14
Mary, 169
Nancy, 83
Samuel, 73
COXE, James, 10, 11, 73, 165
Mark Alexander, 10
Mary, 10, 11
Rebecca, 10
William, 10
CRAGGS, ---, 191
Mrs., 191
CRAIG, Bethiah, 98, 104, 112
Grace, 76
J., 191
John, 98, 191
John A., 95
John D., 191
Julia, 112
Louisa, 98
Margaret, 89
Maria, 104
Mr., 191
Thomas, 98, 104, 112
CRAWFORD, A., 183
Alexander, 10

Alfred, 92
Anna Maria, 197
Anne, 11
Benjamin Bradford, 231
Eliza, 72, 197, 215
Elizabeth, 11
Garvin, 231
Hugh, 231
James, 11
Jane, 10
Jane Ormsby, 231
John, 163, 191, 227
Margaret, 10
Maria Louisa, 231
Mr., 155
Rachel, 197
Robert, 11, 73
William, 158
CRAWLEY, Margaret, 78
CREA, Susanna, 87
CREARY, Catharine, 197
CREATON, John, 191
CREERY, Hans J., 191
J., 191
John, 211
Jonathan, 191
Wealthy Ann, 211
CRERAR, John, 93
CRERRY, Jonathan, 216
CRISFIELD, William, 93
CROCKET, Margaret, 77, 91
Sarah, 76

CROCKETT, George, 87
CROMWELL,
  Comfort, 10
  Nathan, 10
  Phebe, 10
CRONE, Elizabeth, 78
CROOK, Betsey, 180
  Charles, 91
  Walter, 191
CROSBY, Caroline, 13
  George, 13
  Hannah, 13
  Henry Payson, 13
  Josh, 215
  Josiah, 13
CROSS, A., 191
  Andrew, 191, 231
  Andrew Boyd, 197
  Barton, 73
  Catharine, 14
  Eliza, 197
  Elizabeth, 198
  Fances E., 97
  Jane, 198, 231
  Jane Young, 231
  John, 10, 231
  Margaret, 14, 197
  Martha, 197
  Mary, 14, 77
  Mr., 191
  Phillis, 197
  Rachel, 197, 231
  Richard J., 197, 198
  Robert, 14, 73, 191
  Ruth, 73
  Samuel, 10
  Sarah P., 96
  Sarah Patterson, 198
  Susanna, 10
  Trueman, 92
  William, 191
  William S., 191
CROW, Richard B., 92
CRUSES, Elizabeth, 75
CRUSEY, Isaac, 95
CUMMING, Emily, 182
  Emma, 182
CUMMINGS,
  Hannah, 237
  Jane, 198
CUMMINS, Jane, 197
  Joseph, 90
  Thomas, 197
CUNNINGHAM,
  Ann Margaretta, 212
  Arabella, 11
  Bethiah, 84
  Captain, 191
  D., 156
  Frances, 11
  H., 191
  Jane, 79
  Jane Augusta Wilson, 14
  John, 11, 12, 13, 14, 73, 191
  John Brown, 13
  John Mather, 12
  Joseph Mather, 13
  Margaret, 11, 12, 13, 14
  Sarah, 76
CUNNYNGHAM,
  Captain, 191
  John, 224
  Margaret, 224
CURRY, Eleanorra, 86
CURTIS, Jacob, 74
  Nelley, 77

-D-

DAGAN, Fanny, 16
  George, 16
  Mary Magdalene, 16
DAILEY, Ann Jane, 199
  William F., 199
DAILY, Elizabeth, 230
DALE, Samuel, 199
DAME, Augusta Temple, 125
  Thomas, 125
  William, 125
DAMESON, Sarah Jane, 95
DANCE, Augusta, 132, 142
  Augusta T., 142, 178
  Mary Carroll, 132
  Mr., 153, 154
  Mrs., 159
  Thomas, 89, 132, 142
DANE, Mary, 74
DANIELS, Ann, 17
  Anna Maria, 17
  Anthony, 17, 74
  Harriet, 17

INDEX

John, 17
DARE, Elizabeth, 216
  Nathaniel C., 215
DARLING, Isabella, 233, 235
  Margaret, 235
DARRACH, Margaret, 219
DASHIELS, Elizabeth, 17
  Maria, 17
  Rachel, 17
  Richard, 17
DAUGHERTY, Hannah, 14
  Hugh, 14
DAULL, Susannah, 76
DAVIDSON, Abraham, 191
  Agness, 17
  Andrew, 17, 74
  Daniel, 191
  Delia, 215
  James, 191, 226, 233
  Margaret, 17
  Mary, 17, 75
  Mary Ann, 199
  Mrs., 198
  Rev. Dr., 165, 167
  Robert, 74, 226
  Sarah, 17
  William, 74
DAVIES, ---, 224
  Elizabeth, 72
  Elizabeth Glen, 16
  Jacob, 17
  John, 16, 17
  Josiah, 74
  Mary Ann, 72
  Sarah, 16, 17
  William B., 215
  William Glen, 17
DAVIS, ---, 185
  Caroline, 149
  Caroline Augusta, 149
  Eliza Jane, 149
  Elizabeth, 211
  Jeremiah Perry, 102
  Margaret Matilda, 149
  Mary, 149
  Moses, 74
  Phoebe, 199
  Robert, 94, 149
  Sarah, 103
  Thomas, 211
  William, 74
  William S., 103
DAVISON, Jane, 16
  Samuel, 16
  Sarah, 218
  William, 16, 97, 218
DAWES, Agnes B., 228
  Francis N., 228
  Henry, 228
  Henry Dickson, 228
  Hetty, 166
  James, 166
DAWSON, Elizabeth, 80
  William C., 93
DAY, George, 92
DE LA ROCHE, George F., 88
  Jane, 199
DE VRIES, Christian, 103, 107, 111
  Henry, 103
  Jannatie, 103, 107, 111
  Mary, 111
DEAGAN, Catharine, 80
  Elizabeth, 74
DEANE, Hezekiah, 74
DEATH, Maria S., 87
DEAVER, Anne, 15
  Honora, 199
  Hugh, 74
  John, 15
  Martha, 15
  Mary, 15
  Nathan, 15
DEBARTHALL, Sarah, 199
DEBARTHALT, Catharine, 214
  Sarah, 214
DEBARTHOLDT, Catharine, 173
  Sarah, 174
DEBARTHOLT, Catharine, 182
  Sarah, 182
DECALOUR, James, 151
DECKER, Elizabeth M., 178
DECTER, Susannah, 75
DEGOFF, Sophia, 74

DELACOUR,
  Amanda Virginia, 136
  David, 86, 119, 122, 125, 131, 136, 173
  Eliza, 125, 131, 136
  Elizabeth, 119, 122, 173
  J. D., 169
  James, 187
  James Philips, 122
  Joanna, 156, 169
  John David, 125
  Marguerite Ann, 119
  William Lewis, 131
DELISLE, John Baptist Godart, 74
DEMANGIN,
  Charles, 87
  Elizabeth, 170
DEMONGIN, ---, 74
DENISON, Deborah, 119
  Edward, 119
  Eliza., 119
  Mary Deborah, 119
  Robert Miller, 119
DENNISON,
  Edward, 86, 168
  Eliza, 168
  Richard, 168
DENNY, William, 74
DENOS, Augustine R., 86
DENTON, Elizabeth M., 92
DERICKSON,
  Margaret, 216

DESELDING, Helen, 236
DESHEN,
  Christopher, 191
DESHON,
  Christopher, 191
DESPEAUX,
  Hannah, 124
  Isabella, 124
  Thomas, 88, 124
DEVONSHERE,
  Henry, 74
DEWEY, Silas, 86
DEWIT, Thomas, 191
DEWITT, Elizabeth, 15
  John, 15
  Thomas, 15
DICK, David, 16, 17
  Elizabeth, 16, 17
  Jane, 16
  John, 17
  Mary, 16, 17
DICKENSON,
  Eleanor, 84
DICKEY, George S., 191
  Robert, 85
  Sarah, 85
DICKINSON, Anne, 81
  Mary, 93
DICKSON, ---, 191
  J., 198
  Thomas, 191, 232
  W., 198
DIDIER, ---, 225
  Edmund, 92
DIFFENDERFFER,
  John, 191

DILLWORTH,
  Martha, 79
DINSMORE,
  Andrew, 178
  Charlotte, 175
  Elvin M., 175
  John M., 199
  Margaret, 199
  Mr., 191
  Mrs., 156, 198
  Patrick, 191, 198
  Thomas, 74, 151, 153
DISERT, Ruth, 164
DIXON, ---, 191
DOAK, Hannah, 124
  John, 124
DOAKE, James, 74
DOAKS, James, 17
  Jane, 17
  Joseph, 17
  Mary, 17
DOBBIN, George, 191
  Mrs., 198
  Thomas, 191
DODD, Hannah, 74
DODDY, Mrs., 191
DOHERTY, Mrs., 198
DONALDSON,
  Catharine Ann, 124
  Catherine, 108, 111, 116
  Charles Henry, 116
  Frances, 15, 16
  Francis, 16
  Henrietta, 108
  John Johnston, 16

Joseph, 15, 16, 108, 111, 116, 124, 187
Maria, 111
Maria Lowry, 181
Marion L., 96
Mr., 158
Samuel Johnston, 15
DONNELL, John S., 96
DONNELLY, James, 191
DONOGH, John, 225
DONOVAN,
  Jeremiah, 167
  Sarah, 167
DOOLEY, Sarah, 82
DORAN, James, 14
  Margaret, 14
  William, 14
DORMAN, Cornelius, 74
DORRANCE, James, 199
DORRENCE, Sarah, 172
DORRITY, Joseph, 15, 74
  Margaret, 15
DORSEY, Elias, 74
  Job, 93
  Joseph, 74
  Joshua, 191
  Lloyd, 199
  Mary, 76
  Rebecca, 199
  Sally Ann, 217
DORTON, Sarah, 81
DOUGHERTY, Jane, 199

John, 87, 191
Mr., 155
DOUGHTY, James
  Henry, 95
DOUGLAS, Samuel, 169
DOUGLASS, Fanny, 89
  Richard H., 91
DOWELL, Elizabeth, 86
  G. M., 224
  Susannah M., 161
DOWNER, Frances Ida, 177
DOWNES, Thomas, 74
DOWNEY, John, 74
  Margaret, 14
  Mary, 14
  Thomas, 14
DOWNING,
  Alexander, 103
  Ann Eliza, 141
  Catherine, 103, 164
  William, 103, 164
DOWNS, Ann, 91
  Anna, 173
  Dion, 199
DOWSON, Joseph, 86
DRABELLE, Joseph, 93
DRAPER, Ann Maria, 138
  Charlotte, 138, 142
  Charlotte Ann, 142
  Garretson, 93, 138, 142, 168
  Riley, 168

DREW, Joseph, 199
DRUMMOND, John, 15
  Mary, 15
  William, 15
DUBOIS, Edmund C., 199
  Jane Elliott, 199
DUFF, Mrs., 198
DUFFIELD, William, 102
DUFFY, John, 14
  Mary, 14
DUGAN, Abigail, 80
  Cumberland, 16, 74, 191, 221, 225
  Eleanor, 172
  Frederick, 159
  Frederick J., 225
  Hammond, 221
  Janet, 226
  Margaret, 16, 225
  Rebecca, 16
DUGDALE, Ellen M., 229
  George, 229
  Mary M., 229
DUGENT, Francis, 199
DUHAM, Elizabeth, 15
  Jacob, 15
  Samuel, 15
DUKE, James, 98
  John Winning, 98
  Mary, 98
DUKEHART,
  Edward W., 215
  Elizabeth, 199
  Elizabeth B., 219

Henry, 191
Mary Ann, 92
Mr., 217
Sarah Ann, 215
DULANY, Andrew, 89
DULL, Elizabeth Ann, 217
Jane R., 217
DUMERTE, Anna Elizabeth, 16
Catharine Virginia, 17
Elizabeth, 15, 16, 17, 18
Elizabeth Genevieve, 17
George Keeports, 18
Henrietta Maria, 18
Jacob Adrain, 18
John, 15, 16, 17, 18, 74
John Paul, 15
Sophia, 16
DUMEST, ---, 168
J. Adrian, 157
Mrs., 151
DUMESTE, Elizabeth, 87
DUNBAR, Fanny, 137
Frances, 128, 137, 141, 171
G. T., 157
George L., 128, 141
George T., 137
Henrietta F., 97
Henrietta Frances, 128
Joseph, 141

Louisa, 184
Maria Louisa, 128
DUNCAN, Abigail, 15
Agness, 15
Ann Maria, 18
David, 16
Debby, 17
Edward, 17
Elizabeth, 15, 83
Esther, 15, 77
Fanny, 97
Hugh, 16
Janit, 15
John, 16, 191
Margaret S., 181
Mary, 15, 16, 17, 18
Mr., 151, 152, 153, 154, 155, 159, 169, 233, 234, 235
Rebecca, 15, 16
Rebecca Dobson, 17
Samuel, 16
Sarah, 16
William, 15, 16, 17, 18
William Scott, 16
DUNCE, Alexander, 233, 234
Catherine, 233
Jane, 234
Margaret, 234
DUNGAN, Mr., 160
DUNGEN, Esther, 71
DUNKE, F. Dunken, 132
G. L., 132
Mary Eliza, 132
DUNKIN, L. H., 229
Levin H., 94

DUNLAP, James, 15
Sarah, 15
DUNN, Cathrine, 74
Elizabeth, 199, 233
Jane, 199, 231
Margaret, 233
DUNSHEAF, Jane, 82
DUNSMORE, Charlotte, 16, 17
Samuel Henry, 16
Thomas, 16, 17
DUNWOODY, R., 191
Robert, 191
DUPORT, Ann, 84
DURKEE, P., 191
DUVALL, Lemmuel E., 217
Mary Jane, 217
DYKES, Agnes, 176
Asa, 150
James Somervell, 17
Margaret, 17
William, 17
DYSARD, Cornelius, 15
John, 15
Ruth, 15
DYSART, Hester, 152
Mrs., 151

-E-

EADES, John, 84
EAGAN, John, 88
EASTBURN, Hetty, 79

INDEX

EASTMAN, Jonathan S., 219
EASTON, Elizabeth, 77
  Jane, 180
  Mrs., 191
  N. W., 191
  William, 86
EATON, Margaret, 169
  Mary, 119
  Richard Keys, 119
  William, 86, 119
EDDES, Mary Jane, 176
EDDY, James, 139
  Letitia, 139
  Rebecca, 172
  Susan, 172
EDEN, Robert, 74
EDES, Agnes Maria, 129
  Benjamin, 121, 125, 129, 133, 158, 221
  Benjamin Caldwell, 129
  Elizabeth, 125
  Elizabeth W., 96, 180
  Ellen Cross, 133
  Martha, 172
  Mary, 125
  Mary Ann, 121, 129, 133, 172
  Mary Jane, 97, 121
  Mary R., 172
  Mrs., 158
  Peter, 157
  Richard Andrew, 133
  Sarah T., 175
  Sarah Y., 136, 157
EDGERTON, Abraham Dubois, 135
  C. C., 154
  Charles, 135
  Jane, 135
  Margaret, 172
  Mary Susan, 135
EDIE, William, 93
EDRINGTON, Edmund G., 92
EDWARDS, ---, 191
  Eliza, 18
  Mary, 18
  Mr., 191
  Thomas, 18, 74
  William Adams, 18
EGERTON, C. C., 159
  Charles C., 176
  William, 160, 174
EGNEW, Elizabeth, 72
ELBERGER, Samuel, 191
ELDER, Esther, 104, 152, 164
  James, 104
  John, 104, 164
  Margaret, 86
  Mary, 87, 93, 199
  Mr., 153
ELFRY, Mary, 80
ELKINS, Catharine, 81
ELLICK, Ann, 78
ELLICOT, Anne, 74
  David, 74
  John, 74
  Letitia, 74
  Mary, 72
ELLICOTT, Andrew, 91
  Elizabeth, 74
  H. M., 212
  Hanna M., 211
  Nathaniel, 74
  Susanna, 79
  Thomas, 91
ELLIOT, A. M.
  English, 91
  Catharine, 144
  Henry Alexander, 144
  John, 144, 191
  Mr., 158, 191
  Sarah C., 179
ELLIOTT, Edward, 237
  John, 181
  Joseph, 240
  Margaret, 238
  Martha, 238
  Mary, 233
  Robert, 89
  Thomas, 233, 237, 238, 240
ELVANS, William, 74
ELVINS, Elizabeth, 18
ELWARD, Margaret, 83
ELWERT, Thomas, 75
ELY, E. S., 170
  Eunice, 183
  John C., 183
EMMIT, David, 18
  Isabella, 75

Jane, 18
John, 18
Margaret, 18
Mary, 18
EMORY, Lucretia, 180
ENGLISH, Elizabeth, 18
George, 18
Janit, 18
Margaret, 18, 80
Robert, 18
Thomas, 18
William, 18
ENNIS, Joseph, 191
Mary Jane, 93
ENSOR, John, 74
Temperance, 72
William, 74
ENTNIGGLE, John Joseph, 199
ERSKINE, Jane, 227
Michael, 227
ESPY, Hannah, 219
ETCHBERGER, John, 83
ETON, Elizabeth, 76
ETTING, Eliza, 79
ETTYBURN, Catherine, 75
EVANS, Catharine, 76
Charlotte, 138, 177
Elizabeth, 211
Hannah, 93, 176
John, 74
Joseph, 74
Martha, 74
Mary, 72
Rebecca, 80
W., 191
EVERHART, Ester, 199
EVERITT, Christiana, 139
G. W., 139, 156
EVERTON, Henrietta, 84
EWING, Anne, 77
Dr., 18
Mr., 45
EYRES, Mary, 82

-F-
FACKNER, Daniel, 20
James, 20
Jane, 20
FAIRBAIRN, Tabothy, 86
FALCONER, John, 187
FALLS, Dorothea, 176, 214
Jane, 20
Maria, 101, 179
Moor, 20, 75, 160, 181
Moore, 101, 105
Moore Nielson, 105
Rebecca, 20, 101, 105, 176
Sarah, 20
Stephen Wilson, 20
FAREL, Anne, 76
FARNHAM, Catharine, 200
FAUQUENIER, James, 236
FAY, Julius A., 183
Margaret, 184
FENBY, Alley, 199
Ann, 200
Ann Jane, 200
Elizabeth, 230
John Breckenridge, 230
Mary Jane, 230
Peter, 191, 199, 230
Peter Fletcher, 230
Richard D., 200
Samuel, 199
Sarah, 200
Theodosia, 199, 200, 230
FENN, Lydia Maria, 90
FERGUSON, Agnes, 91
Alexander Oscar, 137
Ann, 106, 111, 163
Catharine, 95, 142, 171, 211
Catherine, 130, 133
Catherine E., 95
Eleanor, 88
Elizabeth, 91, 129, 137
George Robb, 142
James, 87, 130, 133, 142, 160
James Smith, 133
Jane, 106
John, 129, 137
John Robertson, 111
Margaret Jane, 130
Robert, 106, 111, 163, 191

William, 89
FERGUSSON,
  Catharine, 120, 123
  Catharine
    Elizabeth, 123
  James, 120, 123
  Margaret J., 219
  William Robb, 120
FERRILL, Harriet, 174
FEW, Priscilla, 84
FINLATER,
  Alexander, 19, 20
  Anne, 19
  Eliza, 166
  Elizabeth, 19
  James, 19
  Jane, 19, 20
  Margaret, 19
  Mary, 19, 20
FINLEY, ---, 161
  A. P., 127
  Alexander, 120
  Amelia Frasier, 139
  Ann C., 178
  Ann Catherine, 117
  Ann P., 121, 130, 139
  Ann Perry, 106, 114, 117
  Ann Rebekah, 127
  Anna C., 95
  Catharine, 114, 119
  Catherine, 117, 166
  E. L., 129, 131, 153
  E. W., 131
  Eben L., 127, 138
  Eben LaFayette, 157
  Ebenezer, 19, 20, 102, 114, 117, 119,
151, 152, 163, 166, 186
  Eliza O'Donnell, 127
  Eliza W., 127, 129, 138, 174
  Elizabeth Margaret Didier, 139
  Isham Randolph, 114
  James, 114
  Jane, 102, 106, 163
  Jane McKnight, 226
  Jenny, 19, 20
  John M., 122
  John William, 130
  Joseph Washington, 20
  Mary, 122
  Mary Jane, 127, 184
  Mary Randolph, 131
  Mary V. L., 122
  Mrs., 157
  Polly, 19
  Randolph J., 175
  Robert Smith, 139
  Rosalie O'Donnell, 129, 226
  S. L., 157
  Samuel, 102, 121
  Sarah Chew, 138
  Sophia H., 97, 178
  Sophia Hanson, 119
  Sylvester Larned, 127
  Thomas, 84, 106, 114, 117, 121, 127, 130, 139, 168, 170, 187, 188, 191
  William Reynolds, 139
FISHER, Ann, 117, 170
  Anne, 120
  Basil, 75
  Catharine Eve, 120
  Edward G., 177
  Henry, 117
  Henry M., 191
  John, 86, 117, 120, 170
  Joseph, 75
  Mary, 183
FISHWICK, Fanny, 84
FLAHAVEN,
  William, 189
FLANAGAN,
  Elizbeth, 73
  Mary, 184
FLEMING, Anne, 18
  Sarah, 18
  William, 18
FLEMMING, Eliza, 85
FLETCHER,
  Elizabeth, 84
FOLGER, Franklin, 19
  Frederic, 19, 75
  Frederick, 222
  Isabella, 19
  Sophia Maria, 19
  Mary, 19
  Thomas Cale, 19
FOOT, Andrew, 94
FORBES, Rachel, 233

268 PRESBYTERIAN RECORDS OF BALTIMORE, MD

FORD, Charlotte, 173
  Elizabeth Neale, 86
FOREMAN, Ann, 176
  Evelina, 176
  Francis, 176
  Mary, 184
  William Lee, 191
FORESTER, Robert, 234
FORMAN, Ann E., 93, 131
  Ann Elizabeth, 111, 113, 117, 120, 127, 166
  Caroline, 127
  Eliza, 20
  Elizabeth, 111
  Evinlina, 113
  Francis, 111, 113, 117, 120, 127, 131, 166, 188
  Francis Keller, 120
  Jane, 19, 20, 97, 164
  Jane Hollins, 20
  John Spear, 20
  Margaret, 19
  Mary Immell, 131
  Mary Jane, 117
  Sarah Emory, 19
  Sophia, 19
  William, 97
  William Lee, 19, 20, 75, 97, 164
  William Raymond, 127
  William Spear, 19
FORNEY, Barbara, 89

FORREST, Sarah G., 88
FORSYTH, Alex, 158
  Alexander, 191
  Isaac, 75
  Jane, 82
FORSYTHE, Maria, 201
FORTE, Thomas, 84
FORWOOD, Mary, 89
FOSTER, Ann Swift, 136
  B. W., 135, 136
  Benjamin Wood, 135
  David Wood, 135
  Elizabeth, 80
  Elizabeth Allen, 136
  Hannah, 135, 136
  Hannah Maria, 135
  Sarah, 212
FOULKS, Mary, 219
FOWLER, William H., 182
FOXWALL, Susan, 215
FOXWELL, Julia A., 161
FRAIL, John, 191
FRANCIS, Andrew, 178
  Ann, 95
  Christopher James, 145
  Jane, 144
  John L., 89
  Mary A., 200
  Robert, 94, 144, 146, 176
  Thomas, 96, 156

  William John, 144
  William M., 178
FRANCISUS,
  Margaret, 72
FRANK, Sarah, 177
FRANKLIN,
  Charlotte A., 92
FRANSISCUS, J., 191
  J. M., 199
  John, 191
  Mr., 191
FRASER, Alexander, 18
  Christiana, 18
  Donald, 98
  Elizabeth, 18
  Francis, 75
  Hugh, 18
  James, 18, 107
  Margaret, 98, 102, 107, 115
  Mary, 19
  Mary Anne, 18
  Matthew, 115
  Nancy, 102
  Robert, 18
  Ruth, 18
  William, 18, 19, 98, 102, 107, 115
FRASIER, Mary, 83
FRAZER, Eliza J., 218
  Elizabeth R., 219
FREEMAN, William H., 191
FRENCH, ---, 168
  Daniel, 75
  Mary, 19
  Robert, 19

FREYER, Eleanor, 200
FRIDGE, A., 224
  Alexander, 188
FRINK, Mrs., 152
FRIZZEL, Mary, 234
FROMENTIN,
  Betsey, 164
  Elegins, 164
FROST, John, 75
FRY, Elizabeth Jane, 20
  Isabella, 20
  Thomas, 20
  Thomas Cousins, 20
  William Irvin, 20
FRYATT, William Th., 88
FULFORD, Ailsey, 83
FULLARTON,
  George, 234
  Susanna, 234
FULLERTON,
  Elizabeth, 240
  George, 238, 239, 240
  Margaret Ann, 239
  Mary Jane, 238
  Samuel, 238
  Susanna, 240
FULTON, A., 191
  Amelia, 91
  Andrew, 101
  David, 191
  J., 191
  James, 75
  John B., 185
  Mary, 101
  Mary Ann, 87
  William, 75, 101, 191
FURLONG, William, 75

-G-
GABBY, John, 235
GABLE, Mr., 191
GALBACH, Sophia, 95
GALBRAITH,
  Margaret, 162
GALLAGER, A., 200
GALLAGHER,
  Alexander, 21, 22, 99, 191
  Betsey, 99
  Elizabeth, 21, 22, 227
  George Washington, 22
  Hugh, 22
  James, 21
  Martha, 22
  Mary, 99
  Peter, 21
  Thomas, 22
GALLOWAY, Anne, 20
  Francis, 75
  James, 20, 21, 191
  Janit, 21
  John, 83
  Mary, 20, 21
  Mary Anne, 81
  Moses, 21
  Susanna, 20
GAMBAL, R., 191
GAMBLE, George Reed, 131
  Margaret, 77, 131, 179
  Mr., 191, 200
  R., 191
  T., 191
  Thomas, 75, 131, 191
  Thomas Buchanan, 131
GAMBRILL, Mary A., 201
GARDINER, Obed, 75
  Samuel, 85
GARDNER, Ann, 72
  Anna, 122
  Elizabeth, 22
  John, 191
  John Hamish, 186
  Margaret, 22
  Mary Bunker, 22
  Mr., 157
  Obed, 22
  Sarah, 89
  Timothy, 22
  W., 157
  William, 75
  William Henry, 22
GARLAND,
  Catherine, 147
  Catherine G., 148
  Eliza Jane, 147, 148
  James, 147, 148
  Sarah, 147, 148, 183
  Sarah J., 94
GARNONS, William, 87
GARRETSON,
  Cornelius, 21
  Mary, 21

William Martin, 21
GARRISON,
  Benjamin, 21
  Hannah, 21
  John, 21
GARROLD,
  Elizabeth, 78
GARROWAY, Ann, 240
  Jane, 236
  Samuel, 236, 240
GARRTSON,
  Cornelius, 20
  John, 20
  Mary, 20
GARTY, Mary, 77
GARTZ, Elizabeth, 80
GEDDES, ---, 161
  Alexander, 143
  Ann Eliza, 138
  Eliza Ann, 144
  Ellen, 146
  James, 138, 139, 143, 144, 160
  James William, 138
  Margaret Ann, 138
  Mr., 157
  Sarah, 138, 139, 143, 144, 146, 176
  Sarah Jane, 139
GEDDIS, George, 75
GELBACH,
  Elizabeth, 95
GEORGE, A., 229
  Archibald, 191, 200
  Eliza, 201
  Elizabeth, 200
  Isabella, 200
  James, 229
  Jane, 200

  Samuel K., 97, 200
  Sarah, 200
  Sophia, 201
  William, 200
GERSONDERFFER,
  Eliza, 88
GETTIS, Catherine, 100
  Jane Inglis, 100
  Mary Maxwell, 100
  Sarah, 100
  William, 100
GHANT, Ann, 89
GHENT, Ann, 89
GIBBES, Emily, 135
  Robert M., 92, 135
  Robert Oliver, 135
GIBBONS, Philip, 75
GIBBS, A. C., 213, 214
  Andrew C., 213
  Eliza L., 213
  Maria Ellen, 214
GIBSON, Agnes, 136
  Alexander, 22
  Anna, 150
  Captain, 191
  Charlotte, 94
  Elizabeth, 20, 22, 102
  G. S., 154, 155
  George, 137
  George S., 134, 137, 175
  George Sanderson, 150
  J., 229
  James, 22, 75, 102, 191
  Maria, 134, 137

  Mary, 20, 136, 175
  Mary Elizabeth, 150
  Mary Tyson, 134
  Mrs., 200
  Patrick, 95, 150, 180
  Robert, 20
  Sophia Finley, 150
  Tyson Irvin, 225
  William, 102, 136, 191
  William Francis, 136
GIESE, J. H., 191
  W. H., 191
  W. Hy., 191
GIFFORD,
  Alexander, 130, 191
  Elizabeth, 93
  Hugh, 130
  James, 130
  Mary, 130, 173
  Robert, 130
  Thomas, 93
  William, 130
GILBERT,
  Catherine, 94
  Mary S., 200
  Mr., 155
GILBREATH,
  George, 191
GILBURG,
  Charlotte, 168
GILES, Ann, 200
  Jacob, 200
  W. F., 200, 209
GILL, Angelica, 183
  Elizabeth, 136
  Elizabeth A., 131, 133, 155
  Esther, 22

INDEX

John, 22
John P., 157
John Purviance, 133
Nancy, 80
Nesbit Hawthorn, 136
Oliva Lowry, 131
Thomas, 22
W. L., 156, 157
William, 179
William L., 90, 96, 131, 133, 136, 175, 187
GILLESPIE, Catharine, 201
GILLIS, Mille, 74
GILLMAN, J. S., 191
GILMAN, J. S., 191
GILMOR, Ann, 90, 100
Charles Smith, 126
Elizabeth, 21
Elizabeth S., 97, 184
Elizabeth Sherlock, 126
Jane, 21, 89
Louisa, 21
Louisa Airy, 105
Mary Ann, 100, 105, 110, 126, 164, 181
Robert, 21, 110, 151, 162, 164, 186, 188, 221
Sarah, 182
Sarah Reeve, 168
William, 100, 105, 110, 126, 156, 164, 167
GILMORE, ---, 224

John, 75
Louisa A., 92
Mary Ann, 95, 115, 129
Susan Smith, 129
Thomas, 21
William, 115, 129
GIRKEY, Frederick, 22
Margaret, 22
Sarah, 22
GISSE, Peter, 75
GIST, Independent, 21
Mary, 21
Mordecai, 21, 75
GITTEAU, S., 210
GITTINGS, James, 75
Louisa, 21, 87
Mary, 21
Richard, 21, 75
GLASER, Jacob, 191
GLENDY, Dr., 151, 152, 153
John, 101, 191
Miss, 191
GLENN, James, 76
John W., 191
GLYN, James, 75
GODFREY, Mary, 77
GODIN, Francis, 75
GODMAN, Louisa, 173
GOLD, Sarah Ann, 200
GOLDEN, John, 22
Maria, 22
Susanna, 22

GOLDER, Robert, 178, 211
GOLDSBOROUGH, Anna Maria, 215
Elizabeth G., 144, 179
Henrietta Eugenia, 215
Louis M., 94, 144
Sarah Elizabeth, 215
William Wirt, 144
GOLDSMITH, Joseph, 98
Rachel, 98
William, 98
GOODMAN, Sarah, 82
GOODRICK, Mary A., 96
GOODRIDGE, Mary, 82
GORDON, Alice, 20
Anna Maria, 101
Anne, 74
Catharine, 20, 21
Charles, 21
Duncan, 75
Edward, 200
George, 21
Harriet, 21
Jane, 200
John, 20, 21, 101, 191
Mary, 20
Michael, 75
Sabrey, 21
Sarah, 21
William, 21, 191

William Alexander, 101
GORE, Ann, 183
  John, 95, 183
  Mary Ann, 144
  Sarah, 144
  William, 144
GORSUCH, Mary, 77
  Urith, 74
GOSLIN, William, 75
GOTTIER, Deborah, 75
GOULD, ---, 183
  Jane, 200
  Sarah Ann, 200
GOULDING, Mary, 73
GOURLEY, George, 202
  Mrs., 202
GRABLE, Jacob, 11
  Jane, 11
  Martha, 11
GRAHAM, ---, 225
  Agness, 76
  Andrew, 234, 235, 238, 239, 240
  Ann, 219
  Campbell, 97
  Charlotte, 99
  David, 191
  Dr., 191
  Eliza, 239
  Elizabeth, 102
  H., 191
  Hamilton, 22, 191, 200
  Henrietta, 216
  Hugh, 235
  Isabella, 235
  James, 99, 191
  Jane, 102, 200
  Janet Malcom Bell, 238
  Jenny, 22
  John, 22, 99, 102
  Laura, 240
  Margaret, 234
  Mary, 22, 80, 162, 200, 235
  Matilda, 173
  Nelly, 235
  Rach. J., 200
  Rachel, 158, 200
  Robert, 22, 191
  William, 191
  William T., 191
GRANGER, George, 217
  George W., 216
  Mary, 216
GRANT, Angus, 22
  Charlotte, 87
  Daniel, 22
  Elizabeth, 22
  Frances Jane, 22, 89
  Isaella, 22
  Janit, 22
  John, 92
  Moses, 96
  Mrs., 191
GRASCUP, Joseph, 216
GRASS, Henry, 75
GRAVES, Ebenezer, 75
GRAY, Affy, 114
  Daniel, 114
  Elizabeth, 79
  George, 114, 155
  George Lewis, 107, 110
  H. W., 191
  James, 200
  James Farwell, 107
  Joanna, 114
  Juliana Penn, 107, 110
  Kitty Maria, 114
  Mary, 200, 201
  Phoebe, 201
  Robert Hamilton, 110
  Samuel, 75
  Walton, 191
GRAYSON, Eliza, 183
  John, 88, 124
  Martha, 124
  Thomas Way, 124
GREATHOUSE, Eve, 78
GREEN, Brandy, 214
  Elizabeth, 78
  Henry, 75
  Julian, 93
  Mary, 214
  Rev. Dr., 165
  Robert, 94
  Thomas, 96
GREENE, Russell, 75
GREENWAY,
  Edward M., 88
GREENWOOD,
  Melinda, 96, 132, 173
GREER, Susan, 88
  Thomas, 191
GREGG, Alexander, 229

INDEX

Andrew, 174
Esther, 180, 213
Jane, 180
John, 229
Mr., 191
GREGORY, Rebecca P., 218
GREIER, Alexander, 20
Alice, 20
James, 20
GREIG, Agnes, 234
Margaret, 235
GRENIER, Gabriel, 88
GREY, George, 99
Isabella, 99
Jane, 99
Sarah Eliza, 231
GRIDLEY, Mrs., 201
GRIEVES, James, 191
GRIFFEE, Susanna, 73
GRIFFIN, Dr., 171
E. D., 164
York, 75
GRIFFITH, Harriet, 211
Henry A., 95
Mary Ann, 182
Ruth Maria, 216
William A., 94
GRIMES, James, 84
GROSCUP, Joseph, 216
GROSS, Simon, 75
GROTON, Phoebe, 201

GROVES, George B., 89
Mary, 81
GUISHARD, Catharine, 22
Louisa, 22
Mark, 22, 75
Pamela, 22
GUITEAR, S., 203
GUITEAU, Mr., 191
GULLEY, Catharine, 212
Mr., 212
Mrs., 212
Phillip, 213
Sarah, 212
William, 212
GUNN, James, 84, 191
GUTHRIE, Martha, 168
Mrs., 153
GUYTHER, George, 96
GWIN, John, 75
GWINN, Charles, 126
Eliza, 126
Elizabeth, 183
Emily Ann, 126
Susan, 90
GWYNN, Charles, 122, 126, 133, 170
Charles John Morris, 133
Eliza, 122, 126, 170
Elizabeth, 133
Elizabeth Maria, 122
Emily Ann, 126

Sarah Matilda, 122

-H-

HABERSETT, Henry, 202
Phoebe, 202
HADEN, Elizabeth, 215
HAGERTY, Elizabeth, 79
HAGGERTY, Elizabeth, 155
HAHN, Ann, 75
HAING, Benjamin, 76
HALIDAY, Sarah Ann, 234
HALL, Alexander, 165
Alexander F., 27
Alexander Fraser, 23
Ann, 116, 131, 134, 138, 141, 143, 172, 201
Ann Eliza, 139
Ann Maria, 141
B. W., 131, 134, 138, 141, 143
Benedict W., 120
Benedict William, 26, 86, 90, 117, 125, 168, 174
Charles, 191
Charlotte J., 134
Charlotte S., 139
Churl J., 145
Edward Gwinn, 116
Eleanor, 25
Eliza, 168

Elizabeth, 165
Elizabeth Buchanan, 123
Elizabeth Smith, 25
George, 24
H. Y., 145
Hannah Elizabeth, 25
Henry, 90, 134, 139
Isaac, 76
James, 191
Jane, 164, 202
Jane Smith, 95
Janet, 117
Janit, 25, 26
John, 23
Josiah Carvil, 26
Josias Carvil, 25, 164, 166
Levin, 191
Lydia, 138
Lydia Calhoun, 120
Margaret, 87
Margaret Louisa, 134
Mary, 27, 117, 120, 125, 168, 185
Mary Calhoun, 125
Mr., 191
Mrs., 201
Philip, 23, 24, 25
R. W., 168
Richard W., 170
Richard Wilmot, 87
Sarah, 23, 24, 25
Sergeant, 167
Sophia McHenry, 134
Susanna, 77

Syndey Calhoun, 131
Washington, 116
William Carvel, 143
William J., 76
William White Ramsey, 145
HALLECK, ---, 191
HALLOCK,
  Margaret, 74
HAMAN, Isabella, 202
  Margaret, 202
  Martha, 202
HAMELTON, Mary, 134
  William, 134
HAMILTON, Agness, 76
  Alexander, 191
  Bridget, 25
  Catharine, 178
  Eleanor, 22
  Ellen, 201
  J., 191
  James, 22, 191
  Jane, 201, 219
  John, 25, 173
  John A., 191
  John Agnes, 25
  John W., 181
  Margaret, 25
  Mary, 22, 174
  Matthew, 25
  Mr., 201
  Mrs., 201
  Oliver, 124
  Rebecca, 124, 202
  Robert, 22
  Sarah Ann, 181

William, 124, 154, 174, 202
HAMMET, Jane, 26, 99
  Jesse, 99
  Maria Rosina, 26
  Thomas, 26, 76
HAMMETT, Jane, 27
  Jesse, 27, 76
  Margaret, 27
  Rosanna, 27
  Thomas, 27
HAMMILL, Alex, 201
  Charles, 191
  Olivia, 201
HAMMOND,
  Catharine, 172
  Ephraim, 155, 176
  George, 76
  Harriet, 168
  Matilda, 93
  Nancy, 175
  Sarah Ann, 218
HAMNER, James G., 211
  Jane, 211
  Mary L., 211
HANA, Thomas, 76
HANCOCK,
  Jonathan, 88
HANDLING, Ellen, 84
HANEL, Mary, 73
HANNA, ---, 191
  A. B., 191
  Alexander B., 191
  Andrew, 191
  James, 191
  John, 191

INDEX

Margaret P., 93, 176
William, 95
HANNAH, Caleb, 26
  Edward, 27, 76
  Elizabeth, 24, 81
  Grisel, 23
  Grissel, 24
  Isabella, 23
  Jane Catharine, 27
  Mary, 26
  Mrs., 201
  Rebecca, 27
  Thomas, 24
  William, 23, 24
HANSON, Anna Maria, 79
  E. M. M., 88
HANTSZCHE, John S., 201
  Mrs., 201
HANWARD, Mary, 76
HARDESTER, Jacob, 145
  Mary Ann, 145, 181
  Mrs., 160
  Sarah Jane Carroll, 145
  Thomas Henry Austin, 145
HARDESTY, Mr., 159
HARDIN, Mary Ann, 97
HARDY, Abigail, 93
HARMAN, John M., 93
HARNAUGH, Catharine, 26
  Christian, 26
  John, 26
HARPER, Charles C., 191
  Eliza, 170
  Robert G., 153
HARRINGTON, John, 92
HARRIS, Ann J., 91
  Ann Somervell, 99
  Antoinette, 147, 184
  Benjamin, 24
  Charles, 23, 24
  D. C., 200
  David, 23, 24, 25, 76, 99, 105, 109, 113, 116, 124, 130, 151, 164, 165, 221, 222
  David Caldwell, 113
  Eliza, 24
  Eliza S., 175
  Eliza Stary, 136
  Esther, 174
  Esther Morrison, 105
  George, 23
  George Washington, 116
  Harriet, 93
  James, 76
  James Morrison, 124
  Jane, 164
  John, 25
  John M., 176
  John Montgomery, 109
  Margaret, 23, 76
  Maria, 86
  Marietta Eliza, 216
  Matthew, 23
  Molly, 24
  Mr., 160
  Rebecca, 23, 24
  Sally, 99, 105, 109, 113, 116, 164
  Samuel, 86, 153
  Sarah, 23, 24, 124, 130
  Sooty, 23
  Thaddeus Mason, 167
  Thomas Montgomery, 130
  William, 23, 152
HARRISON, Hall, 191
  Heziah, 117
  Margaret M., 95
  William, 165
  William G., 191
HART, Catharine, 81
HARTSHORE, Mary, 166
  William, 166
HARVEY, Anne, 26
  Catharine, 218
  Ellen Harvey, 150
  Harriet, 150
  Henry D., 150
  James, 26, 76
  Joshua, 218
  Lydia, 26
  Margaret, 26
  William, 76
HARWOOD, James, 87
  Margaret, 183
  Mary, 185

HASKELL, John, 125, 148
John H., 187
Marietta Camilla, 125
Mary Allen, 148
Minerva, 148
Minvera, 183
Polly, 125
HASKILL, John, 133, 173
John H., 136, 175
Mary, 133, 174
Theodore Joseph, 133
HASKINS, Joseph, 191
HASLET, Alexander, 26, 27, 76
Andrew, 25
Anne, 24
Elizabeth, 23, 26, 27
George Salmon, 26
Hannah, 25
John, 24
Jonathan, 23
Joseph, 24
Kesisah, 78
Kessina, 24
Kissinah, 23, 25
Mary, 23
Moses, 24, 25, 26
Rachel, 26
Samuel, 23, 24, 25
Sarah, 24, 25, 26
Solomon, 24
Susanna, 27
William, 23, 25, 26, 83
William Duncan, 27
HASLETT, Hannah, 85
James, 191
Rebecca Mercer, 72
William, 191
HASLOPP, John, 191
HASSAN, J., 201
Rebecca, 201
HASSELBAUGH, John, 189
HASSON, John, 201
Maria, 201
Mary, 201
HATCH, Mr., 156
Nancy, 83
HATHAWAY, Ann, 127
Ebenezer, 127
Jethro, 76
Sarah W., 127
HATTON, Henry, 92
HAWK, Stephen, 76
HAWKINS, Agness, 23, 24
Elizabeth B., 87
Elizabeth D., 94, 177
Frances, 24
John, 23, 24
Mary, 24
Matthew, 23
William, 24
HAY, Andrew, 25
Elizabeth, 88
Janey, 77
John, 24, 25
Martha, 24, 25
Mary Bond, 24
HAYES, Isabella, 75
Reverdy, 86
HAYNES, D. F., 191
Mr., 191
HAYS, Davis, 229
William, 191, 201
HAYWARD, Mary Ellen, 224
HAZELHURST, Alexander, 120
Andrew, 84, 106, 114, 119, 121, 122, 159
Emma, 119
Frances, 106, 114, 119, 120, 121, 122
Frances Jane, 106
Henry, 114
Julianna, 114
Lauretta, 123
Robert, 114
Samuel, 120
HAZELTHORPE, Edward, 202
Elizabeth, 202
HAZELTON, Hugh, 192
HAZLEHURST, Andrew, 116
Frances, 116
Frances Jane, 184
Mary, 116
HEAFLICK, Jacob, 87
HEIDE, George, 170
HEILHOLTZ, Magdalina, 88
HELM, Abraham Mayberry, 225
Ann, 79, 225

Anne, 24
Frances, 23, 24
George, 23, 24
Henry, 23
Margaret, 24
Mary, 23
Mayberry, 221
HEMAN, Isabella, 202
Martha, 202
HENDERSON,
  Caroline Jane, 91, 101
  Elizabeth, 24, 25, 176
  George, 26
  Isabella, 26
  J., 202
  John, 25
  Mary A., 175
  Mary Ann, 218
  Phebe, 101
  R., 227
  Robert, 24, 25, 101
  Robert E., 228
  Robert M., 153
  William, 26
HENDRIX, Thomas J., 97
HENLON, Elizabeth, 77
HENNAMAN, Sarah Ann, 92
HENNING, David, 94
  Rose Ann, 94
HENNINGS, Ernest A., 97
HENNYMAN, H., 212

Hannah, 212
HENRAY, Michael, 76
HENRICH, Eliza, 113
  Jacob, 113
  James, 113
  Walter, 113
HENRY, Christian, 26
  John, 26
  Mary, 26
  Polly, 74
  Robert Jenkins, 76
HENSHAW, Mr., 157, 158
HEPBURN, John M., 89
HERON, A., 240
  James, 192
HERRING, Barb., 202
  James, 202
HERRON, James, 192
  R. B., 192
HESLIP, John, 191
HEWES, Daniel, 90
HEWITT, Eli, 94
  Rezin D., 93
HEYES, Phebe, 73
HIGHJAH,
  Elizabeth, 76
HILDEBRAND,
  Catharine, 73
HILL, A., 192
  Ann, 202
  Anne, 227
  Catharine, 202
  Eliz., 202

Elizabeth, 227
Jane, 25, 26
Jeremiah, 25
Jonas, 25, 26
Joseph, 26
Margaret, 202
Martha, 25
Mary, 26
Susan, 201
T. G., 192
Thomas G., 192
Washington, 227
William, 26, 76
HILLS, Eudocia, 137
  Eudocia Gelston, 137
  Samuel, 137
HINES, Sarah, 72
HIPSLEY, Patience, 72
HISDALE,
  Catharine, 81
HISS, ---, 192
HISSEY, Mary, 89
HITE, Nancy, 83
HITZELBERGER,
  Mary Ann, 94
HIXON, Flemming, 95
HOBBS, James, 76
HOBBY, Maria M., 91
HOBSON, George, 192
HODGES, Joseph, 192
  Lucinda, 174
HOFFMAN,
  Elizabeth, 89
  John, 192

Louisa Howard, 185
Philip Rogers, 96
Samuel O., 92
HOGAN, John, 76
HOGEN, Abraham, 76
HOGG, Jane, 84, 179
  William, 179
HOIT, Israel, 76
HOLBROOK, Darby, 74
  Joseph, 192
  Josh., 192
HOLLAND, M., 202
HOLLIDAY, Charles, 23
  James, 23
  Janit, 23
  John, 76
  Mary, 23
  William, 23
HOLLINGSHEAD, Margaret, 182
HOLLINS, ---, 192
  C. Dugan, 228
  Cordelia, 201
  Frederick Wilson, 147
  George, 147
  George N., 95
  George Nicholas, 27
  Georgiana, 228
  Georgiana S., 201
  J. S., 192
  J. Smith, 192
  Jane, 159, 226
  Janit, 25, 26, 27
  John, 25, 26, 27, 76, 154, 192, 221, 226

John Smith, 192, 221, 228
  Margarett, 94
  Margaretta, 27
  Maria, 147, 183
  Marsha, 201
  Mary Jane, 27
  Molly Buchanan, 26
  Mr., 192
  Rebecca, 228
  Robert, 26
  Robert S., 202
  William, 25
HOLMES, Ann, 226
  Anne, 26
  John, 26, 226
  Lemuel, 171
  Malinda, 171
  Mary, 234
  Nancy, 166
  Patience, 170
  Samuel, 170
HOLSTEIN, ---, 161
  Sarah, 175
HOLSTON, Hamilton R., 89
HOLT, Ann E., 150
  Daniel, 150
  Henry, 150
HOLTY, John, 96
HOMANS, Isaac Smith, 93
HOMBLEDON, Jane, 82
HONORA, John Anthony, 25
  Julia, 25
  Mary, 25
HOOHARD, John, 89
HOOK, Mr., 192

HOOKS, Alexander, 23
  Andrew, 23
  Margaret, 23
HOOPER, Elizabeth P., 212
  Ellen C., 217
  Robert, 217
  William, 192
HOPKINS, Cassandra, 74
  Elizabeth, 73
  Elizabeth M., 157
  Lydia, 73
  Philip, 76
HORNE, Priscilla, 88
HOUSTON,
  Elizabeth, 27
  James, 236
  John, 27
  John Lewis, 27
  Mary, 236
  William, 236
HOWARD, Ann Williams, 136
  B. C., 138, 155
  Benjamin C., 89, 128, 131, 132, 136, 140, 145, 147
  Ellen, 145
  J. G., 138
  Jane, 131, 132, 136, 140, 147, 172
  Jane G., 128, 145
  Jane Gilmor, 136
  John E., 192
  John Eager, 224
  Juliana McHenry, 140
  Marian Gilmor, 132

INDEX

Rob., 202
Robert, 192
Robert Gilmor, 128
Robert Gilmore, 151
Sophia, 131, 186
William Gilmor, 138, 147
HOWDEN, Juliana, 170
Paris, 170
HOWLAND, Gardiner Greene, 93
HOWLING, Daniel, 76
HUBBERD, William, 192
HUBER, Ellen, 120, 121, 124
Henry, 120, 121, 124
Jane, 121
Maria, 124
William, 120
HUDGINS, J., 192
HUGHES, Aquilla D., 219
Christopher, 192
Daniel, 24, 76
John, 76
Margaret, 80
Sarah, 87
Susanna, 24
William, 192
HULL, John, 91
HUMES, Mrs., 201
HUMPHREYS, Sarah, 85
HUNGERFORD, Thomas B., 218

HUNRAMAN, Mrs., 202
HUNTER, Agness, 27
Alexander, 101
Ann, 101
Elizabeth, 168
Hannah, 26
Jane, 163
John, 27, 84, 85, 168
Margaret, 27
Sarah Jane, 237
Thomas, 237, 241
Thomas Henry, 26
William, 26, 101
HURD, Ruth, 82
HURDEVANT, Miss, 202
HURTON, John, 76
HUSTON, William, 234
HUTCHESON, Sarah, 76
HUTCHINS, Susan, 202
HUTCHINSON, Mr., 159
HUTSON, John, 192
HUTTON, Bell, 25
J., 192
James, 192
Margaret, 25, 201
Miss, 201
Mr., 192
William, 25, 227
HYDE, Adelaide Morton, 127
Ann, 150
Ann Catharine, 132

Anna Maria, 149
Benjamim Dove, 129
David, 123
Edward Ingle, 149
Eliza M., 174
Elizabeth M., 94
Francis, 96, 123, 127, 129, 132, 153, 169
Francis T., 188
Joseph, 181
Mahitabel, 123
Mehitabel, 127, 129, 169
Mehitable, 132
Moses, 149, 178, 187
Sophia, 94, 174
HYNSON, Henrietta, 94

-I-

IMBRIE, James, 185
INGLES, Silas, 76
INGLIS, Anna Maria, 163
George S., 176
George Salmon, 112
J., 118
J. S., 118
James, 28, 83, 97, 101, 103, 112, 153, 156, 162, 163, 164, 186
Jane, 97, 101
Jane Swan, 103, 112, 162
John Auchincloss, 118

Mary, 163, 175
Mary S., 160
Matilda, 86, 166
Mrs., 156
Rev., 192
Susan, 172
Susan Maria, 103
William, 154
William Cowper, 101
INGLISS, James, 107
Jane Swan, 107
INGRAM, Andrew, 192
Clark, 76
John, 76
IRVIN, James, 76, 108
John, 27, 108
Margaret, 108
Sarah, 27
IRWIN, James, 101, 103
Jane, 101
Matilda, 169
Sarah, 101, 103
IRWING, Catharine, 180
Margaret, 185
ISAACKS, Elizabeth, 75
ISETT, Elizabeth, 105, 111, 114, 158, 165
Emmeline, 111
Henrietta, 114
Henry J., 153
Henry Jacob, 105
John, 105, 111, 114, 165

Maria, 93, 167
IVES, Eliza Jane, 95

-J-
JACKSON, ---, 161
Ann, 79, 109
B. R. M., 97
Bethiah, 113, 131, 174
Bolton, 89, 130
Collin, 28, 77
Diana, 169
Elizabeth, 82
Elizabeth Russel, 105
Frances Jane, 130
Helen, 105, 109, 111
J., 192
James, 28, 85, 105, 109, 111, 113, 131, 178, 192
Jane, 28
John, 28, 218
John Grant, 130
Julianna, 131
Margaret, 91
Mary, 77, 178
Miss, 157
Nathaniel, 77
Sally, 82
Sarah, 113, 176
JACOBS, George, 192
Mary, 82
Mr., 150
JAFFRAY, James, 221
Mary, 81

JAFFRIES, James, 28
John, 28, 77
Margart, 28
Sarah, 28
JAMES, Adeline, 93
Elizabeth, 28, 77
Jane, 229
Janit, 28
John, 28, 192, 229
Margaret, 28
Mary, 79
Wiliam, 28
William, 28, 77
JAMIESON, Hannah, 141, 179
JAMISON, Amelia, 87
John, 89
Joseph, 192
JANEWAY, Rev. Dr., 168
JANVIER, Catharine, 202
P., 192
Perigo, 202
JARBER, Juliet, 88
JARBOE, Juliet, 88
Susanna, 88
JARRATT, Harriet, 132
James, 132
JARVIS, Elizabeth, 183
John, 77
JEFFORDS, George, 77
JENNEY, Anna Maria, 28
Elizabeth, 27

INDEX

John, 28
Nathanael, 27, 28
Sarah, 27, 28
JENNINGS, Ann, 95, 178
JESSOP, Charles, 77
JEVIS, Cassandra, 78
JEWRY, Elizabeth, 212
JOB, Ann, 75
JOHNS, Jacob, 95
  Rev., 192
JOHNSON, A. M.
  Elizabeth, 135
  Ann M., 203
  C., 132
  Caleb, 28, 77
  Chris., 154
  Christopher, 132, 153, 161
  David Hezekiah, 28
  Elijah, 77
  Eliza, 132, 173
  Elizabeth, 77
  Elliot, 135
  Frances, 89
  Francis, 77
  George, 88
  Isaac, 203
  J., 202
  James, 192
  Jane, 28, 89, 202
  John, 76
  Listy, 90
  Lucy, 132, 153, 173
  Margaret, 203
  Mary Stith, 132
  Matthias, 85
  Mr., 152
  Mrs., 156, 202
  Nancy, 202
  Robert, 93
  Sally, 75
  Thomas D., 135
  William, 85
  William T., 91, 213
JOHNSTON, Ann, 28
  Ann Elizabeth, 28
  Christopher, 27, 28, 134, 162, 186, 188, 221
  Edward, 27, 77
  Eliza, 134, 168
  Eliza S., 89
  Elizabeth, 28
  Hannah, 27
  James, 121
  Jane Swan, 83, 121
  Janit, 27
  John, 27, 28
  John Griffin, 27
  Margaret, 27
  Maria Stith, 162
  Mary Stith, 27
  Robert Nelson, 28
  Susanna, 27, 28
  Susannah, 162
  Thomas, 160
  Thomas D., 91
  William, 27
  William Hyde de Venville, 134
JOICE, Pierce, 77
JOINER, Rebecca, 88
JONES, Anna
  Barbara, 225
  Anna P., 89
  Anne, 72
  Anne Maria, 94
  Eleanor, 202
  Jane, 185
  Levin, 77
  Maria, 185
  Mary, 90
  Mrs., 192
  Samuel, 93
  Talbot, 192
  Talbot D., 94
  Thomas, 77, 169
  William, 77
JOOTLE, James, 171
JORDAN, Ann, 86
  Catharine, 218
JOURDAN, Charles
  Alfred, 128
  George Edwin, 128
  Jonathan, 128
  Mary Ann Delacour, 128
  Susan, 128, 171
  William Ford, 128
JOYCE, Joshua, 77
JUDAH, Hannah, 82
JUSTICE, Elizabeth, 78

-K-

KANE, Amelia S., 230
  Amelia Sophia, 216
  Ann, 230
  Captain, 192
  John K., 230
  John M., 192, 230
  Samuel K., 230
KASSON, Joseph M., 93
KAUFMAN, Mr., 156

KEAN, Thomas O., 159
KEARNEY, Eliza, 29
　Richard, 77
KEARNS, John, 192
KEATH, Jane, 80
KEATON, Eleanor, 76
KEELAND, Rebecca, 80
KEENE, Jesse L., 85
　Lawrence, 85
KEENER, Elizabeth H., 218
　Emily F., 220
　William C., 218
KEEP, Samuel, 156
KEEPORTS,
　Elizabeth, 74
　George P., 222
　Jacob, 223
KEHO, Daniel, 192
KEIRSTED, Luke, 192
KEITH, Isaac S., 71
　Patrick, 77
KELLER, Mary, 185
KELLOG, O., 160
KELLOGG, Eleanor Ann, 140, 144
　Henry, 140
　Mary Richard, 144
　Orson, 93, 140, 144
KELLY, Carvil, 154
　Eliza, 174
　Jane, 94
　Susan, 159, 174
KELSO, Elizabeth Augusta, 203
　Ellen, 134, 135, 142, 145, 159, 203
　Ellen Rich, 145
　G., 224
　George L., 145
　George S., 134
　George Y., 90, 134, 135, 142, 155
　James, 28
　Jane Young, 134
　John, 28, 142
　Margaret, 74
　Rebecca, 28
　Rebecca Rich, 135
　Sarah, 28, 79
KELSY, Henry, 192
KELTY, Elizabeth, 90
KELZO, Jane, 203
KENDALL, Mr., 151
KENEDY, J., 192
KENNEDY, Agness, 30
　Andrew, 29
　Ann, 232
　Ann Clayton, 163
　Bridget, 84
　Charity, 29
　J., 192
　James, 29
　John, 29, 30, 163, 192, 231, 232
　John Pendleton, 29
　Nancy, 29
　Sophia, 73
　William, 29
KERL, Henry, 192
KERR, Agness, 29
　Archibald, 203, 206
　Arichbald, 192
　Harriet, 29
　James, 84
　Jane, 29
　Joseph, 29
　R. J., 192
　Thomas, 29
　William, 29
KEVILE, Matthew M., 94
KEY, Andrew, 29
　Ann, 160
　Emily Louisa, 96
　Francis Scott, 222
　Jane, 29
　Marand, 29
　Margaret, 29
　Philip Hunter, 224
　Thomas, 29
KEYES, John F., 169
KEYS, Bayley, 89
　Bayly, 214
　Emilia, 214
　James, 110, 114
　Jane, 85, 110, 114
　John F., 121, 187
　Joseph, 218
　Margaret, 121
　Mary, 86, 110, 169
　Mary Jane, 216
　Priscilla, 214
　Richard, 169
　Richard William, 121
　William Barr, 114
KIDD, Anne, 29
　Hugh, 29
　John, 29
KIERSTED, Luke, 192

INDEX

KILPATRICK, John, 77
KIMBO, Mary Ann, 80
KINEAR, Alexander, 234
  Sarah, 234
KING, Elizabeth Anne, 29
  Jacob, 230
  James, 29
  Jane, 203
  M. A., 203
  Mary, 88
  Susan Jane, 203
  William, 29
KINGAN, Elizabeth, 29
  Thomas, 29
KINGSTON, Abigail, 29
  George Peter, 29
  Harriet, 29
  Margaret, 29
  Nathaniel, 29
  William, 29
KINNIER,
  Alexander, 235, 237
  Jane, 237
  Mary, 235
KINSTEAD, Luke, 203
KIRBY, Sarah, 77
KIRK, Jehosheba, 72
KIRKLAND, David, 192
KIRKPATRICK,
  Eliza, 29
  Elizabeth, 29
  Jer., 192

Jeremiah, 29
KITTERS, John, 77
KNAP, Rebecca, 29
  Samuel, 29
KNEELAND,
  Hannah, 177
  Henry, 95
KNIGHT, Ann Eliza, 145
  Elizabeth, 141
  M., 157, 159
  Mary, 140, 141, 179
  Mary Catharine, 140
  Michael, 92, 140, 141, 177
  Peregrine, 88
KNIPPENBERG,
  Andrew, 121
  Andries, 119, 121, 125
  Elizabeth, 119, 121, 125
  Mary Jane, 119
  Susan Maria Inglis, 121
KNOW, Mrs., 205
  Sam, 106
KNOWLTON,
  George W., 93
KNOX, Alexander, 77
  Anne, 76
  David, 229
  Elizabeth, 29
  Jane H., 90
  Samuel, 192
  William, 29, 77
KONICKE,
  Frederick, 77
KRAP, Sarah, 75

KREBS, William, 192
KRIBS, R., 192
  William, 192
KYLE, ---, 192
  A. B., 203
  Adam B., 192, 203
  Adam E., 192
  Isabella M., 203

-L-

LA REINTRIE, John Louis Roy, 86
LABESIUS, Anne, 73
LACAZE, Nancy, 83
LAFFERTY, Edward K., 95
LAINTEN, Cloe, 76
LAMBIE, James, 135
  John, 135
  Mary, 135
LAMSON, Henry, 152, 172
LANCASTER, R.
  Kent, 224
LANDER, Alexander, 228
LANDES, Alexander, 31, 32
  Anne, 31
  Frances, 32
  Jane, 31
  John, 32
  Mary, 31, 32
  Mary Ann, 32
LANDON, Susanna, 77
LANDSBOROUGH,
  Mary, 235
LANDY, Richard, 192
LANE, Benjamin, 169
  Elizabeth, 73

LANGHEAD, Adam, 31
  Elizabeth, 31
  Sarah, 31
  Thomas, 31
LARRANT, Fenn E., 95
LASON, Francis, 31
  Marieanna Lambert, 31
LATIMER,
  Catharine, 146
  Catharine H., 181
  James B., 89
  Mary, 90
LAUDENSLAGER,
  Jacob, 192
LAUDENSLAYER,
  Jacob, 192
LAUGHLIN,
  Elizabeth, 30
  James, 237, 241
  Jane, 30, 236
  John, 236, 241
  John Gib, 241
  Maria, 236
  Mary, 237
  Robert, 30, 236, 241
  Sarah Jane, 241
LAW, A., 192
  Anthony, 78
  Elizabeth, 31, 32
  Jacob Davies, 31
  James, 31, 32, 192
  Mary Crawford, 31
  Rachel Davies, 32
  Samuel, 211
LAWDER,
  Alexander, 163
  Mary, 163

LAWRENCE, Daniel, 30
  David Howland, 31
  Elizabeth, 31
  John Myer, 31
  Mary, 30
  Rachel, 30, 79
  Richard, 31
  Samuel, 95
  Thomas Leggat, 31
LAWRY, Anne, 30
  John, 30
  Margaret, 30
  Mary, 30
  Robert, 30
  Robert McNight, 30
  Thomas, 30
LAWSON, Charles, 78
  Elizabeth, 104
  G., 152
  Louisa, 104
  Robert, 104, 192
LAYMAN, Thomas, 192
LEA, Sarah, 77
LEACHE, Mr., 192
LEADER, Charles, 78
LEAGUE, Eliza A., 97
LEAHRY, John, 77
LEAHY, Miss, 158
LEAKEY, James, 239
  Richard Henry, 239
LEAKIN, Thomas J., 87
LEAKY, James, 235, 239, 240
  Richard Henry, 239
  Sarah, 235

  Sarah Jane, 240
LEAMAN, Thomas, 192
LEARY, Eliza, 77
LEATHERBERROW,
  William, 78
LECKEY, Hugh, 84
LECOMPTE, Mary, 215
LEE, Elisha, 159
  Eliza, 127, 171
  Harriet A., 92
LEECHE, William, 213
LEERE, Elizbeth, 82
LEGARD, Eliza, 95
LEGG, John, 220
LEMMON, ---, 192
  R., 192
  William, 159
LEMMOND, John, 30
  Martha, 30
  William, 30
LENNAS, Phebe, 173
LENNOX, Sarah, 226
LESLIE, Ann, 144
  Eliza Ann, 144
  Robert, 91, 144
LESTIE, ---, 185
LEUTHWAITE,
  Agnes, 84
LEVERING, ---, 183
  Augusta Virginia, 96
  Eliza B., 136, 217
  Elvin B., 174
  Enoch, 78
  Jesse, 84
  Mary Ann, 136, 217
LEWIS, Ann, 203

INDEX

Charles, 31, 32
Charles George, 32
Cossy, 169
Elijah, 77
Elizabeth, 80
John, 77
Margaret, 31, 32
William Barron, 31
Willoughby, 203
Willowby, 184
LEWTHWAITE,
  Christopher, 78
LIDIARD, John, 77
LIGGAT, Alexander,
  31
  Jane, 31
  Samuel, 31, 77
LIGGETT, ---, 192
LIGHT, John, 84
LIGHTBODY, John,
  203
  Mrs., 203
LIGHTNER, Eliz.,
  203
LIMES, Margaret, 71
LINDON, Elizabeth,
  72
LINDSAY, Adam, 30
  Mary, 30
  Mary Anne, 30
LINKINS, Elizabeth,
  87
LINN, Andrew, 30
  David, 30
  Rachel, 30
LINNARD, Thomas
  M., 192
LINTON, Elizabeth,
  172

LITCHFIELD, Mary,
  85
LITTLE, Alexander,
  30
  Anne, 72
  Harriet, 30
  John, 187
  Martha, 30
  Mary L., 87
LITTLEJOHN,
  Ellenora, 217
  John, 217
  Miles, 77
LITZINBERGER,
  John, 77
LITZINGER,
  Elizabeth, 140, 178
  John, 140
LIVINGSTON, J.,
  167
  John, 203
LLOYD, John, 77
LOCHERD, Ann, 83
LOCKARD, Francis,
  30
  Jane, 30
  Martha, 30
  Thomas, 30
  William, 30
LOCKERMAN, Eliza,
  94
LOGAN, James, 203
  Mary, 203
LOLSON, Joseph, 93
LONG, Andrew H.,
  96
  Elizabeth, 30
  Emmaline, 203
  Henry, 192
  Jane, 30

John, 30
John Edwards, 30
K., 192
Kennedy, 192
Margaret, 30
Mary, 30
Robert, 30, 77
Robert C., 96
Robert Carey, 192
Thomas, 30
LONGBORN,
  Elizabeth, 32
  George Hunter, 32
  Kennedy, 32
LONGHEAD, Adam,
  31
  Elizabeth, 31
  Sarah, 31
  Thomas, 31
LORD, Joseph L., 89
  Lydia, 203
LORMAR, Amelia,
  230
  David, 230
  James M., 230
  William, 230
LORRIANCE, ---, 224
LORTON, Patience,
  71
LOUGHRIDGE,
  John, 192
LOURY, Coloney,
  192
  Samuel, 192
LOVE, Mary Ann T.,
  92
  Miss, 192
  William, 203
LOVEJOY, Amos,
  150, 183

Ann Isabella, 150
Rosabella Sutton, 150
William Henry, 150
LOVELL, Elizabeth, 91
Elizabeth Ann, 169
Henrietta, 175
Mr., 192
William, 169
LOW, James, 163
Mrs., 203
LOWE, Cornelius, 77
LOWNDES, Rebecca, 74
LOWRY, Jane, 31
Mary, 30
Olivia, 31
Robert McNight, 30
Thomas, 30
William, 31
LUCAS, Frances M., 218
LUDDEN, Lemuel, 87, 125
Margaret, 125
Mrs., 154
Rosalber, 125
LUNDY, Richard, 192
LURNMAUX, Hetty, 89
LYFORD, Margaret, 203
Mary Ann, 203
LYMAS, Charles, 89
LYNCH, James, 149
Jane, 149
John B., 149
Mary, 87
William, 77

LYON, Ann, 110
Anna M., 158
Anna Mary, 141, 179
Catharine, 31
Catharine H., 89
Charles Grahame, 31
Edward Dorsey, 32
Elihu Hill, 31
Elisha James, 106
Elizabeth Russell, 133
George Armstrong, 107
Hester, 32, 102, 107
Jacob Broom, 107
James, 78, 110, 113, 118
James Broom, 102
John, 102, 113
Joseph, 31
Mary, 32
Mary C., 133
Mordecai S. D., 94
Mr., 192
Mrs., 158
Rachel, 95
Rachel Broom, 102
Rebecca, 110, 113, 118
Robert, 31, 32, 77, 90, 106, 133
Samuel, 32, 102, 107
Samuel Chew Hall, 106
Susan McCullough, 133

Susanna, 31, 32, 106
William, 186, 187
LYONS, William, 77
LYSON, Robert, 30
Susanna, 30
William, 30

-M-

MCALISTER,
Agness, 36, 38
Elizabeth, 38
John, 36, 38, 204
Mrs., 204
Phebe, 36
MCALLISTER,
James B., 85
John, 192
Mary, 82
MCBEATH, Andrew, 33
James, 33
Jane, 33
MCBLAIR, Alice, 85
Charles, 97
Michael, 192
MCBRIDE,
Archibald, 34
Florence, 34
MCCABE, ---, 216
Ann, 92
Catharine, 75
John, 33, 34, 192
Mrs., 203
Phebe, 33, 34
Thomas, 33
Thomas B., 79
William, 218
MCCAFFER, Nancy, 89

MCCAGHNEY,
  Agnes, 239
  Anges, 241
  James Duncan, 241
  Janey, 239
MCCALISTER, John, 192
MCCAMMON, Anne, 39
  Joseph, 39, 79
  Sarah, 39
MCCANDLESS, Ann
  Christian, 109
  Charles, 105
  George, 33, 34
  Ignatius Perry, 40
  James, 34
  Lavinia, 103
  Mary, 42
  Rachel, 40, 42, 100, 103, 105, 109, 166
  Robert, 40, 42, 103, 105, 109, 166
  Robert Patterson, 100
  Sarah, 33, 34
MCCANDLEY,
  Elisabetth, 37
  Jane, 37
  John, 37
MCCANN, Mary, 205
MCCARD, Julia, 72
MCCARRAL, John, 95
MCCARTY,
  Cornelius, 78
  John, 78
  Letitia, 38
  Margaret, 38
  William, 38, 78

MCCASKEY, Ann, 77
  Hetty, 73
  Mary, 73
MACCAULAY,
  Patrick, 91
MCCAY, Agness, 41
  Elizabeth, 41
  John, 41
MCCHARD, Anney, 36
  Isabella, 36
  John, 36
MCCHORD, Anney, 36
  Isabella, 36
  James, 36
  John, 36
MCCLAIN, Mary, 88
MCCLANAHAN,
  Mr., 192
MCCLEARY, William M., 192
MCCLEERY, Robert, 192
MCCLELLAN, Anna, 226
  Catharine Jane, 117
  Catharine Maria, 128
  Daniel, 204
  David, 222
  Eliza, 121, 124, 128, 132
  Henry Clay, 132
  Jane, 165
  John, 222, 226
  M., 192
  Malvina, 172
  Maria, 172
  Mary, 166, 226

  R., 192
  Rachel Wagner, 128
  Robert, 117, 226
  Samuel, 121, 124, 128, 132, 152, 192, 221
  Samuel Wagner, 121
  Sarah, 117, 226
  William, 221
  William Wellington, 124
MCCLENACHAN,
  Ann, 113
  Elijah, 99
  Elizabeth Scott, 113
  James, 113
  James Boyles Murray, 113
  Josiah, 99
  Martha Murray, 113
  Mary, 99
MCCLENAGHAN,
  Mary, 170
MCCLERAN, ---, 192
MCCLEVE, William, 192
MCCLINTICK,
  Martha, 77
MCCLISH, Nelly, 88
MCCLURE, John, 222
MCCOHN, Anne, 37
  Dennis, 37
  Mary, 37
MCCOLLUM,
  Gilbert, 233
  Mary, 233
MCCOMB, Jane, 163
MCCONKEY, ---, 192

Agnes, 102
Agness, 40, 41
James, 40, 41, 79, 102, 192
James Swan White, 102
John, 40, 192
Mr., 192
Mrs., 192
Rebecca, 40
Thomas, 41
W., 192
William, 40, 192
MCCONKY,
Caroline, 94
Margaret, 177
Mary, 38
Rebecca, 38
Willaim, 38
MCCONNELL,
Andrew B., 124
Eleanor, 88
Euphemia, 124
John D., 124
Robert, 85
MCCORKEL,
William, 205
MCCORMICK, Jane, 72
Letitia, 235
Margaret, 92
Maria N., 237, 241
Mary Jane, 241
William, 192
MCCOY, Dorcas A., 168
Henry, 168
John, 78
Rachel, 77
Rebecca Maria, 168

S. M., 169
Samuel, 88
Sarah Matilda, 90
MCCREA, Nancy, 170
Robert, 88
MCCREERY, Letitia, 169
MCCREIGHT,
Rebecca, 219
MCCULLOCH,
Alexander, 79
Hugh, 39
James, 37, 38, 39, 85
James H., 163
James Hugh, 38
Margaret, 37, 38, 39
Samuel, 170
Sarah, 37
MCCULLOH, James H., 91
James R., 221
MCCULLOUGH,
Elizabeth, 89
J. W., 152
John, 103
Sarah, 179
William, 103
MCCURDY, ---, 192
Grace, 40
Hugh, 40, 79, 192
James, 235
Letita Grace, 40
Letitia, 91, 171
Mary J., 172
Mrs., 192
MCDERMONT,
Annasia, 99
Jane, 99

Thomas, 99
MCDERMOT,
Thomas, 79
MCDERMOTT, Ann, 204
Jane, 204
MCDONALD, ---, 183
Alexander, 101, 105, 110, 188
Col., 192
Elizabeth, 101
Gen., 192
Jenny Margaret, 110
Jn., 192
Lexy Christina, 105
Martha, 205
Mary, 71, 101, 105, 110
Maxwell, 166
Mr., 157, 192
P., 192
Ruth, 166
William, 192, 203, 229
MCDONNEL,
Andrew, 36
Catharine, 36
Daniel, 36
MCDONNELL,
William, 78
MCDONOGH,
Margaret, 165
MCDONOUGH,
Elizabeth, 34, 35, 37, 38, 39, 80
James, 37
Jane, 83
Janit, 34

John, 34, 35, 37, 38, 39, 221
Joseph, 35
Lavinia, 204
Margaret, 38, 87
Mary, 34, 73
William, 39
MCDORMET,
  George, 87
MCDOWEL, Dr., 192
MCDOWELL,
  Elizabeth, 42, 172
  George, 40, 41, 42, 101, 103, 109, 113, 180
  George Hanse, 109
  John B., 180
  Mary, 40, 82, 175
  Mary Ann, 93, 113, 174
  Maxwell, 111, 186, 221
  Ruth, 111, 158
  Sarah M., 172
  Sarah Maria, 103
  Sus., 103
  Susan, 172
  Susanna, 40, 41, 101, 109, 113
  Susanna G., 184
  Susanna Greer, 111
  Susannah, 173
  Susannah M., 161
  William, 41
MCDOWLIN, Maria, 92
MCELDERBERRY,
  John, 156
MCELDERRY, ---, 192

Ann, 123, 204
Ann W., 129
Elizabeth, 37, 38, 39, 40, 41, 42
Hugh, 38, 192
Jane, 38
John, 37, 123, 129, 204
Margaret, 37, 217
Mary, 40
Robert, 42
Samuel Evans, 123
Sarah, 215
Sarah Ann, 234
Thomas, 37, 38, 39, 40, 41, 42, 78, 192
William, 41
MCELDERY, Henry, 205
  Sarah, 205
MCELDIN, Mr., 192
MCELIVEE, John, 192
MCELROY, James, 79, 106
  Mary, 106
  Nancy, 81
  William, 79
MCELWAE, Mary, 204
MCFADDON, James, 36, 37
  James Jennings, 36
  John, 37
  Rebecca, 36, 37
MCFADEN, John, 41, 79
  Margaretta, 41
  Priscilla, 41
MCFADON, Ann, 39

Antoinette, 121
Eliza, 110
Emily Ann, 91
James Wilson, 110
John, 39, 110, 131, 157
John Henry, 121
Louisa, 91, 110
Margaret, 93
Priscilla, 110
William, 39, 131
MCFALL, Mrs., 205
MCFANIN,
  Elizabeth, 37
  Jane, 37
  John, 37
MCFARRIN, Mary, 78
MCFEADON,
  William, 78
MCFEERRAN, Ruth, 212
MCFERRAN, James Rodgers, 39
  Jane, 38, 39, 40, 235
  John, 38, 39, 40
  Ruth, 211
  Samuel, 40
MCGIBBON, A. A., 153
  Mr., 153
  Mrs., 155
MCGILL, Agnes, 238
  Christiana, 234, 238
  Will, 234, 238
  William, 238
MCGRAY, William, 171
MCGREW, Agness, 33

Dolly, 33
Dorothy, 33
Joseph, 33
Robert, 33
MCGUECH, Andrew, 85
MCGUIRE, Anthony, 36
Mary, 36
P., 192
Patrick, 192
Thomas, 78
MCGUIRK,
  Margaret, 205
MCGUYER, P., 192
MCHENRY, Agness, 37
MACHENRY, Anna, 85
MCHENRY, Daniel, 119
  Daniel William, 36, 86
MACHENRY,
  Frances, 108
  Francis Deane, 108
MCHENRY, Grace, 36
MACHENRY, Helen, 108
MCHENRY, James, 36, 37, 38, 162, 163, 188, 222
  James Howard, 129
  John, 37, 129, 151, 172, 188
  Juliana, 129
  Margaret, 36, 37, 38, 159, 163
  Margaretta, 38

Ramsay, 119
Sophia, 168
Sophia H., 119
MCHOSSEY, James, 34
  Janit, 34
  Robina Kennedy, 34
MCILHENNY, Mrs., 157
MCILLROY,
  Margaret, 73
MCILROY,
  Alexander, 34
  Alice, 34
  Fergus, 34
  James, 91
  John, 192
MCILVAIN,
  Alexander, 38, 39, 40, 104, 106
  Andrew, 39
  Angeline, 91, 106
  Caroline, 104
  George, 40, 153
  Maria, 180
  Robert, 38
  Sally, 104
  Sarah, 38, 39, 40, 104, 106
MCILVAINE,
  Alexander, 116
  Gilbert, 33
  Hugh, 33
  Maria, 116
  Rosanna, 33
  Sarah, 116
MCINNALLY, Grace, 109, 167
  John, 79, 109

Sarah Ann
Pennington Rutt, 109
MCINTIRE, Agnes, 240
  Augusta, 240
  Catharine, 204
  David, 204
  Eliza, 233
  Elizabeth, 237
  George Whyte, 237
  James, 233, 237, 238, 239, 240, 241
  John, 84, 107, 192
  Laetitia, 239
  Lilly Ann, 107
  Margaret, 89, 239
  Mary Ann, 238
  Sarah, 107
  Sarah Ann, 204
  Sarah Jane, 241
  Sloan, 233
MCINTOSH,
  Alexander, 37
  Donald, 99
  Duncan, 37
  Elizabeth, 37
  James, 37
  Mary, 99
MCJILTON, John F., 215
  Philis, 205
  Phoebe, 214
MACK, Ellen, 34
  Hannah, 33, 34, 35, 36
  James, 33, 34, 35, 36
  John, 33
  Margaret, 35

William, 36
MCKAY, John, 157, 171
Rev., 192
MCKEAN, Ann, 110
John, 79, 110
Mary McClellan, 110
MCKEE, Joseph L., 204
MCKEEN, Ann, 39, 40, 41, 101, 104, 114, 170
Ann Maria, 173
Anna Maria, 40
Edward Parish, 114
Elizabeth, 39
Jane Buchanan, 104
John, 39, 40, 41, 101, 104, 114, 165, 170, 175, 182, 186, 187, 211
Mary, 184
Rebecca, 101
William Swan, 41
MCKELDIN, Joseph, 229
MACKENRY, Ann, 109
MCKENZIE, C., 192
MACKENZIE, Colin, 123
MCKENZIE, Colin, 42, 79
MACKENZIE, Henrietta, 205
MCKENZIE, James, 83
MACKENZIE, James Smith, 123

MCKENZIE, John Pinkerton, 42
Ruhamah, 205
MACKENZIE, Sarah, 123
MCKENZIE, Sarah, 42
T. M., 192
MCKEOWN, Henry M., 229
Mary J., 229
Mary Jane, 229
MCKEY, George, 79
MCKIM, Agness, 33
David, 196
David Telfair, 39
Elizabeth, 40
Emily, 156
Isabella, 41, 83
Jane, 39
John, 39, 40, 41, 192
Margaret, 39, 40, 41
Martha, 204
Mary, 33
Mary Ann, 205
Miss, 204
Mrs., 192, 204
Robert, 33
Samuel, 192, 231
W. D., 192
William D., 192
MCKINKEY, Jont., 204
Mrs., 204
MCKINLEY, Jane, 153
MCKINNELL, John, 192

MCKINNON, Mary, 217
Robert, 219
MCKINSEE, John, 78
MACKLASCEY, Hannah, 82
MACKMEE, Rosanna, 84
MCKOCHNIE, Agnes, 234
MCKONKEY, Margaret, 204
Maria L., 204
Mr., 192
Mrs., 160, 203
William, 203
MCLANAHAN, Ann, 205
Ann M., 205
MCLAUGHLIN, Catharine, 73
Colonel, 192
M., 192
Major, 192
Matthew, 192
Mr., 192
Robert, 192
Sidney, 172
W. W., 236
MCLEAN, Alexander, 78
Charles, 192
Mr., 154
MCLELLAN, Ann, 42
David, 32, 33, 34, 78, 169, 170
Effe, 42
Elizabeth, 32, 33, 167

Janit, 32, 33, 34
John, 32, 42, 165
Maria, 170
Mary, 32
Robert, 42
Walter, 34
William, 33
MCLENAHAN,
  Elijah, 41
  Mary, 41
  Washington, 41
MACLEVAIN,
  Alexander, 78
MCLINE, John, 79
MCLURE, David, 34, 78
  Elizabeth, 34, 77, 80
  Margaret, 34
  Rebecca, 76
MCMAHON, Biddy, 88
  Mary, 74
MCMAN, Eleanor, 85
MCMECHEN,
  Alexander, 32, 33, 34
  Elizabeth, 32, 33, 34
  James Morgan, 33
  Mary, 32
  Rebecca, 33
  Sarah, 34
MCMILLAN, Ann B., 92
  Ellen, 164
  Isabella, 36
  Janit, 36
  John, 36
  Margaret, 156, 172

MCMULLAN, Ann, 171
  Eleanor, 80
MCMULLEN, Peggy, 83
MCMYER, Cornelia, 76
MCMYERS, John, 79
MCNAMMEE, John, 78
MCNAUGHTON, F. W., 239
MCNEAL, Elizabeth, 230
  James, 230
  Mrs., 158, 203
MCNEALE, John, 84
MCNEIL, James, 192
MCNEILL, James, 34
  John, 34
  Mary, 34
MCNEILLY, Agness, 39, 40
  Jeremiah, 39
  John, 39, 40
MCNIGHT, Anne, 34
  James, 34
  John, 33
  Martha, 33
  Mary, 34
  William, 33
MCNULTY, ---, 204
  Ann Maria, 88
  Elizabeth, 204
MCOREDEN, Isaac, 233
MCPHERSON,
  Duncan, 33
  Malcolm, 33
  Mary, 33
MCREA, Jane, 32, 33

Mary, 32, 33
Samuel, 32, 33, 78
MCTAGGART,
  Alexander, 125
  James, 125
  Mary, 125
MCTHOWEN, Jane, 88
MCTIBBALS, Auzi, 90
MACTIER,
  Alexander, 37, 38, 41, 42, 97, 102, 106, 109, 158
MCTIER, Alexander, 170
MACTIER, Ann, 90
  Dorothea, 91
  Dorothy, 173, 38
  Eliza, 42, 91
MCTIER, Eliza, 171
MACTIER, Frances, 37, 38, 41, 42, 89, 97, 102, 106, 109
MCTIER, Frances, 153
MACTIER, Grace, 93, 102
MCTIER, Grace, 175
  Jane J., 175
MACTIER, Janit, 37
  Samuel McKean, 106, 109
  William McKean, 106
MCWHORTER,
  Alexander, 164
MCWILLIAM, John, 192

INDEX

MCWILLIAMS, Miss, 204
MAFFITT, Mary, 204
MAGEE, Mrs., 202
MAGRUDER, John Stricker, 117
  Laura Maria, 123
  M., 117
  Maria, 114, 123
  Martha Helen, 114
  R. B., 117
  Richard B., 85, 114, 123
  Thomas William, 123
MAHANY, Mrs., 214
MAHARRY, Mrs., 214
MAHOLL, Elizabeth, 41
  Isabella, 41
  Thomas, 41, 79
MAHOLLIN,
  Charles, 38
  Elizabeth, 38
MAHOOL, Eliza, 205
  Elizabeth, 40
  Emily, 204
  Isabella, 204
  James, 40
  Sarah, 205
  Thomas, 40
MAJOR, James, 78
  Mary, 82
  Rebecca, 33
  Robert, 33
  Thomas, 33
MALCHELL, Jane, 205

MALCOM, Jenny, 233
  Peter, 233
MALLONNEE, John, 95
MALLOY, Grissell, 39
  Jane, 39
  Peter, 39
MALTIMORE,
  Robert, 92
MAN, Charles, 106
  Charles Little, 106
  Isabella, 106
MANN, Mary White, 224
MANNING, Samuel, 93
  Sarah, 109
  Thomas, 109
MANSON,
  Catherine, 101
  Evinline, 101
  William, 101
MAREAN, Thomas, 193
MARK, Mr., 155
MARR, Charles, 164
  Isabella, 164
MARRON,
  Catharine, 41
  William, 41
MARSH, Susannah, 74
MARSHALL, Anne, 33, 34, 35, 40
  Elizabeth, 34
  Fanny, 35
  James, 33, 34, 35
  John, 40

Martha, 40
Mary, 33
Rebecca, 35
Sarah, 34
William, 78
MARTIN, Alexander, 39
  Ann, 40, 42, 93
  Anne, 39
  Dubois, 159
  Elizabeth, 35, 36, 111, 163
  Eveline Blair, 111
  Francis, 39
  George, 39, 40, 42, 79
  Hannah, 36
  Henry, 168
  Henry Y., 97
  J., 193
  James, 36, 38, 163, 193, 227
  John, 35, 36, 111, 163
  John B., 85
  Margaret, 72
  Maria, 85
  Mary, 36, 38, 42, 89
  Nancy, 39, 79
  Rebecca, 35
  Samuel, 164
  Susan, 227
  William, 78
  William Blair, 35
  Young, 86
MASK, Isaac, 102
  Mary, 102
MASON, Leah, 83
  Mary, 169
  Peter, 89

MASSEY, John E., 97
MATCHETT, Jane, 205
MATHER, Anne, 37
  Arabella, 224
  Dorothy, 35, 36, 37
  John, 35, 36, 37
  Joseph, 224
  Margaret, 73
  Robert, 35, 36
MATHERS,
  Catharine, 204
  Maria, 142, 180
  Mary, 183, 204
MATHEWSON,
  Martha, 85
MATHISON, Ann, 233
MATTHEWS, Ann Maria, 181
  Susanna, 75
  William P., 79
MATTOCKS,
  Catharine H., 92
MAUGHLIN, Ann, 234
  James, 234, 239, 240
  Mary Ann, 236, 239
  Rebecca, 241
  W. W., 241
  William W., 236, 240
MAUND, John, 168
MAXWELL,
  Elizabeth, 205
  Isabella, 111, 166
  J. W., 205
  Mary Swan, 111
  Moses, 193
  Mr., 150
  Mrs., 151
  William, 111, 165, 166
MAY, Abbey, 38
  Abraham, 36
  Abraham Duryee, 37
  Benjamin, 36, 37, 38, 39
  Elizabeth, 36, 37, 38, 39, 72
  James, 34, 35
  Jane, 35
  Juliann, 39
  Mary, 34, 35
  Rachel Anne, 38
  Rebecca, 79
MAYBEN, John, 94
MAYDWELL,
  Alexander, 193
MAYER, Elizabeth, 40
  Mary, 40
  Mrs., 158
  Robert, 40
MAYHEW, Mrs., 153
  William E., 91
MEASE, Anne, 76
MEEK, Margaret, 75
MEGAFF, Sarah, 76
MEGARRITY,
  Thomas, 79
MEGEE, John C., 202
MEHOOL, Ann Jane, 99
  Elizabeth, 99
  Thomas, 99
MENZIES, Ede V., 93
MERCER, Charles H., 193
  Rebecca, 81
MERCIER, Richard, 78
MEREDITH,
  Charles, 130
  Elizabeth Sarah, 123
  Emily, 116
  Emma Claudine, 128
  George Salmon, 112
  Gilmor, 132
  Hannah, 108, 112, 114, 116, 122, 123, 128, 130, 132, 165
  Jonathan, 85, 108, 112, 114, 116, 122, 123, 128, 130, 132, 165, 188, 221
  Louisa Sophia, 93, 114
  Mr., 152
  Rebecca S., 93
  Rebecca Salmon, 108
  William Wellington, 122
MERRYMAN,
  Elizabeth E., 96
  Nicholas R., 94
MESSITER, Sarah Ann, 215
MESSONIER, Mr., 152
MEYERS, George, 193, 205
  Mary Ann, 230

INDEX

Myer, 230
Nicholas, 230
Susan, 230
MEZICK, ---, 193
B., 193
Babtist, 193
MICHARD, Eloisa, 184
MICKLE, Robert, 79
MIDDLEMORE, Juliana, 218
MILES, George, 193
John, 238, 239, 240
Margaret, 240
Mary Anne, 239
William, 238
MILFORD, James, 79
MILLAR, Mrs., 153
MILLEMAN, Mr., 193
MILLER, Alexander, 40, 41
Ann, 89
G. W., 193
Jacob, 193
James, 193
John, 84
Mary Ann, 41, 171
Rev., 193
Rev. Dr., 135, 165
Robert, 160, 193
Samuel, 163, 193
Susanna, 40, 41
MILLHOLLAND, Sarah, 205
MILLIKEN, Anna, 234
Robert, 234, 235
MILLIKIN, Anna, 234

Robert, 234
MILLIMON, George, 193
Mr., 193
MILLS, Eliza D., 124, 128
Georgina Maria, 128
Margaret, 171
Margaret Ann, 94
Mr., 154
Richard, 171
Robert Henry, 124
Thomas, 124, 128, 151
MILNOR, Mary, 219
MILTENBERGER, Charles A., 97
MILTONER, Dr., 205
MIMM, Grace, 115, 164
MINCEY, Anna Maria, 74
MINSKER, Catharine, 83
MITCHEL, Alexander, 42
Eliza Maitland, 42
Elizabeth, 42
MITCHELL, ---, 193
A., 203
Alexander, 79, 98, 102, 193
Charles Jeffrey, 98
Edward, 78, 193
Eleanor, 75
Eliza, 98, 102
Francis J., 193
J. A., 204
James, 165

James R., 112
Jane Ann, 112, 165
John, 95
Keturah Ann, 112
Margaret, 204
Mary, 92
Richard B., 86
MITCHESON, Mary, 73
MITTONER, Dr., 205
MIX, Thomas Bell, 79
MOALE, Emily Louisa, 146
Frances Halton, 76
J. C., 159
John C., 92, 137, 139, 144, 146
Julia A., 137, 139
Juliet A., 144
Juliet Ann, 146
Mary Armistead, 144
Richard, 139
Richard Henry, 139
Samuel, 193
William Taylor, 137
MOCKEBOY, Kinsey, 86
MOFFAT, Thomas, 78
MOFFITT, Elizabeth, 204
MOILES, John, 233
MONAHAN, Mary, 217
MONK, Ann, 204
MONROE, Emily Frances, 213
Isaac, 193
J., 193

Jane Hastings, 213
Mary Ann, 213
Mary Eliza, 213
Mr., 193
MONTEITH, John, 193
MONTELL, Mary G., 205
MONTGOMERY,
James Nicholson, 115
John, 78, 115, 155, 167
Maria, 115, 167
Mary, 83, 235
Sarah Jane, 241
Stewart, 236, 241
MOODY, ---, 137
Edward P., 155
Elizabeth, 41
Frances, 73
Harriet, 170
James, 41
Mr., 193
William, 160, 177
MOONEY, Daniel, 144, 205
Elizabeth, 144
Sarah, 144
MOOR, John, 193
MOORE, Agness, 40
Bertha, 85
Bethea, 38
Eleanor, 205
Elizabeth, 34
Ellen, 163
Hellen Ranney, 39
Isabella, 36
John, 193
John Lee, 193
Maria, 100
Mathias, 100
Mrs., 196, 198
Nicholas Ruxton, 79
R., 193
Robert, 34, 35, 36, 78, 193, 205
Ruth, 35
Samuel, 193
Sarah, 38, 39, 40
Stephen, 35
Susanna, 34, 35, 36, 82
Thomas, 193
Violet, 100
William, 35, 38, 39, 40
MOOREHEAD,
David, 35
Jane, 35
Michael, 35
MOPPS, Mr., 156
MOREHEAD, John, 125, 236
Mary, 125
William, 125
MOREN, Elizabeth, 85
MORGAN, Arthur, 83
James, 78
MORRIS, ---, 188
Ann, 177
Anna, 183
Anne, 97
Catharine, 205
Edward, 78
George, 177, 187
Isabella, 183
Samuel, 78
William, 233
MORRISON,
Alexander Martin, 139
Eleanor, 32, 33, 80
Elizabeth, 35, 134, 139, 142
Elizabeth Wallington, 134
George, 91, 134, 139, 142
Hans, 35
Hans Hohnes, 35
Hugh, 35
Hugh Holmes, 35
James, 35
John, 32, 33
Joseph, 35
Margaret, 35
Mary, 33
Mr., 155
Mrs., 207
Richard Tellies, 35
Rosina, 205
Samuel, 35
Susanna, 35
MORROW, Ann, 212
Hugh, 40
J., 193
James, 193
John, 193, 212
John Frederick, 212
Kennedy, 40, 79
Mary, 40
MORTIMER, John, 236
Tamerine, 236
MORTON, A. B., 193
Alexander, 85

INDEX

Charles Anderson, 109
G. C., 224
George Copeland, 109
Margaret, 216
Mary Adelaide, 92, 109
Mrs., 204
Nathaniel, 109
Robert, 216
Sarah, 86, 109
MOSHER, Ann, 41, 42, 102, 106, 109
Anne, 37, 38, 39, 41
Anney, 37
Benjamin, 38
Col., 131
Edward Johnson, 109
Elizabeth, 36, 37, 38, 173
Frances, 37
Francis, 36
George, 42
Henry, 106
Isabella, 39, 183
James, 36, 37, 38, 39, 41, 42, 89, 102, 106, 109, 163, 187, 221
Jane, 38, 167
Joanna, 101
Johanna, 39, 40, 41, 42
John, 42, 101
Louis, 41
Mary, 36
Mary Ann, 102, 155
Philip, 36, 37, 39, 40, 41, 42, 78, 101
Samuel, 37
William, 41
MOSHIER, James, 193
MOSSMAN,
Archibald, 34
Elizabeth, 34
Mary, 34
MOYERS, George, 193
MUIR, Dr., 2, 28, 38, 48, 58, 83
Marion, 91
Mary Ann, 171
MUNCASTER, ---, 184
Harriet, 148
Rachel, 147
MUNDELL, Mrs., 203
MUNN, Eli, 151
MUNROE, Agnes, 238
Catharine, 237, 238, 239
Catherine, 233
Daniel, 237
Mr., 193
MUNSON, Ann 41
George Clarke, 41
Joel, 41, 193
MURDOCH,
Alexander, 144, 146, 180, 188
Alexander Fridge, 133, 144
Alice, 137
Ann Fridge, 147
Annie, 146
Elizabeth Jane, 237
Helen, 144
James Campbell, 149
John, 146, 233, 237, 238
John Cole, 139
Louisa Cole, 149
Margaret, 147
Marion, 144
Martha Crawford, 238
Mary, 135, 145, 146, 147, 149
Mary Ann, 132, 233
Mary C., 149
Mary E., 132, 133, 135, 137, 139, 142, 144
Rebecca Campbell, 146
Russel, 149
Susan, 144, 145, 146
Thomas, 96, 146, 149
W. F., 142, 144, 145, 156
William, 146, 147, 149
William F., 132, 133, 135, 137, 139, 147, 149, 179
William Morris, 142
MURDOCK,
Alexander, 92, 137, 138, 142, 147
Charles Nisbet, 142
Mary, 176

Mary Nisbet, 147
Susan, 137, 138, 142, 147
Thomas Fridge, 138
William Turnbull, 137
MURPHY, Adeline, 41
Ann, 105
Anne, 38
Anne Hunt, 229
Eleanor, 37, 38, 39, 42, 100, 229
Eliza, 39
Ellen, 41
John, 37, 38, 39, 41, 42, 100, 229
Mary, 94
Mr., 193
Nancy, 105
Nelson, 37
Samuel, 105
Thomas, 193
W. J., 205
William Lynch, 42
MURRAY, ---, 193
Agness, 89
Amanda, 220
Archibald, 78
Catharine, 178
Elizabeth, 82
Harriet, 157
James E. B., 157
John William Boyles, 38
Mrs., 153
Nicholas, 85
Olivia, 38
W. H., 157
William, 38

William H., 90
MURRY, ---, 193
MUSCHERT, John, 79
MUSGRAVE, Mr., 158, 160, 161
MUSSER, David H., 95
MYERS, Balcher, 32, 78
Barbara, 32
Catharine, 32
Catharine Jarold, 36
Charles, 36, 37, 78
Elizabeth, 36, 37
Emeline, 111
Frederic, 32
George, 111, 204
Isabella J., 94
Jacob, 111
Jane, 111
John, 39
Louisa, 205
Mary, 39
Matilda, 37
Mrs., 158
Polly, 111
Robert, 39, 79
Sarah, 91
Susanna, 111
MYLES, Jane, 88

-N-

NATHANS, Daniel, 91
NAYLER, William, 79
NEAL, Frances, 86
Hugh, 99
Rachel, 99
Rachel Maxwell, 99

NEALE, Ann, 84
NEEDHAM, A., 214
Arabella, 213
Asa, 218
Mary E., 218
NEEDLES, Elisa Martin, 43
Jane S., 226
Nancy, 43
Stephen, 43, 79
NEFF, Isabella L., 137, 138
John Rodolph, 138
P., 156, 160
Peter, 137, 138
William Howard, 137
NEGRO, Coffee, 88
Hagar, 90
Hector, 85
Henry, 119
Hester, 87
Jenny, 116
John, 116
Joseph, 116
Lively, 203
Mary, 125
Nancy, 88, 170
Nicholas, 90
Patience, 170
Sally, 85
Shadrach, 87
Shorter, 152
Sydney, 170
NEILL, Agness, 43
Alexander, 42
Cinthia, 43
Elizabeth, 42
Frances, 43
George, 43

INDEX

Hugh, 43, 44
Isabella, 42, 43
James, 79
John, 43
John Smith, 43
Margaret, 43
Mary, 42
Phebe, 43
Rachel, 43, 44
Robert Callender, 42
William, 42, 43, 44, 187
NEILSON, Caroline, 118, 119, 121, 125, 128, 168
Caroline Helena, 125
Gilbert, 43
H., 168
Harreit, 114
Henry Payson, 119
Hugh, 193
James, 43
Jane, 43, 128
Mrs., 193
Oliver, 121
Oliver H., 118, 128, 151
Oliver Hugh, 119, 125
Rebecca Virginia, 118
Robert, 91
William, 114
William Gwynn, 121
NELSON, Felty, 153
John, 193
Mary, 85
Rebecca, 82
Sarah, 81

NESBIT, James, 43
John, 43
Margaret, 43
Robert, 193
NEVINS, Anna Key, 138
Louisa Emily, 141
M. H., 160
M. U., 138
Mary, 132
Mary D., 135, 176
Mary L., 141
Philip Barton Key, 132
Rev., 193, 211
William, 90, 127, 132, 135, 138, 141, 171, 186, 193, 224
William Russell, 135
NEWCOMB, Cath., 181
NEWELL, Charles, 205
Sarah, 205
NEWMAN, Ann, 108
Ann Jane, 109
Joseph, 108, 109
Lason, 193
Lawson, 193
Sally Ann, 108
NEWTON, Arad B., 95
William, 79
NIBLER, Maria, 217
NICHOL, Agness, 79
NICHOLAS, Cary Ann, 43
George, 42, 43, 79
Jane, 44
John Hollins, 226

John Separ, 95
John Smith, 226
Margaret, 43, 44
Margaretta, 43
Mary, 42, 43, 44
Mary Buchanan, 43
Mary Jane Carr, 226
Philip N., 44, 79
Robert Carter, 44
Sarah E., 177
Wilson Cary, 43, 44, 79
NICHOLS, Maria, 170
NICHOLSON, Francis, 147
Helen Tiernan, 145
James, 158
James D., 91
Joseph, 147
Joseph J., 92, 144, 145
Joseph James, 222
Laura, 147
Laura C., 144, 145
Margaret, 89
William Carmichael, 144
NICKERSON, Charles Vashan, 99
Elizabeth, 99, 103
Elizbeth, 89
Jane Lewis, 103
Lewis, 99, 103
Pamelia Ann, 180
NICOLL, Catharine, 44
David, 44, 99
Dorcas, 44, 99

Isabella, 99
Jane, 77
Margaret, 96
NIELSON,
  Catherine, 86
  Oliver H., 170
NIGHT, Agness, 42
  Edward, 42
  Sarah, 42
NISBET, Alexander,
  85, 113, 116, 120,
  124, 127, 174, 188
  Ann Tweddie, 120
  Cassandra Owings,
  120
  Charles, 113
  Colegate Deye, 113
  Fanny Owings, 124
  John, 155
  John Owings, 127
  Judge, 90
  Mary, 120, 124, 175
  Mary C., 116
  Mary Cockey, 113
  Mary Nisbet, 127
  Thomas Deye, 116
NOLEN, Alexander,
  220
  Henry, 220
NORCOM, Ann
  Eunice, 214
  John, 214
NORQUAY,
  Magness, 79
  Magnus, 165
NORRIS, Alexander
  Brown, 115
  John, 115
  Margaret, 205
  Mary, 205

Mrs., 193, 197
Nancy, 115
William, 79, 193
NORTH, Rebecca, 72
  Sophia, 73
NUCOLL, Christian,
  42
  Grizel, 42, 43
  Thomas, 43
  Thomas Young, 43
  William, 42, 43
NUGENT, Ann, 43
  David, 43
  John, 43
  Mary, 43
  Sarah, 43

-O-

O'BRIEN, Solomon,
  95
O'DONNEL,
  Columbus, 44
  Henry, 44
  Mary Eliot, 85
O'DONNELL,
  Deborah, 44
  Deborah H., 87
  Elisa White, 45
  Elliot, 45
  John, 44, 45, 134
  Mary, 44, 134
  Sarah, 44, 45
OGIER, Frances
  Canoze, 45
  John, 44, 45
  John Stevenson, 44
  Mary, 44, 45
OGLE, Catharine H.,
  91
  George, 98

James, 107, 130
Mary, 130
Michael Van Kuik,
  107
Nelly, 98
Sarah, 107
William, 98, 107
William Edward,
  130
OLER, Margaret,
  115, 117
  Peter, 115, 117
  Philip, 115
OLIVER, Charles, 44
  Eliza, 44, 45, 99,
  105, 166
  Emily, 92, 105
  George, 44, 45
  Henry, 45
  Hugh Thompson, 44
  Jane, 45
  John, 45, 152
  Margaret, 86
  Mrs., 152
  N., 193
  Peggy, 44, 166
  Robert, 44, 45, 99,
  105, 160, 166
  Thomas, 99
OLLER, P., 154
OLLIPHONT, Jane,
  85
OLO, Janet, 226
  William, 226
ORD, George, 84
ORMSBY, Robert,
  231
  William Crawford,
  231

ORR, Alexander, 233, 237, 238, 239
　Ann, 233
　Anne, 239
　Jane M., 238
　Janet Russell, 238
　William Morris, 237
ORRICK, Mary, 44
　Nicholas, 44
　Sydnee, 44
　William, 44
OSBORN, Charles, 143
　John, 140, 143
　John Henry, 140
　Sarah, 140, 143, 178
　William, 89
OSBORNE,
　Catherine, 82
　Eleanor, 44
　James, 44
　James Haly, 44
　Sarah, 44
OSTON, Mr., 193
OTTERSON, Matilda, 185
OULD, Lancaster, 187
OWEN, Asalom, 211
　Caleb, 181, 211
　Capt., 148
　David, 181, 211
　G., 202
　George, 146
　Henry Duning, 146
　Henry Dunning, 148
　Jane, 181, 211
　John, 96, 145
　Joshua, 205, 211
　Lucy Gray, 148
　Lucy Grey, 146
　Mary, 79, 146, 180
　Mr., 160
　Rebecca, 78
　William, 156
OWENS, Rev. Mr., 145
OWINGS, Betsy, 74
　Mary C., 85
　Ruth, 74

-P-

PAGE, ---, 183
　Dr., 193
　Elizabeth, 77
　James, 193
PAINE, Sarah, 77
PAIRO, Charles W., 97
PAISLEY, David, 45
　Margaret, 45
PALMER, Mary, 181
　Thomas, 80
PAMPHILON, Thomas, 80
PAMPILLION, Mary, 80
PANNEL, Ann, 175
　Edward, 159
　Jane, 84
PANNELL, Ann Pierce, 49
　Benjamin, 47
　E., 225
　Edward, 47, 48, 49, 160
　Eliza, 48
　Elizabeth, 46, 47, 48
　George Washington, 48, 49
　Hugh, 47
　J., 193
　James, 47, 193
　John, 46, 47, 48
　Margaret, 46
　Sarah, 47, 48, 49
　William, 47
PARADISE, Sophia, 75
PARISH, William, 88
PARK, Alexander, 181
　Harriet, 181
PARKER, ---, 183
　Abraham, 86
　Elizabeth, 78
　James, 80, 91
　Jane, 77
　Mr., 158, 161
　William S., 206
PARKES, Abraham, 86
PARKHILL, Jane, 185
PARKIN, Ann, 81
PARKS, A., 193
　Andrew, 49, 193
　George Washington, 49
　Harriet, 49
　John, 193
PARLEY, David, 80
PARMELE, J. H., 88
　James H., 167
PARR, Elisha, 193
PARSONS, Deborah H., 181

Deborah Hopkins, 144
PATE, Margaret, 87
PATRICK, Hugh, 80
PATTEN, Margaret, 235
PATTERSON, ---, 193
  A., 193
  Andrew, 112, 193
  Ann, 49
  Augusta Sophia, 48
  Caroline, 49
  Dorcas, 46, 47, 48, 49
  Edward, 47, 87
  Eliza A., 206
  Elizabeth, 47
  Esther, 48
  George, 48, 49
  Henry, 49
  Isabella, 153
  James, 80, 212
  John, 47, 48
  Joseph Wilson, 47
  Margaret, 122
  Margaretta, 48
  Mary, 112
  Mary Ann, 180
  Mary Ann Jeromia, 108
  Nicholas, 112
  Octavus, 108
  Rebecca, 48
  Rev., 193
  Robert, 46, 151
  Walter, 49, 193
  William, 46, 47, 48, 49, 80, 91, 108, 160, 188
PATTISON, Hope Margaret Moncrieff, 130
  John, 130
  Rebecca, 130
  Samuel, 218
PATTON, Abraham, 45, 46
  Benjamin, 47
  Elizabeth, 86
  Esther, 47
  James, 47, 88
  Jane, 45
  John Dyer, 46
  Margaret, 46
  Martha, 45, 46
  Mary, 46
  Matthew, 46, 47, 79
  Rebecca, 46, 47, 214
  Sarah, 45
  William, 46
PAWSON, Mary, 205
PAYSON, ---, 193
  Abigail, 227
  Eunice, 227
  Henry, 193, 227
PEABODY, James A., 206
PEACHIM, Mr., 155
PEACOCK, Constant Love, 79
PEALE, William, 80
PEARSON, Andrew, 95
  David, 80
  Elizabeth, 160, 165
  Hannah A., 97
  Joseph, 180, 221, 228
  Mary, 84, 180
PEASELY, Margaret, 78
PECHIN, William, 193
PECK, Elizabeth, 76
  Margaret, 77
PEDAN, Ann, 235
PEERSON, Henry, 80
PELLOY, William, 88
PENDERGRASS, Robert, 80
PENDEXTER, Mr., 209
PENDLETON, Peter, 218
  Robert W., 182
PENNIMAN, Mr., 153
PENNINGTON, H., 193
PENROSE, Eliza, 95
PEREGO, Joseph, 80
PERKINS, Eveline, 94
  Joseph, 179
  Mary, 75
  Miss, 154
PERRY, Albert, 206
  Joshua, 205
  Mr., 159
  Mrs., 193
  Susan, 206
PETERS, D., 193
  Daniel, 193
  Joseph F., 182
PETERSON, Nancy, 88
PETTICON, Catherine, 173
PETTICORE, ---, 131

INDEX

Catherine, 137, 173, 176
John, 129, 172
Mr., 156
PETTINGALL,
Margaret, 115
Robert, 115
PETTIT, E. M., 206
Obediah, 206
PHILBROOK,
Thomas, 177
PHILIPS, Elizabeth, 105
Ephraim Robinson, 105
George, 193
William, 84, 105
PHILLIPS, E. R., 155
Elizabeth, 110, 130, 186
Elizabeth Robinson, 130
Sarah M., 95
William, 110, 130, 158
William E., 228
William Edwin, 110
PHILPOT, Clarissa, 94, 174
John, 93
PHIPPS, Thomas, 85
PIERCE, Betsy
Williamson, 49
Clarissa, 152
Humphrey, 80
Humphrey, Mrs., 153
Israel, 49
Letitia, 49

Levy, 80
William, 49
PIERPONT, John, 122, 169
Juliet, 122
Mary, 122, 169
PIERSON, Anne, 46
Elizabeth, 45, 46
Henry, 48
John, 45, 46
Mary, 45, 46, 48
Rebecca, 46
Robert, 45
Thomas, 46
PILKINGTON, Mary, 179
PILSON, Robert, 93
PINCKNEY, W., 193
PINDELL, Frances, 88
PINE, John, 79
PINKERTON, Sarah, 79
William, 193
PIT, Elizabeth, 79
PITCHER, Hannah, 73
Sarah, 78
PLEASANTS, Ann Cleves, 146
Elizabeth, 146
W. A., 146
William A., 95
PLOWMAN, Anne, 45
Jonathan, 45, 187
Mary, 45
Mr., 193
Rebecca, 45
Sarah, 45

POCOCK, Drusilla, 87
POE, ---, 193
Amelia, 111
Bridget, 102, 108, 111, 112
David, 46, 47, 48, 193, 222, 228
Edgar Allan, 225, 228
Elizabeth, 46, 47, 48
George, 102, 108, 125
George Washington, 46
Harriet, 84
Jacob, 84, 102, 108, 111, 112, 121, 193
James Mosher, 121
John, 108
John Hancock, 46
Mary, 47
Mr., 193
Neilson, 112
Samuel, 47
W. H., 157
William, 46
POGUE, Arthur, 206
Elizabeth, 48, 49, 99, 174
George, 49
James, 48, 49, 80, 99
John, 48
Joseph, 49
Maria, 99
Robert, 49
Sarah, 206
William, 48
POLE, David, 171

POLK, David, 80, 89, 160
David P., 90
POLKINHORN, Henry, 84
POLKINSON, Richard W., 169
POLLOCK, Agness, 47
George, 47, 48, 225
John, 48
Susanna, 47, 48
William, 47
POOR, Charles Henry, 118
Charles M., 85, 113, 166
Charlotte, 118, 121, 167
Deborah, 120
Deborah Hibernia, 168
Deboran, 123
Dudley, 87, 120, 123, 168
Elizabeth, 113
Elliott O'Donnell, 123
Frederick James, 118
George Henry, 118
Jane Eliza, 113
John H., 87
John Kirkland, 121
Moses, 118, 121, 167, 168
Sarah Eliza, 120
William Augustus, 118
POPE, Sarah, 218

PORTER, Ann, 185
Ann Pannel, 120
David, 48, 49, 222
Edward Pannell, 123
Isabella, 120, 154
Jane, 103, 111, 120, 123, 175, 183
Jane Eliza, 106
John, 49
Luisa, 49
Margaret, 206
Margareta, 206
Mary Ann, 111
Miss, 205
Mr., 205
Mrs., 205
Peggy, 49
Polly, 48
Ralph, 84
Rebecca, 48, 49
Sarah McCulloh, 120
Sarah Pannel, 103
Tarissa, 49
William, 84, 103, 106, 111, 120, 123
POST, Electa M., 229
Isabella, 229
Rev., 141
Russell, 229
Silas, 229
POTCHER, Walter, 206
POTTER, Elizabeth, 91
POUTENAY, Sarah, 78
POWEL, Charles R., 96

Peter, 80
POWELL, Charles, 148, 183
Mary Catherine, 148
PRAT, Benjamin, 48
Eliza, 49
James, 48, 49, 80
Sarah, 48, 49
PRENTICE, Alexander, 98, 102, 107, 165, 225
Margaret, 95, 98
Mary A., 225
Nancy Ann, 102
Rosanna, 102, 159, 165
Rosina, 98
Rossanna, 107
Susan, 107
PRENTISS, Margaret, 173
Mary, 173
Susanna, 72
PRESBURY, Hannah, 78
Jane, 177
PRICE, Elizabeth, 72
Ellin, 72
James, 80
Rachel, 87
PRICHARD, John, 80
PRIESTLEY, James, 163
PRUCY, Mary Ann, 88
PUE, Margaret Rutter, 206
PUGH, John, 79
PURL, Hannah, 170

INDEX

PURLE, Mary, 73
PURVIANCE, ---, 193
 Abigail, 98, 102, 105, 111, 113, 116
 Augusta Jemima, 127
 Catharine, 46
 Charles Degen, 130
 Eliza, 49, 104, 106, 163
 Elizabeth Isabella, 86, 163
 Emily Jane, 125
 Frances, 45, 46, 84, 104, 154, 162, 226
 Frances Ann, 120
 Frances Susan, 113
 Francis, 150, 175
 George D., 178
 Hugh, 46, 196
 Hugh Young, 49
 Isabella, 46, 73
 James, 45, 49, 80, 104, 106, 163, 180, 193, 222
 Jane, 46, 81
 Jane J., 178
 Jane S., 160
 Jane Stewart, 105
 Jemima, 120, 125, 127, 130
 John, 45, 80, 98, 102, 105, 111, 113, 116, 188
 John Cumberland, 102
 Letitia, 163
 Margaret S., 178
 Margaret Smith, 111
 Robert, 45, 46, 86, 98, 104, 162, 186, 187, 188, 221, 226
 Samuel, 45, 46, 80, 187
 Susanna, 45
 William, 120
 William T., 127
 William Y., 125, 130
 William Young, 46
 Wilson Cary, 49

-Q-
QUAY, William, 80
QUIMBY, Benjamin, 128
 John Robert, 128
 Magaretta, 128
QUINLON, Patrick, 80

-R-
RABORG, Ann, 214
 C., 193
 Christopher, 193, 221
RAMSAY, Agnes V., 206
 Amanda, 206
 Anabella, 53
 Arabella, 227
 Arrabella, 53
 Charlotte, 170
 Charlotte J., 90
 Elizabeth, 50, 51, 53, 206, 227
 James, 50, 157, 193
 Jane, 227
 Jefferson, 206
 Letty, 206
 Margaret, 95
 Miss, 206
 Mrs., 193, 206
 Nathaniel, 167, 222, 225
 Sarah, 206
 Sophia H., 86
 Thomas, 50, 51, 53
 Thomas W., 227
RAMSEY, Anne, 71
 Joseph, 206
 Margaret, 85
RANDALL, Aquila, 80
 Ellin, 72
 Margaret, 215
 Maria Elizabeth, 213
 Stephen, 87
RANKIN,
 Christopher, 91
 Hugh, 80
 Juliana, 93
 Julianna, 174
 Mrs., 193
 Samuel, 90
 Sophia, 95
RANY, Jane, 52
 John, 52
 Robert, 52
RARETON,
 Margaret, 76
RATIEN, Dederick, 51
 Thomas, 51
 Wilhemina Dorothea, 51
RAWLINS, Eliza, 103

REA, Ann, 217
READ, William, 90
READE, William R., 96
READELL, John, 193
READY, Elizabeth, 99
  James, 99
  John, 99
REAM, Charlotte, 170
  Elijah, 170
REARDON, Mary, 81
REDGRACE, Ann, 177
REDGRAVE, John, 89
REDMAN, Forbes, 218
  James, 94
REED, Hugh, 80
  James, 80
  Samuel, 80
REEDER, Ann W., 206
REESE, Hezekiah, 80
REEVES, Robert, 80
REGAN, Elizabeth, 77
REID, John C., 178
  John P., 174
  Mr., 236
REIDOUT, Sophia, 96
REINAGLE, Alexander, 84
REISINGER, Amanda, 182
RELP, Anne, 81

RELPH, Sarah, 78
REMMAGE, Margaret, 82
RENEY, Alexander, 51
  Mary, 51
  Sarah, 51
RESIDE, Edward, 52
  Jane, 52
  William James, 52
REVELL, John, 88
REYNOLDS, John, 89
  V., 193
  William, 186
RICAUD, Martha Jane, 122
RICE, Anne, 75
  Catharine, 51
  Charlotte, 92
  John, 51
  Mary, 51
RICH, Ellen, 90, 171
  John, 152
  Mathias, 221
  Matthias, 150, 166
  Mrs., 155
  Rebecca, 166, 172
  Sarah R., 170
RICHARDS, Elias Zachariah, 143
  Margaret, 143, 180
  Martha, 143, 184
  Mary, 143
  Percy, 184
  Pierce Ann, 143
  Sarah, 53
  William, 53
  William Penn, 143

RICHARDSON, Elizabeth, 50
  Hiram, 94
  Janit, 50
  Josiah, 213, 216
  Mary, 50
  Reliance C., 213
  Samuel, 50
  William, 50
RICHART, Betsey, 52
  Mary, 51
  Sarah, 51, 52
  William, 51, 52
RICKEY, W., 193
RIDDELL, Alexander Hawkesworth, 52
  Amelia, 52
  Louisa, 51
  Maria, 51
  Mary, 51, 52
  Mary Fraser, 52
  Nancy, 51
  Robert, 51, 52
RIDDLE, Elizabeth Amelia, 138
  Ellen Weld, 138
  John, 138, 142
  Mary, 142
  Mary Ann, 138, 176
  Mr., 157
RIDELL, James, 80
RIDGELEY, Mrs., 170
RIDGELY, William A., 87
RIDGLEY, Captain, 193
  Mrs., 88

RIDLEY, Catherine, 51
  Matilda Frances Sherboure, 51
  Matthew, 51
RIDOUT, John, 133, 136, 183
  Pru T., 183
  Prudence G., 133, 136
  Samuel, 133
RIEGART, ---, 183
RIGBY, Elizabeth Grace, 115
RING, Hannah, 211
  Thomas, 193
RIPPLE, Mr., 152
ROACH, James, 94
ROAN, John, 80
ROBB, Catharine, 52
  Catherine, 87
  Charles Gartry, 52
  David Elphinston, 52
  Elizabeth, 52, 53, 84, 163
  George, 53
  Mary Ann, 52
  Patrick, 52
  Rebecca, 52
  William, 52, 53, 80, 163, 188
ROBBINS, Roger, 80
ROBERTS, Charles, 89
  Elizabeth, 75, 85
  Henry James, 95
  Mary, 185
ROBERTSON, Lucy Ann, 182

ROBESON, Alexander, 53
  Angelica, 53
  Johanna, 52
  John, 52
  Margaret, 52
  Priscilla, 53
ROBINETT, Richard, 81
ROBINSON, ---, 225
  Archibald, 53
  Agness, 50, 51
  Alex., 105
  Alexander, 51, 52, 53, 98, 112, 146, 165, 185
  Alexander C., 94, 144
  Alexander Charles, 112
  Alverda, 90, 98
  Andrew, 50, 51
  Angelica, 52, 53, 89, 98, 112, 165
  Ann, 86, 206
  Aug., 105
  Catharine, 52, 53, 77
  Catherena, 52
  Charles, 53
  Charlotte, 184
  Charlotte Ramsay, 105
  Dr., 161
  E., 228
  Elizabeth, 52, 84, 206, 236
  Elizabeth Ann, 241
  Hannah, 82
  Harriet, 50, 51, 142

  Henry, 124
  James S., 142
  Jane, 80
  Johanna, 78
  John, 52, 53
  Laura, 142
  Laura Wirt, 146
  Louisa, 124
  Lydia, 83
  Martha E., 182
  Mary, 134, 142, 174, 179, 214
  Mr., 152
  Mrs., 208
  Nancy, 51
  Priscilla, 51, 52, 87
  Robert Lyles, 52
  Rosa, 146
  Rosa E., 144
  Sarah, 83, 236
  Thomas, 124, 236, 241
  William Wirt, 144
ROBISON, Agnes, 171
  Agnes E., 92
  Agness, 51
  Agness Eve, 53
  Anne, 52
  Charlotte Christena, 52
  Charlotte Christiana, 87
  Elizabeth, 51
  Ephraim, 51, 52, 53
  Ephraim Allen Rothrock, 53
  Esther, 53
  Eve, 51, 52, 53
  Jesse, 51

ROCHE, Cecilia, 211
  Eliza, 213
RODGERS, Agnes,
  146, 147
  Alexander, 50
  Anne Plat, 50
  Edwin, 229
  Elizabeth, 50
  George Henry, 146
  J. O., 193
  John, 50, 146, 147,
  178, 183
  Louisa, 185
  Martha Ann, 147
  Mary, 229
  Mary Catharine,
  146
  Richard, 193
ROGAN, Johanna, 80
ROGDERS, John,
  187
ROGERS, Alexander
  Mason, 218
  Allen, 80
  Eliza, 218
  Elizabeth, 18, 50,
  53, 74
  George, 86
  J. C., 193
  John, 50
  Mary, 159
  Moses Elvins, 53
  Mr., 193
  R., 193
  Rachel, 50
  Richard, 193
  Sophia, 123
  William, 18, 53, 80,
  236
  William Reed, 18

RONEY, Alice, 206
  John, 206
  William, 85, 193
ROOKER, Harriet,
  181
  Rebecca, 181
ROSE, Grace, 154
ROSISON, Ann, 112
  Susan, 112
  William, 112
ROSS, Anne, 50
  B. C., 193
  Benjamin C., 193
  Elizabeth, 109
  Hannah, 51
  James, 51, 53, 227
  Jane, 52
  John, 50, 51
  Margaret, 50
  Mary, 52
  Mr., 150, 193
  Oliver Bond, 53
  Patty, 86
  R., 193
  Robert Lockhart, 80
  Rose, 53, 227
  Samuel, 109
  Sarah, 50
  Thomas, 52
  Washington William
  Alexan, 109
  William, 193, 230
ROUSE, Js., 193
ROWE, Elizabeth, 84
  Spencer, 216
RUARK, Mary, 140,
  178
  Mrs., 155
  Nancy, 95
  Samuel, 140

RUDULPH, Zebulon,
  122, 169
RUSK, David, 50, 51
  David Lewis, 50
  Elam, 50
  Elizabeth, 50
  Helen, 50
  Mary, 50, 51
  Mr., 150
  Samuel, 50, 51
  Sarah, 50
  William, 50
RUSSEL, Eliza, 235
  Elizabeth, 105
  Esther, 235
  James, 105
  Jane, 234
  John, 105
  Margaret, 206
  Samuel, 235
RUSSELL, Eliza, 236
  Elizabeth, 132
  Esther Ann, 239
  James, 51
  Jane, 51, 52, 53,
  238, 239, 240, 241
  Janet, 132
  John Walker, 240
  Joshua T., 169
  Lydia, 87
  Margaret Elizabeth,
  239
  Mary Ann, 169
  Mary Catherine,
  241
  Robert, 51, 52, 53
  Sarah Jane, 238
  Thomas, 52
  Walter, 132
  William, 80

INDEX

RUST, Elizabeth, 82
RUTHERFORD,
  Alexander, 91
RUTTER, Anna
  Altehia, 206
RYAN, Thomas, 193

-S-
SABBY, Mrs., 193
SAILORS, Hannah,
  81
SALMON, George,
  81, 162, 186, 188
SALTONSTALL,
  Nathaniel, 193
SANDERS, Ann, 181
  Beverly C., 181, 214
  Charlotte, 181, 214
SANDERSON,
  Thomas, 97
SANDISON,
  Alexander, 62, 81,
  98
  Andrew, 98
  Jane, 62
  Meron, 62
SANDS, Bethiah, 140
  Ellen, 140
  John, 140, 156
  Mary Cecilia, 140
SANFORD, Joseph
  L., 179
SANGER, Catharine,
  61, 62, 98
  Eloisa Bentalou, 61
  Lucy Margaret, 62
  Seth, 61, 62, 81, 98
SANKEY, William,
  193

SAPPINGTON,
  John, 92
SAUNDERS, ---, 183
SAUNDERSON,
  Betsey, 169
  Francis, 55
  Jesse Lukens, 55
  Margaret, 55, 169
  Robert, 55
SAVAGE, Frances,
  75
  Susanna, 86
SAWBRIGHT,
  Elizabeth, 78
SCARBOROUGH,
  John A., 175
  John Americus, 136
  Samuel H., 176
SCHAEFER,
  Christian A., 188
SCHAFFER, Sarah,
  79
SCHICK, John D.,
  174
SCHLATER,
  Susanna, 76
SCHLEY, Ann B.,
  127
  Anna B., 129, 136,
  175
  Eunice, 225
  George Jacob, 129
  Jacob, 89, 127, 129,
  136, 154, 222, 225
  Laura Ann, 136
  Mary Eliza, 127,
  225
SCHMINKE, Anna,
  123, 126

  Emilie Wilhelmine,
  126
  George, 123, 126
  Sophia Margaretta
  Charlot, 123
SCOBEY, Ann, 122,
  125, 170
  Elizabeth, 122, 174
  Emma, 122
  John, 122, 125, 151,
  170
  Mary, 92
  Mary Ann, 122
  Rachel, 97, 125, 181
SCOTT, Andrew, 57
  Ann, 100
  Anna, 83
  Catharine A., 207
  Eleanor, 172
  Eliza, 63
  Elizabeth, 58, 60,
  61, 100, 104, 108
  Jane, 63, 207
  John, 60, 63, 81
  Maria Jane, 179,
  182
  Mary, 56, 57, 58,
  104
  Mary Ann, 180, 182
  Mrs., 155, 207
  Nancy, 73
  O'Neal, 60
  Robert, 58, 60, 61,
  100, 104, 108
  Sarah, 78
  William, 56, 57
SCRIVENER,
  Janetta Sophia, 161

SCROGGS,
  Alexander, 61, 63, 81, 107
  Allen, 59
  Ann, 61, 63
  Anna, 107
  E. S., 233
  Frances, 59, 61
  Jane, 61
  John, 59, 61
  Margaret, 59
  Mary, 59
  Mary Ann, 63
  Robert Allen, 107
  William Alexander, 107
SEAMON, Caroline, 94
SEARLEY, Sophia, 207
SEARS, James, 193
SELIVGE, Mrs., 159
SELVAGE, Mr., 160
SEMON, David, 137
  Harriet, 137
  Maria Ann, 137
SENSENY, Jane, 185
SETH, Margaret, 150
SEWARD, Ann, 182
SEWELL, E., 208
  Henrietta Eliza, 212
SEYMOUR, Mr., 171
SHAHANASEY,
  Charlotte Frazier, 88
SHANLEY, Jeffry Dillon, 193
SHANNON, William, 95
SHARP, Peter, 81
SHAW, Ann, 170
  Archibald, 234
  Elizabeth, 105, 170, 234
  Esther, 140, 143
  Gilbert Pigot, 105
  Hester, 91
  James, 143
  John, 193
  Lucy, 61
  Mary, 81
  Matthew, 95
  Moses, 96
  Mr., 193
  Mrs., 170, 193
  Pigot, 105
  Robert, 61
  Sarah, 80
  Sarah Ann, 140
  Thomas, 140, 143, 178
  William, 61
SHEDDEN, J., 163
  John, 193
SHEERER, Robert, 240
SHEPHARD, Ann, 96
SHEPHERD, Anne, 55
  James, 55
  John, 55, 81, 84
SHEPPARD, James, 234
  Sarah Ann, 93
  Susan, 93
  Thomas, 193, 217
SHEPPERD, Thomas, 193
SHERER, Elizabeth, 239
  Mary Ann, 240
  Robert, 235, 239, 240
  William, 235, 240
  William George, 240
SHERMERDINE,
  Joseph, 62
  Robert Clement, 62
  Sarah, 62
SHERWOOD, Ann, 207
SHIELDS, Caleb, 55, 81
  David Brown, 55
  James S., 97
  Jane, 55, 77
  Rachel, 80
SHIPLEY, Agness, 56
  Benjamin, 81
  Eleanor, 56
  Henry, 56
  Jane, 177
  Talbot, 81
SHOCKNESEY,
  Margaret, 75
SHORE, Joseph, 193
SHORT, Agness, 81
  Rebecca, 72
SHORTER, Harriet, 91
SHOW, Mary, 207
SHUSTER, Eliza, 207
SHUTER, Mr., 207
  Mrs., 207
SIDDALL, Jane, 226
SIEMSEN, John Jacob, 88
SILENCE, Susannah, 87

INDEX

SILVERS, John, 193
SIMKINS, David P., 95
SIMMONS, Mrs., 208
  William, 81
SIMPSON, David Boyd, 59
  George Clingon, 58
  James, 58, 59
  Jane, 58, 59
SIMUND, Andrew, 177
  Ann, 177
  Elizabeth Ann, 177
SINARD, John, 81
SINCLAIR, Andrew Mease, 55
  Jane, 88
  Jennet, 85
  Margaret, 54, 55, 75
  Margery, 99
  Nancy, 99
  Rachel, 54
  Robert, 99
  Susanna, 55
  Thomas, 193
  William, 54, 55
SINTON, Mr., 155
SITLER, Eliza A., 95
  Isabella, 95
SIXSMITH, Simeon, 81
SKILLING, William, 181
SKILLMAN, Robert, 81
SKINNER, John Stuart, 222
SLAPPY, Agness, 59
  Elizabeth, 58
  Jacob, 58, 59, 60, 61
  James, 60
  Jane, 58, 59, 60, 61
  Sally, 62
  William, 61
SLATER, Joseph, 81
  Margaret, 72
  Samuel, 193
SLEMMER, ---, 193
  C., 193
  Christian, 193
SLEMONS, John, 164
  Mr., 7
SLEPPY, Jacob, 60, 61, 100
  James, 60
  Jane, 60, 61, 100
  Sally, 62
  William, 61
SLIMMER, ---, 193
SLINGLUFF, Jesse, 97
SLOAN, ---, 193
  Charles, 61
  Elizabeth, 56, 59, 61
  Elizaeth, 60
  J., 193
  James, 56, 59, 60, 61, 159, 193
  Jane, 61
  Mary, 60
SLOON, Elizabeth, 57
  Elizbeth, 56
  James, 56, 57
  William, 57
SLY, Peggy, 75
SMALL, ---, 137
  Agness E., 141
  Ann, 89
  Caroline, 95
  Isabella Robinson, 141
  Jacob, 193
  William F., 92, 141, 158, 174
SMALLWOOD, George, 88
SMART, Anna Maria, 236
  J. G., 236
  John G., 240, 241
  John Gardiner, 241
  Margaret, 241
  Rev., 235
SMILEY, Eliza, 60
  Isaac, 60, 62
  Margaret, 60, 62, 236
  Mary, 236
  Mary Ann, 62
SMITH, A., 193
  Ann, 101, 104, 110, 134, 165
  Anna Maria, 61
  Anne, 61
  Anne Brent, 57
  Arnold, 193
  Arthur, 81
  Campbell, 53
  Caroline, 60
  Catherine, 57
  Conrad, 53
  David, 54
  Dr., 193
  Edward Jenner, 101
  Eleanor, 134, 207

Elizabeth, 53, 56, 61, 62, 81, 180
Elizabeth Louisa, 58
Elizabeth T., 213
Esther, 53, 81
F. H., 138, 158, 159
Flora Caldwell, 110
Frances S., 82
Frances Stevenson, 54
Francis H., 138, 140, 143, 178
Francis Hopkinson, 138
George, 60
Hannah, 54, 78
Henrietta, 57
Henry, 88
J. S., 193
James, 56, 57, 101, 104, 110, 116, 164, 165
Jane, 54, 75, 130, 173
Jane Hollins, 61
Jane Swan, 116
Janet, 76
Jeremiah, 81
John, 53, 54, 56, 61, 62, 148, 186, 187, 193, 221, 225, 233, 235, 237
John Buchanan, 59
John C., 176
John Conrad, 53
John Davidson, 104
John Porter, 55
John Spear, 158, 221
John Stephens, 62
Johnston, 57
Joseph, 56, 58, 130, 193, 222
Joseph Elliott, 58
Joseph Hopkinson, 138
Joseph, Mrs., 193
Laura Sophia, 58
Lavinia, 183
Legh Richmond, 140
Lewis Buchanan, 55
Lina, 54
Margaret, 53, 55, 56, 57, 58, 59, 60, 61, 62, 79, 81, 99, 101, 164
Margaretta Galbraith, 58
Maria, 169
Marshall Pike, 143
Mary, 53, 54, 56, 57, 60, 61, 79, 82
Mary Ann, 61
Mary Ann, 207
Mary Blaikley, 116
Mary Buchanan, 57
Mary Williams, 99
Mr., 193
Mrs., 207
Nathaniel, 54, 55, 158, 164, 187, 222
Nicholas, 83
Phebe, 173
Rachel, 83
Ralph, 154, 193
Rebecca, 53, 54
Richard, 60, 61, 81
Robert, 58, 59, 60, 61, 62, 81, 99, 101, 130, 164, 188, 221, 228
Sally, 73
Samuel, 54, 55, 56, 57, 58, 59, 61, 62, 81, 89, 164, 188, 193, 222, 225
Samuel W., 134
Sarah, 54, 55, 56, 57, 58, 81, 148, 164, 184
Sarah M., 176
Sidney, 59, 87
Sophia, 89
St. John, 55
Susan, 207, 213
Susan F., 178
Susan T., 138, 140, 143
William, 53, 54, 57, 60, 162, 186, 187, 207, 221
William Buchanan, 53
William Carvil, 62
William Spear, 56
SMULL, D. B., 193, 229
David Burke, 62
Dr., 193
Eliza, 229
Elizabeth, 62
Frances Amelia, 229
Jacob, 62
Richard Johns, 62
SNETHERS, J. R., 220
Maria, 220
SNIDER, Amelia Jane, 111

INDEX

Ann Mary, 117
Margaret, 111, 117
Nicholas, 111, 117
SNIDES, John, 81
SNOWDEN,
 Nathaniel, 32
 Rezin H., 93
 Susanna, 74
SNUGGRASS,
 William, 81
SNUGGRESS,
 Catharine, 62
 Juliana, 62
 William, 62
SOLOMON, Abigail, 59, 60, 62
 Ednery, 60
 Elkin, 193
 Elkins, 59, 60, 62
 L., 193
 Mr., 193
 Sarah, 62
 William, 59
SOMERVELL, Ann, 164
 James, 81, 164
SOMERVILL, James, 193
SOMERVILLE,
 Mary, 74
SOMMERVILLE,
 Caroline O., 207
SOUTHARD,
 Captain, 193
SOUTHGATE,
 Ursula, 207
SOUTHWARD,
 Captain, 193
 William, 193
SPARKS, Agness, 73

SPEAR, Barbara, 54, 63, 81, 97
 Dorcas, 80
 Elizabeth, 53, 54, 55, 56
 Jane, 75
 John, 55, 56, 81, 221
 Joseph, 63, 81, 97, 193
 Margaret, 81
 Mary, 54, 55, 79
 Mr., 193
 Mrs., 206
 Robert, 53
 William, 53, 54, 97, 187
SPEDDEN, Ellonora, 218
 Mary Jane, 216
SPENCE, Elizabeth Jane, 139
 John, 81, 139, 140, 143, 159, 189
 Mary Catharine, 140
 Mrs., 193
 Tracy, 139, 140, 143
 William Henry, 143
SPENCER, Anna, 78
 Miss, 207
 Robert, 193
 Susan, 207
SPERRY, Regina Maria, 218
SPICER, Sarah, 79
SPIES, George Washington, 126
 John Peter, 126
 M., 126

SPILLMAN, James, 206
 Maria Ann, 207
SPREKLESON, Ann, 207
SPRIGGS, ---, 137
 Betsey, 176
SPRINGER, David C., 207
SPROLE, Eliza, 94
 William F., 176
SPURRIER, William T., 193
STABLER, Amelia, 61, 90
 John Merriam, 104
 Margaret, 61, 63, 99, 104
 Rebecca, 99
 William, 61, 63, 99, 104
 William Cooper, 63
STABLES, Amelia, 90
STAFFORD,
 Elizabeth Jane, 180
 Francis Asbury, 118
 Mary, 118
 William Josephus, 118
STANSBERY, Ann, 207
STANSBURY, ---, 194
 Ann, 207
 T. A., 87
STAPLER, John, 134
 John Craig, 134
 Margaret, 134
 William Taylor, 134

STAPLES, Rebecca, 215
STAPLETON,
  Joshua, 194
  Mary, 72
STAR, Henry, 194
STARR, ---, 206
  Catharine, 207
  Eliza, 60
  Henry, 194
  Louisa, 62
  Margaret Deaver, 61
  Obadiah, 60, 61, 62, 81
  Ruth, 60, 61, 62
STEEL, Anne, 81
  Archibald, 57
  Jane, 57
STEENE, Matthew, 194
STEIGAR, Andrew, 55
  Mary Anne, 55
  Samuel, 55
STENHOUSE,
  Aleander, 187
STEPHENS, Alex, 142
  Alexander, 131, 133, 139
  Alexander William, 142
  Elizabeth, 131, 133, 139, 142
  James, 133
  Lucinda Baptist, 139
  Mary, 88, 139
  Rebecca, 85
  Rebecca Baptist, 139
  Sarah, 131
STEPHINS,
  Elizabeth, 207
STERATT, Joseph, 87
STERETT, Andrew, 55
  Augusta Temple, 60
  Benjamin, 153
  Charles Ridgely, 56
  Deborah, 54, 55, 56
  Eliza, 55, 79
  George, 54
  Harriet, 55, 75
  James, 54, 56
  James William, 115
  John, 54, 55, 56, 222
  Joseph, 54, 115
  Juliet, 55
  Maria R., 95
  Mary, 54, 59, 75, 115
  Mary H., 94
  Mary Harris, 115
  McLure, 54
  Mr., 194
  Rebecca, 59, 60
  Samuel, 59, 60, 159, 222
  Sophia, 56
STERLEY, Maria, 88
STERLING, Dr., 194
  Elizabeth, 58, 101, 106, 163
  Isabella Maria, 90, 101
  James, 58, 101, 106, 163
  Jane, 165
  W., 194
  William, 194
STERRATT, Augusta Temple, 89
  James, 86
STERRET, Frances
  Mary, 103
  George, 155
  Harriet, 178
  James William, 109
  Joseph, 103, 109, 161, 167
  Josephine, 109, 154
  Mary, 103, 109
  Molly, 167
  Rebecca, 108
  Samuel, 108
  Sarah Caroline
  Sears, 108
STERRETT, Augusta Temple, 124
  Benjamin, 131, 170
  James, 186, 187
  John, 187
  John Y., 131
  Joseph, 119, 150, 221
  Louisa Sherlock, 121
  Margaret, 170
  Maria Ridgeley, 119
  Mary, 119
  Mary B., 90
STEVENS,
  Alexander, 60, 90
  Elizabeth, 73
  J., 194

INDEX

James, 58, 60, 226
John, 81
Mary, 58
Mr., 194
Rebecca, 58, 60, 226, 227
William, 60
STEVENSON, Ann, 88
Anne, 55, 57
Anne Henry, 55
Elizabeth Jane, 230
Esther, 58
Frances, 53, 54
George B., 96
George P., 81
George Pitt, 53, 58, 221
George Pitts, 226
Gertrude, 57
Henry, 53, 54, 55, 57
James, 54, 230
John, 81
Martha, 76
Mary, 78
Rachel, 54
William, 54
William Henry, 54
STEWARD, Sarah Ann T., 145
STEWART, ---, 224
A., 194
Adam, 115
Alexander Wilson, 56
Andrew, 59
Ann, 59, 61, 62, 63, 115
Anne, 57, 58

Anne Philpot, 56
Archibald, 58, 60, 63, 81, 104, 116, 159
Ark, 115
Caroline Matilda, 98
Catharine, 207
Catharine Isabella, 56
Catherine, 80, 118, 183
Charlotte, 115
Colonel, 194
Couden, 61, 62
Cowden, 58
D. C., 194
David, 55, 56, 57, 62, 63, 92, 105, 109, 112, 115, 148, 160, 162, 164, 177, 186, 187, 221
David C., 118, 166, 194
David E., 81
David Reed, 61
David, Mrs., 155
Dorothea Margaret, 115
Edward, 62
Eleanor, 58, 73, 115, 208
Eleanor Reed, 63
Eliza, 98
Elizabeth, 55, 56, 57, 105, 109, 112, 115, 118, 139, 164, 213, 240
Elizabeth Ann, 63, 90, 94
Ellen, 92, 135, 137, 140, 173, 207

Harriet Murray, 112
Helena, 63, 164
Hugh, 56
Isabella, 63, 92, 207
James, 57, 58, 59, 60, 61, 62, 63, 81, 92, 115, 135, 137, 140, 154, 157, 194, 207
James Caldwell, 57
James Moir, 139
James, Mrs., 194
Jane, 62, 63
John, 55, 57, 60, 63, 139, 194
John Archibald, 135
John Couden, 59, 60
John Cowden, 61
John Cowder, 81
Joseph, 207
Joshua, 115
Jospeh O., 207
Letita J., 90
Letitia Jane, 62
Letitia M., 176
Letitia McCreery, 104
Margaret, 61
Mary, 55, 58, 59, 60, 61, 62, 109, 152, 165, 166, 175
Mr., 194, 217
Mrs., 206
Peggy, 56
R., 194
Richardson, 194
Robert, 57, 58, 60, 61, 194, 235, 240

Robert Henry, 98
Robert Nelson, 140
Sarah, 58, 60, 63, 104
Susan J., 93, 174
Susanna, 56, 57, 58, 60, 61
Susanna Isabella, 105
Thomas, 58, 82, 194
W., 194
William, 56, 62, 98, 158, 194
William John, 59, 115
William Plunket, 55
STICKNEY, J. H., 186
John, 194
STIFF, T., 194
STILES, Anna Maria, 59
Anne, 57, 58, 59
Betsey, 55
Bettie M., 230
Bettie Mark, 230
E., 194
Edward, 97, 194
G., 194
George, 57, 58, 59, 81, 97, 194
Harriet, 57
John Steel, 57
Joseph, 54, 55
Joseph Graybell, 58
Lee, 230
Louisa, 59
Mary, 97, 194
Mr., 194
Nancy, 54

Nannie Lisle, 230
Phebe, 54, 55
STINE, Julian, 92
Mariah Rosanna, 76
STIRLING, ---, 224
Archibald, 62, 142, 145, 146, 179, 188
Elizabeth, 57, 60, 62, 63, 94, 146, 176
Elizabeth Ann, 142, 145, 179
James, 57, 60, 62, 63, 123, 187, 221
Jane, 160
John, 57
Margaret Yates, 145
Mary, 123
Robert, 63
Thomas, 60
W., 194
William, 123, 194, 207
STOCKDELL, Eleanor, 81
STOCKEN, Mrs., 194
STOCKTON, ---, 161
C., 171
Catharine, 158
STOKES, Anne, 74
STONE, Ann, 91
Eleanor, 93
John P. R., 94
Joseph W., 91
Mary Ann, 79
Mr., 160
STORR, Catharine, 207
STORY, John, 61
Mary, 61
William, 61

STOUT, Mr., 154
STOWE, Harvey, 208
Jeremiah, 208
STOXALL, Emy, 74
STRATTON, Amanda, 184
STRAWBLE, Ann, 78
STREET, William, 96
STRICKER, ---, 225
Ann Eliza, 90, 166
Anne Elizabeth, 57
Catharine, 170
Catherine, 56
Charlotte, 62, 155
George Bedford, 59
Jane Henrietta, 60
John, 56, 57, 58, 59, 60, 61, 62, 63, 100, 103, 153, 164, 173, 188, 222
Juliana, 91
Julianna, 61
Laura C., 92
Laura Caroline, 103
Maria, 85
Martha, 56, 57, 58, 59, 60, 61, 62, 63, 100, 103, 164
Susanna, 58
William Bedford, 100
STRONG, Erastus, 115, 116, 167
Erastus Albert, 115
Martha Eloisa, 116
Nabby Wright, 115, 116
STUART, Margaret, 54
Mr., 194

Robert, 54
William R., 183
STUBBS, George L., 219
STUBS, Joseph, 217
STULL, Grete, 75
STUMP, John, 81
STURDEVANT, Miss, 202
STUTSON, Sophia, 88
SULLIVAN, Mary, 77
Mr., 157
SUMMERS, Jacob, 60
James, 60
Jane, 60
SUMMERSON, Seth S., 95
SUMWALT, George, 89
SURRELL, E., 208
SUTHERLAND,
David, 81
Elizabeth Jane, 125
Isbella, 125
Samuel, 212
William, 125
SUTOR, James, 89
SUTRINE, Annette
Caroline Colim, 88
SWAIN, Howard, 96
SWAN, ---, 194, 229
Agness, 58, 63
Ann, 59, 163
Anne, 56, 58
Eleanor, 134
Elizabeth, 57, 58, 59, 127, 134

George Maxwell, 58, 59
J. E., 194
James, 59, 106, 127, 134
James Christopher, 106
Jane, 106
John, 57, 58, 59, 102, 127, 151, 156, 194, 222
John E., 194
John Maxwell, 58
Joseph, 58, 59, 63, 163
Matthew, 56, 58, 59, 221
Robert, 57
Robert Joseph, 63
Susan J., 93
Thomas, 58
William Glassell, 59
SWANN, Anne, 57
Elizabeth, 94
James, 188
John, 188
Matthew, 57
William, 57
SWANWICK, Rose, 76
SWARTZ, P., 194
SWEARER, Elizabeth, 184
SWEETING, Ann Barbara, 63
Catharine, 63
Thomas, 63, 81, 194
SWIFT, Mary, 169
William R., 169

SWINDALL, Peter, 81
SWITZER, Elizabeth, 93

-T-

TAGART, ---, 194
Anne Calwell, 65
Elizabeth, 65
John, 65, 66, 106, 166
Mary, 65, 106
Mary Lyon, 65, 66
William, 66
TAGERT, James Inglis, 98
John, 82, 98
Mary, 98
TAGGART, Cardiffe, 103
Catharine, 158
Grizzel, 162
John, 103, 123, 162, 187
Margaret M., 180
Mary, 103, 123, 162
Samuel Hall, 123
TALBOT, Mary Ann, 139, 178
TALBOTT, Rebecca B., 220
TARR, L. S., 194
Levin, 194
Levin S., 194
TARTAR, Charlotte, 93
TATE, Agness, 64
Andrew, 64
Elizabeth, 64
James, 82

Jane, 64
Margaret, 64
Mary, 64
TAWSON, Rachel, 77
TAYLOR, ---, 184
　Adeline M., 92
　Adeline Margaret, 105
　Anne, 63
　Catharine, 65, 208
　Cornelia Clinton, 117
　Edward, 185
　Eliza, 87
　Elizabeth, 235, 237
　Ellen, 239
　Esther, 64
　Frances, 65
　Grace, 79
　Hannah, 164
　Hannah Russell, 213
　Hugh, 238
　Isaac, 63
　Isabella, 213, 234
　Isabella Norris, 213
　J., 224
　James, 235, 238, 239
　James Duncan, 64
　Jane, 170, 218
　Jane E., 87
　Jane Etting, 65
　John, 66
　John B., 194
　Joseph, 64, 170, 176
　Julia A., 92
　Julian, 66
　Juliet Ann, 172
　Louisa, 66

Louisa Watson, 66
Lucia, 165
Margaret, 220
Maria, 66, 88, 105, 112, 117, 165
Martha, 63
Martha Ann, 94
Mary, 63, 73
Mary Ann, 129, 239
Mary Patterson, 213
Mrs., 234
Priscilla, 89
Robert, 65, 213
Robert A., 129
S., 208
Samuel, 234, 238, 239
Samuel George, 238
W. W., 117, 224
William, 66, 82, 105, 164, 169, 194
William James Whyte, 239
William McKesson, 112
William W., 112, 158, 165, 187, 221
William Wallace, 129
TENNANT, H., 208
TENNAR, John, 85
TENNIS, Jacob, 82
TEPLER, Elizabeth A., 211
TERR, L. S., 194
TERREL, Harriet A., 97
TERRILL, Elliot Buckingham, 133

Harriet, 174
Harriet Abigail, 133
Lawrence Hitchock, 133
Virginia Caroline LaFayet, 133
TERRY, Luther, 183
　Sarah, 232
　William, 232
TEVIS, Cassandra, 78
THECKER, Walter, 194
THOMAS, Ann, 107
　Caleb, 208
　Daniel L., 85
　Ellen, 128
　Jane, 213
　Joel, 220
　John, 128
　Matty Augusta Lindsay, 107
　Mr., 150, 214
　Mrs., 151, 214
　P. E., 194
　Philip, 89
　Robert, 88, 128, 151, 156, 169
　William, 107
　William Henry, 214
THOMPSON,
　Alexander, 64
　Ann, 65, 66
　Anne, 65
　Deborah, 78
　Eleanor, 66, 99, 165
　Eliza, 65
　Elizabeth, 64, 66, 233

INDEX

Elizabeth
Susannah, 118
Ellen, 174
Frances, 63
George, 65, 66
Hugh, 168
Israel P., 89
J. P., 157
James, 65, 108, 114, 118, 194, 233
Jane, 63, 64
Jane Eliza, 108
Janet, 234
John, 63, 64, 65, 66, 132
John T., 132
Josias, 82
Margaret, 66
Maria, 66
Mary, 64, 65, 66, 108, 114, 118
Mary Ann, 66
Moses, 82
N., 194
Nathaniel, 65, 66, 194
Robert, 64, 65
Sarah, 65
Susan, 87
Thomas J., 94
William, 66, 99, 114, 194
THORNBURGH,
  Mary Ann, 79
  Sarah, 91
THORNELL, George, 65
  Jane, 65
  Robert, 65
  Sarah, 65

William, 65
THORNHILL, ---, 161
  Jane, 167
  Mr., 152
THORNTON, A., 194
  Ann, 130
  Rose, 130
  Sam, 130
TILDEN, Mary R., 96
TODD, Ann, 208
TOLLEY, James W., 94
TOOGOOD, Edward, 88, 155, 169
  Nancy, 169
TOOLE, James, 82
TOOTLE, James, 171
TOPHAM, Matthew, 82
TORANCE, Mary, 64
TORRANCE, ---, 225
  Anne, 64
  Charles, 63, 64, 65, 66, 151, 163, 165
  Dorcas, 64
  Eleanor, 149, 180
  Eleanor Fulford, 149
  Eliz. R., 208
  Eliza, 79
  Elizabeth, 63, 64, 65, 66, 165
  George, 64, 149
  Harriet, 65
  James, 63, 65
  John, 65, 158
  Louisa, 66, 171
  Mary, 174
  Mary C., 180

Mary S., 208
Mrs., 156
TORRENCE, John, 222
TOTTEN, Joseph, 82
TOWER, George, 194
TOWSER, Jonathan, 82
TOWSON, Jacob, 64
  Jacob T., 82
  Jane, 64
  Lydia, 64
  Rachel, 77
TOY, Ammael, 89
TRAPNELL, William, 82
TRAVERS,
  Elizabeth, 65
  Jane, 64, 65, 66
  Mary, 65
  Matthew, 64, 65, 66
  Matthews, 82
  Nancy, 78
  Rebecca, 64
TRAYSER,
  Margaretta, 218
TREGO, Adeline, 219
  Albert, 219
TRIEV, Herman, 82
TRIMBLE, ---, 194
  Mrs., 208
  Rebecca B., 208
  Sarah, 72
  William, 194
TRIPPE, Capt., 198
  James, 194
  Joseph E., 96, 208
  Mr., 197
TROTMON, Jane, 79
TROTT, Mrs., 208

TROXEL, Isabella, 208
TUCKER, Helena
Anna, 225
James, 225
Louisa, 225
Rebecca, 86
TUMBLESOME,
Elizabeth, 64
James, 63, 64
Janit, 63, 64
John, 64
Mary, 64
Samuel, 64
William, 63, 64
TUMBLESON,
William, 82
TURINE, Nancy, 72
TURNBULL, Alison, 95
Alison M., 179
Andrew, 65, 66, 82
Ann, 149, 171
Anna G., 184
Betsey, 171
Caroline, 175
Elizabeth, 66, 149
Grame, 149
Hannah, 65, 66
Henry, 175
Henry C., 149, 187
Jane, 66
Mrs., 159, 171
Sally, 65
Susan, 92, 172
William, 151
TURNER, ---, 43
Asa, 143
Elizabeth, 90, 143
Flora, 170
Irvine, 92
Jane, 63, 146, 149, 183
John, 63
John Nicholas, 43
Lydia Calhoun, 149
Martha, 143
Samuel, 63
Thomas Shirley, 146
W. F., 149
William F., 146
William Fitzhugh, 95
TURNPAUGH, John, 82
Mary, 73
TUSTON, Albert, 65
Elizabeth, 65
Septimus, 65
William, 65
TUTTON, Mr., 194
TYRREL, Lawrence, 161
TYRRELL, Harriet, 184
TYSON, ---, 202
Amanda, 215
Jonathan, 208, 217
Mary S., 218
Nathan, 82
Philip T., 91

-U-

UHLER, George M., 217
ULERY, Aust, 82
UNDERWOOD, Hannah, 85
UNICK, Eleanor, 80
USHER, ---, 194

-V-

VALENTINE,
Charlotte, 78
VAN BIBBER,
Abraham, 67
Mary, 67
VAN LASSEL, Peter, 84
VAN LILL, Ann, 111
Henry, 111
Stephen York, 111
VAN NOEMES,
Susanna Johanna Geradina, 72
VAN WYCK, William, 194
VANBIBBER,
Abraham, 222
VANCE, Jno., 194
William, 194
VANDERVOORT,
Edward M., 179
VANSANT, Agness, 66
Eleanor, 66
Elizabeth, 66
Isaiah, 66
James, 66
Mary, 66
Rebecca, 66
Susanna, 66
VARLEY, Agness, 82
VARNER, Henry, 94
VARNUM, J. B., 194
VASHON, Halson, 92
VAUGHN, Ruth, 82
VICKERS, B. Albert, 218

Elizabeth W., 218
Geraldine Sarah, 215
Joel, 217
VICKERY, Dorothy, 66
Eleanor, 67
Elizabeth, 66, 67
Stephen, 66, 67
Steven, 194
VINCENT, John, 86
VON DEN HEAVELL,
Remptje, 26
Richard, 26
Romelis Wilhelmus, 26
VON KAPFF, ---, 224
VONKAPFF, Mrs., 151
VOSER, Thomas, 167
VOWELL, John D., 87

-W-
WADDELL, Margaret, 174
WADDLE, David, 70
James A., 70
Sarah, 70
William, 70, 83
WADE, Sarah, 78
WAGERS, Thomas, 83
WAITE, Mr., 159
WALKER, Elizabeth, 67
George Read Hollins, 139
Harriet, 135, 139
Isabella, 67
James, 67, 91, 135, 139
James P., 174
James Perry, 135
Jane, 67
John Matthew, 128
John Wesley, 128
Joseph, 67, 83
Julianna, 135
Mary, 160
Mary Jane Elizabeth, 128
Mr., 152
Rachel, 128
Robert, 67
S., 194
Samuel, 82
Sarah, 89, 122
WALL, Anne, 68, 69
John, 68, 69
WALLACE, Andrew, 69, 70, 169
Eleanor, 68
Elizabeth, 68, 208
Esther, 231
George Gillespie, 69
J., 194
Jane, 68
John, 68, 83
Joseph, 194
Joseph A., 169
Ruth, 69, 70, 168
Thomas, 231
William, 70
WALLENDER, Elizabeth, 177
WALLER, Eleanor, 84
WALTER, Ann, 227
James L., 227
WALTERS, Elizabeth, 75
WANNALL, Mary, 179
WARD, Ebenezer, 122, 125
Elizabeth, 125
Elizabeth Jane, 120
Francis, 82
George, 122
James, 120, 167, 169
Lucretia, 120
Lucy, 169
Margaret, 122, 125
WARDEN, James B., 209
James E., 209
Robert M., 209
WARFIELD, ---, 184
Ann, 176
Daniel, 90
Julia Ann, 218
WARLEY, Mr., 159
WARNER, Elizabeth, 115
George, 194
John, 115
Margaret, 115
Thomas, 194
WARREN, Isaac, 84
WASHINGTON, General, 194
WATERS, Alevda, 172
Alverda, 133
Ann, 179
Horace W., 90, 133
Mr., 194

Rebecca Angelica, 133
WATKINS, William, 83
WATSON, Agness, 70
  David, 70
  Elizabeth, 85
  Frances, 69
  Frances Anne, 69
  Francis, 70
  Isabella, 70
  Isabella Freeman, 96
  James, 182
  Joseph, 69
  Margaret, 85
  Mary, 70
  Mrs., 131, 152
  R., 224
  Robert, 87, 151
  Robert, Mrs., 160
  Sarah, 69
  William Price, 131
WATTS, John, 183
WAY, John, 167
  Mary, 167
WEARY, Rebecca, 80
WEAVER, Catharine, 209
  Mary, 76
WEBB, George, 209
  Hannah, 209
WEBER, Joseph Aloysius, 223
WEBSTER,
  Elizabeth, 67
  Hannah, 67
  John, 67
  John A., 88
  Mrs., 198
  Rebecca, 91
  Sarah, 67
WEDGE, Ann M., 209
WEEKS, Samuel, 194
WEEMS, Maria L., 180
  Mary Ann, 209
WEER, Catherine, 67
  Eleanor, 67, 73
  Jane, 72
  Janit, 78
  Thomas, 82
  William, 67, 82
WEILEY, Mary, 83
WEIMER, Agness, 67
  George, 67
  Jemima, 67
  Matthias, 67
WEIR, George, 173
  Joseph, 208
  Mary, 173
  Sarah, 209
WELCH, David Smith, 68
  George, 67, 68
  James Cox, 68
  John, 68
  Margaret, 67, 68
  Mary, 67
  Rebecca, 68
  Susanna, 82
WELLFORD, Robert Y., 87
WELLINS, Maria L., 219
WELLS, Anne, 73
  Elizabeth, 76
  Lewis, 89
  Micah, 82
  Rachel, 74
  Robert K., 209
  Thomas, 82
WELSH, James, 82
  Walter, 82
WEST, Benjamin, 82, 104
  Catharine, 209
  Dr., 16
  Frances, 82
  Harriet, 71, 172
  Helen A., 180
  Helena Anna, 104
  Isabella, 219
  J., 194
  James, 70, 71, 100, 104, 112
  Maria L., 70, 71
  Maria Louisa, 100, 104, 112, 167, 225
  Mary, 70, 100
  Mr., 155
  Nancy, 74
  Samuel H., 86
  William Henry, 104
WESTBY, Eleanor, 68
  Nathaniel, 67
  Rebecca, 67, 68
  Robert, 68
  Susanna, 67
  Thomas, 67
  William, 67, 68
WESTERMAN, Mr., 157
WESTERN, Eleanor, 75
WHANN, William, 194

INDEX

WHEATON, John R., 82
WHEELER, Agness, 70, 71
 Anne Eliza, 71
 Greenberry, 82
 Honor, 82
 Jane, 103
 Jesse, 70, 71, 100, 103
 Maria, 100
 Mary Ann, 92
 Nancy, 100, 103
WHITACAR,
 Elizabeth, 80
WHITE, ---, 194
 A., 238
 Andrew, 69
 Ann, 90, 170
 Betsey, 69
 Charlotte, 169
 Deborah, 116
 Decimus, 71
 Dr., 194
 Edward, 69
 Eliza Maria, 116
 Elizabeth, 71, 85
 Henry, 82, 86, 88, 116, 119, 154
 Isabella, 94, 233
 J. C., 194, 208
 J. Campbell, 97
 James, 69
 John, 69, 116
 John C., 194, 230
 John Campbell, 71, 163, 194
 Joseph, 69, 116
 Kissina, 69
 Letitia, 69
 Margaret, 68, 116, 119, 215
 Mary, 68
 Mary Lucy, 131
 Mr., 156
 Mrs., 154, 208
 Rebecca, 69
 Rezin, 84
 Robert, 68, 69
 Samuel, 69, 215
 Samuel K., 131
 Sarah J., 209
 Susanna, 69
 Thomas, 194
 William, 96, 119
WHITEFORD,
 William D., 94
WHITELOCK,
 Agness, 70, 71
 Elizabeth, 70
 John, 83
 Martha, 71
 Moses, 70, 71
 Mr., 155
WHITELY, Charles, 194
WHITEMAN, A., 209
 Ann, 185
WHITMARSH, ---, 184
 George, 143, 181
 James, 185
 Mary, 143, 180
WHITNEY,
 Margaret, 180
 Solomon, 87
WHYTE, A., 235
 Archibald, 237
 Susan N., 235
WICKES, Ann, 105
 Benjamin, 105
 Frances, 105
WICKS, Frances J., 151
WIGHT, Harriet, 94
WILCOX, Ann B., 145, 181
 Grafton Hayne, 145
 James, 145
 Wesley Banningson, 145
WILEY, Alexander, 194
 Robert, 83
 Samuel F., 237
WILKINS, Elizabeth, 71
 James, 67
 Mary, 67
 Thomas, 67
WILKINSON, Ann, 208
 Elizabeth, 208
 Hezekiah, 92
 James, 208
 Mr., 155
WILLEY, Henry, 82
WILLIAMS, Amos A., 188, 194
 Andrew, 83, 97
 Ann, 129, 173
 Ann Gilmor, 96
 Benjamin, 86, 116, 177, 211
 Edward G., 90, 155
 Edward Greene, 69
 Edward T., 129
 Elizabeth, 67, 97, 123
 Esther, 98

Frederic, 83
George, 67, 87
Giles, 84
Henry L., 154
Henry Lee, 70
Isaac, 104
Jacob, 71, 98, 104, 110, 113, 116, 119, 123, 129, 154, 169
James, 119
John, 67, 69, 82, 83, 94, 170
Julia, 92
Julia Ann, 91
Lewis, 93
Margaret, 69
Mary, 67, 69, 70, 71, 97, 98, 104, 110, 113, 116, 119, 123, 129, 185
Mary Smith, 129
Maurice, 71
Mr., 154, 158, 160, 194
N. F., 194
Nancy, 77
Nathaniel, 194
Otho Holland, 69, 70, 82
Peter, 113, 177
Rebecca Anne, 97
Robert Smith, 69
S., 209
Sam, 194
Samantha, 214
Sarah, 82, 116, 172
Stephen, 208
Susanna Mary, 116
Thomas, 110
William, 67, 69
William Elie, 69

Willis L., 95
WILLIAMSON, Anne, 80
Elizabeth, 80
Mary, 82
Mary M., 161
Samuel, 82
Thomas, 82
WILLIS, Ann, 117
John, 83
Mrs., 208
T., 194
Thomas, 117, 194, 208
W., 194
William, 117
WILMER, Ann S., 173
Rebecca A., 217
WILSON, Agnes, 233, 236
Ann, 68, 98, 102
Ann Eliza, 141
Ann S., 96
Anna, 70, 106, 112, 116, 120, 123, 166, 181
Anna Mary, 120
Anne, 69
Armenella, 70
Benjamin, 86
Benjamin Harrison, 116
Benoni, 70
Bethiah, 167
Cassandra, 81
Catharine, 141, 142, 178
Catharine Somervell, 112

Cold, 208
David, 68, 69
Dinah, 209
Eleanor, 68, 69
Elenora, 216
Eliza, 86, 136
Elizabeth, 68, 69, 70, 84, 237
Elvin, 176
Frederick, 106, 160
Hannah, 68
Hugh, 69
Isabella, 69, 84, 208
James, 68, 70, 141, 142, 167, 209, 232, 233, 237
James P., 94, 143
Jane, 68
Jesse, 68
John, 69, 83, 94, 105, 141, 194, 208
John E., 209
John Steward, 123
Joseph, 102
Margaret, 143, 209
Maria, 209
Martha, 235
Mary, 79, 235
Mary Jane Hollins, 143
Matthew, 105
Mrs., 201
Priscilla, 79
Rachel, 75
Rebecca, 68, 69, 70, 75
Robert, 69, 70, 90, 98, 102, 106, 112, 116, 120, 123, 166, 236

INDEX 325

Samuel M., 177
Sarah, 77, 209
Stephen, 69, 70, 82, 98, 188
Stephen S., 91, 159
Susanna, 105
T., 194
Thomas, 68, 83, 142
William, 68, 165, 194
William H., 209
Zechariah Crawford, 70
Zipporah, 68
WINCHESTER,
  Caroline, 209
  Hannah, 123, 157, 170, 226
  Martha Jane, 123, 226
  Samuel, 89
  Samuel G., 93, 175
  William, 123, 151, 170, 226
WINDER, Araminta R., 138
  Arminta, 148
  Arminta R., 143, 177
  Aurelia S., 184
  Charles H., 94
  Charlotte Aurelia, 128
  Esther, 165
  Gertrude, 104, 128, 164, 183
  Lydia H., 148
  Mary Stoughton, 138
  Sarah Rogers, 143

Sidney, 148
W. H., 164
W. S., 138, 143
William, 104
William H., 104, 128, 152
William Sidney, 92
WINEMAN,
  Catharine, 81
WINN, Sarah, 79
WINTER, Robert, 111, 112, 166
  Sarah, 111, 112
  Sarah Ann, 111
WIRT, Agnes C., 157
  Catharine G., 178
  Elizabeth G., 94
  Ellen T., 180
  Rosa E., 94, 179
  William, 160, 179
WISE, Ann, 73
  Levin, 83
WITCHELL, James R., 108
  James Wheland, 108
  Jane Ann, 108
WITNEY, Solomon, 87
WOADEN, Rachel, 76
WOLF, Catherine, 72
WOLFE, Maria, 209
WOLFENDEN,
  Margaret, 91
WOLFORD, Ann Maria, 218
WOOD, Ann, 170
  Anthony, 91
  John, 170

Mrs., 155
Pheonix Nicoll, 93
William, 89
WOODBROUGH,
  John Williams, 82
WOODEN, Letitia, 70
  Margaret, 83
  Mary Ann, 70
  Richard, 70
  Thomas, 70
WOODS, Mrs., 152
WOODWARD,
  George P., 175
  George Powell, 95
  Jemima, 80
  N. B., 159
WORK, Andrew, 69
  James, 69
  Nancy, 69
  William, 69
WORKMAN, Agnes Mary, 241
  James, 240
  John, 235, 239, 240, 241
  Margaret Ann, 239
  Rebecca, 235
  Robert, 82
WORLEY, Ann Maria, 144
  John, 141, 144
  John Amos, 141
  Sarah M., 141, 144
WRAY, John, 167
  Martha, 88
  Mary, 167
WRIGHT, H., 194
  John, 83
  Margaret, 78

   Mary Ann, 214
   Sarah, 80, 86
WYLE, Vincent, 194

-Y-
YATES, Joseph C., 165
   Margaret, 236
YEAGER, John, 88
YEAT, James, 91
YERKESS, David, 194
YERKIS, Stephen, 209
YONCE, Charles W., 93
YOUNG, ---, 224
  Alexander, 84
  Andrew, 92
  Carey, 71
  Catharine, 63
  Charles, 85, 108, 189
  Eleanor, 108
  Eliza, 71, 80
  Elizabeth, 71
  Frances, 86, 163
  Henry, 108, 120
  Hugh, 71, 163, 187
  J., 194
  Jacob, 83
  James, 71
  Jane, 71, 76
  Jesse, 71, 83
  Mary, 71, 120, 156, 165
  McClintock, 71
  Rebecca, 71
  Robert, 71
  Susanna, 72
  William, 63, 71, 83
  William Scott, 63

-Z-
ZIGLAR, Sarah, 219

Other books by the author:

A Closer Look at St. John's Parish Registers [Baltimore County, Maryland], 1701-1801

A Collection of Maryland Church Records

A Guide to Genealogical Research in Maryland: 5th Edition, Revised and Enlarged

Abstracts of the Ledgers and Accounts of the Bush Store and Rock Run Store, 1759-1771

Abstracts of the Orphans Court Proceedings of Harford County, 1778-1800

Abstracts of Wills, Harford County, Maryland, 1800-1805

Baltimore City [Maryland] Deaths and Burials, 1834-1840

Baltimore County, Maryland, Overseers of Roads, 1693-1793

Bastardy Cases in Baltimore County, Maryland, 1673-1783

Bastardy Cases in Harford County, Maryland, 1774-1844

Bible and Family Records of Harford County, Maryland Families: Volume V

Children of Harford County: Indentures and Guardianships, 1801-1830

Colonial Delaware Soldiers and Sailors, 1638-1776

Colonial Families of the Eastern Shore of Maryland Volumes 5, 6, 7, 8, 9, 11, 12, 13, 14, and 16

Colonial Maryland Soldiers and Sailors, 1634-1734

Dr. John Archer's First Medical Ledger, 1767-1769, Annotated Abstracts

Early Anglican Records of Cecil County

Early Harford Countians, Individuals Living in Harford County, Maryland in Its Formative Years Volume 1: A to K, Volume 2: L to Z, and Volume 3: Supplement

Harford County Taxpayers in 1870, 1872 and 1883

Harford County, Maryland Divorce Cases, 1827-1912: An Annotated Index

Heirs and Legatees of Harford County, Maryland, 1774-1802

Heirs and Legatees of Harford County, Maryland, 1802-1846

Inhabitants of Baltimore County, Maryland, 1763-1774

Inhabitants of Cecil County, Maryland, 1649-1774

Inhabitants of Harford County, Maryland, 1791-1800

Inhabitants of Kent County, Maryland, 1637-1787

Joseph A. Pennington & Co., Havre De Grace, Maryland Funeral Home Records: Volume II, 1877-1882, 1893-1900

Maryland Bible Records, Volume 1: Baltimore and Harford Counties

Maryland Bible Records, Volume 2: Baltimore and Harford Counties

Maryland Bible Records, Volume 3: Carroll County

Maryland Bible Records, Volume 4: Eastern Shore

Maryland Deponents, 1634-1799

Maryland Deponents: Volume 3, 1634-1776

Maryland Public Service Records, 1775-1783: A Compendium of Men and Women of Maryland Who Rendered Aid in Support of the American Cause against Great Britain during the Revolutionary War

Marylanders to Carolina: Migration of Marylanders to North Carolina and South Carolina prior to 1800

Marylanders to Kentucky, 1775-1825
Methodist Records of Baltimore City, Maryland: Volume 1, 1799-1829
Methodist Records of Baltimore City, Maryland: Volume 2, 1830-1839
Methodist Records of Baltimore City, Maryland: Volume 3, 1840-1850 (East City Station)
More Maryland Deponents, 1716-1799
More Marylanders to Carolina: Migration of Marylanders to North Carolina and South Carolina prior to 1800
More Marylanders to Kentucky, 1778-1828
Outpensioners of Harford County, Maryland, 1856-1896
Presbyterian Records of Baltimore City, Maryland, 1765-1840
Quaker Records of Baltimore and Harford Counties, Maryland, 1801-1825
Quaker Records of Northern Maryland, 1716-1800
Quaker Records of Southern Maryland, 1658-1800
Revolutionary Patriots of Anne Arundel County, Maryland
Revolutionary Patriots of Baltimore Town and Baltimore County, 1775-1783
Revolutionary Patriots of Calvert and St. Mary's Counties, Maryland, 1775-1783
Revolutionary Patriots of Caroline County, Maryland, 1775-1783
Revolutionary Patriots of Cecil County, Maryland
Revolutionary Patriots of Charles County, Maryland, 1775-1783
Revolutionary Patriots of Delaware, 1775-1783
Revolutionary Patriots of Dorchester County, Maryland, 1775-1783
Revolutionary Patriots of Frederick County, Maryland, 1775-1783
Revolutionary Patriots of Harford County, Maryland, 1775-1783
Revolutionary Patriots of Kent and Queen Anne's Counties
Revolutionary Patriots of Lancaster County, Pennsylvania
Revolutionary Patriots of Maryland, 1775-1783: A Supplement
Revolutionary Patriots of Maryland, 1775-1783: Second Supplement
Revolutionary Patriots of Montgomery County, Maryland, 1776-1783
Revolutionary Patriots of Prince George's County, Maryland, 1775-1783
Revolutionary Patriots of Talbot County, Maryland, 1775-1783
Revolutionary Patriots of Worcester and Somerset Counties, Maryland, 1775-1783
Revolutionary Patriots of Washington County, Maryland, 1776-1783
St. George's (Old Spesutia) Parish, Harford County, Maryland: Church and Cemetery Records, 1820-1920
St. John's and St. George's Parish Registers, 1696-1851
Survey Field Book of David and William Clark in Harford County, Maryland, 1770-1812
The Crenshaws of Kentucky, 1800-1995
The Delaware Militia in the War of 1812
Union Chapel United Methodist Church Cemetery Tombstone Inscriptions, Wilna, Harford County, Maryland

www.ingramcontent.com/pod-product-compliance
Lightning Source LLC
Chambersburg PA
CBHW051036160426
43193CB00010B/962